Dominion and Civility

DOMINION
AND CIVILITY:

ENGLISH IMPERIALISM
AND NATIVE AMERICA, 1585–1685

BY MICHAEL LEROY OBERG

Cornell University Press

ITHACA AND LONDON

First published 1999 by Cornell University Press

First printing, Cornell Paperbacks, 2003

Printed in the United States of America

Library of Congress Cataloging-in-Publication Data

Oberg, Michael Leroy.
    Dominion and civility : English imperialism and native America, 1585–1685
/ Michael Leroy Oberg.
        p.   cm.
    Includes bibliographical references (p.   ) and index.
    ISBN 0-8014-3564-1 (cloth : alk. paper)
        1. Indians of North America—New England—History—Sources.
    2. Indians of North America—Chesapeake Bay Region (Md. and Va.)—
    History—Sources.   3. Indians, Treatment of—New England.
    4. Indians, Treatment of—Chesapeake Bay Region (Md. and Va.)
    5. Indians of North America—Government policy—New England.
    6. Indians of North America—Government policy—Chesapeake Bay
    Region (Md. and Va.)   7. Colonial administrators—United States—
    History—Sources.   8. Great Britain—Colonies—America—
    Administration.   9. United States—History—Colonial period, ca.
    1600–1775.   I. Title.
    E78.N5034   1999
    974'.01—dc21   98-38345

Cornell University Press strives to use environmentally responsible suppliers and materials to the fullest extent possible in the publishing of its books. Such materials include vegetable-based, low-VOC inks and acid-free papers that are recycled, totally chlorine-free, or partly composed of nonwood fibers.

Cloth printing   10 9 8 7 6 5 4 3 2 1
Paperback Printing 10 9 8 7 6 5 4 3 2 1

Contents

Illustrations

Acknowledgments

This book is a study of English efforts to govern the first American frontiers and to incorporate the people living there, Native American and European, into an expanding, Anglo-American, Christian, New World empire. It links events in the Chesapeake and New England together in a single narrative and integrates the history of Native Americans into a broad transatlantic and imperial context. I could not have written it without the assistance of several institutions and a great many people.

A Phillips Fund Grant from the American Philosophical Society, and smaller awards from the Virginia Historical Society and the Research and Creative Endeavor Fund at Montana State University–Billings, provided important financial support for research and writing. Syracuse University provided a four-year graduate fellowship without which I could never have commenced work on this project, and for which I am especially thankful.

In Billings, Paula Duffy and Dona Helmer generously offered their encouragement and assistance; Kristen Anderson-Bricker, Maurice Forrester, Denny Frey, Mary Kelly, Ian McGiver, John Naisbett, Greg Scott, Rich Ver Wiebe, and Bruce Yenawine, colleagues all in the graduate program at Syracuse University, were likewise supportive. Joseph Levine, William Stinchcombe, Ralph Ketcham, and Donald Meinig all read and commented upon an earlier version of the manuscript, as did Helen Rountree and Peter Mancall. My new colleagues in the Department of History at the State University of New York–Geneseo have provided a wonderful and supportive atmosphere for completing this book. At Cornell University Press, Peter Agree has been a tremendous help.

James Roger Sharp and Stephen Saunders Webb have read more drafts than perhaps they care to remember. Throughout, they have been exceptionally generous in their advice. I am grateful to them both as teachers and as friends.

Finally, I must thank my family, and especially Leticia Ontiveros, who was always there when it mattered, and Nathan and Adam, who want to see their names in print.

Abbreviations Used in Notes

AM	William Hand Browne, ed., *Archives of Maryland*, 72 vols. (Baltimore, 1883–1972)
AHR	*American Historical Review*
CR	J. Hammond Trumbull, ed., *The Public Records of the Colony of Connecticut*, 15 vols. (Hartford, 1850)
CSP Col, 1574–1660	W. Noel Sainsbury, ed., *Calendar of State Papers, Colonial Series, America and West Indies, 1574–1660* (London, 1860)
CSP Col, 1661–68	W. Noel Sainsbury, ed., *Calendar of State Papers, Colonial Series, America and West Indies, 1661–1668* (London, 1880)
CSP Col, 1674–75	W. Noel Sainsbury, ed., *Calendar of State Papers, Colonial Series, America and West Indies, 1674–1675* (London, 1893)
CSP Col, 1677–80	W. Noel Sainsbury and J. W. Fortescue, eds., *Calendar of State Papers, Colonial Series, America and West Indies, 1677–1680* (London, 1896)
CSP Col, 1681–85	H. J. Fortescue, ed., *Calendar of State Papers, Colonial Series, America and West Indies, 1681–1685* (London, 1898)
CSP Col, 1708–9	Cecil Headlam, ed., *Calendar of State Papers, Colonial Series, America and West Indies, June, 1708–1709* (London, 1922)
CSP Col, 1710–11	Cecil Headlam, ed., *Calendar of State Papers, Colonial Series, America and West Indies, 1710–June 1711* (London, 1924)
CSP Col, 1717–18	Cecil Headlam, ed., *Calendar of State Papers, Colonial Series, America and West Indies, August 1717–Dec. 1718* (London, 1930)
CSP Col, 1719–20	Cecil Headlam, ed., *Calendar of State Papers, Colonial Series, America and West Indies, January 1719–Feb. 1720* (London, 1933)

CSP Dom. 1547–80	Robert Lemon, ed., *Calendar of State Papers, Domestic Series, of the Reigns of Edward VI, Mary, and Elizabeth, 1547–1580, Preserved in Her Majesty's Public Record Office* (London, 1856)
CSP Dom. Add., 1566–79	Mary Anne Everett Green, ed., *Calendar of State Papers, Domestic Series, of the Reign of Elizabeth, Addenda, 1566–1579, Preserved in Her Majesty's Public Record Office* (London, 1871)
CSP Ireland, 1574–85	Hans Claude Hamilton, ed., *Calendar of State Papers Relating to Ireland, of the Reign of Elizabeth, 1574–1585* (London, 1867)
JAH	*Journal of American History*
JR	Ruben Gold Thwaites, ed., *The Jesuit Relations and Allied Documents: Travels and Explorations of the Jesuit Missionaries in New France, 1610–1791*, 73 vols. (Cleveland, Ohio, 1896–1901)
MBR	Nathaniel B. Shurtleff, *Records of the Governor and Company of Massachusetts Bay in New England*, 5 vols. (Boston, 1853)
MHS Coll	*Collections of the Massachusetts Historical Society*
NHR	Charles J. Hoadly, ed., *Records of the Colony and Plantation of New Haven from 1638–1649*, 2 vols. (Hartford, 1857)
NYCD	E. B. O'Callaghan, *Documents Relative to the Colonial History of New York State*, 14 vols. (Albany, 1853–87)
PCR	Nathaniel B. Shurtleff, ed., *Records of the Colony of New Plymouth in New England*, 12 vols. (Boston, 1853)
RICR	J. R. Bartlett, ed., *Records of the Colony of Rhode Island and Providence Plantations in New England, 1636–1792*, 10 vols. (Providence, 1856–65)
RUC	*Records of the United Colonies of New England*, published as vols. 9 and 10 of *Records of the Colony of New Plymouth* (PCR)
RVC	Susan Myra Kingsbury, ed., *The Records of the Virginia Company of London*, 4 vols. (Washington, D.C., 1906–35)
VCRP	*Virginia Colonial Records Project* (Microfilm copies of British documents), Virginia Historical Society, Richmond
VMHB	*Virginia Magazine of History and Biography*
WMQ	*William and Mary Quarterly*

Dominion and Civility

Introduction

In 1794 George Washington lamented "the insufficiency of the existing provisions of the laws toward the effectual cultivation and preservation of peace with our Indian neighbours." He had hoped to oversee the orderly expansion of American settlement while pursuing a policy "calculated to advance the happiness of the Indians and to attach them firmly to the United States." "Happiness," in this sense, meant peaceful relations with and the Christianization and "civilization" of Native Americans. By 1796, however, Washington thought it unlikely that he would ever attain these goals. Aware always of the necessity "for restraining the commission of outrages upon the Indians, without which all pacific plans must prove nugatory," he confided to his secretary of state that "scarcely anything short of a Chinese wall, or a line of troops, will restrain Land jobbers, and the encroachment of settlers upon the Indian territory."[1]

There is a certain timelessness to George Washington's complaint, and his frustration typifies the experience of metropolitan Englishmen, and later Anglo-Americans, charged with governing the early American frontier and with pursuing a rational and moral Indian policy from the time of the first English settlements in America in 1585. This study explores the relations that developed among and between a variety of Native American and English groups in colonial North America during the critical first century of Anglo-Indian contact. It seeks, at heart, to explain why the Anglo-Indian exchange has so tragic a history. To do so it focuses upon a dynamic transatlantic relationship

---

[1] George Washington to Senate and House, 2 June 1794, Third Annual Address, 25 October 1791, and Fourth Annual Address, 6 November 1792, in *A Compilation of the Messages and Papers of the Presidents*, comp. James P. Richardson (Washington, D.C., 1897), 1:148, 96–97, 119; George Washington to Timothy Pickering, 1 July 1796, in *The Writings of George Washington*, ed. John C. Fitzpatrick (Washington, D.C., 1931–44), 35:112.

I

involving English metropolitans, the English men and women who settled the American frontiers, and Algonquian Indian communities in the Chesapeake Bay and New England. This relationship developed as the English metropolis expanded aggressively outward into a number of foreign "marchlands," "peripheries," and frontiers, beginning in the sixteenth century.

Metropolitan power radiated outward into the marches from London, the seat of royal government, commercial core of the empire, home of the English church, and the center of English Renaissance culture. Metropolitans defined and dictated their policies in colonial and corporate charters, royal decrees, and orders issued by the king-in-council. Colonial governors, ministers, and the officers the governors appointed implemented these policies. Together they constituted a haphazard yet real governing structure intended to incorporate the frontier and its peoples into an Anglo-American, Christian New World empire.

Metropolitan Englishmen in the Americas and in Britain sought to establish dominion and civility along the Anglo-American frontiers. They hoped to derive a profit from their settlements, either for the crown or for their sponsoring organizations. They hoped to secure and defend their colonial possessions from enemies both Native American and European. And they hoped to spread English Christianity and English civility among the native population of the New World.

To obtain these objectives most easily and least expensively, they needed an orderly and peaceful frontier. Only through peaceful means could they establish the lucrative trading relationships and stable agricultural settlements that would benefit colonial promoters or, perhaps, provide the crown with a revenue enabling it to rule without the obtrusive interference of parliaments. Only then could philanthropic Englishmen stay the deadly scourge of the Catholic powers sweeping into North America. Only then could they deliver the Indians they encountered out of the hands of Satan and, in the words of the younger Richard Hakluyt, "wth discrecion and myldenes distill into their purged myndes the swete and lively liquor of the gospell."[2] As English Christendom expanded, Hakluyt's elder cousin and namesake wrote, it would do so peacefully, "without crueltie and tyrannie" and so "best answereth the profession of a Christian, best planteth Christian religion; maketh our seating most void of blood, most profitable in trade of merchandise, most firme and stable, and least subject to remoove by practise of enemies."[3]

Metropolitans, of course, seldom succeeded in bringing order to the Anglo-American frontier. Their failure goes a long way toward explaining the

[2] Richard Hakluyt (the Younger), "The Discourse on Western Planting," in *The Original Writings and Correspondence of the Two Richard Hakluyts*, ed. E. G. R. Taylor, 2 vols. (London, 1935), 214–15.
[3] Ibid., 334.

devastating consequences of the European "invasion" of America, as well as the dynamics of the Anglo-Indian exchange.

This book takes as its subject English metropolitan efforts to govern effectively the first Anglo-American frontiers. The use of the word "frontier" here requires some attention because of the long shadow cast by Frederick Jackson Turner's "Frontier Thesis," and because the concept has recently fallen into disfavor among practitioners of the "New Western History." Patricia Nelson Limerick, for instance, has argued that in making use of the term, too many historians have adopted "the point of view of only one of the contesting groups" that encountered each other along the frontier; Native Americans have often rather cavalierly been relegated to the "other" side of the frontier. This has produced in her view a severely truncated and reductionist perception of American western history.[4]

Yet the concept of a frontier need not suggest a relentless march forward, or simply "the outer edge of the wave, the meeting point between savagery and civilization," as Turner described it.[5] Frontiers are better conceived of as zones of intercultural contact, involving two or more groups, no single one of which can dictate unilaterally the nature of the ensuing relationships. American frontiers should be viewed as zones of cultural interaction and interpenetration along the periphery of European settlement which posed significant problems of governance for Metropolitan Englishmen. The groups that encountered each other along these frontiers saw themselves as dissimilar, owing to a combination of cultural, religious, racial, environmental, and economic characteristics.[6]

Contact in this zone did not always involve conflict, however, as some fine recent studies have shown. Matthew Dennis, for instance, writing of European-Iroquois relations, argues that "war and peace were only extremes on the continuum of relationships among and between various groups. More important was the vast middle range of interactions characterized by neither absolute harmony nor total warfare, neither full understanding nor complete ignorance, neither unmarred competition nor utter contention."[7] This "middle ground," as Richard White describes it, was characterized by a complicated process of accommodation. It depended for its existence "on the in-

---

[4] Patricia Nelson Limerick, "The Adventures of the Frontier in the Twentieth Century," in *The Frontier in American Culture*, ed. James R. Grossman (Berkeley, Calif., 1994), 72–75.

[5] Frederick Jackson Turner, "The Significance of the Frontier in American History," in *Frontier and Section: Selected Essays of Frederick Jackson Turner*, ed. Ray Allen Billington (Englewood Cliffs, N.J., 1961), 38.

[6] Jack D. Forbes, "Frontiers in American History and the Role of the Frontier Historian," *Ethnohistory* 15 (1968):207–9. See also James H. Merrell, " 'The Customes of Our Countrey': Indians and Colonists in Early America," in *Strangers within the Realm: Cultural Margins of the First British Empire*, ed. Bernard Bailyn and Philip D. Morgan (Chapel Hill, N.C., 1991), 117–56.

[7] Matthew Dennis, *Cultivating a Landscape of Peace: Iroquois-European Encounters in Seventeenth-Century America* (Ithaca, N.Y., 1993), 3–4.

ability of both sides to gain their ends through force," and it grew "according to the need of people to find a means, other than force, to gain the cooperation or consent of foreigners."[8]

Complete understanding was not necessary for the middle ground to function. As James H. Merrell has pointed out in his history of the Catawbas, European observers employed more than a dozen different names to identify the Indians of the Carolina Piedmont, a terminological imprecision that revealed "a profound ignorance of Indian polities."[9] Nonetheless, those who would successfully pursue their own objectives along the middle ground, White argues, had "to attempt to understand the world and reasoning of others and to assimilate enough of that reasoning to put it to their own purposes." Indians and whites, through this process, influenced and learned from each other, creating a relationship that, in White's words, could "often guide the course of empires."[10]

Owing to these fine studies, we know more than ever before about the wide variety of relationships that developed, throughout the Americas, between natives and newcomers. Still, this middle ground remained always tenuous and fragile. Violence was ever a possibility beyond the edges of the middle ground; many rituals there, as White points out, were devoted to coping with the difficult problem of intercultural violence. The concept of a "middle ground," in fact, seems to explain best the nature of European-Indian relations during their infancy, when relatively small numbers of Europeans were encountering Native American communities.

Once European settlers began moving into a given region, peaceful relations along the frontier became less likely. The "frontier exchange economy" in the lower Mississippi Valley described by Daniel H. Usner Jr., an analog to White's "middle ground," broke down rapidly after 1763 as immigrants poured into the region. Indian relations in the Ohio country, the Great Lakes region, and the Susquehanna River valley deteriorated in similar fashion as settlers began moving into those areas.[11] So, too, around Chesapeake Bay and in New England. Farmers cleared the land, altering the game potential of what previously had been Indian hunting grounds, and allowed their livestock to roam free and forage in unfenced Indian corn-

---

[8] Richard White, *The Middle Ground: Indians, Empires, and Republics in the Great Lakes Region* (Cambridge, England, 1991), 52.

[9] James H. Merrell, *The Indians' New World: The Catawbas and Their Neighbors through the Era of Removal*, (Chapel Hill, N.C., 1989), 47.

[10] White, *Middle Ground*, 52, xi.

[11] Daniel H. Usner, Jr., *Indians, Settlers, and Slaves in a Frontier Exchange Economy: The Lower Mississippi Valley before 1783* (Chapel Hill, N.C., 1992), 112–13; Eric Hinderaker, *Elusive Empires: Constructing Colonialism in the Ohio Valley, 1673–1800* (New York, 1997); Peter C. Mancall, *Valley of Opportunity: Economic Culture along the Upper Susquehanna, 1700–1800*, (Ithaca, N.Y., 1991).

fields. As settlers began to occupy Indian land, "the common ground contracted almost to the vanishing point."[12]

The Anglo-American frontier experience in general thus was predicated upon a prolonged competition for control of frontier resources between peoples with opposing value systems. Native Americans and Englishmen employed these resources in ways that were seldom compatible. Sometimes, the pursuit of self-interest by Native American and English frontier communities worked to mutual advantage. There existed at some times and in some places a give-and-take and a significant degree of cultural osmosis; natives and newcomers got along, learned from and traded with each other, and propagated children together. But more frequently, tension bred in conflict and competition over access to frontier resources characterized relations on this middle ground. The frontier was a world of pragmatism, exploitation, and, quite often, violence, where English and Native American settlements ultimately stood opposed.

The challenges of governing a frontier were not without precedent in the annals of English maritime expansion, and the problems English metropolitans faced in America were not unlike those they had experienced elsewhere. In the sixteenth century King Henry VIII began a slow and painful process of incorporating the Scottish Borderlands, the Welsh Marches, and Ireland into an expanding Tudor state. This process, continued during the reign of Henry's successors, carried the English into the "Celtic Fringe," a zone of nearly constant conflict and endemic lawlessness where English soldiers and settlers encountered tribal peoples they thought of as backward, barbaric, and irreconcilably different from themselves. While the crown and its officers debated how best to bring Celtic peoples under the authority of the English state, convert them to English Christianity, and maintain order on this frontier, the actual experience of frontier conflict generated a bitterness that heightened the traditional animosity of English settlers toward their Celtic neighbors. A similar clash between frontier and metropolitan interests consistently replayed itself on the first Anglo-American frontiers.[13]

The English effort to govern its first American frontiers, moreover, offers instructive parallels with the experience of other European powers in North America. Like the Spanish, the French, and, to a much lesser extent, the Dutch, the English viewed colonization as part of a broader movement to extend Christianity and civility throughout the world. Each of these nations

---

[12] William Cronon, George Miles, and Jay Gitlin, "Becoming West: Towards a New Meaning for Western History," in *Under an Open Sky: Rethinking America's Western Past*, ed. Cronon, Miles, and Gitlin (New York, 1992), 14.

[13] See A. L. Rowse, *The Expansion of Elizabethan England* (New York, 1955), 1–157; J. G. A. Pocock, "The Limits and Divisions of British History: In Search of the Unknown Subject," *AHR* 87 (1982): 317, 324–25; and W. R. Jones, "England against the Celtic Fringe: A Study in Cultural Stereotypes," *Journal of World History* 13 (1971): 155–71.

claimed dominion over the peoples and territories it settled. European expansion was equated with Christian expansion, and all the imperial powers believed that the native peoples of the Americas ultimately would be incorporated within the Christian empires they hoped to establish in the New World.[14] All recognized a need for peaceful relations with the Indians if their colonies were to prosper. The invasion of America, in this limited sense, was launched upon waves of benevolent intent. Benevolence seldom worked, however, owing to the dramatically different and ultimately incompatible strategies of land use practiced by Native Americans and Europeans, and the inability of metropolitans to manage effectively the nature of intercultural relations.

During the first century of English settlement in America, competition for control of frontier resources in the Chesapeake Bay region and in New England produced tension between English settlers and Indians which resulted in mutual harassment, exploitation, abuse, and a mounting cycle of violence that metropolitans never successfully controlled. As this cycle accelerated, the Anglo-American frontier population demonstrated heightened racial antipathy toward Indians, especially when and where these tensions flared into warfare. War with the Indians undermined the metropolitan program. With farms and plantations set ablaze by an enemy both elusive and effective, colonizing enterprises could neither prosper nor allow the crown to collect customs revenue on provincial products. Trouble with Indians, moreover, provided opportunities for England's imperial rivals to interfere in the English colonies by luring offended natives into alliances—with potentially devastating consequences. Finally, metropolitans could not hope to convert the same Indians they were trying to kill. In resolving these crises, English metropolitans abandoned the more philanthropic elements in their program, effectively accepting the frontier assessment of native worth. Their attempts to bring Christianity to Indians diminished as they became increasingly inclined to view Indians as irredeemable savages. Everywhere in colonial North America the Indian wars left among their legacies the subjugation, dispossession, and, at times, enslavement and execution of the Indians involved. By the end of the 1670s the native peoples of the first frontiers—the coastal Algonquians from New England to the Chesapeake—had lost their independent and autonomous status, and had been forced well along the road to becoming a despised and encircled minority.

As at Roanoke Island in 1585, so too in New England and the Chesapeake ninety years later: metropolitan Englishmen entered with a number of religious, imperial, and economic objectives. Their explicitly Anglo-centric program, they believed, would benefit the English colonists living along the frontiers, the Indians, and the crown. Metropolitan policies, however, di-

---

[14] Anthony Pagden, *Lords of All the World: Ideologies of Empire in Spain, Britain, and France, c. 1500–c. 1800* (New Haven, Conn., 1995), 30–31, 126.

rected toward incorporating the frontier, its resources, and its people into an Anglo-American empire where all would embrace English standards of civility and Christianity, led implicitly to the elimination or, at best, the profound alteration of native cultures that had succeeded in feeding, clothing, and housing themselves and meeting their own spiritual needs for centuries.[15] The power of English ethnocentrism should not be underestimated. Metropolitans were confident that Indians would follow the path of progress that had brought the English to their current and, to them, highly desirable level of civilization. They believed the Indians capable of reason and so assumed that they would make the only reasonable choice—but only if order prevailed along the frontier.

Metropolitans failed to achieve their goal of establishing both dominion and civility along the first American frontiers. Native Americans maintained a rich and powerful cultural heritage. With their own assumptions about polite manners and how strangers ought to treat one another and, more important, with their subsistence systems under siege, Indians in the end had little interest in accommodating to English cultural norms and resisted—violently, at times—the English invasion. The English frontier population, meanwhile, whose subsistence and livelihood depended upon access to and control of frontier resources, resisted metropolitan directives aimed at relieving the pressure they placed upon native lands, and so poisoned relations between the two peoples. The frontier, in this sense, became the crucible in which Anglo-American attitudes and policies toward Native Americans were formed.

The metropolitans' vision of the New World, however ethnocentric, was an inclusive vision. They had hoped initially to bring Indians peacefully into an English society overseas, persuading them to abandon their native savagery in favor of English civility. Metropolitans also tried to impose their plans for a Christian, Anglo-American New World empire upon a frontier population that was locked in competition with natives for control of the land; they could not fully develop and pursue their plans to "improve" the Indians without controlling these colonists. The pressure exerted by this population upon the Indians produced tensions along the frontier which everywhere in English North America flared into full-scale warfare shortly after the plantation of English settlements.

The interplay of the English frontier population, Native Americans, and the English metropolitans who attempted to govern both shaped profoundly the nature of interracial relations in the American colonies, relations between the crown and the provinces, and the history of the cultural margins of the first British Empire.

[15] Richard White, *The Roots of Dependency: Subsistence, Environment, and Social Change among the Choctaws, Pawnees, and Navajos* (Lincoln, Nebr., 1983), xix; Calvin Martin, "An Introduction: Aboard the *Fidele*," in *The American Indian and the Problem of History* (New York, 1987), 8–9.

I   *This New Found Land*

Late in the summer of 1586 Thomas Hariot returned to London after his second and final voyage to the "New Found Land of Virginia." In the service of Sir Walter Ralegh, the promoter of this attempt to secure an English foothold in the Americas, Hariot had participated both in a reconnaissance of the Carolina Outer Banks in 1584 and the attempt to plant a colony at Roanoke Island one year later. He remained there with the soldiers and settlers sent to colonize the island for the entire twelve months of the colony's existence. Then, once again taking up residence at Durham House, Ralegh's headquarters in the Strand, Hariot sought to extract lessons from his New World experience. Over the course of the next few years he thought deeply about Roanoke, not solely about the mineral and agricultural potential of the region but about its people, their culture, and their place in the ordering of all creation.

Hariot had joined the circle of adventurers, soldiers, explorers, and scholars at Durham House by the fall of 1583, after Ralegh began planning his North American enterprise. Initially, Hariot would train Ralegh and his men in navigation. His primary responsibility, however, was to travel to America with the artist John White to discover, he said, "the true pictures and fashions of the people in that parte of America now called Virginia."[1]

The assignment reflected the interest of Ralegh, Hariot, and White in the New World and its inhabitants, an intellectual preoccupation that may justifiably be considered scientific in approach. Hariot and White hoped to learn about the culture and manners of the native peoples they encountered, then to employ this information in an effort both to incorporate these peo-

---

[1] Thomas Hariot, *A Briefe and True Report of the New Found Land of Virginia* (1590), ed. Paul Hulton, (New York, 1972), [36]; John W. Shirley, *Thomas Harriot: A Biography* (Oxford, 1983), 81–82, 96, 101.

ples into a framework of human development understandable to Renaissance Englishmen and to assimilate them into an English, and Christian, society overseas.[2]

Hariot first published his *Briefe and True Report of the New Found Land of Virginia* in 1588. At the urging of his friend and mentor Richard Hakluyt the Younger, the greatest promoter of English overseas expansion, Hariot planned the second edition (1590). Hakluyt saw in the combination of Hariot's words and White's artwork a means to combat fears of the difficulty of survival in a distant colonial outpost. Hakluyt encouraged the Flemish engraver and publisher Theodor de Bry to publish Hariot and White's work. The *Briefe and True Report* described, first, "the Merchantable Commodities" of the Roanoke region; second, "suche commodities as Virginia is knowne to yeelde for victuall and sustenance of mans life"; and finally, "the nature and manners of the people of the countrey." In the course of his discussion Hariot effectively addressed the metropolitan concern for New World profit, security, and conversion. De Bry appended twenty-eight engravings to the text based upon White's artwork.[3]

The work of Hariot, White, and De Bry constitutes the best visual description of any American culture at the dawning of its contact with Europeans. It also testifies with horrifying clarity to the devastation wreaked by European settlement. Disease killed hundreds of natives on the Carolina Outer Banks in the initial months of contact. When the English visited Algonquian settlements, Hariot noted, "within a few dayes after our departure from everie such towne, the people began to die very fast, and many in short space; in small townes about twentie, in some fourtie, in some sixtie, & in one sixe score, which in trueth was very manie in respect of their numbers." Many Indians, he observed, "were perswaded that it was the worke of our God through our meanes, and that we by him might kil and slai whom wee would without weapons and not come neere them."[4]

The spread of disease in some cases weakened attachments to Carolina Algonquian tradition as the remedies proposed by village shamans proved unable to halt the epidemic. Disease, then, along with an array of English technology that, according to Hariot, awed and impressed the natives, disoriented Algonquian society. This "made manie of them to have such an opinion of us as that if they knew not the trueth of God and religion already, it was rather to be had from us, whom God so specially loved then from a people that were so simple, as they found themselves to be in comparison of us."[5]

[2] David Beers Quinn, *Set Fair for Roanoke: Voyages and Colonies, 1584–1606* (Chapel Hill, N.C., 1985), 158, 204, 220.
[3] Paul Hulton, *America 1585: The Complete Drawings of John White* (Chapel Hill, N.C., 1984), 17; Hariot, *Briefe and True Report*, 7, 13, 22, 41; George Brunner Parks, *Richard Hakluyt and the English Voyages*, 2d ed., (New York, 1962), 162–63.
[4] Hariot, *Briefe and True Report*, 28.
[5] Ibid., 27.

Hariot's observations, however, did not lead him to either a blanket de-nunciation of native culture or bold assertions of English superiority. He of course witnessed the natives of the Carolina Outer Banks through a lens of ethnocentrism; his own culture, that of Renaissance England, provided the standard against which he measured all others. He regarded his own reli-gion, the Protestantism of Elizabeth's England, as superior to the untutored beliefs of the natives. Yet nowhere is there present in Hariot's or White's work any suggestion of an innate inferiority of the native tribes. Indeed, Har-iot found much to respect in Indian society. These clearly were intelligent and adaptable people, and Hariot believed that they would easily, and peace-fully, be "brought to civilitie and the imbracing of true religion."[6]

Hariot accumulated enough familiarity with the Carolina Algonquian di-alect to converse with Roanoke priests on matters of some theological com-plexity, and he found the Indians eager to learn about English religion. "Many times and in every towne where I came, according as I was able," Hariot wrote,

> I made declaration of the contents of the Bible; that therein was set fourth the true and onlie God, and his mightie workes, that therein was contayned the true doc-trine of salvation through Christ, with many particularities of Miracles and chiefe poyntes of religion, as I was able then to utter, and thought fitte for the time.

The coastal Algonquians demonstrated "their hungrie desire of that knowl-edge which was spoken of." They reportedly joined the English in prayer and in the singing of psalms. They sought the help of English prayers in com-batting the effects of drought, and they begged an English god for relief from the ravages of epidemic disease. Hariot concluded that conversion would oc-cur without difficulty and that neither force nor compulsion nor subdual would be necessary to bring the Indians to English standards of civility.[7]

Hariot, White, and De Bry conceived of the Native Americans of the Roanoke region in progressive terms. The Indians, they believed, could par-ticipate in the natural historical process whereby all societies moved gradu-ally forward, becoming more civilized as time passed. This paradigm of the development of human societies lay at the heart of White's inclusion in his portfolio of a sampling of Brazilian, Roman, medieval European, Inuit, Turkish, Tartar, Pict, and ancient British figures. The same assumption in-formed the decision to include in the *Briefe and True Report* an appendix containing images "of the Pictes which in the olde tyme dyd habite one part of the great Bretainne." As De Bry wrote,

> The Painter of Whom I have had the first of the Inhabitants of Virginia [White] give my allso thees 5. Figures fallowinge, fownd as hy did assured my in a oold

---

[6] Ibid., 25. De Bry shared these views; see his "Epistle to the Reader," ibid., 41.
[7] Ibid., 25, 27–28, 30.

SOM PICTVRE,
OF THE PICTES
WHICH IN THE OLDE
tyme dyd habite one part of the
great Bretainne.

THE PAINTER OF WHOM J HAVE
had the firſt of the Inhabitans of Virginia, giue my allſo thees 5. Figures
fallowinge, fownd as hy did aſſured my in a oolld Engliſh cronicle, the which
I wold well ſett to the ende of thees firſt Figures, for to ſhowe how that
the Inhabitants of the great Bretannie haue bin in ti-
mes paſt as ſauuage as thoſe of
Virginia.

E

Page introducing Appendix to Thomas Hariot's *A Briefe and True Report of the New Found Land of Virginia* (1590). Courtesy Dover Publications, Inc.

English cronicle, the which I wold well sett to the ende of thees first Figures, for to showe how that the Inhabitants of the great Bretannie have bin in times past as sauvage as those of Virginia.[8]

[8] Ibid., [75], 25.

White and Hariot were likewise of the opinion that humankind had evolved socially from primitive origins and that different peoples in different places evolved at different rates. Believing that the inhabitants of England had been little more than tattooed and woad-stained barbarians at a time when Roman civilization flourished in England, they likened the Carolina Algonquians to the Picts and ancient Britons of the first century B.C. The conviction that all civilized societies had at one time been as "savage" as the natives of North America clearly undergirded their optimism that like their forbears, Indians too would progress. All societies evolve; all societies progress. This paradigm, that all peoples could be understood by their developmental location on a natural historical progression, lay within the core of the metropolitan understanding of the Indian.[9]

I

The English entered slowly the arena of European maritime expansion. Henry VII, seeking access to Cathay and the Spice Islands, granted a charter in 1496 to a syndicate of Bristol merchants headed by John Cabot and his sons. Their early voyages produced some exciting discoveries but generated little interest at home. When Elizabeth ascended to the throne in 1558, England knew little more about the coast of North America than it had fifty years before.

Spain and Portugal, in the meantime, had been far from inactive. The creation of the Portuguese and Spanish empires resulted at least in part from dramatic social changes occurring in Europe. Between the last quarter of the fifteenth century and the middle of the sixteenth, a significant increase in population had led not only to intensified agriculture within Europe but also to intensified exploitation of the Atlantic fisheries. The drive to harvest the sea led in turn to the development of a naval technology capable of supporting longer voyages than ever before. The expansion of the European economy produced as well a dramatic increase in luxury consumption. The desire to satisfy this demand took the Portuguese into their lucrative trading activities in Africa and the Orient, and the desire of the Spanish to break into this trade brought about the European discovery of America.[10]

[9] Ibid. See also J. A. Leo Lemay, "The Frontiersman from Lout to Hero: Notes on the Significance of the Comparative Method and Stage Theory in Early American Literature and Culture," *Proceedings of the American Antiquarian Society* 88 (1978): 203; Alden T. Vaughan, "Early English Paradigms for New World Natives," *Proceedings of the American Antiquarian Society* 102 (1992): 51–53; George Huppert, "The Idea of Civilization in the Sixteenth Century," in *Renaissance Studies in Honor of Hans Baron*, ed. Anthony Malho and J. A. Tedeschal (Florence, Italy, 1971), 760, 768.

[10] J. H. Parry, *The Age of Reconnaissance: Discovery, Exploration, and Settlement, 1450–1650* (New York, 1963), 163; David Beers Quinn, *England and the Discovery of America* (New York, 1974), 193; Kenneth R. Andrews, *Trade, Plunder, and Settlement: Maritime Enterprise and the Genesis of the British Empire, 1480–1630* (Cambridge, England, 1984), 3–5.

England shared in the general economic prosperity of Europe. Its population grew, market forces made substantial inroads into the countryside, and London became a thriving metropolis. Rising population on the Continent increased the demand for English cloth, and the woolens industry in England expanded rapidly to satisfy this need. English merchants, then, had little incentive to devote their energies to the exploitation of the New World. So long as they had access to European markets and the general economic prosperity continued, they felt little need to look westward, save for the yearly fishing voyages that plied the coast of what would become northern New England.[11]

By the middle of the sixteenth century, however, powerful social and economic changes had forced Englishmen to cast their eyes across the Atlantic. Exports of cloth declined significantly in volume during the 1550s, and the ensuing depression resulted in widespread dislocation within several sectors of the economy.[12] The growth rate in England's population slowed for only a short time during the crisis of the 1550s; thereafter, population pressures brought rising food prices, unemployment, and landlessness. For a government that felt itself increasingly responsible for the economic and social stability of the realm, these conditions were a tremendous source of concern. Fearing restiveness and riot on the part of an angry populace, the crown began to search for means of providing for both its growing population and the safety of the kingdom.[13]

While social and economic problems were forcing the English to think about overseas expansion and settlement abroad, the religious turmoil of England's Reformation produced a national hatred of the Catholic Spanish and a desire both to injure the enemies of the realm and to relieve them of their New World riches. The death of the young Protestant Edward VI in 1553 brought the Catholic Mary Tudor to the throne. Her leap into the arms of Felipe of Spain invoked in many a fear of foreign domination and aroused active hostility to her reign long before she began her persecutions for heresy. Risings against the Spanish match hardened Mary's determination to bring the English church back into the Roman fold. The three hundred burnings that followed were indeed a small figure by the monumental standards of European religious bigotry, but they had an enormous impact upon English Protestants. Mary provided Protestant laymen with a cause they could rally around, and she inspired an undying hatred in many English hearts of all things Catholic.[14]

[11] Andrews, *Trade*, 6; C. G. A. Clay, *Economic Expansion and Social Change in England, 1500–1700*, 2 vols. (Cambridge, England, 1984), 2:109–10.
[12] Clay, *Economic Expansion*, 1:16, 2:113–15; L. A. Clarkson, *The Pre-Industrial Economy in England, 1500–1750* (London, 1971), 131. See also Whitney R. D. Jones, *The Mid-Tudor Crisis, 1539–1563* (New York, 1973), 130.
[13] D. C. Coleman, *The Economy of England, 1450–1750* (London, 1977), 18; Jones, *Mid-Tudor Crisis*, 113, 130–34; Whitney R. D. Jones, *The Tudor Commonwealth, 1529–1559* (London, 1970); Andrews, *Trade*, 66.
[14] See William Haller, *The Elect Nation: The Meaning and Relevance of Foxe's "Book of Martyrs"* (New York, 1963).

English New World enterprise, then, addressed the religious, social, and political concerns of the crown and provided an opportunity both to serve the commonweal and strengthen the empire. English metropolitans watched and learned important lessons as their Spanish rivals enriched themselves in America. In fact, in administering its own New World empire, Spain confronted problems and challenges that the English too would soon face.

Spanish colonization in America logically followed from the *Reconquista*, the centuries-long struggle to drive the forces of Islam from the Iberian peninsula. Spanish Catholicism as a result developed a particularly strident and zealous character that shaped Spanish intentions in the New World.[15] Colonization would enrich the crown and at the same time extend Spanish culture, institutions, and religion abroad. Colonization would benefit the crown, the empire, and God, and Queen Isabella emphasized always the importance of spreading the one and only true religion. "Because we desire that the Indians be converted to our Holy Catholic faith and their souls be saved, and because this is the greatest benefit that we can desire for them," Isabella ordered Nicolas de Ovando, her first governor of Hispaniola in 1503, to ensure "that they be instructed in the things of our faith, in order that they will come to a knowledge of it." Convinced of the capacity of the Indians for spiritual improvement and of their willingness to listen to divine reason, Isabella and her supporters assumed that they would readily and freely accept the tenets and teachings of Spanish Catholicism. The Indians, reasoning and rational, fully capable of understanding the superiority of Spanish culture, could be expected to assimilate into a Spanish-American society.[16]

While missionaries worked to harvest native souls, Isabella and her successors hoped as well to extract the mineral wealth of Spain's New World possessions, which they viewed as a divine reward for converting the Indians. These riches could both underwrite further missionary activity and increase the economic power of the empire. To mine gold and silver, however, required an abundant supply of labor. Isabella therefore authorized her agents to compel Indians to labor in the public interest, but she did so with prohibitions against the violation of Indian rights. In return for the privilege of recruiting Indian labor, *encomenderos* agreed to reside on the frontier, protect and support the efforts of missionaries to Hispanicize and Christianize Indians, and provide military service to the crown.[17]

In practice, the efforts of Isabella and her successors to protect the Indians from Spanish colonists met with little success. Spanish conquistadors

[15] David J. Weber, *The Spanish Frontier in North America* (New Haven, Conn., 1992), 20.
[16] Lyle N. McAlister, *Spain and Portugal in the New World, 1492–1700* (Minneapolis, 1984), 108–9; J. H. Parry, *The Establishment of European Hegemony* (New York, 1961), 67.
[17] Anthony Pagden, *Lords of All the World: Ideologies of Empire in Spain, Britain, and France, c.1500–c.1800* (New Haven, Conn., 1995), 34; Parry, *European Hegemony*, 67; McAlister, *Spain and Portugal*, 165; Weber, *Spanish Frontier*, 124–25.

demonstrated a grotesque capacity for violence wherever they went, leaving behind them mangled bodies, ruined lives, and defeated Indians who at times seethed with resentment against their colonial overlords.[18] The pathogens these soldiers carried wreaked even greater devastation than their swords. Virgin-soil epidemics, diseases that Europeans had experienced but to which Indians had no previous exposure, ravaged native communities, carrying away in places 90 percent of the population. At the same time, *encomenderos* exploited Indian labor to a point that threatened native subsistence. Taxes imposed on natives for labor, corn, blankets, and other goods drove Indians in many locations to the brink of rebellion.[19]

Clearly, the imperial structure the Spanish constructed to govern their far-flung empire, although staffed at its highest levels by officers committed to safeguarding Indian rights, was ill-equipped to protect native peoples on remote and distant frontiers. The Spanish crown, in fact, faced enormous practical obstacles to efficient administration. Communication between Seville and the Americas occurred infrequently, given the distance between frontier and metropolis. As a result, the crown knew little of American events and could seldom respond effectively when crises arose. Within the colonies themselves the vast distances separating imperial officials from the Spanish frontier population militated against efficient oversight of Indian-white relations. Colonists, for all practical purposes, could act as they chose. Spain never developed an imperial administrative system capable of securing meaningful control over Indian affairs.

The fact that the crown and the colonists pursued different objectives only exacerbated these problems. Necessity forced the crown of Castile, strapped for resources and mired in religious and dynastic struggles in Europe, to turn over the business of discovery and colonization to *adelantados*, private adventurers who performed much of the work of carving out a Spanish-American empire. Though the crown encouraged these adventurers to see to the spiritual and temporal well-being of the Indians, few listened. Conquerors and settlers, the men sent to occupy the Americas wanted to exploit the natives and become wealthy, and these objectives frequently rendered considerations of native spiritual welfare of secondary importance at best.[20]

---

[18] See, e.g., Bartolomé de Las Casas, *The Devastation of the Indies* (1552), trans. Herma Briffault (Baltimore, Md., 1992).

[19] Among fine local studies treating these problems, see Ramon A. Gutierrez, *When Jesus Came, the Corn Mothers Went Away: Marriage, Sexuality and Power in New Mexico, 1500–1680* (Palo Alto, Calif., 1991); Elizabeth A. H. John, *Storms Brewed in Other Men's Worlds: The Confrontation of Indians, Spanish, and French in the Southwest, 1540–1795* (Norman, Okla., 1975); Andrew L. Knaut, *The Pueblo Revolt of 1680: Conquest and Resistance in Seventeenth-Century New Mexico* (Norman, Okla., 1995); Eugene Lyon, *The Enterprise of Florida: Pedro Menendez de Aviles and the Spanish Conquest, 1565–1568* (Gainesville, Fla., 1976); Charles R. Cutter, *The Protector de Indios in Colonial New Mexico, 1659–1821* (Albuquerque, N.M., 1986). On disease, see Alfred Crosby, "Virgin Soil Epidemics as a Factor in the Aboriginal Depopulation in America," *WMQ*, 3d ser., 33 (1976).

[20] McAlister, *Spain and Portugal*, 79, 81, 91.

On occasion the crown attempted to reform imperial administration and protect the Indians, but these efforts seldom succeeded. Stung by the pointed criticism of the Dominican friar Bartolomé de Las Casas and others, Carlos V in 1542 issued a new body of laws that strengthened earlier prohibitions against enslaving Indians and abolished the *encomienda* system. Carlos ultimately backed down in the face of widespread opposition from *encomenderos* who argued that the institution provided the only sure means for extracting a livelihood from the Americas. In 1573, however, Carlos's successor, Felipe II, promulgated new "Comprehensive Orders for New Discoveries" which reaffirmed the crown's commitment to the peaceful conversion of the Indians, emphasized the importance of preaching the gospel to natives and prohibited violence against them. Felipe thus committed the Spanish to the notion that New World natives were neither animals nor natural slaves but rational people capable of understanding divine reason; they should not, therefore, be destroyed but preserved and incorporated into a Spanish, Christian civilization overseas.[21] Missionaries did in fact enjoy some tremendous successes in persuading Indians to adopt the outward forms of Catholic worship, but these reforms were seldom enforced on the most remote frontiers of the empire, and Indians continued to suffer at the hands of Spanish colonists.

English metropolitans knew of the brutality of the Spanish conquest, and some saw an opportunity to enrich England by exploiting the disaffection of subjects angry with their colonial overlords. With the successes of Sir Francis Drake in Spanish America, enthusiasm for English expansion grew dramatically, and peaceful relations with New World natives became a critical constituent of early English metropolitan thought. These arguments received their most cogent support in the writings of the two Richard Hakluyts, elder and younger cousins.

Together, the Hakluyts tirelessly promoted English overseas expansion. They maintained always a firm belief that the New World would be in better hands under the direction of an English queen rather than a Spanish king. More than any of their contemporaries, the Hakluyts considered the place of Native Americans in England's New World empire and offered suggestions as to how they ought to be treated. Widely disseminated, their opinions are consequently central to any understanding of the ideas about Indians that English metropolitans carried into the New World.

On the eve of Humphrey Gilbert's first American voyage, in 1578, the elder Hakluyt argued that a hostile Indian population could endanger any colonial enterprise. Conversely, trade with natives could keep the colonists alive and, as well, make the colony profitable. "It behoveth," he wrote, "that all humanitie and curtesie and much forbearinge of revenge to the inland people be used, so shall you have firme amitie with your neyghbours, so shal

---

[21] John, *Storms*, 10–11; Weber, *Spanish Frontier*, 95.

you have their inland commodities to maintayne trafficke, and so shall you waxe rich and strong in force."[22]

Later, in 1585, Hakluyt suggested that if numerous Indian tribes inhabited an area, selective alliances should be made with particular groups. This diplomacy opened two possibilities for the colonizers. First, "with a few men," Hakluyt wrote, the English "may be revenged of any wrong offered by any of them." Second, selective alliances offered the English the opportunity, "if wee will proceed with extremitie," to "conquer, fortifie, and plant in soiles most sweet, most pleasant, most strong, and most fertile, and in the end bring them all in subjection and to civilitie." To the elder Hakluyt the purpose of English settlement in the New World should be to plant Christianity among the natives, establish profitable trade relations, and, finally, enlarge "the dominions of the Queenes most excellent Maiestie, and consequently of her honour, revenues, and of her power by this enterprise."[23]

Before they could attain these goals, however, promoters of English maritime expansion needed to resolve questions involving the process by which "rude" or "savage" nations become civilized and adopt Christianity. Englishmen confronted these questions both in Ireland and in the New World, and they applied the answers arrived at in Ireland to the American context. Some argued that the natives must be subdued militarily prior to their religious conversion. Others thought that direct evangelization, preaching, and catechesis, as well as formal education, would suffice to bring the natives to accept the true religion. The sword, in this case, would yield to the word, and force yield to persuasion.[24] "A gentle course," wrote the elder Hakluyt, "without crueltie and tyrannie best answereth the profession of a Christian, best planteth Christian religion; maketh our seating most void of blood, most profitable in trade of merchandise, most firme and stable, and least subject to remoove by practise of enemies."[25] It seldom worked, but no better statement of the English metropolitan perspective exists.

The younger Richard Hakluyt, a clergyman, also believed that the inhabitants of the New World could be brought peacefully to accept English Christianity; in fact, he saw the conversion of the Indians as integral to any successful colonial enterprise. In 1582 he wrote "that Godliness is great riches, and that if we first seeke the kingdome of God, al other things will be

---

[22] Quoted in David B. Quinn, ed., *The Voyages and Colonizing Enterprises of Sir Humphrey Gilbert* (London, 1940), 181–82.

[23] E. G. R. Taylor, ed., *The Original Writings and Correspondence of the Two Richard Hakluyts* (London, 1935), 329–30, 332, 327.

[24] On Ireland, the best contemporary statement is Sir John Davies, *A Discoverie of the True Causes Why Ireland Was Never Entirely Subdued* (London, 1612). See also Brendan Bradshaw, "Sword, Word, and Strategy in the Reformation of Ireland," *Historical Journal* 21 (1978): 475–502; Nicholas P. Canny, "The Ideology of English Colonization: From Ireland to America," *WMQ*, 3d ser., 30 (1973): 575–98; David Beers Quinn, *The Elizabethans and the Irish* (Ithaca, N.Y., 1966); Quinn, "Sir Thomas Smith and the Beginnings of English Colonial Theory," *Proceedings of the American Philosophical Society*, 89 (1945): 543–60.

[25] Taylor, *Writings of the Hakluyts*, 334.

given unto us." The kings and queens of England, Hakluyt argued, "have the name of Defendors of the Faithe: By which title I thinke they are not onely chardged to mayneteyne and patronize the faithe of Christe, but also to inlardge and advaunce the same." This task, he continued, should be thought of not as "their last worke but rather the principall and chefe of all others."[26]

In 1589 Hakluyt published the first edition of his magnum opus, *The Principall Navigations of the English Nation*, a comprehensive collection of information on English exploration of the world. Although he devoted the bulk of the text to voyages that had occurred during his lifetime, Hakluyt traveled far into the English past, discussing the mythical conquests of Ireland, Norway, and Greenland by King Arthur. He thereby contributed to the creation of the national myth that long before such expansion actually had taken place, men of his nation had carried the standard of English liberty far and wide across the globe. With all his brash confidence in the glory of English institutions, Hakluyt believed wholeheartedly in the myth himself. In this harshly Anglo-centric view of the world all peoples, upon receiving education in the virtues of English civilization, would gladly seek the protection and munificence of the English crown.[27]

Englishmen seeking information on the New World and its inhabitants did not need to rely solely upon the works of the two Hakluyts.[28] Still, they remained the most important and central figures in a growing circle of geographers, cosmographers, and promoters of English empire. Theirs was truly a metropolitan concern. When they looked across the Atlantic, they saw the establishment of societies addressing the concerns of both commonwealth and empire. These societies would secure domestic peace and stability at home while enriching the state and weakening its enemies. The New World would provide fruitful employment for those dislocated by the tumultuous social change of the Tudor period. There, colonists could serve both the crown and God as they brought English liberty and the true religion to a people living in darkness, bereft of such advantages. All this would be accomplished without coercion, without violence. It was a highly idealistic view of the New World.[29]

II

The Tudor period in England, with all its attending social, economic, and religious turmoil, coincided with the arrival of Renaissance influences, the

[26] Richard Hakluyt, *Divers Voyages Touching the Discoverie of America* (London, 1582), n.p.; Taylor, *Writings of the Hakluyts*, 215.

[27] J. H. Parry, "Hakluyt's View of British History," in *The Hakluyt Handbook*, ed. David Beers Quinn (London, 1974), 3–7; Taylor, *Writings of the Hakluyts*, 142–43; Edmund S. Morgan, *American Slavery, American Freedom: The Ordeal of Colonial Virginia* (New York, 1975), 16–17.

[28] George Brunner Parks, "Tudor Travel Literature: A Brief History," in Quinn, *Hakluyt Handbook*, 97–132.

[29] See Hakluyt's epistle dedicatory to his edition of Laudonnière's *Notable Historie Containing Foure Voyages Made by Certayne French Captaynes unto Florida*, in Taylor, *Writings of the Hakluyts*, 375–76.

strength of which had been intensified by the New World discoveries of the late fifteenth and early sixteenth centuries. The Renaissance resulted from "two overlapping modes of discovery," Charles Trinkhaus wrote, that of the classical past and that of the unknown continents. Much more now could be known about other peoples, across both time and space. Europe could observe America through one of two lenses, with both images inherently narcissistic: it could view America as a reflection of its own ideal past, an Edenic setting uncorrupted by the vice, greed, and corruption of an increasingly cosmopolitan Europe; or, as they did increasingly over the course of the sixteenth century, Europeans could see in America their own actual past—a time when the inhabitants of Europe, like the contemporary inhabitants of America, remained as yet uneducated in the benefits of Christian religion and civil society.[30]

Several traditions of thought equipped Europeans to comprehend, in their own fashion, the dramatic intellectual changes occurring around them. Renaissance humanism made them acutely conscious of societies and civilizations not their own: those of the classical world. Knowledge of the Greeks and Romans, far removed in time, gave Renaissance Europeans a new sense of temporal perspective which aided them in comprehending the societies of the New World, far removed in space. Especially important, Europeans rediscovered the classical notion that the earliest men had been naked forest dwellers, which provided a foundation for the development of an idea of human progress. Yet however open-minded the Europeans of the Age of Discovery, they remained strongly wedded to their Christian beliefs, and thus many looked upon the inhabitants of the New World primarily as souls to be saved. The discovery of new worlds, moreover, strengthened the providentialist interpretation of history as a progressive movement that would culminate in the conversion of all mankind, as contrasted with the older cyclical theory of the rise and fall of civilizations. The New World discoveries, then, encouraged a linear and progressive tendency in Christian thought.[31]

The conjunction of Christian and classical traditions initiated a process through which such self-validating representations of the "other" as "barbarian" or "wildman" or "savage" were replaced in the metropolitan mind by more transhistorical concepts placing the New World inhabitants within a larger matrix of human development. This process moved slowly and

[30] Charles Trinkhaus, "Renaissance and Discovery," in *First Images of America: The Impact of the New World on the Old*, ed. Fredi Chiapelli et al., 2 vols. (Berkeley, Calif., 1976), 1:4–5; John H. Elliott, "Renaissance Europe and America: A Blunted Impact?" in Chiapelli et al., *First Images*, 1:20; David Beers Quinn, "Renaissance Influences in English Colonization," *Transactions of the Royal Historical Society*, 5th ser., 26 (1976): 73; J. R. Hale, "Sixteenth-Century Explanations of War and Violence," *Past and Present*, no. 51 (1971): 5.

[31] Elliott, "Renaissance Europe and America," 1:18; Margaret T. Hodgen, *Early Anthropology in the Sixteenth and Seventeenth Centuries* (Philadelphia, 1964), 184; Arnoldo Momigliano, "The Place of Herodotus in the History of Historiography" in *Studies in Historiography*, (New York, 1966), 137–38; J. H. Rowe, "Ethnography and Ethnology in the Sixteenth Century," *Kroeber Anthropological Society Papers* 30 (1964): 7; J. H. Elliott, *The Old World and the New, 1492–1650* (Cambridge, England, 1970), 51–52.

would nowhere approach its completion during the period here under discussion. Yet there developed in the sixteenth century a tendency to view Indians by a set of standards that might safely be called "paganism," a concept that referred to much more than religion; it also contained assumptions about human nature and the assimilability of other peoples. Since both biblical prophecy and the course of history showed that pagans had been converted and assimilated, the concept of paganism allowed sixteenth-century Europeans to incorporate the peoples of America into both their spiritual and their secular world views.[32]

The sum of this new information on peoples living in different times and in different places encouraged Europeans to think comparatively about the diversity of humankind. This is not to say that Europeans had previously been uninterested in the variety of cultures they encountered. "Curio-collecting," the assemblage of tiny pieces of material culture in cabinets for display, had a long history. In the sixteenth century, however, Europeans expanded the hobby of collecting to include descriptions of human manners. In this endeavor, arising out of the interest in the variety of humankind, one can find the foundations of modern anthropological inquiry, in the application of a scientific method to the study of culture and society.[33]

The circle of intellectuals, scientists, and scholars around Sir Walter Ralegh were the English exemplars of this Renaissance inquiry. Ralegh immersed himself fully in the culture of the English Renaissance and succeeded in gathering at Durham House a talented group of men whose interests complemented his own desire to settle and occupy the New World. There were soldiers in this group but also historians, scientists, philosophers, and artists. Hariot, as we have seen, was residing at Durham House by 1583, "maintained," according to Hakluyt, "at a most liberal salary."[34] John White, the artist and Hariot's partner, was probably there too. Ralegh provided a subsidy as well to support the French artist Jacob Le Moyne du Morgues, a survivor of the short-lived Huguenot colony in Florida.[35]

[32] The concept of paganism is central to Michael T. Ryan, "Assimilating New Worlds in the Sixteenth and Seventeenth Centuries," *Comparative Studies in Society and History* 23 (1981): 524–25. See also Elliott, "Renaissance Europe and America," 1:19.
[33] Hodgen, *Early Anthropology*, 8, 116; Christian F. Feest, "The Collecting of American Indian Artifacts in Europe, 1493–1750," in *America in European Consciousness, 1493–1750*, ed. Karen Ordahl Kupperman (Chapel Hill, N.C., 1994) 324–60. On the Spanish, see Elliott, *Old World*, chap. 2; and Anthony Pagden, *The Fall of Natural Man: The American Indian and the Origins of Comparative Ethnology*, (Cambridge, England, 1982).
[34] Hakluyt's dedication to Ralegh of his edition of Peter Martyr's *Decades of the New World*, in *The Roanoke Voyages, 1584–1590: Documents to Illustrate the English Voyages to North America under the Patent Granted to Walter Ralegh in 1584*, ed. David Beers Quinn, 2 vols. (London, 1955), 86.
[35] Taylor, *Writings of the Hakluyts*, 42; Paul Hulton, "Images of the New World: Jacques Le Moyne du Morgues and John White," in *The Westward Enterprise: English Activities in Ireland, the Atlantic, and America, 1480–1650*, ed. K. R. Andrews, Nicholas P. Canny, and P. E. H. Hair (Detroit, Mich., 1979), 198; Quinn, *Set Fair*, 183.

The historian William Camden also likely visited Durham House. Camden maintained a long correspondence with the circle of geographers and mapmakers around Abraham Ortelius in Flanders, an attachment he shared with Hakluyt. Both Hakluyt and Camden were intensely patriotic and passionately loyal to the Protestant establishment. Both employed precedents drawn from the past to understand contemporary events.[36]

Camden revolutionized the writing of history in late Tudor and early Stuart England. In his most important work, the *Britannia* (1586), he surveyed the history of England from the time of the Saxons through the Norman Conquest, thus promoting an interest in the ancient inhabitants of Britain. As the primitive character of these peoples slowly dawned upon Tudor intellectuals, English scholars became increasingly aware of the possibility that the early Britons bore similarities to the primitive peoples they were then encountering in Ireland and America. The result, apparent in Camden and increasingly so in the work of late Tudor and early Stuart antiquarians, was the emergence of a new historical consciousness, one characterized by a tendency to look at history as a continual process of development in both societies and cultures. With this came an awareness of the relativity of social customs, institutions, and values across time. Hariot and White wrestled with this problem in the De Bry edition of the *Briefe and True Report*. Camden, too, by suggesting that the Britons, after being civilized and converted by the Saxons, became a great and powerful people, laid the foundation for a developmental view of English history.[37]

It thus became possible for Englishmen, drawing from a number of influences, to comprehend the Indian tribes of the New World within a context broader than that framed by the exigencies of securing survival on the English Atlantic frontier. The apocalyptic tradition in Christianity called for the conversion, and thus due consideration, of all the world's peoples. The humanist scholarship that dominated the universities and the Renaissance rediscovery of the classical past encouraged the view of a European society that had developed from primitive origins. The discovery of real primitives, pagans, in North America allowed men such as Ralegh, Hariot, and Camden, immersed in the culture of the English Renaissance, to conclude that much like the ancient inhabitants of their own island, the natives of America occupied a distinct stage in a process of development undergone by every human society.[38]

[36] Parry, "Hakluyt's View of British History," 1:4.
[37] I have used the first English translation of the *Britannia*: William Camden, *Britain, or a Chorographicall Description of England, Scotland and Ireland, Beautified with Mappes*, trans. Philemon Holland (London, 1610). See also F. J. Levy, "The Making of Camden's *Britannia*," *Bibliothèque D'Humanisme et Renaissance* 26 (1964): 89; Arthur B. Ferguson, *Clio Unbound: Perception of the Social and Cultural Past in Renaissance England* (Durham, N.C., 1974), x, 110, 380–381; T. D. Kendrick, *British Antiquity* (New York, 1970), 121.
[38] Ferguson, *Clio Unbound*, 357, 381. On Ralegh sharing this view, see Maxwell Ford Taylor Jr., "The Influence of Religion on White Attitudes toward Indians in the Early Settlement of Virginia" (Ph.D. diss., Emory University, 1970), 72–133.

Certainly there existed sound, pragmatic reasons for learning about the natives of the New World. Only by communicating with them could Englishmen learn what valuable commodities a given territory might contain and its inhabitants' degree of willingness to part with them. Friendly social relations and the knowledge of Indian languages, moreover, would facilitate the conversion of the Indian tribes to Christianity. And as the writings of the Hakluyts make clear, friendly relations with the natives were a necessary prop supporting the theory of English New World imperialism; disaffected Indians would pose a powerful and intimidating threat to any colony.

Yet even in these considerations, the question of the native in a prospective English society overseas was placed within the larger context of an emerging metropolitan paradigm. Trade relations were discussed in terms of securing the economic and, increasingly, the social and political health of the commonwealth. The conversion of the natives was framed in the context of the religious turmoil of the sixteenth century and a desire to bring the gospel to all peoples. The primitive nature of the Indians was understood within an anthropology slowly coalescing around the idea of a natural and progressive developmental process. Taking these elements together, Englishmen assumed that the natives, once having recognized the superiority of English culture, would readily accept English religion, English laws, and English social organization.

III

Ralegh was not the first Englishman to try to settle in the New World. By the middle of the 1570s Martin Frobisher had scraped together the funds necessary to search for a northwest passage to Cathay. Between 1576 and 1578 Frobisher would lead three voyages to the inhospitable region surrounding the bay that now bears his name.

On his first voyage, on an island near Baffin Land, Frobisher found a quantity of ore that assayers in England determined to contain gold. He returned the next year with a larger expedition of eleven ships and took home some two hundred tons of the ore, which excited great interest in London and at court. A third voyage followed, this time under the supervision of the crown, to plant a mining colony of one hundred men, but bad weather forced them to return after several months of inconclusive exploration. Meanwhile, back in England, continued examination proved the ore worthless, and Frobisher's Cathay Company collapsed.[39]

Frobisher had spent his entire life on England's maritime frontier, encountering alien cultures in Ireland, Africa, and the Levant. His crew left a detailed description of what could happen when men of his experience en-

[39] William McFee, *The Life of Martin Frobisher* (New York, 1927), 1–114.

countered aboriginal peoples in a frontier setting. After a period of distrust and suspicion passed, according to Frobisher's lieutenant, George Best, the Inuits "exchaunged coates of Ceale and Beares skinnes, and suche like, with oure men, and received belles, loking glasses, and other toyes in recompence thereof againe." Then something went wrong:

> After great curtesie, and manye meetings, Our Mariners, contrarie to their Captaines dyrection, began more easily to trust them and five of our men, going a shoare, were by them intercepted with their boate, and were never since hearde of to this day againe.

Frobisher quickly took a hostage, hoping to force the release of his men. Sighting several Inuits nearby, he drew them close to his ship by ringing "a pretie cowbel." He then proceeded to pluck one man, kayak and all, onto the deck of his ship.[40]

On his second voyage Frobisher again took captives in order to secure the release of his men. Again he failed. Since in all likelihood the five were dead, Frobisher returned with his human cargo to Bristol, where the Inuit "family"—a man, a woman, and a child—sparked tremendous interest in educated circles. They were subjected to experiments, and observers recorded their cultural attitudes and child-rearing practices, motor skills and coordination, and anatomy and physiology.[41]

John White, who may have accompanied Frobisher's second voyage, painted the trio in two of his earliest known watercolors. Michael Lok, Frobisher's principal financial backer, compared the appearance of the male "to the tawney Mores; [or Ra]ther to the Tartar Nation, whereof I think he was." A chronicler of Frobisher's voyage, Christopher Hall, also likened them to Tartars, perhaps a product of the wishful thinking of men who sought a passage to the Orient. The Inuit woman reminded William Camden of the inhabitants of an older England. She was, he wrote, "painted about the eyes and balls of the cheek with a blue color like the ancient Britons."[42]

The attention paid to the three captives of 1577—all of whom died shortly after their arrival in England— and to the solitary male captured the year before raises some intriguing questions about metropolitan interest in Native Americans. Lok, as treasurer of Frobisher's Cathay Company, recorded the

---

[40] George Best, *A True Discourse of the Late Voyages of Discoverie, for the Finding of a Passage to Cathaya, by the Northwest, under the Conduct of Martin Frobisher Generall* (London, 1578), 49–50.

[41] Ibid., 11–12; Dionyse Settle, *A True Reporte of the Laste Voyage into the West and Northwest Regions &c., 1577, worthily atcheived by capteine Frobisher* (London, 1577), 17–20.

[42] See Hulton, *America 1585*, plates 63–64. For White accompanying Frobisher, see Quinn, *Set Fair*, 183–84. Lok quoted in William C. Sturtevant and David Beers Quinn, "This New Prey: Eskimos in Europe in 1567, 1576, and 1577," in *Indians and Europe: An Interdisciplinary Collection of Essays*, ed. Christian F. Feest (Aachen, Germ., 1987), 72; Hall and Camden quoted in Neil Cheshire et al., "Frobisher's Eskimos in England," *Archivaria* 10 (1980): 29.

disbursements of funds to pay for the care of the Inuits and to commission paintings of them; perhaps he hoped that by showing the natives to Elizabeth and her courtiers he might generate financial support for the economically troubled company. [43] This, however, does not explain the intense curiosity aroused by the four captives. What is clear is that metropolitans, from the time of the earliest English contacts, became absorbed in what may tentatively be called the anthropology of aboriginal peoples.

Long before Frobisher's Eskimos were exhibited by the side of the River Avon, Sir Humphrey Gilbert had begun to nourish his own plans for New World settlement. Like Frobisher, he hoped to find a passage to Cathay, but the desire to settle, to plant a colony that would serve as the basis for an English agrarian community in the Americas, weighed heavily in his plans. [44]

In 1566 Gilbert began a military career in Ireland which would culminate four years later when he was knighted on the field at Drogheda. Gilbert demonstrated a tremendous capacity for violence during his tenure in Ireland. Thomas Churchyard, his chronicler, recorded that when Gilbert entered enemy territory, "he killed manne, woman, and child, and spoyled, wasted, and burned by the ground all that he might." He coupled these scorched-earth tactics with a systematic program of terror designed to rob the Irish of their will to resist. "His manner," wrote Churchyard,

> was that the heddes of all those (of what sort soever they were) whiche were killed in the daie, should bee cutte of from their bodies, and brought to the place where he incamped at night: and should there bee laied on the ground, by eche side of the waie leadyng into his owne Tente: so that none could come into his Tente for any cause, but commonly he muste passe through a lane of heddes, which he used *ad terroram*, the dedde feelyng nothyng the more paines thereby: and yet it did bring greate terrour to the people, when thei saw the heddes of theyr dedde fathers, brothers, children, kinsfolke and freends, lye on the grounde before their faces. [45]

Gilbert felt little but contempt for the Irish and "thought his dogges eares to good, to heare the speeche of the greateste noble manne emongst them." [46] The Irish, in his eyes, were irredeemable savages, incapable of understanding anything but force; they could be kept in subjection to "cyvill governance" only through the power of the sword. Gilbert proposed that the children of Irish noble families be seized and transported to England to receive education and to serve as security for the good behavior of their parents, and that "upon eche haven of Ireland fortresses to be made to be kept with a garrison of English souldiers and the licke in every notable porte towne and this

---

[43] Portions of Lok's account book are reprinted in William Brenchley Rye, ed., *England as Seen by Foreigners in the Days of Elizabeth and James the First* (New York, 1967), 205–6.

[44] Morgan, *American Slavery*, 21.

[45] Thomas Churchyard, *A Generall Rehearsall of Warres*, (London, 1579).

[46] Ibid.

to be done in every quarter of Ireland Easte, west, north and Southe."[47] In North America, however, pragmatic considerations dictated against pursuing so draconian a policy. Neither Gilbert nor the administrative apparatus of the Tudor state had the means to engage in a military conquest of the New World. The most evident military reality there would be the settlement of small numbers of Englishmen in the midst of large numbers of natives. Gilbert thus needed to pursue peaceful relations with the American tribes.

According to George Peckham, the leader of a Catholic subcommunity within Gilbert's patent, the settlers "should doo theyr best endevour to take away such feare as may growe unto" the natives from the presence of the English colony. Peckham referred to his countrymen as "Christians," and the conversion of the Indians for him unquestionably comprised a principal part of the colony's mission. Conversion could not be reconciled with the use of force, and, according to Edward Hayes, who composed a narrative of Gilbert's final voyage, was "an action doubtlesse not to be intermedled with base purposes." Hayes believed that the expedition intended to win the Indians to Christianity "by all faire meanes possible."[48] Peckham also believed that the natives "shalbe reduced from unseemly customs to honest maners, from disordered riotous rowtes and companies, to a wel governed common wealth," through education rather than compulsion. The natives could be taught "mechanicall occupations, artes, and lyberal sciences" and thus made productive members of a colonial Anglo-American society.[49]

We have no evidence on the extent to which Gilbert shared these views— his writings seldom touched upon the subject—but they were common currency among the literate members of his crew. Though the Irish experience may well have disillusioned Gilbert about the capacity of primitive peoples to abandon their "savage" customs, it is more likely that he looked to America as an arena where his colonization schemes could be carried out free from the legacy of bitterness that characterized Anglo-Irish relations. As yet unfamiliar with the American Indians, he had not the contempt for them that he bore toward the Irish. Native Americans, if they could be persuaded to cooperate, would occupy an integral, if subordinate, role in Gilbert's agrarian utopia.[50]

In June 1578 Gilbert received the letters patent from the crown allowing him "to discover searche finde out and viewe such remote heathen and barbarous landes countries and territories not actually possessed of any Christian prince or people."[51] The voyage was a disaster: the fleet scattered in

[47] Quinn, *Voyages of Gilbert*, 126–27.
[48] Ibid., 389–90, 396, 451.
[49] Ibid., 468.
[50] See Morgan's discussion in *American Slavery*, 21, and Gilbert's notes on the examination of David Ingram—an English sailor set ashore after the Battle of San Juan Ulloa, who reportedly walked from the Gulf of Mexico to New England—in Quinn, *Voyages of Gilbert*, 296–97.
[51] Quinn, *Voyages of Gilbert*, 188.

search of prizes, its mission forgotten. A second voyage in 1583 reached the coast of North America, but Gilbert stayed for only a short time. He would not have another opportunity to settle the New World. Characterized most appropriately by his queen as "a man noted of not good happ by sea," Gilbert went down with his ship on the return voyage.[52]

IV

Gilbert's half-brother, Sir Walter Ralegh, received the exclusive right from the queen "to discover search fynde out and viewe" any New World lands "not actually possessed of any Christian Prynce and inhabited by Christian people" in March 1584. Ralegh placed two members of his own household, Philip Amadas and Arthur Barlowe, in charge of the reconnaissance voyage which departed on April 27. Sometime around July 4 the expedition coasted along the Carolina Outer Banks, landing finally at Roanoke Island.[53]

Barlowe composed a glowing panegyric to the New World's potential. The abundance of wildlife on the island impressed him, and he described the soil as "the most plentifull, sweete, fruitfull, and wholesome of all the world." More important, however, Barlowe found the native inhabitants of "the country Wingandacoa" friendly and gracious, "in their behaviour as mannerly, and civill, as any of Europe." Granganimeo, the brother of the Roanoke *weroance* Wingina, was especially impressive, "very just in his promise," and a man with whom the English could deal faithfully. The Indians quickly began trading with the explorers, exchanging skins, furs and pearls for English pots, pans, and tools. They also brought fruit, vegetables, and meat to the expedition, and Barlowe wrote that "we were entertained with all love, and kindnes, and with as much bountie, after their manner, as they could possibly devise." He thought his hosts a "people most gentle, loving and faithfull, void of all guile, and treason, and such as lived after the manner of the golden age."[54]

Barlowe could retain this optimism because his brief sojourn on the Outer Banks precluded the sort of environmental conflict that later would sour relations between Indians and Englishmen. The members of his expedition remained for so short a period in the New World that they did not have time to develop the sense of disillusionment and distaste for the natives generated by planting an isolated settlement so far from home.

Amadas and Barlowe returned to England in September 1584. They carried with them Manteo, a native of Croatoan, and Wanchese, a Roanoke and perhaps an adviser to the *weroance* Wingina. Both lodged with Hariot at

[52] Ibid., 339.

[53] Quinn, *Roanoke Voyages*, 86, 91–94.

[54] Ibid., 106, 96–97, 105, 108. Wingina himself did not greet Barlowe and Amadas because he was recovering from battle injuries.

Durham House. In the meantime, Ralegh obtained parliamentary confirmation of his rights in the New World and engaged the younger Hakluyt to prepare for the queen's consideration "a particular discourse concerninge the greate necessitie and manifolde comdyties that are like to growe to this Realme of Englande by the Westerne discoveries lately attempted."[55] Through these means he hoped to persuade the queen to provide the capital necessary to establish an English settlement overseas. Hakluyt presented the "Discourse on Western Planting" to the Queen on October 5, shortly after the return of Amadas and Barlowe.

Nothing terribly original appeared in the document, but it did summarize the concerns that drove metropolitans westward across the Atlantic. Hakluyt recognized that social and economic forces had transformed Elizabeth's England. There were, he wrote, "many thousandes of idle persons . . . in this Realme, wch havinge no way to be sett on worke be either mutinous and seeke alteration in the state, or at leaste very burdensome to the common wealthe and often fall to pilferage and thevinge and other lewdnes." America offered hope for those that "for trifles may otherwise be devoured by the gallowes." The jails were stuffed full of such unfortunates, he argued, the victims of a general constriction in opportunity. Social order and the peace of the commonwealth demanded a solution.[56] Neither could Hakluyt ignore the strategic value for England of possessing a defensible naval station from which to raid Spanish shipping, as well as a fine source of the raw materials England previously had obtained from the crown's rivals.

The Indians, Hakluyt continued, must be converted to Christianity. Because hostile Indians could threaten any settlement, armed men must be part of the colonial population to protect the colonists and provide a secure base for English missionaries. Still, in order to bring the "infinite multitudes of these simple people that are in errour into the righte and perfecte waye of their salvacion," Hakluyt clearly proposed a patient program of education and catechesis. Missionaries must first "learne the language of the people nere adjoyninge . . . and by little and little acquainte themselves wth their manner, and so wth discrecion and myldenes distill into their purged myndes the swete and lively liquor of the gospell."[57]

Elizabeth appreciated Hakluyt's efforts but offered Ralegh little other than the use of one of her ships, the *Tyger*. Undaunted, Ralegh continued to nurture his plans for a second expedition to survey the interior, undertake experiments in agriculture, and secure an English base in the New World for privateering raids and future full-scale settlement.[58] Hariot, meanwhile, set himself the difficult task of learning the Algonquin language from his two

[55] Taylor, *Writings of the Hakluyts*, 211; David Beers Quinn, "Preparations for the 1585 Virginia Voyage," *WMQ*, 3d ser., 6 (1949): 73–93.

[56] Taylor, *Writings of the Hakluyts*, 317, 319, 234.

[57] Ibid., 214, 215.

[58] David Beers Quinn, *Ralegh and the British Empire* (London, 1947), 67.

new companions, Manteo and Wanchese, while he, in turn, instructed them in English. He may even have begun developing an Algonquin alphabet.[59] White's activities cannot be traced during this period, but it is likely that he remained close to Hariot. Both would return with the 1585 voyage to continue their investigations.[60]

The expedition that departed Plymouth on April 9, 1585, consisted of seven ships, carrying more than five hundred persons, of whom well over half were soldiers and sailors.[61] The expedition's military cast corresponded with advice Ralegh had received as he began planning the venture: an anonymous set of notes written in late 1584 or early 1585 encouraging him to employ martial law in his colony. To secure an orderly settlement, the adviser wrote, the governor must have the authority "to commaund absolutly within the forte and without all matters marshall, to geve all offices in the geovernement, to punnyshe any man by Commandment but not to prosead to deathe of any man but by order of law." The proposed laws ranged in subject from the maintenance of military discipline in the colony to the preservation of the good will of the Indians. Soldiers should never "stryke or mysuse any Indian," enter "any Indians howse without his leave," or force an Indian "to labour unwillyngly." The settlement would better be able to maintain peace, the adviser suggested, by outlawing those actions which might invite retaliation from offended natives.[62]

Ralegh vested Ralph Lane, the colony's governor, with the recommended power, and there is little doubt that the content of the anonymous notes would have sounded familiar to many members of the expedition. The leading figures at Roanoke were military men, hardened on battlefields in Europe, the East, and Ireland.[63]

For Lane the question of relations with natives was primarily a military one. He defined the limits of the possible by the force available to achieve it. Hariot spoke of bringing the Indians with relative ease to English standards of civility. Lane, surveying the Outer Banks, thought that the land was "fytte

---

[59] John Aubrey, *Aubrey's Brief Lives*, ed. Oliver Lawson Dick (Ann Arbor, Mich., 1957), 123; Vivian Salmon, "Thomas Harriot (1560–1621) and the English Origins of Algonkian Linguistics," *Historiographia Linguistica* 19 (1992): 25–56.

[60] Ralegh's instructions to White have been lost, but they likely resembled those given to the artist Thomas Bavin by Sir Humphrey Gilbert: to "drawe to lief one of each kinde of thing that is strange to us in England . . . all strange birdes beastes fishes plantes hearbes Trees and fruictes . . . also the figures & shapes of men and woemen in their apparell as also their manner of wepons in every place as you shall finde them differing" (quoted in Hulton, *America 1585*, 9). See also Hariot, *Briefe and True Report*, 4.

[61] See William S. Powell, "Roanoke Colonists and Explorers: An Attempt at Identification," *North Carolina Historical Review* 34 (1957): 202–26.

[62] Quinn, *Roanoke Voyages*, 136, 138–39. On the identity of the author, see 19–22.

[63] On the general importance of the military establishment in English overseas expansion, see Stephen Saunders Webb, *The Governors-General: The English Army and the Definition of Empire, 1569–1681* (Chapel Hill, N.C., 1979).

to bee cyvylly, and Chrystyanly inhabyted" and that once "inhabited with English," "no realme in Christendome" would compare to Virginia. There is no talk here of civilizing and Christianizing Indians.[64]

Lane had had many years of experience soldiering along the marchlands of the English Atlantic. In 1583, after almost two decades of military service, the crown sent him to Ireland to build fortifications to protect the southwest coast from a threatened Spanish invasion. Over the course of the next two years, commanding garrisons in Kerry, Clanmorris, and Desmond, he dispatched his duties with both ruthless efficiency and a pronounced desire for personal gain.[65]

It is likely that many of the soldiers on board had served with Lane in the Irish wars. Ireland had been under nominal English jurisdiction since the twelfth century, but it was not until the Tudor period that intense efforts were made to bring the kingdom firmly under crown control. This resulted in the creation of a frontier zone in which English and Celtic cultures stood opposed, not only along the fringes of the English Pale around Dublin in Ireland but also in the Scottish lowlands and Welsh marches. The state of nearly continual warfare that characterized this violent region generated a deep and bitter hostility among English settlers toward the inhabitants of "the Celtic Fringe."[66]

Few Englishmen questioned the inferiority of the Irish, but most thought that they could be assimilated into an Anglo-Irish colonial society.[67] Sir Thomas Smith, more than many other promoters of settlement in Ireland, firmly believed that the "wild Irish" could be brought to adopt English standards of civility. Classical precedent informed Smith's own ideas on colonization, and he viewed the English role in Ireland as akin to that of the Romans in ancient Britain. England, he believed, had once been as wild and untamed as Ireland "until colonies of Romans brought their laws and orders," bestowing upon a savage society peace and civilization.[68]

Smith greatly overestimated the enthusiasm of his Irish wards for the gift of English religion and common law. The forces of the O'Neills frequently overran his plantation, and his son was suddenly attacked and "unhappily

---

[64] Lane to Walsingham, 8 September 1585, and Lane to Hakluyt the Elder, 3 September 1585 in Quinn, *Roanoke Voyages*, 213, 208.

[65] Lane was an expert in fortification. See *CSP Ireland, 1574–85*, 423; Quinn, *Ralegh*, 74. White painted two of the fortifications Lane built in Puerto Rico; see Hulton, *America 1585*, plates 3, 4. For biographical material on Lane, see Edward E. Hale, ed., "Original Documents from the State Paper Office, London, and the British Museum Illustrating the History of Sir Walter Raleigh's First American Colony and the Colony at Jamestown," *Transactions and Collections of the American Antiquarian Society* 4 (1860): 317–45.

[66] W. R. Jones, "England against the Celtic Fringe: A Study in Cultural Stereotypes," *Journal of World History* 13 (1971): 156–57. See also J. G. A. Pocock, "The Limits and Divisions of British History: In Search of the Unknown Subject," *AHR* 87 (1982): 311–36.

[67] Bradshaw, "Sword," 482.

[68] Smith quoted in Quinn, "Sir Thomas Smith," 546.

and treacherously slain" by his own Irish churls, who chopped up the body, boiled it, and then fed it to their wolfhounds.[69]

Most of the Old English community in Ireland, descendants of the original Anglo-Norman settlers, also favored the persuasive approach pursued so unsuccessfully by Smith. English officials, however, became increasingly disillusioned with such reform proposals. Each new failure in Ireland, each new rising against royal power, led to harsher evaluations of the Gaelic culture the English hoped to transform. Familiarity bred contempt, and the idea that reform could be effected through gentle means lost ground to the more sanguinary notion that change could be achieved only through force.[70]

The writings of Barnabe Rich symbolize this shift. Born in Essex sometime around 1540, Rich enlisted in the army as a boy and saw action in France and the Low Countries. His Irish service began in 1573, and he would spend the majority of his remaining years on the Anglo-Irish frontier. Rich believed that there was no inherent difference between the Irish and the English, and that the inferiority of the Irish could be explained purely in cultural terms. It was not, he wrote, "either the Country or the Countryman, that maketh me either to love or hate, it is their manners and conditions that maketh mee both to prayse or dispraise." That the Irish were "rude, uncleanlie, and uncivill" Rich attributed not to their "natural inclination" but to their education: they were "trained up in Treason, in Rebellion, in Theft, in Robery, in Superstition, in Idolatry, and nuzeled from their Cradles in the very puddle of Popery."[71]

Rich came to believe, however, that the Irish could not be persuaded to abandon their culture; they "have ever beene, and still are, desirous to shake off the English government." Frustrated, he concluded that a gentle approach could never work.

> But Alas! their judgements are both blinde and lame, and they are deafe to all good counsels, they are falne into a blind arrogancy, and they are so generally bewitched with Popery, that they will neither draw example nor precept from the English.[72]

Rich certainly was not alone in holding such views. Englishmen in Ireland increasingly believed that only an iron hand could bring a savage people to civility. Sir John Davies, in one of the classic contemporary statements on

---

[69] John Strype, *The Life of the Learned Sir Thomas Smith* (Oxford, 1820), 133; Stephen G. Ellis, *Tudor Ireland: Crown, Community, and the Conflict of Cultures, 1470–1603* (London, 1985), 267.

[70] Nicholas P. Canny, *Kingdom and Colony: Ireland and the Atlantic World, 1560–1800*, (Baltimore, Md., 1988), 31–32; Bradshaw, "Sword," 484; Quinn, *Elizabethans and the Irish*, 132.

[71] Barnabe Rich, *A New Description of Ireland, wherein Is Described the Disposition of the Irish* (London, 1610), epistle dedicatory, 15–16.

[72] Ibid., 20, 27.

England's failure to conquer Ireland, wrote that "a barbarous Country must be first broken by a warre, before it will be capeable of good government, and when it is fully subdued and conquered, if it bee not well planted and governed after the Conquest, it will est-soones return to the former Barbarisme."[73]

Even Sir Edmund Spenser, the poet and friend of Ralegh, argued that to subdue the Irish "the first thing must be to send over into that realm such a strong power of men as that shall perforce bring in all that rebellious rout of loose people which either do now stand out in open arms or in wandering companies do keep the woods spoiling and infesting the good subjects."[74] For Spenser, the basic problem was the unsettled and seminomadic quality of Irish life. Settling these people on the land, he thought, could civilize them, but this could be effected only through force and conquest.[75]

Barnabe Rich never went to America. Neither did Spenser or Davies. But Ralph Lane did, and so too did Richard Grenville, the expedition's naval commander. Historians long have recognized the importance of Ireland as a model for the colonization of America. The important point for our purposes, however, is that of the men Ralegh actually impressed or recruited or sent to the New World, a large number bore in their minds a set of attitudes toward native and "savage" peoples at odds with the concerns of metropolitan-minded men such as Hariot, Ralegh, and Hakluyt.

V

The Algonquin-speaking peoples among whom Lane and his men settled on the Outer Banks proved no more willing than the Irish to accept English cultural domination. A large number of Algonquian groups inhabited the coastal Carolina region. Essentially village communities, they sometimes joined together under powerful leaders and at other times followed independent courses. Political authority changed over time as villages shifted their allegiance from one *weroance* to another through conquest and maneuver.

The Roanokes, under their *weroance* Wingina, resided in "a village of nine houses, built of Cedar, and fortified round about with sharpe trees to keepe out theyr enemies," on the island that bore their name, as well as in the adjacent mainland villages of Dasemunkepeuc and, at times, Pomeiooc. Farther south, along the strips of coastal territory to the north and south of the Pamlico River, the Secotans inhabited several villages. Aquascogoc, a town later burned by the English, most likely was a Secotan village.

---

[73] Davies, *True Causes*, 5.
[74] Edmund Spenser, *A View on the Present State of Ireland*, ed. W. L. Renwick (Oxford, 1970), 95–96.
[75] Bradshaw, "Sword," 482–83, 490; James Muldoon, "The Indian as Irishman," *Essex Institute Historical Collections*, 111 (1975): 275.

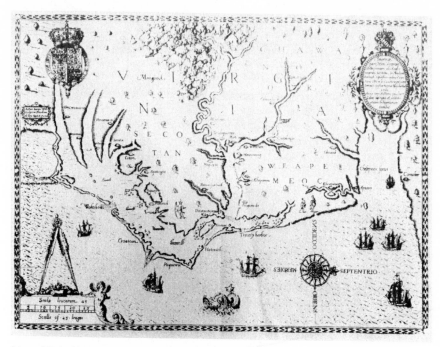

Map of Ralegh's Virginia engraved by Theodor DeBry, from Hariot's *A Briefe and True Report of the New Found Land of Virginia* (1590). Courtesy Dover Publications, Inc.

According to Barlowe, the Secotans clashed frequently with the Pomeioocs, led by Piemacum, who in turn had leagued with an unnamed *weroance* of the Neusioks. All these groups, apparently, had fought against Wingina in a "mortall warre" two years before the 1584 Barlowe expedition.[76] The Weapemeocs inhabited a number of towns along the northern coast of Albemarle Sound, between the Chowan River and Currituck Sound. They may have owed allegiance to the powerful Choanokes, whose main village lay farther to the west, between the Chowan and Roanoke Rivers. The Moratucs lived to the south, along both banks of the Roanoke River. The Mangoaks, an Iroquoian people (probably Tuscarora), occupied the territory to the west of the Choanokes and Moratucs. Skiko, the son of the Choanoke *weroance* Menatonon, suggested to the English that the Choanokes and Mangoaks had been at war shortly before the English arrived.[77]

---

[76] Quinn, *Roanoke Voyages*, 107, 113–14.

[77] Ibid., App. 1 and 2, pp. 841–72, 110–11; 258–59, 270, 279. On the identity of the Mangoaks, see Thomas Parramore, "The Tuscarora Ascendancy," *North Carolina Historical Review* 59 (1982): 307–9. For a general view, see David Sutton Phelps, "Archaeology of the North Carolina Coast and Coastal Plain: Problems and Hypotheses," in *The Prehistory of North Carolina: An Archaeological Symposium*, ed. Mark A. Mathis and Jeffrey J. Crow (Raleigh, N.C., 1983), 1–51.

Carolina Algonquians located their village communities on the waterside, thus ensuring access to the greatest possible variety of environmental and subsistence resources in the coastal region. Coastal waters teemed with fresh and saltwater fish, shellfish, and crustacea, and provided habitat for a great variety of waterfowl as well. The Indians, accordingly, built fish weirs and fish traps in the rivers and marshes, harvesting much of their food from the surrounding waters. From these villages, Hariot reported, Algonquian hunters also moved into the interior to stalk a variety of mammals, including deer, squirrels, rabbits, and opossum.

Agriculture, however, formed the basis of Carolina Algonquian subsistence. The coastal zones where, according to Lane, native towns were "scytuated upon moost delicate plattes of grounde" contained the best soil in the region for simple hoe agriculture. In fields surrounding and on small plots within the villages, natives grew corn which, complemented with squash and beans, met most of their dietary and subsistence needs, providing them with enough food to survive even the predictable annual periods of scarcity.[78]

Carolina Algonquians, then, lived in relative comfort, drawing sustenance from various subsistence resources in the region. Still, a certain tension characterized Algonquian relationships with nature and the environment. Indians both exploited and revered nature's life-sustaining power, and Algonquian religion and ritual assisted Carolina natives in maintaining a fragile balance within their environment.[79]

English observers such as Hariot and Barlowe reported with great interest upon the active and vibrant spiritual life of coastal Algonquians. At times self-serving and always ethnocentric, the English accounts reveal nonetheless that the peoples of the coastal Carolina region maintained a complex, complete, and functional cosmological order at the time the English arrived. The concept of *mantoac*, or power, described by Hariot as the "many Gods . . . of different sortes and degrees" the Indians believed in, rested at the heart of their assumptions about the functioning of the cosmos. Power, as Gregory Evans Dowd has shown in his study of religious awakening in eighteenth-century native communities, meant survival, an abundant harvest, a successful hunt, and a safe return from war. Power occurred in many forms throughout the Indians' universe, and some things and beings possessed more power than others.[80]

In order to acquire and harness this life-sustaining power, Algonquians on the Carolina Outer Banks, and elsewhere, celebrated a tremendous variety of rituals which they believed were gifts taught to mortals by benevolent

[78] Christian F. Feest, "North Carolina Algonquians," in *Handbook of North American Indians*, vol. 15, *Northeast*, ed. William C. Sturtevant (Washington, D.C., 1978), 271.

[79] Christopher Vecsey, "American Indian Environmental Religions," in *American Indian Environments: Ecological Issues in Native American History*, ed. Christopher Vecsey and Robert W. Venables (Syracuse, N.Y., 1980), 12–13.

[80] Hariot, *Briefe and True Report*, 25; Gregory Evans Dowd, *A Spirited Resistance: The North American Indian Struggle for Unity, 1745–1815* (Baltimore, Md., 1992), 3.

forces in the cosmos. A Roanoke Indian told Hariot that a "few yeares before our comming into the countrey" a "wicked man" had died and was buried. The next day he rose from his grave and "made declaration where his soule had beene." The wicked man had traveled toward *Popogusso*, the Algonquian hell, "a great pitte or hole, which they thinke to bee in the furthest partes of their part of the worlde toward the sunne set, there to burn continually." He came "very neere entring into *Popogusso*, had not one of the gods saved him and gave him leave to returne againe, and to teach his friends what they should doe to avoid that terrible place of torment."[81] The wicked man brought back sacred knowledge that enabled his people to escape the wrath of evil forces in their universe.

Barlowe in 1584 reported that Carolina Algonquians engaged in elaborate public rituals prior to warfare. One year later Hariot reported that when the Indians "have escaped any great danger by sea or lande, or be returned from the warr in token of Joye they make a great fyer abowt whiche the men, and woemen sit together." There, with gourd rattles and song, the Roanokes "make merrie."[82] Tobacco rested at the center of much Algonquian ritual activity. Tobacco, Hariot wrote, "is of so precious estimation amongest them that they thinke their gods are marvelously delighted therwith." Sometimes, he continued, "they make hallowed fires & cast some of the pouder therein for a sacrifice; being in a storme uppon the waters, to pacifie their gods, they cast some up into the aire and into the water; so a weare for fish being newly set up, they cast some into the aire likewise." All this they did "with strange gestures, stamping, sometime dauncing, clapping of hands, holding up of hands, & staring up into the heavens, uttering therwithal and chattering strange words & noises."[83]

Through their religious activities, natives on the Carolina Outer Banks maintained an essential balance with their larger environment. English settlement disrupted this balance. Not all Indians responded in the same way to the arrival of the English, but in all cases their beliefs about power influenced the nature of their response to the dramatic and drastic changes unleashed by English settlement at Roanoke.

Grenville and the fleet arrived off Florida sometime around June, 20, 1585, and coasted northward over the course of the following week. On June 23 the *Tyger* nearly wrecked off the "Cape of Feare" and three days later anchored off Wococon Island, some distance south of Roanoke.[84] Things began badly for the colonists. On June 29 Grenville attempted to bring the *Tyger*, a ship of 160 tons, into the harbor at Wococon. It struck ground and, wrote one chronicler, "beat so manie strokes upon the sands, that if God had not miraculouslie delivered him [Grenville], there had beene

---

[81] Hariot, *Briefe and True Report*, 26.
[82] Quinn, *Roanoke Voyages*, 112–13; Hariot, *Briefe and True Report*, 62.
[83] Hariot, *Briefe and True Report*, 16.
[84] Quinn, *Roanoke Voyages*, 188–89; Shirley, *Thomas Harriot*, 128–29.

no waie to avoid present death." Salt water poured into the hold of the ship so "that the most part of his corne, salt, meale, rice, bisket, & other provisions . . . was spoiled." According to Hariot, the accident left the colonists with food for only twenty days, giving the entire question of survival new meaning. Unless they could obtain food from the Indians (for they had arrived too late in the year to plant their own), the newcomers would face the prospect of starvation. Ralegh's Roanoke Colony was born in crisis.[85]

Grenville sent word to Wingina, the "king" at Roanoke, on July 3, announcing the arrival of the English at Wococon. Exploration of the area began shortly thereafter. On the July 11 Grenville fitted out an expedition to cross Pamlico Sound and explore the mainland. The next day his three boats reached the palisaded village of Pomeiooc; a day later they arrived at Aquascogoc, and on July 15 they rowed up the Pamlico River to the principal seat of the Secotans.[86] White at this time made drawings of Pomeiooc and Secotan, as well as some of the Indian men and women he encountered there.[87]

On July 16 most of the expedition began the return trip to Wococon, where they arrived two days later. One vessel, however, under the command of Philip Amadas, returned to Aquascogoc; an Indian there reportedly had stolen a silver cup from the expedition, and Amadas was sent to demand its return. "Not receiving it according to his promise," an anonymous member of the crew reported, "we burnt, and spoyled their corne, and Towne, all the people being fledde." The first breach with the Indians had occurred.[88]

Grenville considered Wococon nothing more than a temporary station, to be held while he made repairs to the hull of the *Tyger*. By July 21, with these repairs completed, the fleet "wayed anker for Hatoraske," or Port Ferdinando, which it entered on the 27th. Shortly thereafter Grenville decided to establish the English settlement at the northern end of Roanoke Island, not far from Wingina's village. It is likely that Granganimeo, the brother of the Roanoke *weroance* and the host of Amadas and Barlowe's 1584 reconnaissance voyage, influenced this decision.[89]

The colonists spent the following weeks transferring goods from ship to shore at Roanoke and building a fortified settlement. Lane's expertise in this regard must have been of immense help to the colonists, who apparently feared a Spanish assault as much as an Indian one.[90] Grenville sent one of the faster ships to England to inform Ralegh that the expedition had arrived safely but that a serious shortage of supplies would soon develop. Some of

[85] Quinn, *Roanoke Voyages*, 176–77; Hariot, *Briefe and True Report*, 31.
[86] Quinn, *Roanoke Voyages*, 190–91.
[87] See Hulton, *America 1585*, plates 32–40.
[88] Quinn, *Roanoke Voyages*, 191.
[89] Ibid., 191–92.
[90] For Spanish efforts to locate the English settlement, see Paul E. Hoffman, *Spain and the Roanoke Ventures* (Raleigh, N.C., 1987), 18–70.

the other ships, too, must have been planning to return, for on August 12
Lane wrote three letters home. Grenville would return home with the *Tyger*,
probably because he had been unable to find an adequate harbor to serve as
a base for privateering raids; he had hoped to make more money plundering
Spanish shipping in the Caribbean. Lane would remain with 107 others. Because of the destruction of the expedition's provisions, they planned to live
off the land or acquire food from the Indians until supply ships could be
sent.[91] Lane thought their prospects for success were good. Although he
complained that he was in the "myddest of infynytt busynesses, as having,
emongst sauvages, yᵉ chardge of wylde menne of myne owene nacione," he
called the territory "the goodliest soil under the cope of heaven."[92]

With the departure of the *Tyger* on August 25, Lane and his men were left
alone at Roanoke. Lane quickly initiated an energetic program of exploration. He hoped to follow up the earlier reconnaissance voyages in the Pamlico River region and in Albemarle Sound, and to move toward Chesapeake
Bay as well. The harbors so far discovered left him unimpressed, and he
thought it possible that one more suitable might be found to the north.[93]

Little is known of the voyage toward the Chesapeake, for Lane mentioned
it only in passing. The expedition—probably under the command of Amadas
and including Hariot and White—reached the mouth of the Chesapeake Bay
and apparently encamped in the region of present-day Norfolk through the
winter. Hariot there encountered representatives of the "Mandoages, Tri-
panicks, and Opossians," the first an Iroquoian- and the other two Algonquin-speaking peoples. According to Lane, these "all came to visit the
Colonie of the English, which I had for a time appointed to be resident
there."[94] Information on this outpost may have been suppressed by either
Lane or Hakluyt, who, like Ralegh, wanted to prevent any news of a desirable harbor from reaching England's enemies.[95] Lane awaited the return of
this group before he launched his own exploration of the Chowan and
Roanoke Rivers sometime late in February or early March 1586.

During the summer and fall of 1585, relations between Lane's colonists
and the Roanoke Indians appear to have been peaceful; none of the extant
sources record any problems. Before Lane's spring departure, however, relations began to deteriorate between the English settlers and Wingina's
people. Although it is impossible to locate the origins of the breach with any
certainty, Wingina's subsequent actions suggest that the colonists' demands
for maize had surpassed what he could safely provide without risking injury
to his own people, among whom disease already had taken an enormous
toll, and that the violence characteristic of English actions in the region had

[91] Quinn, *Roanoke Voyages*, 167–68, 192, 202–4, 256–57.
[92] Ibid., 204–5, 207–10.
[93] Ibid., 273–75.
[94] Ibid., 245–46, 257–58.
[95] As Quinn has suggested (ibid., 245–46).

alienated many Roanokes.[96] The colonists, apparently unable or unwilling to grow their own crops, could hunt to meet some of their needs, though, as Hariot implied, this would not have provided for the entire settler population. The Englishmen then had to resort to begging, borrowing, stealing, and trading to obtain the food necessary to keep the colony alive.[97]

At first, the Roanokes eagerly engaged in trade with the settlers and, in doing so, extended native concepts of power to things English; this extension enabled them to incorporate components of English material culture into their daily lives. Many trade items manifested power—*mantoac*—to the natives. Although Hariot comprehended Roanoke *mantoac* in terms analogous to the English "God," to coastal Algonquians it denoted a power higher than that of humans, a sacred power that could manifest itself in both *things* and *beings*. Indians sought English trade goods for reasons beyond their utilitarian and functional value, Hariot wrote, viewing them as "rather the workes of god then of men." Acquiring these things from the English voyagers thus provided Carolina Algonquians with a means to acquire sacred power.[98] When, for instance, Granganimeo hung "a bright tinne dishe" that he had acquired from Barlowe around his neck, he did so out of a belief that this metal item "would defend him against his enemies arrowes," a clear indication that to him it contained a significant degree of beneficent power.[99]

English technology played a vital role in shaping the Roanoke Indians' perception of the colonists. Though incomplete, the evidence suggests that they viewed the settlers as powerful people bearing magical and otherworldly items permeated with *mantoac*, a power that allowed them, in Bruce White's apt phrase, "to do things that ordinary human beings could not."[100]

[96] J. Frederick Fausz, "Patterns of Anglo-Indian Aggression and Accommodation Along the Mid-Atlantic Coast, 1584–1634," in *Cultures in Contact: The Impact of European Contacts on Native American Cultural Institutions*, ed. William W. Fitzhugh (Washington, D.C., 1985), 233; Andrews, *Trade*, 208, 221. John White in 1587 reported that the Croatoan Indians begged the English not to "gather or spill any of their corne," suggesting the scope of English predation the year before. See Quinn, *Roanoke Voyages*, 526.

[97] Hariot, *Briefe and True Report*, 6.

[98] See the discussion in Constance A. Crosby, "From Myth to History, or Why King Philip's Ghost Walks Abroad," in *The Recovery of Meaning: Historical Archaeology in the Eastern United States*, ed. Mark P. Leone and Parker Potter (Washington, D.C., 1988), 184–98; Hariot, *Briefe and True Report*, 27.

[99] Quinn, *Roanoke Voyages*, 100–101; Christopher L. Miller and George R. Hamell, "A New Perspective on Indian-White Contact: Cultural Symbols and Colonial Trade," *JAH* 73 (1986–87): 311–28; George R. Hamell, "Mythical Realities and European Contact in the Northeast during the Sixteenth and Seventeenth Centuries," *Man in the Northeast* 33 (1987): 63–87; Hariot, *Briefe and True Report*, 27.

[100] Bruce M. White, "Encounters with Spirits: Ojibwa and Dakota Theories about the French and their Merchandise," *Ethnohistory* 41 (1994): 378. For similar treatments of other native communities, see Bruce G. Trigger, *The Children of Aataentsic: A History of the Huron People to 1660* (Montreal, 1976), 429–31, 566; James W. Bradley, *Evolution of the Onondaga Iroquois: Accomodating Change, 1500–1655* (Syracuse, NY, 1987), 142, 166–70. See also Rebecca Kugel, "Of Missionaries and Their Cattle: Ojibwa Perceptions of a Missionary as Evil Shaman," *Ethnohistory*, 41 (1994): 227–44; James Axtell, *The Invasion Within: The Conquest of Cultures in Early America* (New York, 1985), 10–13.

Although English technology impressed the natives, the power manifested in English disease frightened and perplexed them. Sickness that ravaged Indian communities but left the English unscathed "wrought so strange opinions of us that some people could not tel whether to thinke us gods or men."[101] Native shamans and healers—"notable enchaunters" to Hariot, "well stricken in yeers"—found that traditional cures failed to halt the spread of disease. Under assault from what they considered the "invisible bullets" of the English, many Roanokes apparently took steps to harness the superior power that allowed the colonists to flourish while Indians declined.[102]

Some Roanokes sought the assistance of English prayers—English ritual—to preserve their corn during a period of drought. Others beseeched the English to send disease among their native enemies so that they "might in like sort die." Still others, Hariot wrote, "when as wee kneeled downe on our knees to make our prayers unto god . . . went abowt to imitate us, and when they saw we moved our lipps, they also dyd the like." Wingina, he said, joined the English in prayer and the singing of psalms "hoping thereby to be partaker of the same effectes which wee by that meanes also expected." When on two occasions Wingina became "so grievously sicke that he was like to die, and as he lay languishing, doubting of anie help by his owne priestes," he called upon the English "to praie and bee a meanes to our God that it would please him either that he might live, or after death dwell with him in blisse." Others, believing strongly in a connection between English power and the Bible, desired "to touch it, to embrace it, to kisse it, to hold it to their breasts and heades, and stroke over all their bodie with it." To Hariot this behavior demonstrated a desire for Christian religion, but the Roanokes desired Christianity less than they did access to the sacred power that enabled the English to prosper on the Outer Banks while Indians suffered.[103]

The devastation wreaked as a result of English settlement on Roanoke Island, as well as the widespread belief among Indians on the Outer Banks that the English possessed great power, generated divisions within the Roanoke community. Though they could agree that they had declined relative to the English, Roanoke Indians divided over how best to respond. Colonization produced devastation, but clearly not apathy and acquiescence. Natives on the Carolina Outer Banks responded variously to the changes rending their communities. Some, such as Granganimeo and Ensenore, a "savage father" to Wingina, apparently accepted that the English were more powerful than they and hoped to secure their survival through accommodation to and cooperation with the colonists. Others, such as Wingina and Wanchese, who quickly abandoned the English, tried initially to understand the sources of

---

[101] Hariot, *Briefe and True Report*, 29.

[102] Ibid., 29, [48]; Crosby, "From Myth to History," 196.

[103] Hariot, *Briefe and True Report*, 27–28.

English spiritual power and to incorporate those sources into their accustomed ways of living.

For Wingina this effort appears to have been nothing less than profoundly disillusioning. Buffeted in a world of rapid change, he experimented with English cultural forms in order to secure the power that preserved and bestowed so many benefits upon the settlers. English power, however, provided few answers for beleaguered Algonquians, and Wingina moved rapidly away from the accommodationism of Granganimeo and Ensenore. As deaths from disease continued, and Lane's settlers, particularly during the lean months of late winter and early spring, placed increasingly dangerous strains upon finite Roanoke food supplies, Wingina concluded that contact with the English was the source of Algonquian problems. Soon he began to work toward effecting a complete separation between the Indian and white worlds on the Carolina Outer Banks.

After the death of his brother Granganimeo, sometime during the winter of 1585–86, Wingina changed his name to Pemisapan and began making plans to abandon Roanoke Island. The precise significance of the name is unclear. James A. Geary, who assembled a glossary of Carolina Algonquian words, suggests that the name might reflect the vigilant attitude of one who watches from a distance, or one who supervises, "as if that were his office."[104] Although Lane noted that the new name was taken upon Granganimeo's death, it is not likely that it reflected a change in Pemisapan's political status. Barlowe in 1854 clearly indicated that Wingina already was "king" at Roanoke. Wingina's adoption of a new name, however, may be related closely to Roanoke spirituality and the *weroance*'s perception of the English. Pemisapan, one who watched closely, may have recognized clearly that his people's survival was dependent upon separating themselves from the English, whose arrival on the Carolina Outer Banks, more than the powerful items they carried with them, had initiated drastic and devastating changes in his community. Lane said little about the meaning of the name change, and believed that Pemisapan began at this time organizing a conspiracy with Indians throughout the coastal Carolina region to exterminate the English settlers. Pemisapan's privileged position with respect to English trade, the story goes, would have provided him with enough English copper to attract a large following. Knowing that Lane intended to sail into Albemarle Sound, Pemisapan, according to Lane's own self-serving account, sent a warning ahead to the Choanokes and Mangoaks that Lane and his expedition intended to attack and kill any Indians they encountered; therefore the natives should abandon their villages, remove their corn, and so starve the English. Lane could not have been aware of the details of this plot when he departed Roanoke, however, for at that time, by his own account, he took seriously Pemisapan's dire warning that a "confederacie against us of the

[104] Quinn, *Roanoke Voyages*, 893–94.

Choanists and Mangoaks" was assembling upriver with the intention of destroying the English settlement.[105]

Lane and his men sailed in a pinnace to the head of Albemarle Sound and there, early in March, boarded smaller vessels for the ascent of the Chowan River. This was the territory of Menatonon, the *weroance* of the Choanokes. What Lane saw there impressed him. "Choanoke," he wrote, "it selfe is the greatest Province and Seignorie lying upon that River," with a town able to field seven hundred fighting men, not to mention forces gathered from the outlying tributary villages.[106]

When Lane arrived at Chowanoke he chanced upon a meeting of representatives from the Weapemeocs, Moratucs, and Iroquoian Mangoaks. Believing that he had encountered the Choanoke-Mangoak confederacy of which Pemisapan had spoken, Lane stormed the gathering, seized Menatonon, and held him hostage. For the next two days Lane interrogated the Choanoke *weroance*, who provided "more understanding and light of that Countrey then I had received by all the searches and salvages that before I or any of my companie had had conference with."[107]

Menatonon provided Lane with exciting information on the geography of the region. Three days farther up the Chowan River and then four days overland, he said "a certaine Kings countrey, whose Province lyeth upon the Sea," would be found. This sounded to Lane like a route to Chesapeake Bay, but he decided to put off following it until fresh supplies arrived from England, for Menatonon's reports of what lay farther up the Roanoke River were of more immediate interest.[108] Forty days upstream at the head of the river a "huge rocke" stood so close "unto a Sea, that many times in stormes (the winde coming outwardly from ye Sea) the waves thereof are beaten into the said fresh streame, so that fresh water for a certaine space, groweth salt and brackish." Lane also heard from Menatonon that the natives in this region panned for "a marveilous and most strange Minerall" that sounded curiously like gold.[109]

Lane decided to follow the Roanoke River course outlined by Menatonon. He released the *weroance* but took his son Skiko hostage to secure Menatonon's good behavior. Lane also concluded what he regarded as a "league" with the representatives of the Moratucs and Mangoaks. He then returned to the head of Albemarle Sound, sent Skiko back to Roanoke Island in the pinnace, and prepared to ascend the Roanoke River "with two double wherries" and forty men.[110]

---

[105] Quinn, *Roanoke Voyages*, 265–66.

[106] Ibid., 259.

[107] Ibid., 265–66. Lane must have had Hariot or Manteo with him during the expedition. Given Hariot's remarks at the conclusion of the *Briefe and True Report*, 30, it is possible that he witnessed Lane's treatment of the invalid Menatonon and found this display disturbing.

[108] Quinn, *Roanoke Voyages*, 259, 261–63. Lane referred to the Roanoke as "the River Moratico" (263).

[109] Ibid., 264, 268.

[110] Ibid., 266, 264 n, 264.

Short of food, Lane hoped to obtain supplies from the Moratucs and Mangoaks as he moved westward; this, he believed, had been the substance of his agreement with them. Three days into his journey, however, he began to think "that we were betrayed by our owne Savages, and of purpose drawn foorth by them, upon vaine hope to be in the ende starved."[111] He found "all the Countrey fledde before us." Both the Moratucs and Mangoaks had "retyred themselves with their [women], and their corne within the mayne; insomuch . . . we could not meete a man, nor finde a grain of corne in any their Townes."[112]

Later, of course, Lane would attribute this betrayal to the influence of Pemisapan, who he believed had circulated among the neighboring villages vicious rumors regarding hostile English intent.[113] One need not, however, attribute the withdrawal of the Moratucs and Mangoaks from their villages to the scheming of Pemisapan. Menatonon, while Lane's hostage, admitted that Pemisapan had sent messengers onto the mainland to organize opposition to the English. Yet Menatonon had ample reason to say precisely what he thought the English governor wanted to hear, for Lane already suspected that Menatonon was actively conspiring against the English; he believed that in Choanoke he had uncovered the "confederacie against us of the Choanists and Mangoaks" mentioned by Pemisapan, and he would likely have confronted Menatonon with this information. The Choanoke *weroance* could easily have turned the charge around to implicate Pemisapan. Indeed, Lane at one point described his expedition into Albemarle Sound as "my voyage that I had made against the Chaonists, and Mangoaks."[114] That Lane took Skiko as hostage to secure the future good behavior of the Choanokes indicates that he was not yet entirely convinced of the veracity of Menatonon's story.

The Moratucs and Mangoaks, for their part, having observed the precipitancy with which Lane seized a neighboring *weroance*, interrogated him, and made off with his son, had ample reason to stay clear of the English party. When confronted by Lane at Chowanoke, they too may have agreed to whatever Lane demanded in order to free themselves of him as quickly as possible. The Choanokes, Moratucs, and Mangoaks, moreover, may even have found the idea of aligning themselves with Pemisapan unappealing. Pemisapan, by virtue of proximity, maintained a stranglehold on Indian trade with the English and, according to Lane, had acquired enough wealth through this trade to purchase the allegiance of the neighboring Algonquian

---

[111] Quinn (*Roanoke Voyages*, 267n, 266) believes that Lane here was referring to the Roanokes and Pemisapan, but there is no reason to think that at this point Lane did *not* suspect treachery on the part of the Choanokes and Mangoaks, with whom he had arranged a league only three days before.

[112] Ibid., 267, 266.

[113] Ibid., 265.

[114] Ibid., 276. See also Michael L. Oberg, "Indians and Englishmen at the First Roanoke Colony: A Note on Pemisapan's Conspiracy, 1585–1586," *American Indian Culture and Research Journal* 18 (1994): 75–90.

bands. Cross-cultural exchange is clearly evident in White's artwork, and it is not unlikely that other native groups wanted to break into this trade.[115]

No conspiracy is needed to explain the reaction of the Carolina Algonquians to Lane. He began his ascent of the Roanoke River early in the spring, normally months of dearth in native corn cultures. During this time of the year Algonquian villagers customarily were forced to forage, and at times split up, in search of food to tide them over until the first corn harvest. That this was a year of drought, as Hariot suggested, would only have intensified food shortages among the Roanoke villagers and reduced their ability to meet the needs of hungry English colonists. These considerations alone help explain the timing of Pemisapan's disaffection with the English. Disease, moreover, had already ravaged the Roanokes, and the Indians Lane encountered, having likely heard of or even encountered Europeans previously, acted accordingly when approached by an angry, and hungry, European force.[116]

Menatonon, in any case, convinced Lane that Pemisapan had instigated a conspiracy to eliminate the English presence in the New World by starving them and had organized a powerful Indian confederacy to help him achieve this end.

Lane attempted to continue up the Roanoke River, despite the shortage of food. After consuming both their watch dogs and an emergency diet of boiled sassafras leaves, however, Lane and his men decided to return to Roanoke Island. The voyage was difficult and the threat of starvation real, but Lane and his men found enough fish in the weirs of deserted Weapemeoc villages to see them home. They arrived back at Roanoke on April 4, 1586.[117]

Whether Pemisapan hoped to eliminate Lane by sending him into the center of an aboriginal hornets' nest or intended to use Lane to eliminate some of his most powerful native rivals, it seems unlikely that he expected his hungry and aggressive nemesis to return. During the early spring months the native corn supply was at its lowest ebb, and the fact that the colonists had little corn and even less aptitude in hunting and fishing could not have impressed a native leader grown weary of these intolerant, violent, infectious, and dependent strangers. Pemisapan and his followers, then, according to Lane, "raised a bruite among themselves, that I and my company were part slayne, and part starved by the Chaonists, and Mangoaks."[118] Further, the Indians "began to blaspheme," Lane wrote, "and flatly to say, that our Lord God

[115] Hulton *America 1585*, plates 33, 45.

[116] For evidence of drought, see Hariot, *Briefe and True Report*, 27–28; and David W. Stahle et al., "The Lost Colony and Jamestown Droughts," *Science* 280 (1998): 564–67. On early European encounters with Indians in the coastal Carolina region, see J. Leitch Wright, *The Only Land They Knew: The Tragic Story of the American Indians of the Old South* (New York, 1981), 27–52.

[117] Quinn, *Roanoke Voyages*, 272.

[118] Ibid., 276–77.

was not God, since hee suffered us to sustaine much hunger, and also to be killed of the Renapoaks, for so they call by that generall name, all the inhabitants of the whole mayne, of what province soever."[119]

Believing himself rid of Lane and thoroughly disaffected with the English, Pemisapan rallied support among the Roanokes and convinced many that the English god lacked spiritual power. Therefore, he argued, the Indians ought to turn their backs on the English. The Roanokes had actively pursued English power, but the costs of this pursuit had been unacceptably and devastatingly high. To stop paying that price, they must separate themselves from these people who were burdening Algonquian subsistence resources to a dangerous degree. Abandoning the island would lead to the destruction of the remaining colonists, Pemisapan knew, for the English could not feed themselves. Lane too was aware that his position was vulnerable, "for at that time," he wrote, "wee had no weares, neither could our men skill of the making of them, neither had wee one grayne of corne for seede to put into the ground."[120]

Lane's return, however, forced Pemisapan to forgo his plans to leave the island and generated renewed divisions within the Indian community on Roanoke. Since the colony's governor had demonstrated his power by returning from an expedition into the territory of "those whose very names were terrible unto them," accommodationist Indians such as Ensenore argued that any hostile action taken against the English would be dangerous. According to Lane, Ensenore had warned those "amongst them that sought our destruction" that instead they "shoulde finde their owne, and not be able to work ours." Ensenore's counsel that the English "were the servants of God" and that the colonists "were not subject to be destroyed" by the natives carried new weight after Lane's return.[121]

Perhaps Pemisapan shared in this reassessment of English power. He may have been among those Roanokes who during this period sought the assistance of English prayers to combat the effects of drought. At any rate, certainly at Ensenore's urging, he planted a crop of corn for the English and helped them construct fishing weirs. Carolina Algonquian *weroances* clearly had limitations upon their power and could do little without first establishing a community-wide consensus.

A few days later, however, on April 20, Ensenore, "the only frend to our nation that we had amongst them," succumbed to disease, discrediting in Pemisapan's eyes the accommodationist path he had followed. Ensenore's death was full of meaning for the Roanokes. Those who had worked most closely with the English, he and Granganimeo, had both died. Accommodationism with the superior power of the English, then, had brought the

---

[119] Ibid., 277.

[120] Ibid., 276–77. See also Morgan, *American Slavery*, 40; Oberg, "Indians and Englishmen"; and David Stick, *Roanoke Island: The Beginnings of English America* (Chapel Hill, N.C., 1983), 131–40.

[121] Quinn, *Roanoke Voyages*, 278.

Indians nothing but destruction. Pemisapan, tired of colonists who threatened Algonquian subsistence and who spread English disease, renewed his plans to abandon Roanoke Island and thus effect a total separation between the English and the Indians.[122]

Early in May 1586 Pemisapan, after destroying the weirs he earlier had provided the colonists, crossed over to Dasemunkepeuc and there, according to Lane, saw to the planting on the mainland of another corn crop. He also reportedly paid with the copper he had obtained through English trade for military assistance from a large Weapemeoc faction, the Moratucs, and the Mangoaks. All told, Lane believed, some 1,500 warriors from different tribes would be assembling at Dasemunkepeuc on June 10 for an assault on the Roanoke colony. He obtained this information from Skiko, Menatonon's son, who had reason to implicate Pemisapan in a conspiracy against the English. It is significant that of the tribes supposedly gathering at the rendezvous, Skiko did not mention Menatonon's Choanokes; in fact, Skiko persuaded Lane that he could count on the Choanokes for support.[123]

Meanwhile, by breaking up the weirs, Pemisapan forced Lane "to disband my company into sundry places to live," and there to forage for shellfish and crabs and whatever else could be obtained.[124] Scattering his men in small contingents across the Outer Banks, Lane knew, made them easy targets for hostile Indian attack, but without the prospect of food for the next two months his situation was critical. By the middle of May he had resolved to act before Pemisapan could gather his forces. Lane sent word to Pemisapan that he intended to go to Croatoan because he had heard of the arrival of the supply ship—though in truth he "had neither heard nor hoped for so good adventure." He asked Pemisapan if his men would fish for him and sell him four days' provision to serve the voyage.

Pemisapan had little interest in helping Lane. All his actions indicate a desire to separate his people from the colonists. Having abandoned Roanoke and left the English to their own devices, he apparently had no desire to return. But Lane, deeply suspicious of Pemisapan's actions, planned a night raid to steal all the canoes on Roanoke, thus cutting off Pemisapan's communication with his allies still on the island. Lane sent a number of men under the command of one of his lieutenants

to gather up all the Canoas, in the setting of the sunne, & to take as many as were going from us to Adesmocopeio [Dasemunkepeuc], but to suffer any that came from thence to land; he met with a Canoa going from the shoare, and overthrew the Canoa, and cut off 2 savages heads: this was not done so secretly but hee was discovered from the shoare, whereupon the cry arose: for in trueth,

122 Ibid., 275.
123 Ibid., 281–82, 284–85.
124 Ibid., 283.

privie to their owne villanous purposes against us, held as good espial upon us, both day and night, as we did upon them.[125]

Lane's men, approaching by water, killed three or four natives in the ensuing skirmish. A return volley of Indian arrows had little effect.

The next morning Lane continued the offensive. With twenty-seven others he crossed to Dasemunkepeuc on the pretext that he needed to complain to Pemisapan of the attempt of one Osocan, a lesser Roanoke *weroance*, to free his hostage Skiko.[126] Lane entered the village and found himself in the midst of seven or eight of Pemisapan's principal men. After quickly noting his surroundings and chances for success, Lane gave the watchword, "Christ our victory," and withering gunfire assured that the Roanokes "had by the mercie of God for our deliverance, that which they had purposed for us."

Pemisapan fell quickly and was mistaken for dead, but while Lane's men "were busie that none of the rest should escape," he managed despite his wound to spring to his feet and run for the woods. Another bullet fired by Lane's "Irish boy" struck Pemisapan "thwart the buttocks" but failed to stop the fleeing *weroance*. Edward Nugent, another Irishman, pursued Pemisapan into the forest. Lane, hearing nothing, feared that he had lost his man, but a short while later Nugent emerged from the woods with Pemisapan's head in his hand.[127]

VI

Pemisapan died on the first day of June 1586. Less than three weeks later the English abandoned Ralegh's first Roanoke colony.[128] For Lane, Roanoke must in many ways have seemed Ireland all over again. The same disillusionment, frustration, and anger in dealing with a native people are discernible in his actions. If Lane could speak of the potential of the New World in his letters home during the first two months of the colony's existence, by the following summer he had lost hope that anything could be achieved peacefully with the natives.

Lane had learned the rules of survival in a frontier world where the normal rules did not always apply. His was a world of violence, of savagery, and of harsh reprisals committed on all sides. His world view was harshly pragmatic as well, recognizing the occasional necessity of cooperation between natives and newcomers. Yet for Lane the exigencies of survival in a world untamed by English standards would always govern the resulting relationships. He never understood Pemisapan's situation. He began his ascent of Albemarle

[125] Ibid., 286.
[126] Ibid., 287.
[127] Ibid., 287–88.
[128] Ibid., 294.

Sound and the Roanoke River during the late winter and early spring, a period of dearth in native corn cultures when natives normally dispersed in small groups to search for and gather shellfish, crabs, berries, and other wild foods. When Lane found empty villages, however, he assumed the worst, and with his men outnumbered and hungry, he sought justification for the failure of the colony that Ralegh had charged him with governing. To rationalize his failures, Lane was only too ready to believe that Menatonon and, later, Pemisapan were conspiring against the English encampment on Roanoke Island.

Thomas Hariot came to Roanoke from a different world. He found Lane's brutality in dealing with the Indians repellent. Bullying Menatonon, kidnapping his son, and killing Pemisapan were, in Hariot's view, all careless, all unnecessary. "Some of our companie towardes the ende of the yeare," he wrote, "shewed themselves too fierce, in slaying some of the people, in some towns, upon causes that on our part might easily have been borne withall." He recognized that the actions of his countrymen had alienated the coastal Algonquians.[129]

At no time did Hariot ever doubt that the Indians could be assimilated into a Christian, Anglo-American society in North America. If "meanes of good government bee used," he wrote, "they may in short time be brought to civilitie and the imbracing of true religion." There was, indeed, "nothing at all to be feared."[130] Hariot had not lost hope. Unlike Lane, he did not find fault with the natives; rather, he questioned English methods. Only by approaching the Indians peacefully could the English persuade them to abandon their customs and habits in favor of Christianity. The events at Roanoke, where frontier attitudes toward the Carolina Algonquians prevailed over those held in the metropolis, disappointed Hariot. He hoped that future English voyagers to the west would learn the lessons of Roanoke.

The younger Richard Hakluyt shared his friend's disappointment and continued to believe that the Indians of England's New World were an intelligent and adaptable people. Writing in 1587, Hakluyt concluded that if properly treated, "they will easilie embrace the Gospell, forsaking their idolatrie, wherein at this present for the most part they are wrapped & intangled."[131]

But Ralegh's Roanoke colony began a pattern that would be repeated on subsequent American frontiers. English metropolitans called for the incorporation of the Indians into the Anglo-American society they hoped to establish. Their plans ended in failure because so few of the actual colonists were able to appreciate these metropolitan concerns, and because such intense pressure was placed upon Native American subsistence systems by English colonists.

[129] Hariot, *Briefe and True Report*, 30.
[130] Ibid., 25, 30.
[131] Taylor, *Writings of the Hakluyts*, 375.

Walter Ralegh, Thomas Hariot, and Richard Hakluyt, as part of their metropolitan vision, had called for the fair and just treatment of the New World's inhabitants. Only through these means, they recognized, could a colony be planted in a distant and foreign land. Only through these means could Indians be assimilated into a Christian, English New World empire. Yet to people his colony, Ralegh sent soldiers, men who lived by violence and whose beliefs about "savage" peoples had been forged along the marchlands of the empire. Seldom were men of this cast of mind capable of sharing the broader vision of a Thomas Hariot or a Richard Hakluyt, ultimately so out of place on the Anglo-American frontier.

2 Master Stockam's Opinion

So unlike Thomas Hariot, Captain John Smith had long questioned the wisdom of the English effort to civilize and Christianize American Indians. Shortly after arriving in 1607 at the marshy encampment his countrymen would call Jamestown, Smith recognized the incompatibility of the instructions issued by the colony's promoters with the demands for survival on the Anglo-American frontier. The Indians among whom the English settled had corn, whereas the colonists succumbed rapidly to disease as their food supplies dwindled. Smith believed that "by trade and courtesie there was nothing to be had" from the natives, and he soon embarked upon a policy of forced trade and intimidation. Within weeks he had coerced from the Indian tribes of Powhatan's chiefdom hundreds of bushels of corn.[1]

As Smith swaggered about the Chesapeake, he proved a keen observer of the Algonquian bands he hoped to subjugate. Long interested in the diversity of human cultures, before his arrival in Virginia he had encountered a variety of peoples in Europe, Africa and the Middle East. In 1596 and 1597 he had fought with English Protestants in the Low Countries against the Catholic forces of Felipe II. By 1600, however, Smith had grown uncomfortable with the fratricidal quality of European religious warfare. Uninterested in the theological debates then rending Christian Europe, he traveled to Hungary to join in the ideologically less complex warfare of Christian against infidel. He quickly distinguished himself on the battlefield and in

---

[1] John Smith, *The Generall Historie* (1624), in *The Complete Works of Captain John Smith*, ed. Philip L. Barbour, 3 vols. (Chapel Hill, N.C., 1986), 2:324, 144; Edmund S. Morgan, *American Slavery, American Freedom: The Ordeal of Colonial Virginia* (New York, 1975), 77; Stephen Potter, *Commoners, Tribute, and Chiefs: The Development of Algonquian Culture in the Potomac Valley* (Charlottesville, Va., 1993), 181; J. Frederick Fausz, "The Powhatan Uprising of 1622: A Historical Study of Ethnocentrism and Cultural Conflict" (Ph.D. diss., College of William and Mary, 1977), 242.

personal combat, but in 1603 his luck ran out. Wounded and then captured, Smith was sold into slavery in Constantinople and Tartary. After beating his owner to death with a threshing flail, he escaped through Russia and returned to England in 1604.[2]

Smith's biographers argue that his experience with "various world cultures" placed him "in a better position to appreciate individual Indians and Indian culture than most of his English contemporaries." Smith, they argue, believed "in the comparative method and stage theory of civilization," which characterized the writings of men such as Thomas Hariot.[3] These statements, however, ignore the context in which Smith encountered other cultures.

John Smith was an adventurer, a soldier of fortune. Turks and Tartars he knew only as soldier or slave. The nature of religious warfare against the infidel rendered the gaping cultural chasm separating him from his enemies nearly unbridgeable. He could comment, much later, on the customs of Turks and Tartars, but he never thought in the terms necessary to assimilate them into an organized matrix of human development. As in the East, so in Virginia. Smith was a product of the frontier, a world of pragmatism, exploitation, and violence. His interest in the Indians, accordingly, was neither philanthropic nor philosophic.[4]

Smith later claimed that for the "constancy and conversion" of the Indians, "I am and ever have beene of the opinion of Master Jonas Stockam, a Minister in Virginia." Stockam, who had sailed for Virginia in September 1620, saw little hope of converting the native tribes. "I confesse you say well to have them converted by faire meanes," he wrote to the Council of the Virginia Company, "but they scorne to acknowledge it . . . and though many have endeavoured by all meanes they could by kindnesse to convert them, they finde nothing from them but derision and ridiculous answers." Stockam concluded, "I can find no probability by this course to draw them to goodnesse; and I am perswaded if Mars and Minerva go hand in hand, they will effect more good in an houre, than those verball Mercurians in their lives."[5]

As Stockam's letter reveals, different groups of Englishmen developed fundamentally different sets of attitudes toward the Algonquian bands of the

---

[2] Alden T. Vaughan, *American Genesis: Captain John Smith and the Founding of Virginia* (Boston, 1975), 3–13.

[3] Quoted material is from J. A. Leo Lemay, *The American Dream of Captain John Smith* (Charlottesville, Va., 1991), 116–17. The same interpretation informs Philip L. Barbour, *The Three Worlds of Captain John Smith* (Boston, 1964); and Karen Ordahl Kupperman, ed., *Captain John Smith: A Select Edition of His Writings* (Chapel Hill, N.C., 1988), 133–204.

[4] Morgan, *American Slavery*, 76–77; Nicholas Canny, " 'To Establishe a Common Wealthe': Captain John Smith as New World Colonist," *VMHB* 96 (1988): 220.

[5] Smith, *Generall Historie*, 2: 285–86. On Stockam, see George Maclaren Brydon, *Virginia's Mother Church and the Political Conditions under Which It Grew*, 2 vols. (Richmond, Va., 1948), 1:40–51.

Virginia Tidewater. At Jamestown the mores and values of an expansive, commercially minded, and aggressive frontier population prevailed over the religious and imperial concerns of metropolitans both in London and Virginia. The rigid determination with which the frontier population devoted itself to the cultivation of tobacco undermined the efforts of the Virginia Company's last governor, Sir Francis Wyatt, to promote expansion through ordered settlement, martial discipline and peaceful relations with the Indians. The aggressiveness of the English frontier population destroyed as well George Thorpe's plan to educate and assimilate the Powhatan Indians into an English and Christian New World empire. Frontier pressures produced a crisis in the form of the Indian uprising of 1622, which stunted the growth of the colony, contributed to the dissolution of the Virginia Company of London, and forced metropolitans to abandon any notion of a philanthropic Indian policy. As John Smith noted, in the months and years following the rising of 1622, Master Stockam's opinion prevailed.

I

King James I chartered the Virginia Company of London in April 1606, granting Richard Hakluyt the younger and "divers others" of the king's "lovinge subjects" the right "to make habitacion plantacion and to deduce a Colonie of sondrie of our people into that parte of America commonly called Virginia."[6] The sponsors of this enterprise were closely connected to the circle that had supported Ralegh's colonizing activities two decades earlier. Hakluyt remained the most important holdover from the Roanoke ventures.[7] In 1606 he helped frame instructions for the colony, which reflected his understanding of the causes of the failure at Roanoke. The natives, Hakluyt insisted, must be treated fairly. "In all your passages," he wrote, "you must have great care not to offend the naturals, if you can eschew it." Hostile Indians would not provide maize for the colonists.[8]

The metropolitan concerns that had animated Ralegh and his circle remained relevant in 1606. Profits, of course, ranked high on the Virginia Company's list of priorities. Its leaders saw the settlement as a commercial organization. Colonists would search for precious metals, open a lucrative trade with the Indians, and, it was hoped, discover a passage to the Orient. If profits did not result from these endeavors, the investors were willing to

---

[6] Philip L. Barbour, ed., *The Jamestown Voyages under the First Charter, 1606–1609* (Cambridge, England, 1969), 24.

[7] See David Beers Quinn, *Set Fair for Roanoke: Voyages and Colonies, 1584–1606,* (Chapel Hill, N.C., 1985), 341–78. Hariot, apparently, remained active as well. See Alexander Brown, ed., *The Genesis of the United States*, 2 vols. (London, 1890), 1:206.

[8] E. G. R. Taylor, ed., *The Original Writings and Correspondence of the Two Richard Hakluyts* (London, 1935), 494.

pursue the production of glass, iron, potash, pitch, and tar.[9] The promoters of the Virginia venture also hoped that colonization abroad would relieve England's problems at home. They saw America as a refuge from increasing population pressures, dislocating social and economic change, intensified religious controversy, and the rapid commercialization of English life.[10]

Still, a concern for the souls of the Indians lay at the heart of the Virginia Company's program for colonization.[11] The king, in the company's 1606 charter, emphasized the importance of bringing "Christian religion to suche people as yet live in darknesse and myserable ignorance of the true knowledge and worshippe of God." The natives, he said, must be well treated, and "all just, kind and charitable courses shall be holden" so that "they may be the sooner drawne to the true knowledge of God, and the obedience of us."[12] A "True and Sincere Declaration of the Purpose and Ends of the Plantation," published in 1609 by the Council of the Virginia Company, declared that "the *Principal* and *Maine Endes* . . . were *first* to preach and baptize into *Christian Religion,* and by propagation of the Gospell, to recover out of the armes of the Divell, a number of poore and miserable soules, wrapt up unto death, in almost invincible ignorance." A circular letter published by the council three months later noted that "the eyes of all Europe are looking upon our endevors to spread the Gospell among the Heathen people of Virginia."[13] The English, according to one minister, would bring to "those poore and savage, and to be pittied *Virginians,* not onely humanitie, instead of brutish incivility, but Religion also." The first of these gifts, noted another, would "make them *men*: the second *happy men*."[14]

That little occurred in terms of actual missionary activity in the colony's early years should not be taken as evidence either of cynicism or hypocrisy on the part of company leadership. Poor and divided, the English church lacked the means to build a missionary empire in America. Many of its more aggressive elements, however, recognized that the Catholic powers had outdistanced English Protestants in the race to convert the inhabitants of the

---

[9] James R. Perry, *The Formation of Society on Virginia's Eastern Shore, 1616–1655* (Chapel Hill, N.C., 1990), 11; Morgan, *American Slavery,* 44–45.

[10] See, e.g. Daniel Price, *Sauls Prohibition Staide* (London, 1609), B2.

[11] Avihu Zakei, *Exile and Kingdom: History and Apocalypse in the Puritan Migration to America* (Cambridge, England, 1992), 98–119; John Parker, "Religion and the Virginia Company, 1609–1610," in *The Westward Enterprise: English Activities in Ireland, the Atlantic, and America, 1480–1650,* ed. K. R. Andrews, N. P. Canny, and P. E. H. Hair (Detroit, Mich., 1979), 245–70; Perry Miller, "The Religious Impulse in the Founding of Virginia: Religion and Society in Early Literature," *WMQ,* 3d ser., 5 (1948): 492–522; J. Leitch Wright, *The Only Land They Knew: The Tragic Story of the American Indians in the Old South* (New York, 1981), 61; Maxwell Ford Taylor Jr., "The Influence of Religion on White Attitudes Toward Indians in the Early Settlement of Virginia" (Ph.D. diss., Emory University, 1970), 134–93.

[12] Barbour, *Jamestown Voyages,* 25.

[13] Brown, *Genesis,* 1:339, 463.

[14] William Crashaw, *A Sermon Preached before the Lord Lawarre, Lord Governour of Virginea* (London, 1610), D4; Richard Crakanthorpe, *A Sermon at the Solemnizing of the Happie Inauguration of our Most Gracious and Religious Soveraigne King James* (London, 1609), D3.

New World. In the absence of any church organization to plan and orchestrate missionary activity, the Virginia Company provided an opportunity to carry the true religion abroad.[15]

In justifying these missionary efforts, company promoters addressed the question of the English right to Indian soil. Robert Gray, in his *Good Speed to Virginia*, noted that the Indians have "only a generall residencie there, as wild beasts have in the forest," and that they did not recognize private ownership of land, "so that if the whole land should bee taken from them, there is not a man that can complaine of any particular wrong done unto him." A Virginia Company publication argued that "it is not unlawfull, that wee possesse part of their land, and dwell with them, and defend ourselves from them . . . because there is no other, moderate, and mixt course, to bring them to conversion, but by dailie conversation."[16]

The Virginia Company never arrived at, nor did it seek, a definitive solution to the problem of aboriginal title. Conquest alone, the promoters insisted, could not justify settlement on Indian land. Instead, the Company tended to regard English settlement as a *fait accompli* and to justify its continuation on the grounds that the Indians would be converted to Christianity and treated humanely. The conversion process could, and should, be peaceful. Whereas the Spaniards conquered the West Indies "with rapiers point and musket shot, murdering so many millions of naked Indians," wrote Robert Johnson, the English would use "faire and loving meanes, suiting to our English natures."[17] William Crashaw, a London clergyman, noted that "the Israelites had a commandement from God to dwell in Canaan, we have leave to dwell in *Virginea*: they were *commanded to kill* the heathen, we are *forbidden* to *kill* them, but are commanded to *convert* them."[18]

Obeying this command would be dangerous work, and nearly all the company's promoters recognized the need for strong defensive precautions. Still, Robert Johnson argued:

> If you seeke to gaine this victorie upon them by stratagems of warre, you shall utterly lose it, and never come neere it, but shall make your names odious to all their posteritie. In steed of Iron and steele you must have patience and humanitie to manage their crooked nature to your form of civilitie: for as our Proverbe is, Looke how you winne them, so you must weare them: if by way of peace and gentlenesse, then shall you alwaies range them in love to you wards, and in

[15] Parker, "Religion," 269.

[16] Robert Gray, *A Good Speed to Virginia* (London, 1609), C4; [Virginia Company], *A True Declaration of the Estate of the Colonie in Virginia*, (London, 1610) 10.

[17] Robert Johnson, *Nova Britannia* (1609), in *Tracts and Other Papers, Relating Principally to the Origin, Settlement, and Progress of the Colonies in North America*, comp. Peter Force (Washington, D.C., 1836), 13–14.

[18] Crashaw, *Sermon*, F3–F4. Alfred A. Cave argues in "Canaanites in a Promised Land: The American Indian and the Providential Theory of Empire," *American Indian Quarterly* 12 (1988): 277–97, that Englishmen used the Canaanite analogy to justify the dispossession and destruction of the Indians, but it seldom appears in the Virginia material.

peace with your English people, and by proceeding in that way, shall open the springs of earthly benefits to them both, and of safetie to your selves.[19]

Only self-preservation could justify violence against the Indians. Robert Gray found ample justification in the Old Testament for slaying idolaters but thought saving souls better. The Indians, "desirous to imbrace a better condition," provided the English with an opportunity to reclaim millions of souls from eternal damnation. Care should be taken, he observed, that no occasion be given "that the holy name of God should be dishonoured among the Infidels."[20]

A belief that the Indians would readily abandon their own cultural moorings and accept the cultural and religious norms of English society lay at the heart of these discussions. The Indians, thought amenable to persuasion, would easily follow a path of progress that appeared to many of these writers as similar to that followed centuries before by the ancient Britons when confronted by the superior culture of Rome. Europeans had long since abandoned their paganism and accepted Christianity and the benefits of civil society. History, then, provided a clear precedent: the Indians would follow the same progression that had brought the English to their current level of civilization.[21]

In a short poem introducing his *Historie of Travaile into Virginia Britannia* (1612), William Strachey wrote:

Wild as they are, accept them, so we're wee:
To make them civill, will our honnour bee:
And if good worcks be the effects of myndes,
Which like good angells be, let our designes,
As we are Angli, make us Angells too:
No better worck can state- or church-man do.

Strachey believed that "we might yet have lyved overgrowen satyrs, rude and untutred, wandering in the woodes, dwelling in caves, and hunting for our dynners," had not the Romans "reduced the conquered partes of our barbarous iland into provinces, and established in them colonies of old souldiers; building castells and townes, and in every corner teaching us even to knowe the powerfull discourse of divine reason." Even though Indians were surely as barbarous as the ancient Britons once had been, "by a gentle and faire entreaty we may win them to be willing to heare and learne of us and our preachers."[22]

[19] Robert Johnson, *The New Life of Virginia* (1612), in Force, *Tracts*, 18–19.
[20] Johnson quoted in Parker, "Religion," 256. See also George Benson, *A Sermon Preached at Pauls Crosse* (London, 1609), 92.
[21] Among the best contemporary statements is John Speed, *The History of Great Britaine* (London, 1611). See also Bernard W. Sheehan, *Savagism and Civility: Indians and Englishmen in Colonial Virginia* (Cambridge, England, 1980), 120–21.
[22] William Strachey, *The Historie of Travaile into Virginia Britannia*, ed. R. H. Major (London, 1849), B1, 18–19.

Robert Johnson, similarly, noted that "wee had continued brutish, poore and naked Britaines to this day, if *Iulius Caesar* with his Romane Legions (or some other) had not laid the ground to make us tame and civill." William Crashaw reminded his listeners that there was a time "when wee were savage and uncivill, and worshipped the divell, as now they do," before "God sent some to make us civill, others to make us Christians." Had that not happened, he argued, "we had yet continued wild and uncivill, and worshippers of the Divell: for our *civilitie* wee were beholden to the Romanes, for our *religion* to the Apostles and their disciples."[23]

Like Ralegh's circle, these men believed that the relative backwardness of the native tribes owed less to any racial or cultural characteristic than to a want of knowledge. "It is not the nature of men," wrote Robert Gray, "but the education of men, which make them barbarous and uncivill, and therefore chaunge the education of men and you shall see that their nature will be greatly rectified and corrected."[24] Yet though their intentions were good, these intensely ethnocentric Englishmen failed to understand that they had encountered a people as loyal to their own culture as the English were to theirs. English progress offered little to a tribal people existing contentedly beyond the pale of Christian and civil society. To follow the path of progress the English had charted for them would have meant nothing less than the forfeiture of their culture and religion.

That English civility held little attraction for Indians is understandable. Native Americans belonging to the constituent tribes of Powhatan's paramount chiefdom were, like the English, powerfully ethnocentric, and they found little about the English that they considered palatable.[25] As important as native resistance in preventing the attainment of metropolitan goals, however, were the structure of English maritime expansion in the early Stuart period and the demands for physical and economic survival along the Virginia frontier.

II

The first three ships sent by the Virginia Company entered Chesapeake Bay and ascended the James River to the territory of Powhatan in the spring of 1607. The settlers planted their colony at Jamestown in the middle of May, per Hakluyt's instructions, at a site ideally located by European military standards. A narrow and easily defended strip of land connected the

[23] Johnson, *Nova Britannia*, 14; Crashaw, *Sermon*, D.
[24] Gray, *Good Speed*, C2.
[25] Helen C. Rountree, "The Powhatans and the English: A Case of Multiple Conflicting Agendas," in *Powhatan Foreign Relations, 1500–1722*, ed. Helen C. Rountree (Charlottesville, Va., 1993), 178.

uninhabited peninsula they chose to the mainland. Deep water allowed oceangoing ships to tie to trees near the shoreline, yet the location was far enough upriver to promise the colonists ample warning should European invaders attack.

Powhatan felt no immediate threat from the tiny settlement planted on what he considered little more than a marshy wasteland. Far more concerned about powerful Indian enemies to his north and west than a European invasion, he probably looked to the English as potentially useful allies, and the famous scene of Pocahontas "saving" John Smith possibly represented an effort by Powhatan to adopt Smith symbolically and appoint him *weroance* of his new subsidiary "tribe" of Englishmen.[26]

When the English arrived, Powhatan's empire of "Tsenacommacah" had a population of nearly 14,000 of the estimated 20,000 Algonquians in the entire Virginia Tidewater. The nucleus of his domain consisted of the six chiefdoms he had inherited late in the sixteenth century centered upon the confluence of the Pamunkey and Mattaponi Rivers: the Powhatans, Arrohatocs, Pamunkeys, Youghtanunds, Appomatocs, and Mattaponis.[27] From this base Powhatan extended his sway over other bands through conquest, alliance, and intimidation, always moving eastward toward the Chesapeake. His influence ultimately extended to about thirty Algonquin-speaking tribes in some two hundred villages along the entire length of the Virginia coast. By 1608 all the tribes along the James, York, and Panyankatank Rivers and their tributaries, with the exception of the Chickahominys, were part of a complex hierarchical tribal empire governed by Powhatan.[28]

The English arrival placed Powhatan in a delicate position regarding his still-expanding empire. Since at least the middle of the sixteenth century Virginia Algonquians had experienced pressure from foreign nations, both European and Indian. Spanish Jesuits planted a short-lived settlement along the James or York River in 1570. It lasted one year, wiped out in an uprising led by a young Algonquian known to the Spanish as Don Luis de Velasco. The Powhatans likely had heard as well of both the English attempt to settle Roanoke Island and the party of Englishmen who wintered on the Chesapeake in 1585–86. Powhatan in early 1607 may even have massacred the

[26] J. Frederick Fausz, "An 'Abundance of Blood Shed on Both Sides': England's First Indian War, 1609–1614," *VMHB* 98 (1990): 12–13; Nancy Oestreich Lurie, "Indian Cultural Adjustment to European Civilization: The Case of Powhatan's Confederacy," in *Interpreting Colonial America: Selected Readings*, ed. James Kirby Martin (New York, 1978), 42; Ian K. Steele, *Warpaths: Invasions of North America* (New York, 1994), 41.

[27] Helen C. Rountree, *The Powhatan Indians of Virginia: Their Traditional Culture* (Norman, Okla., 1989), 15, 140.

[28] Lurie, "Indian Cultural Adjustment," 45: Rountree, *Powhatan Indians*, 140; Helen C. Rountree, "Who Were The Powhatans and Did They Have a Unified Foreign Policy?" in Rountree, *Powhatan Foreign Relations*, 1–19; Christian F. Feest, "Virginia Algonquians," in *Handbook of North American Indians*, vol. 15, *Northeast*, ed. William C. Sturtevant (Washington, D.C, 1978), 253–55; Fausz, "Powhatan Uprising," 63.

remnants of Ralegh's "Lost Colony," who had removed themselves from Roanoke and settled among the Chesapeake Indians.[29]

As Europeans began to explore the coastal plain, Iroquoian-speaking Massawomecks and Pocoughtaonacks were pressing upon the northern and northwestern boundaries of Powhatan's domain. Tension also existed between the Powhatans and the Piedmont Monacans, a Siouan-speaking group that controlled access to native copper sources in the Blue Ridge Mountains. Copper was charged with symbolic, ceremonial, and political significance for Eastern Algonquians. Competition and maneuver for access to indigenous copper supplies bred conflict between the Powhatans and their western neighbors, and archaeological evidence indicates the presence of substantial warfare on the coastal plain in the centuries before the English arrived. The combined pressure from sporadic European exploration, continuing conflict with other Native American groups, and, perhaps, depopulation caused by European disease may have encouraged Powhatan to extend his control over neighboring tribes in order to protect his original holdings, secure control of trade routes throughout the interior, and circumvent Monacan control of indigenous copper supplies.[30]

Powhatan initially hoped to monopolize trade with the newcomers. Copper brought by the colonists, redder and harder than local varieties, was especially prized in native exchange. A Powhatan *weroance* was expected by his followers to demonstrate his generosity by downward distribution of a portion of the goods he acquired through exchange or tribute. With a monopoly on English copper, Powhatan could resell some to neighboring nations for "100.tymes the value" and use the rest to secure the loyalty of the subsidiary chiefdoms within his empire. Only after the English "begann to plant and fortefye" did Powhatan resolve upon an attack to test their strength. On May 26, between two hundred and four hundred warriors mounted "a very furious assault" against the still unfinished fort. The attackers killed two colonists and wounded perhaps a dozen more before fire from the ships' cannon drove them off.[31]

John Smith had been exploring upriver when Powhatan's forces attacked. Through much of the colony's first year Smith lacked the power to effect the changes he thought necessary in the company's Indian policy. In September 1608, however, following the death or departure of most of his rivals on the governing council, Smith took complete control of affairs at Jamestown. He

[29] David J. Weber, *The Spanish Frontier in North America* (New Haven, Conn., 1992), 72. See also Rountree, *Powhatan Indians*, 142; and Quinn, *Set Fair*, 362.

[30] Jeffrey L. Hantman, "Powhatan's Relations with the Piedmont Monacans," in Rountree, *Powhatan Foreign Relations*, 109–10; Helen C. Rountree, "The Powhatans and Other Woodland Indians as Travellers," in Rountree, *Powhatan Foreign Relations*, 45; Rountree, *Powhatan Indians*, 142.

[31] Barbour, *Jamestown Voyages*, 95, 110; Potter, *Commoners*, 169, 180–81; Rountree, *Powhatan Indians*, 111; Hantman, "Piedmont Monacans," 109–10.

recognized that a want of discipline and general improvidence had contributed to the death of all but 38 of the 104 original settlers in the colony's early months, so he set the colonists to work, refusing to feed those who would not labor. Smith also struggled to restrain colonists and sailors from debasing the value of English goods through careless exchange.[32]

The London Council's orders to treat the Indians with all possible kindness disgusted Smith. He respected the tactics employed by the Spanish in governing the Indians of Central and South America. In 1624 he wrote that the English, like the Spaniards, should have "forced the treacherous and rebellious Infidels to doe all manner of drudgery worke and slavery for them, themselves living like Souldiers upon the fruits of their labors."[33]

Accordingly, late in the fall of 1608 Smith led an expedition to buy corn at Chickahominy, forcing the Indians—who "complained extreamly of their owne wants"—to sell at gunpoint.[34] Later, Smith departed for Nansemond, where the Indians were similarly reluctant to trade. "Upon the discharging of our Muskets," Smith wrote, "they all fled and shot not an Arrow; the first house we came to we set on fire, which when they perceived, they desired we would make no more spoyle, and they would give us halfe they had." Word of English tactics spread up and down the James River. As Smith's forces continued to raid native villages, they found that "all the people were fled, as being jealous of our intents."[35]

Increasing difficulty in obtaining corn from the Indians convinced Smith that "it was Powhatan's policy to starve us." He thus resolved upon a plan "to surprise Powhatan, and all his provision" at Werowocomoco. Powhatan, as well, likely had plans to eliminate the English leader. Smith arrived at Werowocomoco in January 1609, and his ensuing meeting with the great *weroance* showed the extent to which peaceful coexistence between the Indians and the English had become impossible within a year and a half of the first settlement. Powhatan had cut off all trade with the English in retaliation for Smith's brutal assault at Nansemond. Yet he clearly still thought of the English as allies, though subordinate, and he tried to persuade Smith to embrace the principles of reciprocity which he believed should undergird relations within his chiefdom, "we being all friends, and for ever Powhatans."[36]

Smith's attack on Nansemond, Powhatan said, "so much affrighteth all my people as they dare not visit you." He then asked Smith

---

[32] Barbour, *Three Worlds*, 175–76. On mortality at Jamestown, see Carville V. Earle, "Environment, Disease, and Mortality in Early Virginia," in *The Chesapeake in the Seventeenth Century*, ed. Thad W. Tate and David L. Ammerman (New York, 1979), 96–125.

[33] Quoted in Morgan, *American Slavery*, 77.

[34] John Smith, *The Proceedings of the English Colonies in Virginia*, in Smith, *Complete Works*, 1:239.

[35] Smith, *Generall Historie*, 2:191–92.

[36] Ibid., 195. See also 156, and the discussion in Martin H. Quitt, "Trade and Acculturation at Jamestown, 1607–1609: The Limits of Understanding," *WMQ*, 3d ser., 52 (1995): 227–58.

What will it availe you to take that by force you may quickly have by love, or to destroy them that provide you food. What can you get by warre, when we can hide our provisions and fly to the woods? whereby you must famish by wronging us your friends. . . . Thinke you I am so simple, not to know it is better to eate good meate, lye well, and sleepe quietly with my women and children, laugh and be merry with you, have copper, hatchets, or what I want being your friend: then be forced to flie from all, to lie cold in the woods, feede upon Acornes, rootes, and such trash, and be so hunted by you, that I can neither rest, eate, nor sleep.

The English colonists had trade goods of great significance to Powhatan, and he realized that the English needed him as well. Smith's behavior, however, constituted a form of insubordination that Powhatan could not tolerate. "I never use any Weroance so kindely as your selfe," he lectured Smith, "yet from you I receive the least kindnesse of any."[37]

Powhatan failed, however, to persuade Smith to abandon the practices he had learned on the peripheries, the frontiers, of the English world. His appeal to common interest fell upon deaf ears. Smith remained convinced that Powhatan intended to starve the English and that peaceful coexistence was not possible. The meeting with Smith was a telling experience for Powhatan, who learned that the English could not, and would not, engage in relations with native peoples on acceptable and understandable terms. After an attempt to capture Smith failed, the *weroance* fled Werowocomoco. Prior to his own departure, Smith forced Powhatan's people to deliver up their corn and load it aboard his ships.[38]

The English force next sailed up the Pamunkey River, where they met Opechancanough, one of Powhatan's heirs. Relations at first were amicable, but then Smith sensed that he had again sailed into a trap. In a rage he seized Opechancanough and, "with his pistoll ready bent against his breast," led "the trembling king, (neare dead with feare) amongst all his people." If the Pamunkeys did not cast down their weapons, or if they attempted to injure any of his men, Smith announced, "you shall see, I wil not cease revenge (if once I begin) so long as I can heare where to find one of your nation that will not deny the name of Pamaunke." Smith's actions were brutal but effective. By the spring of 1609 he believed that he had successfully subjugated the Indians.[39]

Yet his policy of intimidation could succeed only so long as Smith controlled the men he had compelled to respect his command. As immigration

---

[37] Smith, *Generall Historie*, 196–97.

[38] Quitt, "Trade and Acculturation," 227–58; Frederic W. Gleach, *Powhatan's World and Colonial Virginia* (Lincoln, Neb., 1997), 2.

[39] Smith, *Generall*, 2:253; Helen C. Rountree, *Pocahontas's People: The Powhatan Indians of Virginia through Four Centuries* (Norman, Okla., 1990), 51. The Powhatans, however, apparently thought of the cessation of hostilities as little more than a truce to allow for spring planting.

from England slowly increased the number of colonists, he found it difficult to control the nature of Anglo-Indian contacts. He complained fiercely about "disorderly stragling" as Englishmen fanned out along the rivers to trade with the Indians for corn, offering in exchange firearms, swords, hatchets, and copper. In fact, by effectively monopolizing the trade in English copper, Powhatan strengthened his position relative to the increasingly unwelcome English. As he acquired more English copper, its value naturally fell. At the same time, the value of native maize rose steadily with increasing English demand. Well aware that Smith could not feed all the new arrivals, Powhatan drove increasingly hard bargains for his corn, asking in exchange larger quantities of copper and, tellingly, English weapons.[40]

In an effort to preserve his scarce resources, Smith dispatched new arrivals along the length of the James but was unable to compel "this lewd company" to plant corn. Smith became alarmed as the new arrivals "tormented these poore soules, by stealing their corne, robbing their gardens, beating them, breaking their houses and keeping some prisoners." By the fall of 1609 Smith had lost control of the situation. Seriously injured when a bag of gunpowder ignited in his lap, he sailed for England on October 4, never to return to Virginia.[41]

III

The tremendous loss of life over the course of the colony's first two years provided the Council of the Virginia Company with glaring evidence of the inadequacy of its first charter for governing an English outpost three thousand miles from home. The principal problem, the council believed, was the inability of the governing council in the colony to maintain discipline among the settlers. This, in turn, created a situation where "the poore Indians by wrongs and injuries were made our enemies."[42]

Late in the summer of 1609 violence erupted along the length of the James River. The Powhatans avenged insults suffered at the hands of newly arrived Englishmen by killing more than one hundred colonists between August and November 1609. Then, one month after Smith's departure, Powhatan cut off all trade with the English and encouraged his followers to snipe freely at the settlers. The "Starving Time" followed, "a worlde of miseries" in which the English settlers began "to feele that sharpe pricke of hunger wch noe man trewly descrybe butt he wch hath Tasted the bitternesse thereof." One hundred and ten Englishmen died horribly over the course of the winter, "either

---

[40] Smith, *Generall Historie*, 2:139; Fausz, "Powhatan Uprising," 250; Steele, *Warpaths*, 42; Rountree, *Powhatan Indians*, 111.

[41] Smith, *Generall Historie*, 2:222–23; Rountree, *Pocahontas's People*, 52.

[42] Johnson, *New Life*, 10.

sterved throwe famin or cutt of by the Salvages."[43] Clearly, under the first charter, neither dominion nor civility had been obtained in Virginia.

The Virginia Company never had considered it possible or desirable to attempt immediately to recreate English social and legal institutions in the colony. The exigencies of frontier defense and survival, as well as the fact that most of the colonists were either soldiers or members of the poorest elements in English society, predisposed many promoters of colonization to favor martial discipline. Early in 1609 company officials decided to empower military commanders to reorganize settlement along military lines, and to instruct the sole "governor or principal officer" of the colony to impose martial law. Only then, they argued, could they achieve effective control over the Anglo-American frontier. The company received the charter permitting these changes late in May 1609.[44]

The "military regime" of colonial Virginia consisted of Thomas West, Lord De La Warr; Sir Thomas Gates; and Sir Thomas Dale—not unemployed mercenaries seeking wealth and adventure like John Smith but esteemed and accomplished officers, as close as anything England had yet produced to professional military men. The company hoped that this triumvirate would restore order among the colonists, impose discipline, and thus place the colony on a firm footing. Profits then could accrue to the company's investors, while the Indians received the benefits of the gospel.[45]

The London Council instructed Gates, the first to sail for Virginia, to use extreme caution in his dealings with the Powhatans. He should maintain a close watch over his crops, for if the Indians destroyed "but one harvest or burne yor townes in the night they will leave you naked and exposed to famine and cold." He "must keepe goode watches in the fielde and suffer none of [the Indians] to come nere yor corne in those dangerous seasons and continuall centinells without the walls or uttermost defences in the night." Gates must also force "Powhatan and his Weroances" to pay a tribute to the English in corne, "by wch meanes you shall quietly drawe to yor selves an annuall revennue of every Commodity growinge in that Countrey." The folly of frontier colonists made this measure necessary. "Yf you hope to winne them and provide for yor selves by trade," Gates was told, "you wilbe deceaved for already yor Copper is embased by yor abundance and neglect of prisinge it, and they will never feede you but for feare."[46]

The Council of the Virginia Company clearly had lost respect for Powhatan, telling Gates that he should "no way trust him." Still, the coun-

[43] George Percy, "'A Trewe Relacyon': Virginia from 1609–1612," *Tyler's Quarterly Magazine* 3 (1921–22): 266, 269.

[44] Barbour, *Jamestown Voyages*, 250; Darret B. Rutman, "The Virginia Company and Its Military Regime," in *The Old Dominion: Essays for Thomas Perkins Abernethy*, ed. Darret B. Rutman, (Charlottesville, Va., 1964), 4; Nicholas Canny, "The Permissive Frontier: The Problem of Social Control in Ireland and Virginia, 1550–1650," in Andrews, Canny, and Hair, *The Westward Enterprise*, 18–19.

[45] Rutman, "Virginia Company," 9.

[46] RVC 3:18–19, 118.

cil thought it possible to civilize and Christianize the Indians and to attain the metropolitan imperatives of dominion and civility. Gates must "with all propensnes and diligence, endeavour the conversion of the natives to the knowledge and worship of god and their redeemer Christ Jesus, as the most pious and noble end of this plantacon." To achieve this end the company recommended a twofold policy. First, Gates should "procure from them some convenient nomber of their Children to be brought up in yo[r] language, and maners." Second, he must eliminate their "Iniocasockes or Priestes." Either out "of necessity, or conveniency," the council wrote, "we pronounce it not crueltie nor breache of Charity to deale more sharply with them and proceede even to dache with these murtherers of Soules and sacrificers of gods image to the Divill."[47]

The general tenor of the company's publications in 1609 and 1610 reveal a belief that the conversion of the Indians would quickly follow the elimination of their priests. The first two years of its experiment in colonialism had chastened the Virginia Company's leadership, and Gates's instructions show the London Council attempting to react to the realities of life on the frontier. Still, those instructions remained consistent with metropolitan hopes for the New World. Although the governor was to rule with an iron hand, controlling the nature of Anglo-Indian relations while putting the colony on a firm defensive footing against both aboriginal and European enemies, the company still viewed relations with the Indians within the larger context of missionary Christianity and English imperialism.[48]

Yet Gates, De La Warr, and Dale failed to import in their entirety the metropolitan ideals of the Virginia Company. They each shared in the imperial ambitions of an increasingly aggressive English state, but their prior experiences proved an impediment. The Virginia Company employed as its agents men whose attitudes toward other cultures—like John Smith's—had been forged along the marchlands of the empire, and they together expressed little interest in incorporating Indians into an English colonial society. Thomas Dale, for example, first appears in 1594 in Ireland. He then fought in France and returned to Ireland in 1598 to serve under Essex in an army that also included Gates and De La Warr.[49] The extraordinary brutality, even by English standards, of Essex's campaigns taught these men that violence and terror made for short wars. Upon arriving in America and learning "how little a faire and noble intreatie workes upon a barbarous disposition," Virginia's military regime transported the brutal tactics of the Irish wars to the Anglo-American frontier.[50]

[47] *RVC* 3:14–15, 18–19.

[48] *RVC* 3:17–18; Rutman, "Virginia Company"; Sheehan, *Savagism*, 121–22.

[49] Darret B. Rutman, "The Historian and the Marshal: A Note on the Background of Sir Thomas Dale," *VMHB* 68 (July 1960): 290; Rutman, "Virginia Company," 7.

[50] William Strachey, *A True Reportorie of the Wrack, and Redemption of Sir Thomas Gates, Knight*, in *Hakluytus Posthumus, or Purchas His Pilgrimes*, ed. Samuel Purchas, 4 vols. (London, 1625), rpt. in 20 vols. (Glasgow, 1905–7), 19:62–63; Fausz, "Abundance of Blood," 33.

In June 1609 Gates sailed for Virginia with nine ships and some six hundred men, women, and children. After six weeks at sea, however, the expedition's flagship, the *Sea Venture*, was caught in "a most terrible and vehement storme," the "taile of the West Indian Horocano," and shipwrecked in Bermuda.[51] Gates spent the next eight months trying to extricate the 120 men in his charge from the island. By the time he arrived at Jamestown late in May 1610, the colonists had passed through the Starving Time. Finding the settlement in a state of "desolation and misery"—with the fort a shambles, houses deserted, and the English involved in a war in which "the Indian killed as fast without, if our men stirred but beyond the bounds of their Block-house, as Famine and Pestilence did within"—Gates resolved to abandon the colony. Only the arrival of De La Warr on June 8 prevented the abandonment of Jamestown.[52]

De La Warr and Gates immediately set themselves to the task of reorganizing the colony along military lines. They assigned all males to work companies of fifty men each. They instituted as well the first edition of the *Lawes Divine, Morall and Martiall*, a draconian legal code designed to control the colonists, ensure political stability, and provide the means to manage a war against a dangerous and numerous foe.[53]

Many of the laws regulated and limited contact between colonists and Indians, for mistreatment of the Indians by settlers was recognized as the immediate source of the colony's problems. Now, anyone who provoked hostilities with the natives or who

> shall wilfully, or negligently set fire on any Indian dwelling house, or *Quioquisock* house or temple, or upon any storehouse, or garner of graine, or provision of what quality soever, or disvaledge, ransacke, or ill intreat the people of the country . . . without commandement from the chiefe officers shallbe punished with death.

The penalty for bartering with the Indians without license from the governor was death. A colonist who "shall rifle or dispoile, by force or violence, [and] take away any thing from an Indian comming to trade, or otherwise," would do so "upon paine of death."[54]

Having established the structure through which they would govern the colony and secure frontier order, De La Warr and Gates launched a series of raids in retaliation for Powhatan's successful attacks of the year before. Gates sailed to Kecoughtan, and after ordering a musician who accompa-

---

[51] Gabriel Archer quoted in S. G. Culliford, *William Strachey, 1572–1621* (Charlottesville, Va., 1965), 105.

[52] Sir George Somers to Earl of Salisbury, 15 June 1610, in Brown, *Genesis*, 1:400–401; Strachey, *Reportorie*, 19:44–50.

[53] Rutman, "Virginia Company," 17.

[54] William Strachey, comp., *For the Colony of Virginia Britannia: Lawes Divine, Morall and Martiall, &c.*, ed. David H. Flaherty (Charlottesville, Va., 1969), 37, 15.

nied his men "to play and dawnse thereby to Allure the Indyans to come unto him . . . fell in upon them putt fyve to the sworde wownded many others some of them being fownde in the woods wth Sutche extreordinary Lardge and mortall wownds thatt itt seamed strange they Cold flye so far." He drove off the rest.[55] De La Warr next sent word to Powhatan that the price of peace would be the return of English captives and stolen weapons. Powhatan was unimpressed. Enraged by the principal chief's "prowde and disdayneful Answers," De La Warr ordered the hand of a Paspahegh captive cut off and sent the victim back to Powhatan with an ultimatum. If English captives were not returned along with the "stolen" weaponry—weapons the Powhatans felt had become theirs legitimately in exchange for providing the colonists with food—the neighboring towns would be burned.[56]

After three weeks of silence, De La Warr sent George Percy and seventy men to a Paspahegh town. The English force killed fifteen warriors, burned the village, gathered its corn, and captured the *weroansqua* of the tribe and her children. On the return trip, when the men began to grumble about sparing the hostages, Percy obliged them by throwing the children overboard and "shoteinge owtt their Braynes in the water." Upon arriving at Jamestown, Percy learned that De La Warr wanted the queen burned. Wearied by "so mutch Bloodshedd that day," Percy insisted that she merely be put to the sword. She was led into the woods and stabbed.[57]

The quick and violent nature of these attacks, particularly the murder of Paspahegh women and children, transformed the conflict between English and Algonquian. Powhatan attacks increased in frequency. The year 1611 began with De La Warr advancing up the James to the fall line, though he soon withdrew. The campaign apparently destroyed De La Warr's health, for he returned to England in March, suffering from a particularly unpleasant combination of dysentery, gout, and scurvy. The arrival of Dale two months later with three hundred soldiers, however, strengthened the English settlement, doubling the size of its population.[58]

Finding the colonists deprived of strong leadership, "growinge againne to their former estate of penurie," Dale immediately set them to work repairing palisades, building fortifications, and stockpiling corn under the aegis of an expanded and harsher edition of the *Lawes Divine, Morall and Martiall*. Dale thought that with two thousand men he might "in the space of two yeares . . . render this whole Countrie unto his Majestie," and "so over-master the subtile-mischeivous Great Powhatan, that I should leave him either no roome in his Countrie to harbour in, or drawe him to a firme association

[55] Strachey, *Reportorie*, 19:63; Percy, "Trewe Relacyon," 270.
[56] Rountree, *Pocahontas's People*, 54.
[57] Percy, "Trewe Relacyon," 271–73; Morgan, *American Slavery*, 74.
[58] Fausz, "Abundance of Blood," 39; Rountree, *Pocahontas's People*, 55; "Lord De-La-Warre's Relation," in *Narratives of Early Virginia, 1606–1625*, ed. Lyon Gardiner Tyler (New York, 1907), 210.

with ourselves." Lacking these forces, however, Dale hoped to limit Powhatan's movement by constructing fortifications at the fall line and at the mouth of the James, trapping him between an expanded English settlement and the hostile tribes to the west. This strategy, set in motion in the summer of 1611, did succeed in limiting Powhatan's movement—but it drove the Powhatans and their western enemies, despite their long-enduring hostility, into an alliance against the English. As William Strachey wrote, "Powhatan had manie enemies, especially in westerly Countryes, before we made our Forts and Habitations so neere the Falls, but now the generall Cause hath united them."[59]

Dale attacked the Nansemonds and reoccupied forts that De La Warr had established across the river from Jamestown. Then in August, strengthened by the return of Gates with 250 soldiers, English forces moved up the James. There they fortified a peninsula "which in honor of the noble Prince *Henrie*" soon became known as the City of Henrico. Five miles away Dale laid out an area known as the Bermudas, "a businesse of the greatest hope, ever begunne in our Territories there." The Bermudas soon became the most populous region in all of English America, a fortified zone where "Powhatan . . . remaines our enemie, though not able to doe us hurt."[60]

The English campaigns of 1611 overwhelmed Powhatan, forced him on the defensive, and rendered him either unwilling or unable to attack well-defended English positions. Dale, for his part, wanted to consolidate control over the James before moving into the York River, territory occupied by Powhatan's most skilled warriors.[61] Then, in the spring of 1613 Captain Samuel Argall captured Powhatan's daughter, Pocahontas, at a village on the Potomac River. Dale and Argall both attempted to use their hostage to obtain from Powhatan "all the armes, tooles, swords, and men that had runne away," as well as a sizable supply of corn. But Powhatan would not let paternal affection influence his determination to resist the English; he offered his enemies nothing more than a token response.[62]

In March 1614 Dale and Argall, with a force of 150 soldiers, sailed up the York River into the homeland of the Pamunkeys. As they approached the heart of Tsenacommacah, Opechancanough's warriors dogged and taunted them. The English replied that "although we came to them in a peaceable manner, and would have been glad to have received our demaunds with love and peace, yet we had hearts and power to take revenge, and punish where

---

[59] Smith, *Generall Historie*, 2:239; Dale to Salisbury, 17 August 1611, in Brown, *Genesis*, 1:503; Strachey quoted in Potter, *Commoners*, 183.

[60] Ralph Hamor, "Notes," in Purchas, *Hakluytus*, 19:96–101; Hamor, *A True Discourse of the Present State of Virginia* (London, 1615), 29; Irene W. D. Hecht, "The Virginia Colony, 1607–1640: A Study in Frontier Growth" (Ph.D. diss., University of Washington, 1969), 75; Fausz, "Abundance of Blood," 42.

[61] Fausz, "Abundance of Blood," 42.

[62] Purchas, *Hakluytus*, 19:92–93; Smith, *Generall Historie*, 2:244.

wrongs should be offered." The landing at Pamunkey, however filled with tension, remained free from violence. The English and Pamunkeys negotiated and extended several truces as they awaited Powhatan's response to the English demands. When they received none, the English packed up and returned to Jamestown in order to "set corne for our winters provision."[63]

Though Dale warned that if Powhatan had not responded favorably by harvest time, he "would thither returne againe and destroy and take away all ther corne, burne all their houses upon that river, leave not a fishing *Weere* standing, nor a *Canoa* in any creeke therabout, and destroy and kill as many of them as we could," it is unlikely that he thought another raid into Pamunkey territory necessary. In April 1614, after a year spent among the English at Jamestown, Pocahontas converted to Christianity and married the colonist John Rolfe.[64]

The decision to wed was not an easy one for Rolfe, who wrestled with his conscience prior to marrying such "an unbelieving creature." In the end, however, he decided that marrying Pocahontas would serve God's glory, the governor's honor, "our Countreys good, [and] the benefit of this plantation" by "the converting of one unregenerate, to generation."[65] The marriage, celebrated in the presence of members of both cultures, brought over five years of warfare to an end.

The advent of peace in 1614 heralded what some have called Jamestown's golden age, a period when the Virginia Company seemed close to obtaining the metropolitan objectives of dominion and civility. The peace was not perfect—occasional acts of violence still occurred on both sides—but the general tenor of pronouncements from both the colony and the London Company were optimistic about the future. John Rolfe, for example, wrote later from London that

> the people yerely plant and reape quyetly; and travaile in the woodes a fowling and hunting as freely and securely from feare of danger or treachery as in England.

"The greate Blessings of God," he continued, "have followed the Peace ... every man sitting under his *figtree* in safety, gathering and reaping the fruites of their labors with much joy and comfort." The territorial expansion of the colony after 1614, moreover, inaugurated Virginia's healthiest era to date. As two-thirds of the population moved upriver away from the brackish water of Jamestown, the colony's mortality rate from disease declined sharply.[66]

[63] Hamor, *True Discourse*, 8, 10.
[64] Ibid., 10, 11.
[65] John Rolfe in Tyler, *Narratives*, 240, 243; Hamor, *True Discourse*, 2.
[66] On violence, see Smith, *Generall Historie*, 2:268; John Rolfe, *A True Relation of the State of Virginia Lefte by Sir Thomas Dale Knight in May Last 1616* (Charlottesville, Va., 1971), 4–5; Earle, "Environment," 112; Hecht, "Virginia Colony," 75–76.

Along with its relative political and demographic tranquillity, a modicum of ethnic harmony produced a subtle shift in English attitudes toward the Tidewater Algonquians. Having administered Powhatan the rebuke they felt he deserved, company officials in England once again argued that a policy based on kindness and persuasion, rather than force and intimidation, could be employed to win the Indians to the linked banners of Christianity and civility.[67]

Alexander Whitaker, for example, who in 1612 had shared a generalized colonial antipathy toward Algonquian priests, wrote from Henrico that the "unnurtured grounds of reason" in the Indians should encourage the English

> to instruct them in the knowledge of the true God, the rewarder of all right-eousnesse, not doubting but that he that was powerfull to save us by his word, when we were nothing, wil be mercifull also to these sonnes of Adam in his appointed time, in whome there bee remaining so many footsteps of Gods image.

Whitaker reminded his audience that "One God has created us" and that the natives "have reasonable soules and intellectual faculties as well as wee; we all have Adam for our common parent."[68]

Rolfe, likewise, wrote that "there is no smale hope by piety, clemency, courtysie, and civill demeanor . . . to convert and bring to the knowledge and true worshipp of Jesus Christ" thousands of Indians.

> Wee and they come from one and the same moulde, especially wee knowinge, that they meerely through ignorance of God and Christ, doe runn headlong . . . into destruccion and perpetuall damnation. For which *Knowledge* we are the more bound and indebted to Almighty God (for what were we before the Gospell of Christ shined amongst us?) and cannot better express our Duties and thankfullnes for so greate mercies; then by using such meanes to them, as it pleased him to lend unto others, to bring our forefathers and us into the waies of truth.[69]

To prove his point Rolfe sailed to England in the spring of 1616 with his wife (christened Rebecca), their young son, and an entourage that included Dale and several Indians. Paraded among the best classes of Jacobean London and supported at Virginia Company expense, Pocahontas was entertained by the Bishop of London, in whose jurisdiction Virginia lay, and taken to meet with members of the royal family in hopes of drumming up support for the company's American enterprise. Vulnerable to English disease, Pocahontas died at Gravesend in March 1617 on her way back

---

[67] Alden T. Vaughan, "'Expulsion of the Salvages': English Policy and the Virginia Massacre of 1622," *WMQ*, 3d ser., 35 (1979): 68.

[68] Alexander Whitaker, *Good News from Virginia* (London, 1613), 26–27.

[69] Rolfe, *True Relation*, 12.

to Virginia. Her brief sojourn in England, however, and her marriage to an Englishman, her conversion to Christianity, and her apparent acceptance of English cultural norms seemed to demonstrate the viability of metropolitan plans for Virginia.[70] All societies evolve, Rolfe and Whitaker suggested, and with the proper assistance all societies could progress. Pocahontas seemed proof enough of that. Though the ancient inhabitants of Britain had once been barbarous pagans, they had come to the light and truth of the Gospel. The example of Pocahontas encouraged the supporters of the Virginia Company to expect the Powhatan Indians to do the same. Rolfe and Whitaker, like many others before them, subsumed the development of North American societies within their own providential understanding of England's past. Though this was powerfully ethnocentric and, as shown by Pocahontas's case, left little room for Indians to remain Indian, it nonetheless did include a space for the Powhatan Indians within the Christian empire the Virginia Company hoped to establish in North America.

Yet if representatives of the Virginia Company expressed optimism about converting the Indians and conceived of the colony as an arena suitable for expanded missionary efforts, the colonists in general did not widely share these sentiments. In the wake of Rolfe's first successful attempt at the cultivation of tobacco, the earliest samples of which he shipped to England in March 1614, the frontier population tended to focus on the opportunity to exploit the first profitable commodity produced in Virginia. For the remainder of the Virginia Company's existence, in fact, the London Council steadily lost control of affairs in the colony, as the frontier population committed itself to the cultivation of tobacco.[71]

This fervent commitment boded ill for the future. When Dale departed for England in 1616 he appointed George Yeardly his deputy. Yeardly was not the disciplinarian the colony needed. Where Dale had forced the colonists to plant corn or starve, Yeardly "applied himselfe for the most part in planting Tobacco, as the most present commoditie they could devise for a present gaine." Order collapsed as "every man betooke himselfe to the best place he could for the present purpose." The colonists' cultivation of tobacco and appropriation of Indian land was, in one historian's view, behavior "as aggressive and provocative as any military conquest," an environmental, ecological, and cultural assault that doomed metropolitan hopes and ideals and undermined the quest for an orderly frontier.[72]

Yeardly's replacement, Samuel Argall, arrived in May 1617 to find a dilapidated settlement. Only five or six houses remained standing at Jamestown, according to John Smith's later narrative, with "the Church downe, the Palizado's broken, the Bridge in pieces, the Well of fresh-water

[70] Rountree, *Pocahontas's People*, 62–64.
[71] Ibid., 61; Fausz, "Powhatan Uprising," 305.
[72] Smith, *Generall Historie*, 2:256; Fausz, "Abundance of Blood," 51.

spoiled, [and] the Store-house . . . used for the Church." The marketplace, the streets, and "all other spare places" Argall found planted with tobacco. Meanwhile, the Indians frequently visited the fort, "whereby they were become expert in our armes, and had a great many in their custodie and possession."[73]

Appalled by the state of the colony, Argall immediately took "the best order he could for repairing those defects which did exceedingly trouble us." He ordered a stop to all "private trucking with Savages," "teaching Indians to shoot wth guns," and familiarity with the "perfidious Savages. . . lest they discover our weekness."[74] Argall also sought to lessen the dependence of the colonists upon the Indians for food and resorted to increasingly harsh discipline in order to force the frontier population to plant corn instead of tobacco. Yet Argall could never break the frontier's devotion to tobacco culture. In 1616, for example, only 2,300 pounds of tobacco had been shipped from Virginia. In 1618, Argall's last year as governor, the total surpassed 41,000 pounds.[75]

By 1618 Jamestown and London were following different paths. London advocated secure and regular patterns of settlement, discipline, and peaceful relations with the Indian tribes. The frontier population, committed to the cultivation of tobacco, was bringing tremendous cultural and physical pressure to bear upon the Virginia Algonquians.

IV

A boom in tobacco prices in 1618 doomed Argall's efforts to restrain the colonists from planting tobacco. His attempt to concentrate settlement in order to impose a much-needed discipline over the colony had resulted only in the loss of nearly a fourth of the population to infectious disease within the crowded and unhealthful confines of Jamestown, as well as renewed attacks by shareholders in England upon the manner in which the Virginia Company conducted its business. By the end of 1618 there was a strong demand among stockholders for reform, along with a widespread belief that a change in administration might produce a change in the company's fortunes.[76]

In 1619 the stockholders elected Sir Edwin Sandys as the company's new treasurer. Both the faction led by Sandys and that led by the original treasurer, Sir Thomas Smith, agreed that the colonists' single minded devotion

---

[73] Smith, *Generall Historie*, 2:262.

[74] Ibid.; proclamation dated 18 May 1618, RVC 3:93.

[75] Hecht, "Virginia Colony," 356.

[76] Wesley Frank Craven, *Dissolution of the Virginia Company of London: The Failure of a Colonial Experiment* (New York, 1932), 37–38, 82–83; Richard Beale Davis, *George Sandys, Poet-Adventurer: A Study in Anglo-American Culture in the Seventeenth Century* (New York, 1955), 96–97.

to tobacco must be checked. Both sides agreed, moreover, that the company must provide greater incentives for potential investors and immigrants. Thus in 1618 the two factions combined to implement a series of reforms. English common law replaced the *Lawes Divine, Morall and Martiall*, and the company established an assembly for Virginia as a means to respond more expeditiously to developments within the colony. Finally, the London Council introduced a headright system allowing prospective immigrants to acquire title to land for each colonist they transported to Virginia. The reforms, in total, represent the Virginia Company's first attempt to create a more stable and permanent society in Virginia.[77]

Yet if the election of Sandys brought little in the shape of real changes in policy, a new enthusiasm and energy characterized his tenure in office and inspired renewed efforts to achieve the original goals of the company. The most urgent need appeared to be a rapid increase in population. The company's lands, intended to provide the bulk of its profits and support for all its officials, needed settlers in order to be profitable. Sandys and his party undertook a vigorous publicity campaign to attract all sorts of laboring people to Virginia. The introduction of skilled laborers would, Sandys hoped, address a second company concern: the general overreliance upon tobacco. The "applying so altogether the planting of Tobacco, and the neglect of other more solid commodities," read a company broadside, "have not only redounded to the great disgrace of the Countrey, and detriment of the Colony; but doth also in point of profit, greatly deceive them which have trusted to it." In order to remedy this situation, the tract continued, the company "endeavoured to set up sundry reall Commodities" such as iron, pitch and tar, cordage, silk, wine, and timber.[78]

To increase both the population and the economic strength of the colony Sandys encouraged the establishment of private plantations. "Societies of adventurers" were free to choose a site, with the consent of the governor, at any location not already occupied or settled and were given virtual autonomy in the management of their affairs. Plantations could not be placed within five miles of any of the four boroughs (James City, Charles City, Henrico, and Kecoughtan) or within ten miles of any other plantation.[79]

While Sandys and his party enthusiastically pursued increased settlement, economic diversification, and the stabilization of colonial life, the period of their control also witnessed an increasingly philanthropic Indian policy. Led

---

[77] Perry, *Virginia's Eastern Shore*, 18; Davis, *George Sandys*, 98; Craven, *Dissolution*, 88; Morgan, *American Slavery*, 93–98.

[78] Broadside dated 17 May 1620, *RVC* 3:278.

[79] W. Stitt Robinson, *Mother Earth: Land Grants in Virginia, 1607–1699* (Williamsburg, Va., 1957), 17–18; Craven, *Dissolution*, 59–62.

[80] Fausz, "Powhatan Uprising," 303–4; R. H. Land, "Henrico and Its College," *WMQ*, 2d ser., 18 (1938): 475–79.

by Sandys and John and Nicholas Ferrar, the Virginia Company began planning for an Indian college at Henrico in 1619.[80]

The college project received enthusiastic backing from many company supporters. Late in 1619 it was reported that some £500 had been promised as a gift "towards y[e] educating of Infidles children."[81] In February 1620 an anonymous donor identified only as "Dust and Ashes" bequeathed another £500

> for the mayntenance of a Convenyent number of younge Indians taken att the age of Seaven years or younger & instructed in the readinge and understandinge the principalls of Christian Religion unto the Age of 12 years and then as occasion serveth to be trayned and brought upp in some lawfull Trade wth all humanitie and gentleness until the Age of one and Twenty years, and then to enioye like liberties and pryveledges wth our native English in that place.[82]

Two weeks later the company clarified the provisions of the "Dust and Ashes" bequest. Those Indian children found capable of learning should "be putt in Colledge and brought upp to be schollers, and such as are not shall be putt to trades, and be brought up in the feare of God & Christian Religion." As for obtaining these children, "it was answered and well allowed that a treaty and an agreement be made with the Kinge of that Country concerninge them w[ch] if it soe fall out att any time . . . they may by his Command be returned."[83]

Nicholas Ferrar, one of the most enthusiastic promoters of Indian education, willed £300 to the "Colledge in Virginia to be paid when ther shall be tenn of the Infidles Children placed in itt." Until that time, Ferrar directed that £24 per year "be distributed unto three discreet and Godlie men in the Colony w[ch] shall honestly bringe upp three of the Infidells Children in Christian Religion and some good course to live by."[84] By the end of May 1620 the company had received over £2000 specifically for the college project and remained optimistic that the Indians could easily and peacefully be converted to the true religion and English standards of civility.[85]

The company had sent George Yeardly back to Virginia to replace the discredited Argall as governor and to put the reform policies into effect. He was to choose "a convenient place . . . for the planting of a University at the said Henrico in time to come and that in the mean time preparation be there made for the building of the said College for the Children of the Infidels."[86]

---

[81] Court Book, 1 December 1619, *RVC* 1:278.
[82] Court Book, 2 February 1620, *RVC* 1:307–8.
[83] Court-book, 16 February 1620, *RVC*, 1:311.
[84] Court-book, 17 May 1620, *RVC*, 1:354, 3:117.
[85] Fausz, "Powhatan Uprising," 297.
[86] Instructions to Yeardly, 18 November 1618, *RVC* 3:102.

Yeardly, however, did not believe that conversion would occur soon and wrote to Sandys that "the Spirituall vine you speake of will not so sodaynely be planted as it may be desired, the Indians being very loath upon any tearmes to part with theire children."[87] Nonetheless, the legislative assembly he convened late in July 1619 at Jamestown attempted to secure peaceful relations between the races and begin the process of conversion. The assembly proclaimed "that noe injury or oppression be wrought by the *English* agst the Indians whereby the present peace might be disturbed, and antient quarrels might be revived." In order to lay "a surer foundation of the conversion of the Indians to Christian Religion," the assembly instructed "eache towne, citty Burrough, & particular plantation" to obtain for itself "by just meanes a certaine number of the natives Children to be educated by them in true Religion & civile course of life."[88]

While the assembly acted to fulfill the benevolent expectations of the Virginia Company, it also tried to curtail the activities of colonists which threatened either the security of the settlement or the Indians themselves. It proclaimed theft from Indians a crime punishable by fines and restitution, declared that no colonist should visit any Indian town without permission from the governor, and ordered "that no man do sell or give any Indians any piece of shott, or poulder, or any other armes offensive or defensive, upon paine of being held a Traytor to the Colony, & of being hanged, as soon as the fact is proved."[89]

The arrival of George Thorpe in May 1620, more than anything else, demonstrated the new optimism that characterized company thinking about Indians during the Sandys era. Thorpe, at the company's request, assumed the responsibility of supervising the tenants placed on the "college lands" and seeing that a profit resulted which could be used to establish the school.[90]

Thorpe also quickly took over the role of mediator between the two cultures and Indian recruiter for the company's educational efforts. He found the Indians to be of "a peaceable & vertuous disposition" and explained that the slender harvest of Indian souls was a result of wrongs done the natives by English settlers. There was, he wrote, "scarce any man amongest us that doth soe much as affoorde them a good thought in his hart and most men wth theire mouthes give them nothinge but maledictions and bitter execrations." The Indians were accused by the colonists of "all the wronge and injurye that the malice of the Devill or man can afoord," yet if there was

[87] *RVC* 3:128–29.

[88] H. R. McIlwaine, ed., *Journals of the House of Burgesses of Virginia*, 13 vols. (Richmond, Va., 1905–15), 1:9–10.

[89] Ibid., 13.

[90] Land, "Henrico," 480–81; Wesley Frank Craven, "Indian Policy in Early Virginia," *WMQ*, 3d ser., 1 (1944): 72–73; Fausz, "Powhatan Uprising," 333.

[91] Thorpe to Edwin Sandys, 15–16 May 1621, *RVC* 3:446.

wrong on any side, Thorpe concluded, "it is on oʳˢ who are not soe charitable to them as Christians ought to bee."[91]

Unquestionably, there were colonists who followed company directives to treat the Indians with kindness. Apparently at some plantations natives were welcome to borrow tools and to come and go as they liked. Some of the neighboring Indians, through these means, became attached to the English so closely that they informed the colonists of Opechancanough's impending assault. Nonetheless, Thorpe's policies angered many of his fellow colonists, as when he punished settlers for mistreating Indians and on one occasion ordered several English mastiffs killed because the dogs frightened the Indians. In fact, he felt the need to inform Sandys that complaints about his conduct soon would be forthcoming. "If you chance to heare mee ill spoken of by any that came from hence," he wrote, "I praie you Judge charitabley till you bee better informed for thanke God I have the testimony of good conscience that I have done noe man wronge only I doe desier to bringe drounkennes and some other sinnes out of ffation. If I live," he concluded, "I doute not but I shall doe it."[92]

In attempting to maintain good relations with the Powhatan Indians and encourage discipline among a ragged and disorderly frontier populace, however, Thorpe fought a losing battle. The policies pursued by Sandys and his supporters worked at cross-purposes with the genuine benevolent interests of metropolitans like Thorpe. The Virginia Company of London, under Sandys, encouraged the dispersed settlement of a poorly provisioned frontier populace, largely free from company control.

From 1619 to 1621 the company shipped some 3,500 colonists across the Atlantic. That fewer than 1,200 colonists were living in Virginia at the start of 1622 indicates that at least 3,000 persons had died within those years, a mortality rate of over 75 percent.[93] Many of those remaining complained of hunger, disease, and suffering, and in 1620 Yeardly begged Sandys to send no more settlers unless he could ensure that each came with food for six months. The warning went unheeded; the company continued to dump boatloads of new and mostly ill-provisioned colonists in Virginia.[94]

The poorly equipped immigrants placed enormous strains upon native food supplies, and Sandys's encouragement of private plantation resulted in the appropriation of massive amounts of Indian land. Assured of a profitable market for tobacco, Englishmen fanned out along the James and York Rivers. In 1617 alone over 80,000 acres in land grants had already been doled out by the company. By 1619 forty-four separate patents for "particular plantations" had been issued; twelve more were established between

[92] *RVC* 3:447, 552.
[93] John Wroth, Notes Showing the Number of People Emigrating to Virginia, 1622, *RVC* 3:537.
[94] *RVC* 3: 534; Craven, *Dissolution*, 158–159.

1620 and 1622. By 1622 the English claimed all the banks of the James except for the southern shore from Nansemond eastward to Chesapeake Bay. All the James River tribes had lost their traditional lands along the rivers except for the Nanesmonds, whose tenure upon their lands was precarious at best.[95]

The result was more than the loss to the natives of their prime farmlands, for the English had occupied the link between the two major Powhatan subsistence areas: the hunting and foraging territories inland and the food-producing and reed-gathering regions along the rivers. The Powhatans had always lived "commonly by the water side, in little cottages made of canes and reeds, covered with the barke of trees."[96] Very few of their settlements were located in the interior of the three peninsulas formed by the Potomac, Rappahannock, York, and James Rivers. Waterways provided a critical source of food and means of transportation for the Powhatans, and the best agricultural soils were located most often on narrow strips of land bordering the rivers and streams. From these agricultural sites Indians had been able to exploit and move between both riverine and upland ecosystems. The English coveted the same sites, for they too needed the rivers for transportation and communication, and desired the soft, silty, and sandy loam soils located along the banks.[97]

English settlers demonstrated a tremendous appetite for this land. Though the amount of planted tobacco that an individual farmer could tend was small, the crop quickly robbed the soil of its nutrients; after three years, on average, new soil was necessary. Old tobacco fields could support the cultivation of maize for an additional three years, but then the land would have to lie fallow for two decades before it regained its fertility. As a consequence, the Powhatans found their primary subsistence areas inhabited by trigger-happy, aggressive, and land-hungry English settlers who were not always willing to allow Indians to pass between the rivers and uplands.[98]

The dispersed pattern of English settlement and poor provisioning of the colonists saddled Yeardly's successor, Sir Francis Wyatt, with enormous difficulties. George Sandys, the colony's secretary who sailed with Wyatt, "found at our Comeing over the Country in peace, but in such a peace as

[95] T. H. Breen, "Looking Out for Number One: Conflicting Cultural Values in Early Seventeenth Century Virginia," *South Atlantic Quarterly* 78 (1979): 347; E. Randy Turner, III, "An Archaeological and Ethnohistorical Study on the Evolution of Rank Societies in the Virginia Coastal Plain" (Ph.D. diss., Pennsylvania State University, 1976), 90; Robinson, *Mother Earth*, 44; Hecht, "Virginia Colony," 78–80, 341–63.

[96] Quoted in Lewis R. Binford, *Cultural Diversity among Aboriginal Cultures of Coastal Virginia and North Carolina* (New York, 1991), 76, 78.

[97] Turner, "Evolution of Rank Societies," 31, 135–38; Helen C. Rountree, "A Guide to the Late Woodland Indians' Use of Ecological Zones in the Chesapeake Region" (unpublished paper, June 1989), 15.

[98] Lois Green Carr, "Rural Settlements in the Seventeenth-Century Chesapeake," in *Settlements in the Americas: Cross-Cultural Perspectives*, ed. Ralph Bennett (Newark, Del., 1993), 178; Potter, *Commoners*, 221.

presaged ruyne." The colonists, he wrote, were "dispearsed in small fami-
lyes, farre distant one from another, and like the foolish Arcadians, exposed
to the pray of whosoever would assaile them." Reform of this "mischiefe"
was nearly impossible, Sandys continued, because the private planters had
"Pattents granted from the Court in England to plant wheresoever they
pleased contrarie to all order, discipline, and Example."[99]

Wyatt shared the company's religious mission and hoped to solve the
colony's problems through the imposition of martial discipline. He took to
heart the advice of his father, the soldier-scholar Sir George Wyatt, of the
danger posed by an ill-disciplined body of settlers. He must, wrote the elder
man, "keepe Cesars ruile to his Romans unto your men, that you reccon
more of the danger of one Christian your patriot, then of numbers of pagan
Infidels."[100] Francis Wyatt accordingly took "espetiall Care that no iniurie
or oppression bee wrought by the English against any of the yᵉ Natives of
that Countrie, whereby the present peace may bee disturbed." He also
hoped "to draw the better disposed of the Natives to Converse wᵗʰ oʳ people
and labor amongst them wᵗʰ Convenient reward, that therby they may
growe to a likeing and love of Civillity, and finallie bee brought to the
knowledge and love of God and true religion." Wyatt sent Thorpe on a number of visits to Opechancanough to obtain "by just meanes a Certaine number of the Children of the Natives to be educated by them in true Religion
and a Civill Course of life."[101]

Yet as the colony grew and settlers scattered along the banks of the rivers,
Wyatt found it nearly impossible to keep frontier settlers from abusing Indians. As colonists at the particular plantations bartered with the natives, offering firearms and swords if necessary to procure corn, violent incidents between settlers and Indians occurred more frequently. As one colonist later
reported, the English "under the pretence of frendship and in yᵉ Governors
name, have taken men prisoners, yea sometymes there lives, & goods for
nothing, or at ther owne rates, contrarie to yᵉ equity of God & natures
lawes."[102] Wyatt, no doubt, felt frustration and anger at his inability to control the frontier population. The policies pursued by himself, Thorpe, and
the company did not coincide with prevailing opinion along the frontier,
where competition between Englishmen and Indians for control of the land
determined the nature of day-to-day relations.

[99] George Sandys to Sir Samuel Sandys, 30 March 1623, RVC 4:73.
[100] George Wyatt, in J. Frederick Fausz and Jon Kukla, eds., "A Letter of Advice to the Governor of Virginia, 1624," WMQ, 3d ser., 34 (1977): 114.
[101] RVC 3:469–70, 583–84.
[102] John Penreis to Governor and Council in Virginia, 4, 8 September 1623, RVC 4:277.

V

Angered by continuous English encroachment upon Indian lands, as well as the surly hostility of the frontier population, Opechancanough, Powhatan's successor, in 1621 requested a poison from the Accomac Indians of the Eastern Shore for use against the English.[103] When the colonists caught word of the plot, Opechancanough denied any involvement and worked to relieve them of their suspicions. He assured Wyatt that he intended to maintain the peace that had prevailed since 1614 and suggested to Thorpe that he would allow English families to settle among the Indians and teach them the doctrines of Christian religion.[104]

Opechancanough succeeded in easing the minds of the English. Well versed in Christianity, and certainly skilled in dealing with Europeans, he managed to persuade Thorpe that "he had more motiones of Religione in him, then could be ymagined in soe great blindnes," that he believed that Powhatan religion to be "not the right waye," and that he desired to "bee instructed in ours and confessed that god loved us better then them."[105] Thorpe also learned that Opechancanough and his brother, Opitchapam, had taken new names. Opechancanough now called himself Mangopeesomon, and his brother became Sasawpen. The change of names, which may have signified some preparation for the attack that soon would follow, apparently did not concern Thorpe. Relieved by Opechancanough's apparent disavowal of Powhatan religion and culture and willingness to convert his people to Christianity, the English colonists lowered their guard once again, worked their tobacco, and concluded that the Pamunkey *weroance* posed no threat to the settlement.

On March 22, 1622, Opechancanough and his allies descended upon the colonists "like violent lightening" in a devastating surprise attack. Within several hours 347 English men, women, and children lay dead. The Indians "basely and barbarously murthered, not sparing eyther age or sexe, man, woman, or childe; so sodaine in their cruell execution, that few or none discerned the weapon or blow that brought them to destruction."[106] The Indians "fell upon them and beat out their braines scarce any escaping."[107] Nathaniell Powell, one of the original settlers, was killed alongside the rest of his family, where "butcher-like" the Indians "hagled their bodies, and

[103] Rountree, *Pocahontas's People*, 68; Vaughan, "Expulsion," 71. On the poisoning attempt, see Perry, *Virginia's Eastern Shore*, 21.
[104] Council in Virginia to Company in London, January 1622, *RVC* 3:583–84.
[105] *RVC* 3:584.
[106] *RVC* 4:73; Edward Waterhouse, *A Declaration of the State of the Colony and Affaires in Virginia, with a Relation of the Barbarous Massacre* (London, 1622), 14.
[107] Joseph Mead to Sir Martin Stuteville, 13 July 1622, in Robert C. Johnson, ed., "The Indian Massacre of 1622: Some Correspondence of the Rev. Joseph Mead," *VMHB* 71 (October 1963): 408–9.
[108] Smith, *General Historie*, 2:295.

cut off his head, to express their uttermost height of cruelty."[108] George Thorpe "was little regarded after by this Viperous brood . . . for they not only willfully murdered him, but cruelly and felly, out of devilish malice, did so many barbarous despights and foule scornes after to his dead corpse, as are unbefitting to be heard by any civill eare."[109] After taking the lives of so many colonists, one chronicler wrote, the Indians "fell . . . againe upon the dead, making as well as they could a fresh murder, defacing, dragging, and mangling the dead carkasses into many pieces, and carrying some parts away in derision, with base and brutish triumph." Outlying settlements recently planted in Powhatan territory suffered the heaviest casualties.[110]

Nearly a month passed before the Council in Virginia dispatched a ship for England with news of the attack: "Itt hath pleased God for ou^r manyfold sinns to laye a most Lamentable Afflictione uppon this Plantacon, by the treacherie of the Indyans," who "under the Colour of unsuspected amytie . . . attempted . . . to have cutt us off all and to have swept us away at once through owte the whole lande."[111]

The response of the London Council could not have been less sympathetic. "The great Massacre," they responded, disgraced the colonists, who were "in parte instruments of contriving it, and almost guiltie of the destruccon by a blindfold and stupid entertaininge of it, w^{c}h the least wisdome or courage" would have sufficed to prevent. Nevertheless, abandoning entirely their optimistic view that the Indians might peacefully be incorporated into an English colonial society, the London Council demanded that the colony avenge the deaths of so many Christians. "We must advise you," they wrote, "to roote out from being any longer a people, so cursed a nation, ungratefull to all benefits, and uncapable of all goodnesse." The Indians should be attacked and driven "so farr from you, as you may not only be out of danger, but out of feare of them, of whose faith and good meaning you can never be secure." The children of the Indians should be spared as fit objects for conversion, but otherwise, the colonists must wage "a perpetuall warre wthout peace or truce."[112]

Wyatt knew that the company's shortsighted policies since 1618, which had provided no means for controlling the settlement or activities of the frontier population, were most responsible for provoking Opechancanough's assault. The Sandys administration's support for private colonization, designed to stabilize the colony by planting a diligent and productive population, had actually hastened the development of Virginia's frontier, resulting in increased pressure upon Indian lands. Wyatt com-

---

[109] Waterhouse, *Declaration*, 17.
[110] Purchas, "Occurrents in Virginia," in Purchas, *Hakluytus*, 19:159; Gleach, *Powhatan's World*, 75.
[111] RVC 3:612.
[112] RVC 3:666, 671–72.

plained of the ill discipline of the colonists, their poor provision, and his inability to govern the inhabitants of the private plantations. He thought the success of the Indian attack could be explained by the colony's pattern of settlement. "This Colony was so dispersed and people so straglingly settled," he wrote, "that we were not onely bereft of the friendly converse, and mutuall society one of another in religious duties . . . but were also altogether disabled, any way to provide for the common safety either against forrain or domestick invasion." Consequently, "we were forced to stand and gaze at our distressed brethren, frying in the fury of their enemies, and could not relieve them."[113]

In the days and weeks following the massacre, Wyatt ordered the surviving population concentrated at Jamestown, Kecoughtan, and other well-defended sites.[114] By forcing many colonists, still shocked from the massacre, "to forsayke their howses . . . & to joyne themselves to some great mans plantation," however, he created an atmosphere where food shortages and discipline became problems of critical importance.[115] Believing that only harsh discipline could ensure the colony's survival, Wyatt requested from the London Council "some commission for a Marshall Court" to control the colonists and force them to "subsist of our selves."[116] In order to avert "a relapse into an extreame famine," he ordered all English inhabitants of Virginia to "plant at least a sufficiencie of Corne for themselves and their families, and that they do not hope or rely uppon any supply of Corne, by trade wth the Indians, wch wilbe in vaine."[117]

Wyatt was working to restore metropolitan control over a frontier colony that had grown too quickly, too haphazardly, and whose relentless pressure upon the neighboring Indians had provoked a native response that now threatened the existence of the colony. His objective in the war that followed, then, was first and foremost to preserve English settlement in America. Wyatt recognized that "for the glory of God, and love towards o^r brethren" the Indians must be punished, and he knew that most of the colonists carried an unbridled animosity toward the Indians. Yet aware that a war of extermination would not serve the colony's interests, he adopted instead a pragmatic policy of war when necessary, peace when possible.[118]

---

[113] "Documents of Sir Francis Wyatt, Governor, 1621–1626," *WMQ*, 2d. ser., 7 (1927): 44. See also George Sandys to Mr. Ferrar, March 1623, *RVC* 4:24–25.

[114] Council in Virginia to Company in London, April 1622, *RVC* 3:612; Commissions to Roger Smith and Ralph Hamor, 13 and 15 April 1622, *RVC* 3:609–10; Commission to Roger Smith, 20 April 1622, *RVC* 3:611.

[115] Unsigned letter to Joseph Mead, 4 April 1623, in Johnson, "Indian Massacre," 410.

[116] Francis Wyatt to John Ferrar, 7 April 1623, *RVC* 4:105.

[117] Council in Virginia to Company in London, late April 1622, *RVC* 3:613; Francis Wyatt, Proclamation, 9 May 1623, *RVC* 4:172–73.

[118] Francis Wyatt, Commission to George Yeardley, 10 September 1623, *RVC* 3:678; Fausz and Kukla, "Letter of Advice," 108.

After imposing discipline on the colony, Wyatt launched a series of raids, which would continue periodically for the next year and a half, to obtain corn from the Indians—by force if necessary. The abandonment of so many plantations had meant the abandonment of fields, so corn was not planted in sufficient quantity in the spring of 1622. "The present necessitie of the Colony," he wrote, required "that by all meanes possible, either of warr or trade, Corne be procured from the Indians."[119] Wyatt commissioned each captain to "make warr, kill, spoile, and take by force or otherwise whatsoever boote of Corne, or any thing else he can attaine unto, from any the Salvages o[r] enemies."[120] He hoped by this strategy both to feed his colonists and to starve the Indians, rendering their military position untenable.

The raids succeeded in wearing down Opechancanough's forces. Then, when an English force of sixty soldiers sailed up the York River into the heart of Powhatan territory in the summer of 1624, and there successfully engaged perhaps as many as eight hundred Pamunkey and other Powhatan warriors in a pitched battle that lasted two days, massed English muskets and plate armor proved unbeatable. The shame of losing the encounter probably weakened Opechancanough's influence over his tributaries, and Powhatan resistance tailed off. In two years the English had avenged the deaths of their countrymen many times over.[121] The Indians, their fields either cut down or burned and their villages destroyed, were neutralized as a military threat, and Wyatt could proclaim that they would no longer be able to injure the colony "through theire strength but [only through] o[r] owne carelesnes."[122] Subsequently, Wyatt ordered his captains no longer to "compell y[e] said salvages to trade nor to kill or to offer them violence or injurie" except in self-defense.[123]

VI

Francis Wyatt had saved the English settlement, consolidated English control of the James River valley, and imposed a discipline upon the colony that permitted it to weather the crisis years from 1622 through 1625. Doing so, however, had required him to abandon the philanthropic ideals that he and others such as George Thorpe had carried across the Atlantic. Faced with a crisis on the frontier, he recognized that the instructions he continued to re-

[119] Francis Wyatt, Commission to Ralph Hamor, 23 October 1622, *RVC* 3: 696. See also Commission to "William Eden alias Sampson," 24 October 1622, *RVC* 3:698.
[120] Francis Wyatt, Commission to Yeardly, 678–79. See also commissions printed in *RVC* 3:622, 696–98, 700; 4: 7, 189, 250.
[121] Council in Virginia to Company in London, 20 January 1623, *RVC* 4:9–10; Steele, *Warpaths*, 47.
[122] Wyatt, Proclamation, 167–68.
[123] Francis Wyatt, Commission to Raleigh Crashaw, 16 March 1624, *RVC* 4:470. See also Commission to Ralph Hamor, 19 January 1624, *RVC* 4:448–49.
[124] Council in Virginia to Company in London, 30 January 1624, *RVC* 4:451.

ceive from the metropolis were incompatible with the need for frontier security. Advised by the London Council "to observe rules of Justice wth these barbarous and perfidious enemys," Wyatt and his contemporaries in the colony were necessarily compelled to "hold nothinge iniuste, that may tend to theire ruine, (except breach of faith)." Wyatt's metropolitan vision had been tempered by his experience on the frontier.[124]

After the massacre, many metropolitans in both Virginia and England lost faith that peaceful means could be used to bring the Indians to civility and an acceptance of the Christian faith. "The Savages," wrote Edward Waterhouse, "though never a Nation used so kindly upon so small desert, have in stead of that *Harvest* which our paines merited, returned nothing but Bryers and thornes, pricking even to death many of their Benefactors." They were, he continued, "miscreants" who "put off humanity" for a "worse and more than unnatural brutishness."[125] Plans for Indian education and the college at Henrico were abandoned in the aftermath of the massacre, as metropolitan philanthropy faded.

Much of the sentiment expressed by members of the Virginia Company of London was occasioned by the murder and dismemberment of Thorpe, who, as director of the college project, symbolized their idealism. At a deeper level, however, the expressions of this anger and disappointment reveal a racist contempt for the Powhatans. Christopher Brooke, for example, in "A Poem on the Late Massacre in Virginia," asked his audience to "consider what those Creatures are,"

(I cannot call them men), no Character
Of God in them; Soules drown'd in flesh and blood;
Rooted in Evill, and oppos'd in Good;
Errors of Nature, of inhumane Birth,
The very dregs, garbage, and spawne of the Earth,
Who ne'r (I think) were mentioned with those Creatures
Adam gave names to in their severall natures:
But such as comming of a later Brood,
(Not sav'd in th' Arke) but since the generall Flood
Sprung up like vermine of an earthly slime,
And so have held B' intrusion to this time.[126]

It is not possible to determine how widely held these views were in the years following the massacre, but it should be noted that Brooke's poem was published by the Virginia Company and thus implicitly represented "official" Company opinion. Once viewed by the English as fellow "Sons of Adam," the Powhatans had now been tossed from the Ark. By massacring

---

[125] Waterhouse, *Declaration*, 11; *RVC* 3:551.
[126] Christopher Brooke, "A Poem on the Late Massacre in Virginia," ed. Robert C. Johnson, *VMHB* 72 (July 1964): 262–63.

the Virginia colonists, the Indians had unequivocally rejected the ostensible benefits offered by a supposedly superior English civilization. They had in effect thus rejected a critical element of what English metropolitans thought central to all of *human* history: upward progress from primitive origins. From here, it did not require a great leap to question the very humanity of the natives, or at least their potential for progress.

The metropolitan program of dominion and civility rested at its core upon the ability of officials to govern the Anglo-American frontier effectively. The Jamestown experience between 1607 and 1625 reveals the fragility of that vision. Both from London and in Virginia, metropolitan-minded men had tried to impose their plans for a Christian, Anglo-American New World empire upon a frontier where the actual colonists were more interested in planting tobacco on Indian land. The metropolitans could not pursue their plans to improve the Indians without controlling the frontier population. But this population continually pressed upon Indian land, alienated the Powhatan Indians, undermined the philanthropic program of conversion and assimilation advanced by George Thorpe, and ultimately provoked a violent Indian rising that destroyed the metropolitan program of the Virginia Company of London.

3   *Severe Justice*

Early in September 1638 a crowd gathered in Plymouth to witness the execution of Arthur Peach. A "lustie and desperate yonge man," Peach had fought in the Pequot War the year before, "and had done as good servise as the most ther." Later, however, he apparently fell upon hard times. "Out of means, and loath to worke," Peach soon resorted "to idle courses and company."

Peach and three companions had traveled a short distance toward "the Dutch plantation" when they camped for the night, north and west of Plymouth, in Narragansett country. There they encountered Penowanyanques, a Nipmuck messenger loyal to the Narragansetts, "who had been in the Bay a trading, and had cloth and beads aboute him." Peach invited the Indian to share his tobacco and his fire and to join the Englishmen for the evening. As Penowanyanques drank from the pipe, Peach silently drew his rapier "and rane him through the body once or twise." He then stole the fur and wampum that the Indian was carrying for Mixanno, the son of Canonicus, a Narragansett sachem, and left Penowanyanques for dead.[1]

Peach's bloody crime, coming in the wake of New England's horribly violent war against the Pequots, sent a shock wave through the Narragansett country. The Narragansetts had aided the English during the war. Now, Roger Williams reported, they feared the English, and worried that "there hath been great hubbub in all these parts, as a general persuasion that the time was come of a general slaughter of natives."[2]

---

[1] William Bradford, *Bradford's History of Plymouth Plantation*, ed. William T. Davis (New York, 1920), 344; Roger Williams to John Winthrop, 1 August 1638, in *Winthrop Papers*, ed. Samuel Eliot Morison et al., 6 vols. (Boston, 1929–1992), 4:48–49; Glenn W. La Fantasie, "Murder of an Indian," *Rhode Island History* 38 (1979): 66–77.
[2] Roger Williams to John Winthrop, 1 August 1638, *Winthrop Papers*, 4:48.

William Bradford, the governor of Plymouth, recognized the need to "see justice done" quickly. The failure to do so, he believed, "would raise a warr" with the Indians. With the cooperation of Williams and the approval of metropolitan leaders throughout New England, Peach and his fellows were apprehended, brought to trial, and "hanged by the neck untill their bodyes were dead." But the execution of Peach was not universally popular within the colony. "Some of the rude and ignorante sorte," Bradford wrote, "murmered that any English should be put to death for the Indeans."[3]

The case of Arthur Peach reveals much about the nature of the Anglo-Indian exchange in early colonial New England. That Penowanyanques carried trade goods and stopped to spend his final evening with Peach shows the readiness with which Indians and Englishmen established trading relations. The story also reveals, however, that in New England as in Virginia, different groups of Englishmen developed dramatically different sets of attitudes toward the natives. Metropolitan magistrates sought to exploit the resources of the New World for the benefit of their colonies and their sponsoring organizations, to provide for the security of their settlements, and to civilize and Christianize the Indians, all the while seeing to the orderly and peaceable expansion of the Puritan frontier. To do so, they had to control their own frontier population, a large group often unsympathetic to the Puritan mission. The failure of the magistrates to control this population in the face of competition between Dutch and English and Amerindian interests for hegemony in the Connecticut River valley provoked the Pequot War, a brief but bloody conflict that demonstrated the magnitude of the challenge faced by the metropolitan promoters of settlement in New England.

I

A mixture of worldly and religious concerns influenced the decision made by many English Puritans to migrate to America. The writings of the leading colonists exhibit a passionate religious commitment and a profound sense of spiritual peril, but the impact of dramatic social changes in England also figured prominently in their concerns.[4] Social and economic tension, a collapsing cloth industry, widespread unemployment and landlessness, agrarian unrest, and a spate of bad harvests and plague years in the early decades of the seventeenth century clearly bespoke God's disfavor. If the English church continued to walk in its wicked ways, many English men and women believed, the Lord would pour divine wrath upon England. The recent past persuaded Puritans that England was no longer the elect nation,

[3] Bradford, *History*, 346; PCR, 4 September 1638, 1:97.
[4] See Virginia DeJohn Anderson, *New England's Generation: The Great Migration and the Formation of Society and Culture in the Seventeenth Century* (New York, 1991), chap. 1.

and those who remained at home could no longer claim the mantle of God's chosen people.[5] Only in the New World, wrote the Plymouth separatist William Bradford, could the Pilgrims lay "some good foundations. . . for the propagating and advauncing the gospell of the kingdom of Christ in those remote parts of the world." Only in the New World, wrote John Winthrop, could the Puritans of Massachusetts Bay "be as a citty upon a hill," a model for England's regeneration.[6]

The promoters of colonization in New England believed that there troubled Englishmen could prosper once again in their callings. John Winthrop wrote on the eve of his departure for America that England had grown "weary of her Inhabitants, soe as man, whoe is the most pretious of all creatures, is here more vile & base then the earth we treade upon." In England "it is almost impossible for a good & upright man to mainetayne his charge & live comfortablie." John White of Dorchester, like Winthrop, echoed the concerns of Richard Hakluyt a half-century before when he concluded that "we have more men then wee can imploy to any profitable or usefull labour," creating a "fearfull condition, whereby men are in a sort enforced to perish, or to become meanes and instruments of evill."[7] Migration to New England clearly offered to many an opportunity to escape increasingly bleak spiritual and social conditions at home.

Regarding the natives they would encounter, the promoters of settlement at New Plymouth and Massachusetts Bay took to heart Calvin's admonition "that the whole human race, without exception . . . be embraced with one feeling of charity," and "that here is no distinction of Greek or Barbarian, worthy or unworthy, Friend or foe, since all are to be viewed not in themselves, but in God."[8] In *Mourt's Relation*, one of the earliest accounts of life in Puritan New England, William Bradford and Edward Winslow argued that their settlement must "displaie the efficacie & power of the Gospell both in zealous preaching, professing, and wise walking under it, before the faces of these poore blinde Infidels."[9]

The charter of the Massachusetts Bay Company, issued in the spring of 1629, stated as "the principall ende of this plantacon" to "wynn and incite the natives of the country to the knowledg and obedience of the onlie true God and Savior of mankinde, and the Christian fayth." In the instructions

[5] John Winthrop, "Reasons to Be Considered," in *Life and Letters of John Winthrop*, ed. Robert C. Winthrop, 2 vols. (Boston, 1864), 1:309; Avihu Zakei, *Exile and Kingdom: History and the Apocalypse in the Puritan Migration to America* (Cambridge, England, 1992), 64, 129.

[6] Bradford quoted in Peter Gay, *A Loss of Mastery: Puritan Historians in Colonial America* (Berkeley, Calif., 1966), 31; John Winthrop, "Modell of Christian Charity," in *Winthrop Papers*, 2:282–95. See also David Cressy, *Coming Over: Migration and Communication Between England and New England in the Seventeenth Century* (Cambridge, England, 1987), 74–106.

[7] Winthrop, *Life and Letters*, 1:309–10; John White, *The Planters Plea* (London, 1630), 11.

[8] Calvin quoted in Stephen Foster, *Their Solitary Way: The Puritan Social Ethic in the First Century of Settlement in New England* (New Haven, Conn., 1971), 44.

[9] William Bradford and Edward Winslow, *Mourt's Relation; or, Journal of the Plantation at Plymouth*, ed. Henry Martyn Dexter (New York, 1969), 150.

issued to their first governor, John Endicott, the company's directors noted that "we have been careful to make plentiful provision of godly ministers; by whose faitful preaching, godly conversation, and exemplary life, we trust not only those of our own nation will be built up in the knowledge of God, but also the Indians may, in God's appointed time, be reduced to the obedience of the Gospel of Christ."[10]

Even John Winthrop, the most secular-minded of the Bay Colony's leaders, wrote, "It wilbe a service to the Church of great consequence to carry the Gospell into those parts of the world, to helpe on the comminge in of the fullnesse of the Gentiles, & to raise a Bulworke against the kingdome of Ante Christ wch the Jesuites labour to reare up in those parts." Though he could not be certain whether the Indians would receive English religion, Winthrop thought the effort just and necessary, for "it is the revealed will of god that the gospell should be preached to all nations" and "it is a good worke to serve gods providence in offering it to them."[11]

As with the Virginia Company, interest in converting the Indians appeared not only in the official documents of the colonizing enterprise but in promotional and private literature as well. William Alexander, writing from London on behalf of Plymouth Plantation, argued that

> if the Saints of Heaven rejoyce at the conversion of a Sinner, what exceeding joy would it bee to them to see many thousands of Savage people (who doe now live like brute beasts) converted unto God.

John White, similarly, told his audience that "this is the houre for the worke, and consequently our duty to endeavour the effecting that which God hath determined; the opening of the eyes of these poore ignorant soules, and discovering unto them the glorious mystery of Jesus Christ."[12]

The Puritans never doubted their right to plant on Indian soil. To English eyes the natives had more land than they needed. Much of this land had been left vacant as a result of disease, which, according to John White, had "swept away most of the Inhabitants all along the Sea Coast, and in some places utterly consumed man, woman, & childe, so that there is no person left to lay claime to the soyle which they possessed."[13] Between 1616 and 1619 an outbreak of hepatitis ravaged the eastern coast of New England from Cape Cod to Maine, introduced by European fishermen who frequently visited the region. Because of the relatively high population density maintained by eastern Algonquians, the epidemic spread quickly. Mortality rates reached 90 percent among the Massachusetts and Wampanoags. The

---

[10] *MBR*, 1:17; "Instructions to Endicott," 17 April 1629, in *Chronicles of the First Planters of the Colony of Massachusetts Bay, from 1623–1636*, ed. Alexander Young (Boston, 1846), 142.
[11] John Winthrop, "Reasons," in *Life and Letters*, 1:309, 313.
[12] William Alexander, *An Encouragement to Colonies* (London, 1624), 44; White, *Planters Plea*, 9.
[13] White, *Planters Plea*, 14.

first English colonists consequently found, in Francis Jennings's words, a "widowed land." As early as 1622 Robert Cushman of Plymouth observed that "wee found the place where we live emptie, the people being all dead & gone away, and none living neere 8 or 10. myles." Cushman suspected that "the twentieth person is scarce left alive."[14]

European disease would continue to ravage the natives. In 1634 John Winthrop reported that "for the natives in these parts, Gods hand hath so pursued them, as for 300 miles space, [that] the greatest parte of them are swept awaye by the small poxe, which still continues among them." Disease produced a divine transfer of title from the natives to the English. "The Natives," he wrote, "are near all dead of the smallpox, so as the Lord hath cleared our title to what we possess."[15]

No other orthodox New Englander thought as deeply as Winthrop about the problem of English title to aboriginal land. Rejecting the premise that the English had "noe warrant to enter upon that land wch hath beene soe long possessed by others," he wrote in 1629 that "the whole earth is the Lords garden & he hath given it to the Sonnes of men, wth a gen^l Commission . . . [to] increace & multiplie, & replenish the earth & subdue it." The purpose of this commission, he continued, "is double & naturall, that man might enjoy the fruits of the earth, & God might have his due glory from the creature." Why, he asked,

> should we stand striving here [in England] for places of habitation, etc. (many men spending as much labor & coste to recover or keepe an acre or twoe of Land, as would procure them many & as good or better in another Countrie) & in the meane time suffer a whole Continent as fruitfull & convenient for the use of man to lie waste w^thout any improvement?[16]

Winthrop differentiated between two categories of right to the soil, natural and civil.[17] The natural right to the soil originated "when God gave the

---

[14] Arthur E. Speiss and Bruce D. Weiss, "New England Pandemic of 1616–1622: Cause and Archaeological Implication," *Man in the Northeast* 34 (1987): 71–72; William Cronon, *Changes in the Land: Indians, Colonists, and the Ecology of New England* (New York, 1983), 86–87; Francis Jennings, *The Invasion of America: Indians, Colonists, and the Cant of Conquest* (Chapel Hill, N.C., 1975), 30; Sherburne F. Cook, "The Significance of Disease in the Extinction of the New England Indians," *Human Biology* 45 (1973): 499; Alfred Crosby, "Virgin Soil Epidemics as a Factor in the Aboriginal Depopulation in America," *WMQ*, 3d ser., 33 (1976): 300; Robert Cushman, *A Sermon Preached at Plymouth in New England, December 9, 1621* (London, 1622), A4.

[15] John Winthrop to Sir Simon D'Ewes, 21 July 1634, and Winthrop to Sir Nathaniel Rich, 22 May 1634, *Winthrop Papers*, 3:171–72, 167; Jennings, *Invasion*, chap. 2.

[16] Winthrop, "Reasons," 1:309–10; Chester E. Eisinger, "The Puritans' Justification for Taking the Land," *Essex Institute Historical Collections* 84 (1948): 135. See also Winthrop to John Wheelwright, March 1639, *Winthrop Papers*, 4:102.

[17] Eisinger, "Puritans' Justification," 131–36; John Peacock, "Principles and Effects of Puritan Appropriation of Land and Labor," *Ethnohistory* 31 (1984): 40–41; Neal Salisbury, *Manitou and Providence: Indians, Europeans, and the Making of New England, 1500–1643* (New York, 1986), 176.

earth to the sonnes of men . . . by vertue whereof any man may make use of any part of the earth, which another hath not possessed before him." A civil right to the soil could be obtained only when "men growing into Civill societyes and by attainment of Artes and trades have thereby means to improve more lands." The Indians, he concluded, "have no other but a naturall right, and that is only to so much land as they have means to subdue and improve."[18]

While legitimizing an English claim to Indian lands, Winthrop's arguments implied a belief that societies progressed through distinct phases of property-holding and, consequently, civilization, approaching in the process an ideal exemplified by early Stuart Englishmen. Since the Indians had not improved, by English standards, the land they held, the English had a superior claim based upon their relative civility. With this claim to aboriginal land, however, came a responsibility to assist the Indians in obtaining a level of cultural and material existence that metropolitan Englishmen could consider civil. Like the Virginians, the New Englanders believed that Indians would willingly accept the tenets of English Christianity. They believed that Indians were intelligent and reasonable and that they would ultimately abandon their "savage" habits.

"It is true," John White wrote, "that from the first planting of Religion among men, it hath always held a constant way from East to West, and hath, in that Line, proceeded so farre, that it hath extended to the uttermost Westerne bounds of the formerly knowne world; so that if it make any further passage upon that point of the Compasse, it must necessarily light upon the West Indies."[19] Peter Vincent, writing in the immediate wake of the Pequot War, expressed a strong belief in the Indians' capacity for reason. "Their correspondency of disposition with us," he wrote, "argueth all to be of the same constitution, and the sons of Adam, and that we had the same matter, the same mould. Only art and grace," he continued, "have given us that perfection, which yet they want, but may perhaps be as capable thereof as wee."[20]

Similarly, because nature knew "no difference between *Europe* and *Americans* in blood, birth, bodies, &c. God having of one blood made all mankind . . . and all by nature being children of wrath," Roger Williams firmly believed in the Indians' capacity for improvement. The "Father of Spirits," he wrote,

> who was graciously pleased to perswade *Japhet* (the Gentiles) to dwell in the Tents of Shem (the Jewes) will in his holy season (I hope approaching) perswade

[18] Winthrop to Wheelwright, March 1639, *Winthrop Papers*, 4:102; see also Winthrop, "Reasons," 1:311–12; Bradford and Winslow, *Mourt's Relation*, 147–48; White, *Planters Plea*, 2; Francis Higginson, *New England's Plantation; or, A Short and True Description of the Commodities and Discommodities of That Countrey* (London, 1630), 12; John Cotton, *Gods Promise to His Plantation* (London, 1630), 4–7.

[19] White, *Planters Plea*, 7.

[20] [Peter Vincent], "A True Relation of the late Batell Fought in New England between the English and the Pequot Savages," *MHS Coll*, 3d ser., 6 (1837): 34.

these Gentiles of America to partake of the mercies of Europe, and then shall be fulfilled what is written, by the Prophet *Malachi*, from the rising of the sunne (in *Europe*) to the going down of the same (in *America*) my name shall [be] great among the Gentiles.[21]

Williams's hopes for the conversion and improvement of the Indians were consistent with the convictions of many promoters of colonization, in New England as in Virginia.

Though many historians of Indian relations in New England have cast a cynical eye toward these benevolent professions, the first generation of Puritans did not ignore their Indian mission.[22] Rather, because they believed the Indians to be reasoning and reasonable human beings—albeit misinformed, misled, and potentially dangerous—they hoped to win the Indians to Christianity by example. Nearly a century of English Protestant history had bolstered the New England Puritans' conception of themselves as God's chosen people, members of an elect nation in comparison with whom the Indians would readily recognize their own moral, spiritual, and social inferiority. Faced with the choice of their own inferior culture or the rising glory of Anglo-Saxon institutions, the New England Puritans assumed, the Indians would make the only reasonable choice.[23]

At a more immediate level, Puritans maintained a far more stringent criterion for conversion than Catholics and orthodox Anglicans. The Puritans asked not merely for allegiance or regular attendance at church services but rather for evidence of saving grace, the product of a profound conversion experience—and this experience had to be based upon a deep knowledge of the Bible. Conversion in New England, then, was not a simple process. Still, many believed that if the colonists carried themselves well and walked in observance of the ways of the Lord, the Indians would learn from their example.[24]

The promoters of settlement at Plymouth and Massachusetts Bay sought "persons of wealth and quality" to serve the religious, social, and moral mission they had set for themselves. Like their counterparts in the Chesapeake, the New Englanders hoped to prosper and to protect their settlements from the threat of invasion while bringing Christianity to the New World. This,

[21] Roger Williams, *Key into the Language of America*, in *The Complete Writings of Roger Williams*, ed. James Hammond Trumbull, 7 vols. (New York, 1963), 81, 27–28.

[22] See, e.g., Jennings, *Invasion*; Salisbury, *Manitou and Providence*; Gary B. Nash, *Red, White and Black: The Peoples of Early America*, 3d ed. (Englewood Cliffs, N.J., 1982), chap. 4; Alfred E. Cave, "Canaanites in a Promised Land: The American Indian and the Providential Theory of Empire," *American Indian Quarterly* 12 (1988): 277–97.

[23] See "Instructions to Endicott," in Young, *Chronicles*, 149–50.

[24] On Puritan conversion, see Alan Simpson, *Puritanism in Old and New England* (Chicago, 1955); Edmund S. Morgan, *Visible Saints: The History of a Puritan Idea* (New York, 1963). See also Alden T. Vaughan, *New England Frontier: Puritans and Indians, 1620–1675* (Boston, 1965), 237; William Kellaway, *The New England Company, 1649–1776: Missionary Society to the American Indians* (New York, 1962), 6–7.

they emphasized, required a certain sort of colonist, and the absence of that sort, they believed, had been the downfall of earlier settlements. Edward Winslow of Plymouth, who apparently had learned something from the experience of the Virginia Company of London, wrote in 1624 that three kinds of men "are the overthrow and bane (as I may terme it) of Plantations." The first came with "the vaine expectation of present profit," rather than the desire to serve God's glory. The second came out of ambition, "seeking only to make themselves great, and slaves of all that are under them." The third were colonists sent by those "not caring how they bee qualified: so that oftimes they are rather the Image of men endued with bestiall, yea, diabolicall affections, then the Image of God." Large numbers of "profane men," Winslow wrote, "who being but seeming Christians, have made Christ and Christianitie stinke in the nostrils of the poore Infidels."[25]

New Englanders such as Winslow drew a sharp distinction between their settlements and the earlier ones, and they tried to apply lessons learned from the Virginia Company's experience. Emmanuel Downing, a founder of the Massachusetts Bay Company, wrote that while "those of Virgenia went only for proffitt," the New England colonists came for other reasons, some "to satisfie there owne curiousity in poynt of conscience, others (w[ch] was more gen'all) to transport the Gospell to those heathen that never heard thereof."[26]

His distinction was not necessarily correct, but the point was clear: the success of this enterprise required men of high moral fiber; those who "looke after great riches, ease, pleasure, dainties, and jollitie in this world" should be encouraged not to emigrate. Robert Cushman could "advise and encourage to goe" only those "content to lay out their estates, spend their time, labours, and endeavours, for the benefit of them that shall come after, and in desire to further the Gospell among those poore Heathens, quietly contenting themselves with such hardship and difficulties, as by God's providence shall fall upon them." Only then, Cushman told his audience,

> shall you be a notable president to these poore Heathens, whose eyes are upon you, and who very bruitishly and cruelly doe dayly eate and consume one another, through their emulations, warres, and contentions; bee you therefore ashamed of it, and winne them to peace both with yourselves, and one another, by your peaceable examples, which will preach louder to them, then if you could crie in their Barbarous language.[27]

John White, similarly, suggested that those "chosen out for this employment, ought to be willing, constant, industrious, obedient, frugall, lovers of

---

[25] Edward Winslow, *Good Newes from New England* (London, 1624), A3, B.

[26] Emmanual Downing to Sir John Coke, 12 December 1633, *Massachusetts Historical Society Proceedings*, 2d ser., 8 (1892–94): 383.

[27] Cushman, *Sermon*, A3, 18–19.

the common good, or at least such as may be easily wrought to this temper."
For White the advancement of the true religion was the colony's main end,
and he emphasized the importance of "men of piety and blamelesse life, especially in such a Plantation as this in *New-England*, where their lives must
be patternes to the Heathen, and the speciall, effectuall meanes of winning
them to the love of the truth."[28]

The first generation of New Englanders set high standards for conduct in
their colonies. Although the organizers called for immigrants of good character, they nevertheless recognized that they would have to deal with a rough
and rootless lot of adventurers, mariners, servants, and "lustie young men"
who had little sympathy for the concerns of colonial promoters and little left
to lose in England. Colonial promoters appreciated the dangers involved in
planting a settlement three thousand miles from home, and, as at Roanoke
and Jamestown, emphasized the importance of martial discipline during the
early stages. The Pilgrims wanted to protect Plymouth from both the dangers of Indian attack and the threat of invasion by rival Europeans. Discipline, moreover, would restrain colonists from actions that might threaten
the safety of the colony. To ensure their security they employed military ex-
perts, veterans of the Dutch wars mostly, to supervise the defense of their
plantations, and saw to it that every "freeman" or other male inhabitant of
Plymouth "provide for himselfe & each under him able to bear armes, a sufficient musket, & other serviceable peece for war, wth bandaleroes & other
apurtenances, wth what speede may be."[29]

The need for military discipline was thought no less important at Massachusetts Bay. Unlike the Plymouth separatists, the Massachusetts leadership
had not broken from England's established church. Their claims to represent
the interests of the realm, however, were undermined by a tendency toward
religious and political separatism, the latter symbolized by the Massachusetts Bay Company's decision to take its charter to New England. Though
carrying the charter to America granted the company virtual independence
in its own affairs and a fragile freedom from royal oversight, it also placed
the colonial leadership in a delicate situation. They could not afford to draw
attention to themselves by provoking the natives, and an inability to control
the New England frontier could result in diplomatic and military crises involving either the French or Dutch, or an Indian uprising, any of which
might result in crown intervention. The sensitive political position of the
Massachusetts Bay Company within the English empire thus demanded efficient and effective frontier administration.[30]

---

[28] White, *Planters Plea*, 20.

[29] John S. Erwin, "Captain Myles Standish's Military Role at Plymouth," *Historical Journal
of Massachusetts* 13 (1985): 1–6; Adam J. Hirsch, "The Collision of Military Cultures in Seventeenth Century New England," *JAH* 74 (1988): 1187–88; Cressy, *Coming Over*, 43, 100, 85;
PCR, 2 January 1633, 1:6.

[30] Salisbury, *Manitou and Providence*, 180; Vaughan, *New England Frontier*, 98–99.

The Bay Company's governing council ordered John Endicott, the commander of the first detachment of colonists, to see that "our government and privileges be not brought in contempt, wishing rather there might be such a union as might draw the heathen by our good example to the embracing of Christ and his Gospel, than that offence should be given to the Heathen, and a scandal to our Religion, through our disagreement amongst ourselves." Endicott and, later, John Winthrop were empowered to follow a severe course against the natives when necessary. The company encouraged Endicott "to deal as in your discretions you shall think fittest for the general good and safety of the Plantation, and preservation of our privileges." They reminded him of the duplicity and treachery displayed by Opechancanough in Virginia in 1622. "Our countrymen," wrote Matthew Cradock, a founder of the Bay Company, "have suffered by their too much confidence in Virginia. Let us by their harms learn to beware; and as we are commanded to be innocent as doves, so withal we are enjoined to be as wise as serpents." Order, the company instructed Endicott, would prove "as necessary as food and raiment."[31]

A fear of the natives, then—a belief that the New England colonies might fall prey to a disastrous massacre like that in Virginia—informed the plans for settlement drawn up by metropolitan New Englanders. They ordered nightly armed watches and required every able-bodied male to "have ready 1 L. of powder, 20 bullets, & 2 fathome of match, under penaltie of xˢ for every fault." They organized local militia companies and required them to train "on Saterday in everie weeke." The Massachusetts Bay Court of Assistants ordered "that noe person shall travell single betwixte theis plantacons & Plymouthe, nor without some armes, though 2 or 3 togeather."[32]

Magistrates at both Plymouth and Massachusetts Bay sought to control and regulate relations between Englishmen and Native Americans during the early years of contact. At Plymouth the council maintained the value of English trade goods—in this case the corn, beans, and peas traded to the Northern Abenaki in exchange for furs—by outlawing unlicensed trade with the natives. They never entirely succeeded. William Bradford wrote to the Council of New England in June 1627 complaining of "the irregular living of many in this land, who without either patent or licence, order or government, live, trade, and truck, not with any intent to plant, but rather to forage the country, and get what they can, whether by right or wrong, and then be gone."[33] What most concerned Bradford about these "irregular livers" was their alarming habit of trading weapons to the Indians for furs and

---

[31] "Instructions to Endicott," in Young, *Chronicles*, 149–50, 168; Cradock to Endicott, in ibid., 136.

[32] *MBR*, 12 April 1631, 1:85.

[33] *PCR*, 29 March 1626, 11:4; Bradford to Council of New England, 15 June 1627, *MHS Coll*, 1st ser., 8 (1794): 56. Endicott made a similar complaint from Salem; see *MBR* 1:48.

wampum, a practice no responsible magistrate could ignore. In a bit of clumsy verse penned late in the 1630s, Bradford revealed his concerns:

> For base covetousness hath got such a sway,
> As our own safety we ourselves betray;
> For these fierce natives, they are now so fill'd
> With guns and muskets, and in them so skill'd,
> As that they may keep the English in awe,
> And when they please, give to them the law;
> And of powder and shot they have such store,
> As sometimes they refuse for to buy more;
> Flints, screw-plates, and moulds for all sorts of shot,
> They have, and skill have to use them have got;
> And mend and new stock their peeces they can,
> As well in most things as an Englishman,
> Thus like madmen we put them in a way,
> With our own weapons us to kill and slay.[34]

The Massachusetts court prohibited the trading of guns and ammunition to Indians, outlawed the purchase of land from Indians without the court's permission, required "that noe man shall sell, or (being in a course of trade-ing) give any stronge water to any Indean," regulated the use of Indians as servants, and ordered "that there shalbe a trucking howse appoyncted in every plantacon, whither the Indians may resorte to trade, to avoide there comeing to severall howses."[35] These laws demonstrate the desire of the New England magistracy to secure an orderly frontier by regulating the occasions when Indians and Europeans came into contact. This was the thinking that had formed the core, in part, of metropolitan views of the frontier since the Elizabethan period. And like Hakluyt, Hariot, and Ralegh at Roanoke, and Francis Wyatt and George Thorpe at Jamestown, metropolitans in New England soon found that controlling the frontier would pose an enormous challenge.

In the summer of 1622 Thomas Weston fitted out an expedition of nearly sixty men to settle in the Massachusetts Bay. Weston's men, the dregs of London's streets, had little sympathy for the metropolitan concerns of the Pilgrim fathers.[36] Planting their settlement at Wessagusset, on the bay, Christopher Levett wrote, "they neither applied themselves to planting of corn nor taking fish, more than for their present use, but went about to build castles in the air . . . neglecting the plentifull time of fishing." Soon, the Plymouth

---

[34] William Bradford, "A Descriptive and Historical Account of New England in Verse," *MHS Coll*, 1st ser., 3 (1799), 82.

[35] *MBR*, 28 September 1630, 1:76; 1 March 1631, 1:83; 5 June 1632, 1:96; 2 July 1633, 1:106; 4 March 1634, 1:112; 3 September 1634, 1:127.

[36] Winslow, *Good Newes*, 13–14; Vaughan, *New England Frontier*, 82; Erwin, "Standish's Military Role," 7.

magistrates received complaints from the neighboring tribes about the Wessagusset colonists. Some were guilty, Winslow reported, of "stealing the Indians corne, and other abuses conceived by them."[37]

Bradford and the Plymouth magistrates had been warned about Weston's men. "The people which they cary," wrote Robert Cushman, "are no men for us. . . . I feare these people will hardly deale so well with the Savages as they should." When Cushman's predictions proved correct, Bradford sought to distance Plymouth from the Weston group by informing the Wampanoag emissary, Squanto, and neighboring sachems that the Wessagusset colonists were "a distinct body from us"; Plymouth had "nothing to doe with them" and could neither be "blamed for their facts" nor "warrentie their fidelitie."[38]

By February 1623, however, Bradford recognized that Indian disaffection with the Wessagusset settlers had reached a critical level. Indian hostility toward Weston's men, moreover, had developed into a distrust of Plymouth. When Massasoit, the Wampanoag sachem, informed the Pilgrims that the Massachusetts—along with the Nausets, Pamuts, and others—were planning to strike Wessagusset, Bradford and the governing council decided to send Miles Standish, the colony's leading military officer, with eight companions to seize the leaders of the conspiracy. The head of Wituwamut, one of the "principals" in the plan, was brought back to Plymouth by Standish and placed on a spike atop the palisade.[39]

The Plymouth leaders did not undertake the decision to attack the Massachusetts lightly. Most of the Puritan magistrates would have agreed with the lament of John Robinson, the Pilgrim's original pastor. Writing from Leyden, he exclaimed, "Oh! How happy a thing had it been, if you had converted some, before you killed any." He continued, "You will say they deserved it. I grant it, but upon what provocations and invitments by those heathenish Christians?"[40] Bradford and the magistrates recognized that the Weston group deserved little sympathy, and that the grievances of the Massachusetts Indians were mostly valid. The rash actions of the Wessagusset settlers, however, had created a crisis on the frontier that threatened the colony, and this forced Plymouth to abandon broader, more philanthropic concerns.

The Weston group was not the only threat to security and order along the New England frontier. In 1625 Thomas Morton arrived in New England as the partner of a Captain Wollaston in a private colonizing venture. Wollaston soon departed for Virginia, but Morton remained behind with most of original settlers and servants at the settlement, which he named Ma-re

---

[37] Christopher Levett, "Levett's Voyage, A.D. 1623," *MHS Coll*, 2d ser., 8 (1826): 182; Winslow, *Good Newes*, 14–15; Phineas Pratt, *A Declaration of the Affairs of the English People That First Inhabited New England*, ed. Richard Frothingham (Boston, 1858), 11.

[38] Bradford, *History*, 136.

[39] Vaughan, *New England Frontier*, 83–85; Salisbury, *Manitou and Providence*, 129; Erwin, "Standish's Military Role," 9.

[40] Robinson's letter is printed in Bradford, *History*, 172–73.

Mount. Morton quickly fell into disfavor among the Puritan magistrates for his "riotous prodigallitie and profuse excess," for playing the "Lord of misrule" and maintaining "a schoole of athiesme." They arrested him in 1628 and deported him to England. Returning slightly more than a year later, he was this time arrested by authorities at Massachusetts Bay and banished once again. A decade later Morton would again return, and again be taken prisoner. He died shortly after his release from jail.[41]

Morton's familiarity with the Indians, some historians have argued, may well have frightened the Puritan leadership by reminding them that they were not immune to the "heady desires [Ma-re Mount's] indiscipline epitomized." The Puritan fury that descended upon Morton may well have been the "partial returns of [Puritan] suppressed sexuality."[42] More likely the Puritan leadership found Morton's settlement objectionable on religious grounds. The "Separatists," Morton wrote (his generic term for *all* New England Puritans), "would labore to vilifie; with uncivile termes; enveying against the sacred booke of common prayer," while attacking Morton, "a man that indeavoured to advance the dignity of the Church of England."[43] The existence of an unfriendly religious group on the periphery of their settlement violated the principles of homogeneity, unanimity, and order which informed so great a part of the Puritans' social thought. Morton also suggested that the Puritan magistrates were jealous of his success as a trader.[44]

The settlers and servants at Ma-re Mount did not plant their own crops but lived by trading with the natives. To maintain their "riotous prodigallitie," Bradford wrote—which apparently included drinking, dancing, and sleeping with Indians—they exchanged "peeces, powder, and shotte" for food. Those Indians who chose not to participate in Morton's merrymaking could expect rough treatment, and Puritan magistrates received a "multitude of complaintes against him for injuries doone by him both to the English and Indians." English settlements near Ma-re Mount declared that Morton provided safe haven for "all the scume of the Countrie," and that these settlements would "stand in more fear of their lives and goods (in short

---

[41] Michael Zuckerman, "Pilgrims in the Wilderness: Community, Modernity, and the Maypole at Merry Mount," *New England Quarterly* 50 (1977): 256.

[42] Ibid., 275; Richard Drinnon, *Facing West: The Metaphysics of Indian-Hating and Empire-Building* (New York, 1980), 29.

[43] Thomas Morton, *The New English Canaan, Publications of the Prince Society* 14 (1883): 283.

[44] Howard Buffinton, "New England and the Western Fur Trade, 1629–1675," *Publications of the Colonial Society of Massachusetts*, vol. 18, *Transactions, 1915–1916* (Boston, 1917), 162–63. On homogeneity, see Kenneth Lockridge, *A New England Town, the First Hundred Years: Dedham, Massachusetts, 1636–1736*, (New York, 1970).

[45] "Governor Thomas Dudley's Letter to the Countess of Lincoln, March 1631," in *Tracts and Other Papers Relating Principally to the Origin, Settlement, and Progress of the Colonies in North America*, comp. Peter Force, 4 vols. (Washington, D.C.), 2, no. 4: 11; Bradford, *History*, 238, 241.

time) from this wicked and deboste crue, then from the Salvages them-selves."[45]

Bradford recognized that Morton's settlement of people unsympathetic to the Puritan religious mission and engaged in a potentially deadly trade of al-cohol and firearms to the Indians, threatened New England's safety and destabilized the frontier. "O the horiblnes of this vilanie!" Bradford lamented.

> How many both Dutch and English have been latly slaine by those Indeans, thus furnished; and no remedie provided, nay, the evill more increased, and the blood of their brethren sould for gaine, as is to be feared, and in what danger all these colonies are in is too well known. Oh! that Princes and parlements would take some timely order to prevent this mischeefe, and at length to suppress it, by some exemplarie punishmente upon some of these gaine thirstie murderers, (for they deserve no better title,) before their collonies in these partes be over throwne by these barbarous savages, thus armed with their owne weapons, by these evill in-struments, and traytors to their neighbors and cuntrie.[46]

Morton's behavior could not be tolerated by metropolitan leaders in New England. He was "sett into the bilbowes, & after sent prisoner into En-gland," with "all his goods . . . seazed upon to defray the charge of his trans-portacon, payement of his debts, & to give satisfaccon to the Indians for a cannoe he unjustly tooke away from them." John Endicott tore down the Maypole, symbol of the riotous practices at Ma-re Mount, and burned Mor-ton's home "downe to the ground in the sight of the Indians, for their satis-faccon, for many wrongs he hath done them from tyme to tyme."[47]

II

While the destruction of Morton's estate may or may not have pleased the neighboring Indians, there is no question that the settlement of New En-gland brought crisis and change to native villages throughout the region. The epidemic of 1616–1619 had devastated coastal areas, taking an enor-mous toll in Indian lives. An aboriginal population of at least 75,000 in New England at the end of the sixteenth century fell sharply to less than 20,000 in two decades, a horrifying loss of life.[48]

In addition to its epidemiological significance, the European presence ef-fected more subtle transformations in the contours of aboriginal life. Tradi-

---

[46] Ibid., 240.
[47] *MBR*, 7 September 1630, 1:75; James Axtell, *The Invasion Within: The Contest of Cul-tures in Colonial North America* (New York, 1985), 151.
[48] On aboriginal population figures, see Robert S. Grumet, *Historic Contact: Indian People and Colonists in Today's Northeastern United States in the Sixteenth through Eighteenth Cen-turies* (Norman, Okla., 1995), 61–62.

tionally, native communities in New England had shared many cultural traits. All spoke closely related Algonquin dialects, combined fishing and hunting with maize-beans-squash agriculture, and followed a form of social, political, and religious organization centered upon the village as the basic social unit. Their villages were frequently located along rivers that provided access to the variety of the subsistence resources—good land for cultivation, prime hunting and fishing lands, and areas for gathering shellfish and wild plants—on which New England Algonquians relied. As in the Chesapeake, these villages were not fixed geographic entities; their size and location changed on a seasonal basis. Individuals or groups of families traveled throughout the year to hunting grounds, fishing stations, plant- and shell-fish-collecting sites, and marshes frequented by migratory waterfowl.[49]

The early 1620s, however, brought changes in these settlement patterns. Especially on the southern coasts of New England, Indians began to occupy coastal sites year round in order to harvest the shellfish used in the production of wampum, increasingly in demand by Europeans for its use as currency and value as a trade item. As different native groups were drawn into European exchange networks, heightened rivalry and competition produced unprecedented levels of inter-tribal warfare. Warfare provided a further impulse toward sedentarism: many village groups chose to reside in permanently fortified sites housing relatively dense populations. The Pequot fort on the Mystic River, where a minimum of three to four hundred people lived, may well have been built in response to such circumstances.[50]

These changes occurred even among the Narragansetts and Pequots, two powerful tribes in southwestern New England who had largely escaped the impact of disease between 1616 and 1619. Hostility between the Narragansetts and Wampanoags had precluded the kind of human contact necessary for the spread of hepatitis, so that epidemic did not move west of Narragansett Bay. Though the smallpox epidemic in 1633–34 ravaged both tribes, they remained formidable forces along the periphery of English settlement.[51]

The Narragansett sachems Miantonomo and Canonicus, wrote John Mason, controlled territory that stretched "from the Bay of the same Name, to Pawcatuck River, now the Boundary between the Governments of Rhode Is-

---

[49] The best survey of the literature is Kathleen J. Bragdon, *Native Peoples of Southern New England, 1500–1650*, (Norman, Okla., 1996). See also Bert Salwen, "Indians of Southern New England and Long Island: Early Period," in *Handbook of North American Indians*, vol. 15, *Northeast*, ed. William C. Sturtevant (Washington, D.C., 1978), 160, 164; Cronon, *Changes*, 38–43; Anthony F. C. Wallace, "Political Organization and Land Tenure among the Northeastern Indians, 1600–1830," *Southwestern Journal of Anthropology* 13 (1957): 311.

[50] Lynn Ceci, *The Effect of European Contact and Trade on the Settlement Patterns of Indians in Coastal New York, 1524–1665* (New York, 1990), 135–283; Cronon, *Changes*, 101; Jennings, *Invasion*, 39–40; Salwen, "Indians," 166.

[51] Bradford, *History*, 312–13; John Winthrop, *Winthrop's Journal*, ed. James Kendall Hosmer, 2 vols. (New York, 1908), 20 January 1634, 1:118; Speiss and Weiss, "New England Pandemic," 77.

land and Connecticut." As Daniel Gookin observed later, they thus held dominion "over divers petty governours; as part of Long Island, Block Island, Cawesitt, Niantick, and others; and had tribute from some of the Nipmuck Indians, that lived remote from the sea." Their strength rested at least in part upon their position as leaders of the dominant wampum-producing tribe in southern New England. Wampum, wrote William Wood, allowed these "most curious minters," from whom "the northern, eastern, and western Indians fetch all their coin," to grow "rich and power full and also proud."[52]

Wampum consisted of tubular white and purple beads made from the shell of the quahog, or hard-shell clam, and a variety of conch or whelk shells. Traditionally, natives had employed wampum as ornamentation, for tribute, for ransom, and as compensation for crimes. As time passed, its tributary function appears to have increased in importance.[53]

The Dutch first discovered the value of wampum in 1622, immediately recognizing its usefulness as a trade item. The introduction of European metal drills dramatically expanded the capacity of wampum-producing Indians to manufacture the beads, and Europeans soon saw control of the wampum supply as crucially important for winning Indian trade. Increasing quantities of wampum assured that the beads would be available to greater numbers of individuals, setting in motion an inflationary cycle in the price of prestige items which fueled trade all the more. Competition for control of wampum among natives established new leaders, exacerbated existing intertribal rivalries, and created an atmosphere of tension and competitiveness along the southern New England coast.[54]

Sometime around 1630 the Pequots began to encroach upon the position of their Narragansett rivals. The Pequots and their Mohegan kinsfolk had

[52] John Mason, "A Brief History of the Pequot War," *MHS Coll*, 2d ser., 8 (1826): 122–23; Daniel Gookin, *Historical Collections of the Indians in New England* (1674), rpt. (New York, 1972), 7; William Wood, *New England's Prospect*, ed. Alden T. Vaughan, (Amherst, Mass., 1984), 81; Bradford, *History*, 236; William B. Weeden, "Indian Money as a Factor in New England Civilization," *Johns Hopkins University Studies in Historical and Political Science*, 2d ser., 8–9 (1884): 5; Elizabeth Shapiro Peña, "Wampum Production in New Netherland and Colonial New York: The Historical and Archaeological Context" (Ph.D. diss., Boston University, 1990), 61.

[53] Frank G. Speck, "The Functions of Wampum among the Eastern Algonkin," *Memoirs of the American Anthropological Association* 6 (1919): 56; Peter A. Thomas, "The Fur Trade, Indian Land, and the Need to Define Adequate Environmental Parameters," *Ethnohistory* 28 (1981): 363; Peña, "Wampum Production," 21–23; J. S. Slotkin and Karl Schmitt, "Studies of Wampum," *American Anthropologist* 51 (April–June 1949): 223–36.

[54] Peter A. Thomas, *In the Maelstrom of Change: The Indian Trade and Cultural Process in the Middle Connecticut Valley, 1635–1665* (New York, 1990), 56; Cronon, *Changes*, 95–96; Letter of Isack de Rasieres to Samuel Blommaert (1628), in *Narratives of New Netherland, 1609–1664*, ed. J. Franklin Jameson (New York, 1909), 106.

[55] William A. Starna, "The Pequots in the Early Seventeenth Century," in *The Pequots in Southern New England: The Fall and Rise of an American Indian Nation*, ed. Laurence M. Hauptman and James D. Wherry (Norman, Okla., 1990), 33; Salwen, "Indians," 172; Alfred E. Cave, "The Pequot Invasion of Southern New England: A Reassessment of the Evidence," *New England Quarterly* 62 (1989): 27–44.

occupied the region drained by the Thames River for a substantial period prior to their first contact with Europeans.[55] By the spring of 1631 at the latest, they had commenced a move westward toward the Connecticut River. That April, both Bradford and Winthrop received appeals from Wahginnacut, a sachem of the River Indians, to "have some Englishmen to come plant in his country." Wahginnacut offered to provide the immigrants with corn and pay them a yearly tribute of eighty beaver skins; he assured them they would find the country "very fruitful." More than a desire for English friendship motivated Wahginnacut. Described by Bradford as the leader of "a company of banishte Indeans . . . that were drivene" out of the Connecticut Valley "by the potencie of the Pequents," and by Winthrop as "a very treacherous man, and at war with the Pekoath (a far greater sagamore)," Wahginnacut was clearly seeking English assistance to stave off a Pequot invasion.[56]

Massachusetts Bay declined the harried sachem's offer; Plymouth sent a token force more interested in disrupting Dutch trade than in aiding the River Indians. Soon, therefore, the Pequots, "a very warlike and potent people," had gained control of the Connecticut from the river's mouth to the future site of Windsor in the north. They also conquered "the most southerly inhabitants of the Nipmuck country," as well as the wampum-producing tribes of eastern Long Island.[57]

The Pequot conquest of the Connecticut River and eastern Long Island placed the tribe in position to dominate both the production of wampum on the seacoast and the fur trade flowing down the river. Control of the Connecticut, moreover, permitted the Pequots to regulate access to Dutch traders on the river and enabled them to grow "rich and potent," like the Narragansetts before them, by monopolizing the best source of European trade goods in southern New England.[58] With the advent of English settlement in the Connecticut River valley, however, Pequot hegemony in the region became increasingly untenable.

[56] Bradford, *History*, 300; Winthrop, *Journal*, 4 April 1631, 61. See also Peter A. Thomas, "Squakeag Ethnohistory: A Preliminary Study of Culture Conflict on the Seventeenth Century Frontier," *Man in the Northeast* 5 (1973): 28; Benjamin Trumbull, *A Complete History of Connecticut* (1797), 2 vols. (New London, Conn., 1898), 1:12.

[57] Gookin, *Historical Collections*, 7; Starna, "Pequots," 33–34; Alfred E. Cave, "Who Killed John Stone? A Note on the Origins of the Pequot War," *WMQ*, 3d ser., 49 (1992): 512. By at least 1632 members of the Montauk Confederacy on Long Island had become Pequot tributaries. See Salwen, "Indians," 172; and Marion Fisher Ales, "A History of the Indians on Montauk, Long Island," in *The History and Archaeology of the Montauk Indians*, ed. Gaynell Stone Levine (Lexington, Mass., 1979), 208.

[58] Wood, *New England's Prospect*, 80–81; Bradford, *History*, 235; Ceci, *Effect*, 208–9; Cave, "John Stone," 512.

III

Metropolitan New Englanders had always hoped to engage the neighboring Indians in trade. Exchange with the natives, they believed, would provide their colonies with capital that would free them from debt, finance forts and churches, and allow them to profit.[59] New England magistrates, however, faced an impressive range of obstacles in establishing a profitable trade. Plymouth traders learned in the 1620s that the Narragansetts wanted European goods which the English could provide in neither the quantity nor the quality of those offered by the Dutch. To improve the quality of their trade goods, Plymouth needed capital, and that could come only from the same circle of entrepreneurs who already held the colony in debt. The prospects farther north, however, along the Kennebec and Penobscot Rivers, looked much better. Here the Abenakis, who already had altered their subsistence patterns to meet the demands of French fur traders, needed food, which Plymouth could provide in quantity.[60]

In 1625 Edward Winslow sailed into the Kennebec River and exchanged seven hundred bushels of corn for seven hundred pounds of beaver pelts. This was a profitable but cumbersome trade. Isaac De Rasieres, secretary of New Netherland, introduced wampum to the Plymouth traders in 1627. Rasieres, apparently, feared competition for the region's limited supply of furs and hoped that the English, if provided with a valuable medium of exchange, might occupy themselves in the north, leaving Dutch interests along the Connecticut and on Long Island alone.[61]

He was wrong. Wampum significantly increased the volume of New England's fur trade, and, in doing so, intensified competition not only between the English and the Dutch but among Indian groups as well. The growing numbers of Europeans seeking wampum encouraged producing Indians to drive increasingly hard bargains and to play different groups of traders off one another; they could thus charge higher prices for both wampum and furs. At the same time, the fur supply in the vicinity of Massachusetts Bay entered a permanent decline as a result of overharvesting coupled with the beaver's low fertility rate. By 1633, with the bay region almost valueless for the fur trade, Englishmen in Plymouth and Massachusetts Bay were casting their eyes toward the Connecticut River—a region the Dutch believed belonged to them alone.[62]

The Dutch, who first entered the Connecticut in 1614, had until 1632 enjoyed the fur trade on the river by themselves. Increasingly uneasy about the

[59] Winthrop, *Journal*, 8 September 1636, 187; Ceci, *Effect*, 197–98; Bernard Bailyn, *The New England Merchants in the Seventeenth Century* (Cambridge, Mass., 1955), 24.

[60] Salisbury, *Manitou and Providence*, 146; Bailyn, *New England Merchants*, 24.

[61] Bradford, *History*, 208; Ceci, *Effect*, 197–98; Peña, "Wampum Production," 63.

[62] Ceci, *Effect*, 198, 210; Pena, "Wampum," 63; Bailyn, *New England Merchants*, 26–27; *NYCD*, 1:152, 268.

growing English settlements to the east, however, and aware that claims to the Connecticut by right of discovery would mean little when actively challenged by English settlers, the Dutch West India Company acted to strengthen its claims to the valley. In June 1633 the company purchased from the Pequots the right to plant a fortified trading post at the present-day site of Hartford. The Pequots agreed to allow Indians from other tribes free access to the Dutch post, called the House of Good Hope.[63] Whether they understood this agreement to include their Narragansett rivals is not at all clear, for a short time later the Pequots ambushed and killed several Narragansetts, or Narragansett tributaries, along the path leading to the post. The Pequots could not allow a rival to undermine their hold upon the Connecticut. Both the Dutch and the Narragansetts reacted swiftly and violently. The Dutch seized the Pequot sachem Tatobem and, after collecting a bushel of wampum for his ransom, returned his murdered corpse to the Pequots. Meanwhile the Narragansetts prepared for war.[64]

The Englishman John Stone entered this arena in the winter of 1633–34. By all accounts a man of extremely unsavory qualities, Stone had been banished from the Bay Colony "upon pain of death" for his drunkenness, attempted piracy, insubordination, "braving and threatening speeches," and "being found upon the bed in the night with one Barcroft's wife." Stone hoped to try his luck on the Connecticut before he set out for his new home in Virginia. His luck was bad. Ascending the river, he and his men—seven in all—were attacked and killed by a band of Pequots.[65]

Stone's death was a mistake. The Pequots thought he and his crew were Dutch, and killed them in retaliation for the murder of their sachem. Soon aware of their error, the Pequots sent a delegation to Massachusetts Bay seeking friendship. They offered the English a gift of seventy beaver and otter skins along with four hundred fathoms of wampum. This, they hoped, would adequately compensate the English for Stone's death and also serve as the basis for an alliance in which the English would provide the Pequots the European trade goods they no longer could obtain from the Dutch and defend them from their European and aboriginal enemies. In return, the Pequot delegates offered the English "all their right at Connecticut," wrote Winthrop, "and to further us what they could, if we would settle a plantation there."[66]

---

[63] The deed, dated 8 June 1633, is published in *NYCD*, 2:139–40. See also *NYCD*, 1:287; Jennings, *Invasion*, 188; Allen W. Trelease, *Indian Affairs in Colonial New York: The Seventeenth Century* (Ithaca, N.Y., 1960), 54–55; Cave, "John Stone," 512–13.

[64] Winthrop, *Journal*, 6 November 1634, 139; Jennings, *Invasion*, 189; Trelease, *Indian Affairs*, 55–56; Cave, "John Stone," 512–13.

[65] Winthrop, *Journal*, 12 September 1633, 102, 108, and 21 January 1634, 118; John Underhill, "Newes from America," *MHS Coll*, 3d ser., 6 (1837): 9.

[66] Winthrop, *Journal*, 6 November 1634, 139.

The offer clearly interested the magistrates at Boston, but they demanded first that the Pequots hand over "those men who killed Captain Stone, etc." The Pequots replied that those guilty of Stone's murder had been killed when Stone's ship caught fire and exploded or had died of smallpox—a plausible outcome, given that the attack took place during the height of the 1633–34 epidemic. This answer, however, failed to satisfy the Boston magistrates, who reiterated that they would "send a pinnace with cloath to trade with them" only after they received the wampum, the furs, the title to the Connecticut, and the heads of Stone's killers. Winthrop also stipulated that any ensuing alliance with the Pequots would be limited strictly to trade and "not to defend them." Offered trade, but not protection, the Pequots rejected Winthrop's terms. At war with the Narragansetts, their trading relationship with the Dutch shattered, and suffering the scourge of smallpox, the Pequots recognized that to maintain their hold on the Connecticut, they would have to do so by themselves.[67]

IV

While Massachusetts Bay and Plymouth jockeyed with the Dutch, the Pequots, and the Narragansetts for control of the Connecticut River valley, the English population of New England exploded. During the 1630s 21,000 men, women, and children arrived from England.[68]

As early as 1633 Boston and its environs had become crowded. With pasture and meadowland in particularly short supply, the desire to migrate to the Connecticut seized the inhabitants of Dorchester, Newtown, Watertown, and Roxbury—all towns that felt the pressure of increasing population within the Bay Colony. Led by their minister, Thomas Hooker, the residents of Newtown petitioned the Massachusetts General Court late in the summer of 1634 for the right to emigrate to the Connecticut Valley. Their principal reasons, Winthrop wrote, were "their want of accommodation for their cattle" and a severe shortage of land that left them "not able to maintain their ministers" or to "receive any more of their friends to help them." To people so straitened, Hooker told the court, "the fruitfulness and comodiousness of Connecticut" had tremendous appeal.[69]

The leaders of both Massachusetts Bay and Plymouth feared the geographical spread of English settlement. As early as 1632 Bradford com-

[67] John Winthrop to John Winthrop Jr., 12 December 1634, *Winthrop Papers*, 3:177; Winthrop, *Journal*, 6 November 1634, 138–39; Cave, "John Stone," 514; Salisbury, *Manitou and Providence*, 209–12.

[68] Cressy, *Coming Over*, 63.

[69] John Winthrop to Sir Simonds D'Ewes, 20 July 1635, in *Letters from New England: The Massachusetts Bay Colony, 1629–1638*, ed. Everett H. Emerson (Amherst, Mass., 1976), 154; Winthrop, *Journal*, 4 September 1634, 132.

plained that colonists, conceiving "themselves straitened, or to want acco-modation," were breaking away "under one pretence or other, thinking their owne conceived necessitie, and the examples of others, a warrente suf-ficiente for them." Winthrop and Bradford sought to keep the colonists "knit together" in one body, in a single political unit. The careless expansion of settlement, they believed, would not only threaten the integrity of Winthrop's plan for a "citty uppon a hill" but also create an atmosphere of tension along the frontier that could result in expensive warfare with both aboriginal and European foes.[70]

The Bay Colony magistrates, however, failed to stem the tide of migration toward the Connecticut. In May 1635 they reluctantly granted the inhabi-tants of Watertown and "Rocksbury" the right "to remove themselves to any place they shall thinke meete to make choise of, provided they continue still under this government." By autumn the magistrates recognized that they had no practicable means to control frontier expansion. The emigrat-ing settlers ignored the requirement that they remain within the jurisdiction of the Bay Colony. Since the magistrates could not prevent the growth of the river towns, they hoped to retain some control over the fledgling communi-ties by dictating the structure of their governments.[71] In March 1636 the Massachusetts General Court empowered eight men to "make & decree such orders for the present, that may be for the peaceable & quiett ordering of the affaires of the said plantacon, both in tradeing, planting, building, lotts, millitarie dissipline, defensive warr, (if neede soe require,) as shall best conduce to the publique good of the same."[72]

By then the 250 settlers living at three plantations along the Connecticut River had become a threat to the fragile Pequot hegemony in the region, and by June the settlers were hearing rumors of Pequot hostility. The newly ap-pointed Connecticut magistrates responded by establishing a nightly watch and by ordering every inhabitant to secure a supply of powder and shot.[73]

That the English river settlements generated conflict with the Pequots is not surprising. The limited productive capacity of the land, as well as the dif-fering means devised for its use by Indians and Europeans, necessarily drew the two populations into conflict. Englishmen and Indians, on the Con-necticut frontier as elsewhere, sought to control identical geographical areas but to utilize the resources there in ways that were seldom compatible. The frontier population along the Connecticut River placed significant pressure

---

[70] Bradford, *History*, 293–94.

[71] MBR, 6 May 1635, 1:46; Mary Jeanne Anderson Jones, *Congregational Commonwealth: Connecticut, 1636–1662* (Middletown, Conn., 1968), 28.

[72] MBR, 3 March 1636, 1:170–71.

[73] CR, 26 April 1636, 1:1–4; See also Harold E. Selesky, *War and Society in Colonial Con-necticut* (New Haven, Conn., 1990), 3.

[74] Peter A. Thomas, "Contrastive Subsistence Strategies and Land Use as Factors for Under-standing Indian-White Relations in New England," *Ethnohistory* 23 (1976): 14; Thomas, *Maelstrom of Change*, 89–120.

upon Native American subsistence patterns. In the tense and competitive atmosphere that resulted, the survival of the opposing groups hung in the balance.[74]

As important as the drain English settlers placed upon the limited territorial and environmental resources of the Connecticut River valley was the fact that they had obtained their title to those lands by purchasing it from the local sachems, recently conquered River Indians. The English settlements consequently undermined the Pequots' already tenuous overlordship by establishing direct relations with their tributaries, who were apparently willing to use English power in the region to free themselves from the grip of the Pequots.[75]

From a strictly legal viewpoint, the first Connecticut settlers had squatted on land claimed by a variety of English, Dutch, and Pequot interests. Neither the Massachusetts Bay Company nor Plymouth possessed an unqualified right to plant settlements there. The best English legal title to the river valley belonged to Robert Rich, the second Earl of Warwick. In March 1632 Warwick transferred his rights to a group of Puritan nobles, prominent among them William Fiennes, the first Viscount Saye and Sele; Robert Greville, the second Baron Brooke; and Sir Richard Saltonstall, a founder of the Massachusetts Bay Company. The Warwick patentees offered John Winthrop Jr., the son of the Bay Colony's governor, charge of their American domain on July 7, 1635. He accepted the commission to govern "the River Connecticut and . . . the harbors and places ajoining."[76]

It was not the first time that the younger Winthrop had been enlisted by metropolitans to secure control of a strategically critical tract of frontier land. Shortly after his arrival in America in 1631, Bay Colony authorities, fearing French claims to the coastal region north of Boston, had asked him to plant a settlement there. He did so, at Ipswich, in 1634.[77] This time, Winthrop sent Lion Gardener, a military engineer fresh from service in the Low Countries, to oversee the construction of Fort Saybrook on the western side of the river's mouth. Gardener called it a site suitable "both for the convenience of good harbour, and also for capableness and fitness for fortification."[78]

Historians have argued that the construction of Saybrook, which coincided with the beginning of English settlement in the Connecticut Valley, resulted from a partnership between the Warwick patentees and the Massa-

[75] Salwen, "Indians," 173.

[76] *Winthrop Papers*, 3:198–99; Robert C. Black, *The Younger John Winthrop* (New York, 1966), 85–87; Jones, *Congregational Commonwealth*, 23–24.

[77] John Frederick Martin, *Profits in the Wilderness: Entrepeneurship and the Founding of New England Towns* (Chapel Hill, N.C., 1991), 52–53.

[78] Lion Gardener, "Lieft Lion Gardener His Relation of the Pequot Warres," *MHS Coll*, 3d ser., 3 (1833): 137.

[79] Jennings, *Invasion*, 197–98; Salisbury, *Manitou and Providence*, 217.

chusetts Bay Colony (with John Winthrop Jr. serving as the link between them) designed to monopolize land in Connecticut, and to prevent its appropriation by squatters.[79] One must recognize, however, that to metropolitans such as the Winthrops, Bradford, Lord Saye and Sele, and Saltonstall, the Connecticut was not merely a fertile river offering a source of wealth that could both enrich colonial promoters and solve their financial problems; it was a zone of imperial conflict, where Dutch, English, and Native American groups jockeyed for control of a limited supply of strategically valuable resources. It was a marchland of empire which, if mismanaged, could aid the enemies of the realm while provoking Indian resistance. With this concern in mind, Saltonstall emphasized the importance of building a fort "to secure the Rivers mouth for the defence of them all."[80]

V

Saybrook, conceived initially as a possible refuge for Puritans fleeing England, became under the guidance of John Winthrop Jr. a base from which metropolitans in New England hoped to control the Connecticut River valley. By planting their fortification at the river's mouth, they effectively denied Dutch control of the river, placed themselves in a position to exploit the wampum factories of Long Island Sound, and took advantage of both riverine and coastal trade with Boston. Saybrook became a node of metropolitan control in southwestern New England.

Puritan metropolitans quickly recognized the threat to colonial security posed by the three settlements upriver. Jonathan Brewster, a Plymouth trader based at Windsor, informed the younger Winthrop in June 1636 that "the Pequents have some mistrust, that the English will shortly come against them," a conclusion they had reached, Brewster wrote, because of "indiscreet speaches of some of your people here to the Natives."[81] Winthrop forwarded the Brewster message to Boston, where a standing council—composed of the Bay Colony's governor, Henry Vane; John Winthrop, then deputy governor; and a former governor, Thomas Dudley—considered the message. The council members, who three months before had failed to control effectively the inhabitants of the river towns, now sought instead to protect the settlements by restraining the Pequots. Saybrook would serve as their base for this operation, the younger Winthrop as their agent.

The standing council commissioned John Winthrop Jr. "to trade and conferre with the sayd Pequots . . . in a friendly manner about matters of importance." The Bay magistrates, however, clearly misunderstood the posi-

[80] Sir Richard Saltonstall to John Winthrop Jr., 27 February 1636, in *The Saltonstall Papers*, ed. Robert Moody, 2 vols. (Boston, 1976), 1:126.
[81] Jonathan Brewster to John Winthrop Jr., 18 June 1636, *Winthrop Papers*, 3:270.

tion taken by the Pequots in 1634. They had then withdrawn their offer of wampum and skins, as recompense for Stone's murder and as an inducement to forming a military and trade alliance, when the Bay magistrates expressed no interest in a defensive alliance. Vane and the elder Winthrop, however, still expected both the wampum and the skins to be forwarded by the Pequots as compensation for the murder, as well as the heads of Stone's killers (who, the Pequots insisted, were already dead). To the Bay magistrates, the Pequots' unwillingness to comply with the terms proposed in 1634 savored of "so much dishonour and neglect, as that no people that desire friendship should put them in practice."[82]

Winthrop instructed his son to inform the Pequots that "if they shall cleare themselves of these matters, we shall not refuse to hearken to any reasonable proposition from them for confirmation of the peace betwixt us." But,

> if they shall not give you satisfaction according to these our instructions, or shall bee found guilty of any of the sayd murthers, and will not deliver the actours in them into our hands, that then . . . you . . . declare to them that we hold ourselves free from any league or peace with them, and shall revenge the blood of our countrimen as occasion shall serve.[83]

The younger Winthrop informed the Pequots that they were still responsible for the murder of Stone and that the power to deal with Indians in New England rested not with settlers on the Connecticut frontier but at the metropolitan center at Boston. His meeting with the Pequots ended inconclusively.

That same month another Englishman died at Indian hands. John Oldham was killed near Block Island—not by the Pequots but by their rivals the Narragansetts, or a Narragansett tributary. His body, reported the elder Winthrop, was found "stark naked, his head cleft to the brains, and his hand and legs cut as if they had been cutting them off, and yet warm." Winthrop believed that "all the sachems of the Narragansett, except Canonicus and Miantunnomoh, were the contrivers of Mr. Oldham's death," and that the trader had been killed "because he went to make peace, and trade with the Pekods last year."[84]

Oldham died a victim of competition between the Pequots and Narragansetts for control of southern New England, and his death complicated an already tense situation along the frontier. Metropolitans in New England had entered the Connecticut Valley initially to control their own wayward

---

[82] Henry Vane and John Winthrop to John Winthrop Jr., 4 August 1636, in *MHS Coll*, 3d ser., 3 (1833): 129–31.

[83] Ibid., 133.

[84] Winthrop, *Journal*, 25 and 26 July 1636, 184, 185.

[85] See, e.g., *CR*, 8 March 1638, 1:13–14.

settlers and to harvest the riches of the river for metropolitan ends. They enjoyed little success, however, and the Indians were growing angry. The magistrates had proven themselves unable to prevent emigration. The colonists taking up homes in the valley, moreover, bullied the Indians and subjected local natives to vigilante justice.[85]

At the same time, the metropolitans slowly found themselves drawn into inter- and intratribal rivalries. After the Narragansetts killed Oldham in 1636 because he traded with their Pequot enemies, the situation became even more complicated. Uncas, the leader of the Mohegans, who had a claim to the chief sachemdom of the Pequots by right of marriage and descent from past chief sachems, split from the tribal majority led by Sassacus, the son of Tatobem. Uncas saw the increasing competition between Pequots and Englishmen for control of the Connecticut as an opportunity to assert his claims to the grand sachemdom of the Pequot tribe. By ingratiating himself with the English and using English power, Uncas hoped to establish his position, along with the English and the Narragansetts, as one of three dominant powers in the region.[86]

Lion Gardener, at Saybrook, saw more clearly than anyone else that the situation along the river had slipped from control. The aggressive actions of the Connecticut settlers, he feared, coupled with metropolitan attempts to assert authority over the region, would result in war. He entreated the Bay magistrates "to rest awhile, till we get more strength about us." He had only three acres of corn planted, which he certainly would lose if war broke out. The magistrates, he noted bitterly, would remain safely at Boston, while he and his men would be left "at the stake to be roasted, or for hunger to be starved," and exposed "to the Indians, whose mercies are cruelties."[87]

By late summer of 1636 the stakes along the Connecticut had risen significantly. Since the 1621 treaty between Plymouth and the Wampanoags, metropolitans had equated control of the frontier with the imposition of English law over both newcomers and natives.[88] To obtain justice in the Oldham case, the Bay magistrates sent ninety men under the command of John Endicott to "put to death the men of Block Island . . . but to spare the women and children, and to bring them away, and to take possession of the Island." From there, Endicott was to "go to the Pequods to demand the murderers of Capt. Stone and other English, and one thousand fathom of wampum for damages, etc., and some of their children as hostages, which if

[86] P. Richard Metcalf, "Who Should Rule at Home? Native American Politics and Indian-White Relations," *JAH* 61 (1974): 654–56; Carroll Alton Means, "Mohegan-Pequot Relationships, as Indicated by the Events Leading to the Pequot Massacre of 1637 and the Subsequent Claims in the Mohegan Land Controversy," *Bulletin of the Archaeological Society of Connecticut* 21 (1947): 26–34; William Burton and Richard Lowenthal, "The First of the Mohegans," *American Ethnologist* 1 (1974): 597.

[87] Gardener, "His Relation," 138–39.

[88] James P. Ronda, "Red and White at the Bench: Indians and the Law in Plymouth Colony, 1620–1691," *Essex Institute Historical Collections* 110 (1974): 201–3.

they should refuse, they were to obtain it by force." The magistrates were counting on a demonstration of force to secure the Pequots' submission to their demands. Winthrop later recalled that Endicott was sent against the Pequots "with hope to draw them to parley, and so to some quiet end." They did not envision, nor did they desire, an Indian war. Not only would the costs of such a conflict be enormous, John Higginson warned, but the energy expended would divert metropolitans from the ends for which they settled the New World. "It cannot be conceived," he wrote, "that either building, planting, fishing, trading, colledges, etc. or in a word the good of either Church or Commonweal can flourish, and goe forward" during a war with the Indians.[89]

Endicott landed his forces on Block Island late in August but could find no one to fight. The natives fled to the swamps upon first sighting the English. This left Endicott and his men free to stomp about the Indian settlement, where they burnt houses, destroyed crops, and killed a few dogs the Indians had left behind.[90]

Unable to engage the Block Islanders, Endicott proceeded next to the mouth of the Connecticut, where he used Saybrook as his "rendezvous or seat of war"—to the garrison commander's "great grief." Gardener was furious. He accused Endicott of coming "hither to raise these wasps about my ears, and then you will take wing and flee away." He objected to Endicott's plan to approach the Pequots in force, "but go they did to Pequit, and . . . so they went against our will."[91]

At Pequot Harbor, Endicott reiterated the Bay Colony's demand for "the heads of the murderers" of John Stone. Again, the Pequots explained that the death of Stone was an unfortunate mistake, that they had mistaken him for a Dutchman and killed him to avenge the murder of their sachem. "We know no difference between the Dutch and the English," a Pequot ambassador said. "They are both strangers to us, we took them to be all one; therefore we crave pardon; we have not wilfully wronged the English." Endicott refused to accept the Pequot explanation and resolved to attack. Again, no Indian would stand to fight. The English force "gave fire to as many" of the Pequots "as we could come near, firing their wigwams, spoiling their corn, and many other necessaries that they had buried in the ground we raked up, which the soldiers had for booty."[92]

Endicott's soldiers killed fifty-four Indians, mainly women and children. The expedition failed to secure its principal objective: the extension of Massachusetts Bay's authority over the Pequots and control of the Connecticut

---

[89] John Higginson to John Winthrop, May 1637, *Winthrop Papers*, 3:405–6; Winthrop, *Journal*, 25 August 1636 and 12 May 1637, 186, 214; Underhill, "Newes," 3–4.

[90] Underhill, "Newes from America," 7.

[91] Gardener, "His Relation," 140.

[92] Underhill, "Newes from America," 8–11; Gardener, "His Relation," 141.

[93] Underhill, "Newes from America," 11; Hirsch, "Collision," 1197; Ceci, *Effect*, 210–12.

River valley. Instead, by destroying and pillaging the Indian villages at Pequot Harbor and Block Island, and by killing Pequot women and children, Endicott's ham-fisted actions precipitated the Pequot War.[93]

His assault, in fact, rendered the Pequots' situation desperate. Uncas and the Mohegans had already tendered their assistance to the English. If the Narragansetts joined against them as well, the Pequots knew they could no longer maintain their position along the Connecticut River. Late in 1636, consequently, the Pequots sought peace with the Narragansetts. If the Narragansetts aided the English, the Pequots warned, "they did make way for their owne overthrow, for if they were rooted out, the English would soone take occasion to subjugate them." The Pequots assured the Narragansetts that they would not have to attack the English, but only "fire their houses, kill their katle, and lye in ambush for them as they went abroad upon their occasions, and all this they might easily doe without any or litle danger to them selves."[94]

But even though the Narragansetts may have been "once wavering, and were halfe minded to have made peace" with the Pequots, the likelihood of such an alliance was not great. The Narragansetts would benefit in the short run from the destruction of the Pequots, their principal Native American rival in southern New England. Indeed, as Bradford wrote, when the Narragansetts considered "how much wrong they had received from the Pequots, and what an opportunitie they now had by the help of the English to right themselves, revenge was so sweet unto them, as it prevailed above all the rest."[95]

VI

The establishment of Hartford, Windsor, and Wethersfield in 1635 undermined Pequot hegemony in the Connecticut River valley. The construction of Fort Saybrook at the river's mouth the same year thwarted Pequot access to the wampum factories of Long Island sound, the source of the tribe's wealth and power. By purchasing title to the Saybrook site from the tributary Western Niantics rather than from the Pequots themselves, moreover, the fort's builders further subverted Pequot authority in the valley. Now, confronted by powerful Indian enemies intent upon displacing them, and under attack by English metropolitans determined to secure justice

[94] Bradford, *History*, 338; Mason, "Brief History," 123.
[95] Bradford, *History*, 338; Salisbury, *Manitou and Providence*, 211–13; Vincent, "True Relation," 36. For Roger Williams's claims to have broken up the alliance, see Williams to the General Court of Massachusetts Bay, 14 October 1651 and 5 October 1654; and Williams to Major John Mason and Governor Thomas Prence, 22 June 1670, all in *The Correspondence of Roger Williams*, ed. Glenn W. La Fantasie, 2 vols., (Hanover, N.H., 1988), 1:353–54, 2:408, 611–12.

along the frontier, the Pequots resolved to fight for the territory they had acquired over the course of the preceding decade.

Beginning in the fall of 1636, then, the Pequots set upon Saybrook, the base from which Endicott had attacked them. They ambushed patrols that strayed too far beyond its walls, picked off careless soldiers, and struck down those sent to harvest corn without sufficient weaponry. Gardener lost several men who "went a mile from the house a fowling." A short time later, when he sent a party to gather hay, three men were killed immediately by Indians who "rose out of the long grass." The Pequots captured another of Gardener's men and "roasted him alive." When Master Tilly, the captain of a ship plying the Connecticut, fell into Pequot hands, wrote John Underhill, they "tied him to the stake, flayed his skin off, put hot embers between the flesh and the skin, cut off his fingers and toes, and made hatbands of them."[96]

Late in February the following year Gardener himself nearly fell victim to a Pequot ambush. He had ventured from the fort with ten men "to burn the weeds, leaves, and reeds, upon the neck of land, because we had felled twenty timber-trees, which we were to roll to the water-side to bring home." Three Indians fled from the burning reeds, pursued by Gardener's men. Then, from two directions, "a Great Company of Indians" emerged from the woods. Gardener and his men

> gave fire uppon them yett they run one to the very mussels of our pieces and soe they shott 3 men downe in the place and 3 more men shott that escaped of which one died the same night and if the Lord had not put it into my mind to make men draw their swords they had taken us all alive.

Gardener, who received a wound in the leg, removed an arrowhead from the pierced body of one of his men, and sent it to the Bay, "because they had said that the arrows of the Indians were of no force."[97]

A short time later the Pequots approached the walls of Fort Saybrook, and asked Gardener whether the English had tired of fighting. Then, referring to Endicott's attack at Pequot Harbor, the tribesmen asked "if we did use to kill women and children." Gardener replied that the Pequots "should see that hereafter." The Pequots, according to Gardener, were silent a small space and then declared defiantly,

> We are Pequits, and have killed Englishmen, and can kill them as mosquetoes, and we will go to Conectecott and kill men, women, and children, and we will take away the horses, cows, and hogs.

[96] Gardener, "His Relation," 141–43; Underhill, "Newes from America," 15; Bradford, *History*, 335; Hirsch, "Collision," 1197.
[97] Lyon Gardener to John Winthrop Jr., 23 March 1637, *Winthrop Papers*, 3:381–82; Gardener, "His Relation," 143–44.

When reinforcements arrived at Saybrook in the spring of 1637, the Pequots abandoned the siege. Henry Vane, then governor at Massachusetts Bay, dispatched Captain John Underhill "with twenty lusty men, well armed," to "supply the necessity of those distressed persons, and to take the government of that place for the space of three months." "Seeing there was no advantage more to be had against the fort," Underhill reported, the Pequots "enterprised a new action, and fell upon Watertowne, now called Wethersfield, with two hundred Indians."[98]

On April 23, 1637, the Pequots attacked "some that were sawing, and slew nine more, whereof one was a woman, the other a child, and took two young maids prisoners." The Connecticut settlers then resolved "that there shalbe an offensive warr agᵗ the Pequoitt," with each of the three river towns contributing men, provisions, and supplies. Every soldier would carry "1ᶫᵇ pouder, 4ᶫᵇ of shott, 20 bulletts." Ninety men were organized under Captain John Mason and readied for the voyage to Saybrook at the river's mouth.[99]

Mason, a veteran of England's wars in the Netherlands, left with his forces early in May, accompanied by Uncas and "three score Mohiggoners." Some at Saybrook distrusted the Mohegans, fearing that "in time of greatest trial" they "might revolt, and turn their backs against those they professed to be their friends, and join with the Pequeats." To prove their good faith, the Mohegans "fell upon thirty or forty of the Enemy near Saybrook Fort, and killed seven of them outright." According to Underhill, "this mightily encouraged the hearts of all, and we took this as a pledge of their further fidelity."[100]

Despite the confidence he placed in his Mohegan allies, Mason was reluctant to lead a frontal assault against the Pequots. Instead, he proposed sailing from Saybrook eastward to Narragansett Bay, and marching overland from there to attack the Pequot fortress on the Mystic River. The Connecticut force and its Indian allies marched for two days, camping on the last night a short distance from the Mystic River settlement. At one o'clock the next morning the English set out to surround the fort. Mason led a force to the western side of the Pequot village, while Underhill waited to its south. Their Mohegan allies, augmented by at least two hundred Narragansetts, formed a "ringed battalia" completely enclosing the Pequot fort, placing themselves in an ideal position to capture or kill any Pequots trying to flee from the English assault.[101]

Before the sun rose, the English fell upon the sleeping settlement. Mason's forces "entered the forte with all speede" but found "sharp resistence from

---

[98] Gardener, "His Relation," 145, 148, 185–86; Underhill, "Newes from America," 12. See also Winthrop, *Journal*, 10 April 1637, 212.

[99] CR, 1 May 1637, 1: 9–10; Jennings, *Invasion*, 217.

[100] Underhill, "Newes from America," 15–16; Mason, "Brief History," 133; Gardener, "His Relation," 149.

[101] Underhill, "Newes from America," 23; Mason, "Brief History," 136; Winthrop, *Journal*, 25 May 1637, 220.

[102] Bradford, *History*, 339; Vincent, "True Relation," 39.

the enemie, who both shot at and grappled with them." The English had not expected such fierce resistance and found fighting in the cramped quarters difficult. Lacking "foot-room to grapple with their adversaries," the English set the village afire.[102] As flames quickly consumed the fort, the English withdrew, positioning themselves in a circle about the blazing village.

At least four hundred Pequots died in the fires of Mystic. "So many souls," wrote Underhill, "lie gasping on the ground, so thick, in some places, that you could scarcely pass along." Bradford, too, described the carnage:

> It was a fearfull sight to see them thus frying in the fyer, and the streams of blood quenching the same, and horrible was the stinck and sente ther of; but the victory seemed a sweete sacrifice, and they gave the prays therof to God, who had wrought so wonderfully for them, thus to inclose their enimise in their hands, and give them so speedy a victory over so proud and insulting an enemie.

"Those that scaped the fire," he added, "were slaine with the sword, some hewed to peeces, others rune throw with their rapiers, so as they were quickly dispatchte, and very few escaped."[103]

The violence of the English assault appalled the Narragansetts. "Our Indians," Underhill reported, "cried Mach it, mach it; that is, It is naught, it is naught, because it is too furious and slays too many men."[104] Many of the Narragansetts, in fact, had deserted upon learning that Mason planned to attack the Mystic settlement—inhabited mostly by women, old men, and children—rather than Sassacus's better-defended stronghold at Wienshauks farther upriver.

English writers, however, whether they participated in the attack or witnessed it from afar, had little difficulty justifying the intensity of the assault. "The remembrance of the blood shed, the captive maids, and cruel insolency of those Pequots," wrote one observer, "hardened the hearts of the English, and stopped their ears unto their cries." That the English referred to their Pequot adversaries as "wicked imps," who "like the devil, their commander . . . run up and down as roaring lions, compassing all corners of the country for a prey, seeking whom they might devour," demonstrates the extent to which the war had dampened the philanthropy of metropolitans in New England.[105] The English style of warfare against culturally "backward" peoples had always been horribly violent. And few Englishmen, whether they fought on the European continent, in Ireland, or in America, would have disputed the premise so fundamental to the English way of war: "Severe justice must now and then take place."[106]

---

[103] Bradford, *History*, 338–39; Underhill, "Newes from America," 25.
[104] Underhill, "Newes from America," 27.
[105] Ibid., 15; Vincent, "True Relation," 37.
[106] Vincent, "True Relation," 37.

VII

The Pequot War resulted in the destruction of one of the two most powerful Indian tribes in southern New England. By the end of the month in which Connecticut's troops attacked Mystic, English forces and their Indian allies had killed seven hundred Pequot men, women, and children. Within another month, Underhill reported, "fifteen hundred souls" had been driven "out of their country, and slain by the sword."[107]

The English enjoyed a total victory. The elimination of the Pequots spurred emigration. By 1640 the population of the river towns had reached 3,000, and another 2,500 lived at New Haven, founded along the Quinnipiac River in 1638. Metropolitan control of the Connecticut River valley, it seemed, had been secured.[108]

In the weeks and months following the war the English colonies seized control of wampum production on Long Island Sound and along the coast of southern New England. Although the amount of wampum they collected cannot be reconstructed with certainty, Lynn Ceci has shown that if only known payments and assessments are totaled, the English collected more than 17,000 fathoms of wampum. At prevailing rates of exchange, this sum was equivalent in value to more than £9,500. The amount of wampum collected during the years for which no evidence exists, Ceci suspects, would probably increase this total by at least 100 percent. The seizure of such great quantities of wampum certainly spurred the development of the colonies and unquestionably gave the English a considerable advantage over the Dutch in the fur trade.[109]

The English victory provided opportunities as well for their Indian allies. The Narragansetts, especially, aspired to the position of influence and power held previously by the Pequots, and English observers remarked upon the tribe's ambitious and "very prejudiciall" dealings. First, wrote Israel Stoughton, the Narragansetts "frequently receive wampum of our Enemies without advising with us which our enemies give them to obtayne peace, etc." The truth, Stoughton continued, was that the Narragansetts had "so eagerly sett upon their owne ends, to gett booty etc. and to augment their owne Kingdome etc.," that they were using the threat of English attack "as their stalking horse" to obtain Pequot wampum. As a consequence, Roger

---

[107] Vaughan, *New England Frontier*, 122; Vincent, "True Relation," 40; John Winthrop to William Bradford, 28 July 1637, *Winthrop Papers*, 3:457; Underhill, "Newes from America," 3.

[108] Vaughan, *New England Frontier*, 153.

[109] Ceci, *Effect*, 215, 218.

[110] Israel Stoughton to John Winthrop, 6 July 1637, *Winthrop Papers*, 3:441–42. See also Daniel Patrick to Increase Nowell, 6 July 1637, *Winthrop Papers*, 3:440–41; Stoughton to Governor and Council of Massachusetts, 14 August 1637, *Winthrop Papers*, 3:482; Roger Williams to John Winthrop, 30 June 1637, in Williams, *Correspondence*, 1: 88.

Williams found "a great Itch upon the Souldiers to fall fowle" upon the Narragansetts.[110]

Studies of relations between Europeans and Indians in early colonial New England have failed to capture effectively the complexity of Indian-white relations in southern New England, an arena of conflict where rival European and Amerindian groups competed for access to a limited supply of strategically important resources. At least in part these works have suffered from an insensitivity to the difficult problem of managing a frontier, and from an inability or unwillingness to recognize that not all New Englanders were Puritans, that not all shared in the Puritans' strong sense of mission, and that the nature of relations between Indians and Europeans resulted from the complicated dynamic that evolved as differing groups pursued differing objectives in a limited geographical area.

Metropolitan New Englanders came to the New World with a fervent devotion to Puritanism. They hoped that their colonies would serve not only as spiritual beacons for a corrupt world but as models for the Native American tribes of the region to imitate. Yet these men who located their New Israel along the marchlands of empire, a world of grim practicality, exploitation, and violence, were pragmatists. In order for their colonial experiments to prosper, metropolitans had to secure the good of the whole through the use of governmental power, law, and the threat of force. In order to be safe, they had to remain wary always of the Dutch settlements to their west, the French to their north, and the Indians among whom they settled. In order for their settlements to succeed, they had to tend to both the military and the financial needs of their colonies. In order to meet their objectives—profit for their colonial organizations, the security of their colonies and the King's dominions, and the conversion of the Indians and the spreading of the reformed religion—metropolitans urgently needed to control the New England frontier and superintend the activities of those inhabiting it.

They failed. Worldly concerns would consistently intrude upon the millennial expectations of the Puritan fathers, forcing them on occasion to set aside their hopes for a New Israel in the wilderness, and to confront the earthly and often violent realities of expanding an empire and governing a frontier society.

4   *Edward Randolph's Report*

In June 1676 Edward Randolph arrived in Boston, selected by the Lords of Trade in London to investigate affairs in the Massachusetts Bay Colony. Randolph would report upon the colony's military strength, its social structure and religious practices, and the territorial boundaries claimed by provincial magistrates. He would also investigate "the original cause of the present warr with the Indians," as well as "the advantages or disadvantages arising therby." His mission would provide the crown with the information it needed to mount an assault on the apparently disastrous autonomy enjoyed by the Puritan "commonwealths," an autonomy ultimately inconsistent with the restored monarchy's vision of the proper relationship between colony and empire.[1]

Randolph detested Puritans. His sojourn in New England convinced him that the saints were "generally inclined to Sedition, being Proud Ignorant and Imperious." The Bay Colony's leadership, in his view, had been disloyal, shortsighted, and stupid in provoking an Indian war, and Randolph sniffed contemptuously at their explanation for the massive Algonquian uprising that had set New England's frontiers ablaze. According to the magistrates, Randolph reported, "the great and provoking evils for which God hath given the barbarous heathen commission to rise against them" included the "woeful breach of the fifth commandment in contempt of all authority," the fashion for "men wearing long hair and perriwigs made of women's hair," for "women wearing borders of hair ... and disguising themselves by following strange fashions in their apparel," for "prophaneness in the people

---

[1] Extracts from Edward Randolph's report to the Council of Trade, 12 October 1676, *NYCD*, 3:242; Michael Garibaldi Hall, *Edward Randolph and the American Colonies, 1676–1703* (Chapel Hill, N.C., 1960), 4.

in not frequenting their Meetings," and for "suffering the Quakers to dwell upon them, and to sett up their thresholds by God's thresholds, contrary to their old laws and resolutions." To these arguments Randolph replied smugly that "whatever was the cause the English have contributed very much to their misfortunes."[2]

Randolph did not always have his facts straight. He placed far too much blame for the war upon Massachusetts, when in fact all the Puritan colonies had contributed to its outbreak. Still, Edward Randolph's report testified to the inability of the Bay Colony magistrates, and implicitly all New Englanders, to govern the Anglo-American frontier effectively and to attain for the crown the metropolitan imperatives of dominion and civility.

With England itself immersed in civil war during the middle decades of the seventeenth century, each of the New England colonies had pursued its own Indian policy, each hoping to secure an orderly and expanding frontier of settlement, to control the natives within its bounds, and to bring them gently to the true religion and English standards of civility. The result, predictably, was chaos. After the Pequot War colonists from Plymouth, Connecticut, New Haven, Massachusetts Bay and, to a lesser extent, Rhode Island, jockeyed for control of resources along the southern New England coast. A number of powerful Algonquian groups, led by the Mohegans, the Niantics, the Wampanoags, and the Narragansetts, competed with them. The ensuing competition and conflict would reverberate throughout New England, with consequences that far transcended the borders of the region.

Fully committed to the exploitation of opportunities presented by the destruction of the Pequots, their interests tied firmly to the aggressive expansion of the New England frontier, and unable to curtail the aggressiveness of the English frontier population, the Puritan regimes unwittingly drove these native bands to frustration, anger, and resistance. From 1638 through the middle of the 1670s, in fact, metropolitans in New England steadily lost control of the region. Hoping to secure frontier resources for the benefit of their individual colonies, the fiercely localistic Puritan commonwealths provoked both a massive Algonquian uprising and a royalist and metropolitan response designed to curb provincial autonomy and impose order along the Anglo-American frontier.

I

The defeat of the Pequots created a power vacuum along the coast of Long Island Sound. Both Massachusetts and Connecticut wanted the former Pe-

---

[2] Randolph to Charles II, 20 September 1676, and Randolph to Henry Coventry, 17 June 1675, in *Edward Randolph*, ed. Robert Noxon Toppan, 5 vols., *Publications of the Prince Society*, (Boston, 1898), 2:218, 206–7; NYCD, 3:243.

quot lands. Both also sought to insulate their claims from their English rivals. Settlers soon poured into the territory of the Pequots and their former tributaries.[3]

Connecticut was especially aggressive. The River Colony chose as the agent for its expansion the Mohegan sachem Uncas, who had demonstrated his loyalty to the English during the war. Connecticut replaced Pequot hegemony in the Lower Connecticut Valley with that of the Mohegans. Uncas became an intermediary between former Pequot tributaries and the colonial government, receiving English support as he extended his sway over Algonquian bands in the valley and along the coast. Uncas in turn ceded all his own lands and those of his new tributaries to Connecticut, thus confirming their claim to the Pequot territory and barring that of Massachusetts. Connecticut also received tribute payments from Uncas for the Pequots under his protection.[4]

Like the Mohegans, the Narragansetts too hoped to supplant the Pequots, their longtime rivals, as the dominant aboriginal power in southern New England.[5] The Massachusetts Bay magistrates did not object to the extension of Narragansett influence over the Pequot lands, so long as it strengthened their own claims to the region. The Bay Colony had linked its interests with those of Miantonomo. Connecticut, however, well aware that a Narragansett presence in the disputed territory would strengthen the claims of Massachusetts, acted to separate the Narragansetts from their allies in Boston. "Our friends at Qunnihticut," wrote Roger Williams to John Winthrop, "are strangely bewitched with the subjection of the Pequots to themselves, and are allso as strangely resolved upon fighting and violent Courses . . . unless Miantunnomo come over personally to them to answer for proud Speeches wch they heare of."[6]

Connecticut's demand that he appear at Hartford puzzled Miantonomo, who thought that "all the English in the Land were wrapt up in that Agreement" negotiated with Massachusetts in 1636, securing Narragansett assistance in the Pequot War. Connecticut objected to these articles, wrote

[3] Israel Stoughton to John Winthrop, 9 August 1637, in *Winthrop Papers*, ed. Samuel Eliot Morison, et al., 5 vols. (Boston, 1929–), 3:479; *MBR*, May 1665, 4 (pt. 2): 234; Peter A. Thomas, *In the Maelstrom of Change: The Indian Trade and Cultural Process in the Middle Connecticut Valley, 1635–1665* (New York, 1990), 144.

[4] Neal Salisbury, *Manitou and Providence: Indians, Europeans, and the Making of New England* (New York, 1982), 226; William Burton and Richard Lowenthal, "The First of the Mohegans," *American Ethnologist* 1 (1974): 593.

[5] Roger Williams to John Winthrop, 12 August 1637, in *The Correspondence of Roger Williams*, ed. Glenn W. La Fantasie, 2 vols. (Hanover, N.H., 1988), 1:110; *MBR*, 6 September 1642, 2:23. See also Alden T. Vaughan, *New England Frontier: Puritans and Indians, 1620–1675* (Boston, 1965), 55–66; Francis Jennings, *The Invasion of America: Indians, Colonists, and the Cant of Conquest* (Chapel Hill, N.C., 1975), 259–68; Salisbury, *Manitou and Providence*, 225–35.

[6] Williams to Winthrop, 27 May 1638, in Williams, *Correspondence*, 1:157; Jennings, *Invasion*, 258–59.

Thomas Hooker, because they had been "prejudiciall" to Connecticut's interests. The River Colony magistrates, moreover, feared that the Bay Colony agreement, which had allowed the Narragansetts to hunt in the disputed territories, harbor Pequot refugees, and collect Pequot tribute, would directly undermine Connecticut's own claims to the region.[7]

Miantonomo arrived in Hartford on September 20, 1638, to meet with Governor John Haynes and Uncas. A tripartite agreement emerged binding the Mohegans and Narragansetts to "the English inhabitants within the jurisdiction for ye River Connecticut." Uncas and Miantonomo agreed that if one wronged the other, "they shall not presently revenge it, but they are to appeale to ye [Connecticut] English and they are to decide the same." Both sachems agreed "to doe as is by the said English set downe and if one or the other shall refuse soe to doe it shall be lawfull for the English to compel them and to rise and take part if they see cause agaynst ye obstinate or refusing party." Miantonomo and Uncas recognized Connecticut's dominion in southern New England by consenting not to "possess any part of the Pequots country without leave from the English." They divided evenly between them the Pequot refugees and promised to pay to Connecticut an annual tribute in wampum for the Pequots under their protection.[8]

The Treaty of Hartford moved Connecticut firmly toward control of the Pequot territories. The Narragansetts, who either had been promised by the Bay Colony "the free use of the Pequot countrey for their hunting, etc." or expected that Massachusetts would negotiate with Connecticut a revocation of the provision limiting their access to Pequot lands, found themselves outmaneuvered.[9]

Connecticut's support of Uncas, wrote Plymouth's Governor William Bradford, "did much increase his power and augmente his Greatnes, which the Narigansets could not indure to see." Miantonomo and Canonicus, Williams reported, complained often of "the English Partialitie to all the Pequots at Monhiggin," and felt that the infidelity and opportunism of Uncas compared unfavorably with their own longstanding devotion to the English. Uncas had, in fact, ingratiated himself with authorities in the Bay Colony three months before the meeting at Hartford. In June 1638 he had traveled to Boston with a gift of wampum for Governor Winthrop and a promise to accept English resolution of his differences with Miantonomo. Uncas deftly exploited the diplomatic advantages he had garnered during the Pequot War. His contribution to the English war effort in 1637 had been significant, and

---

[7] Hooker to John Winthrop, c. December 1638, *Winthrop Papers*, 4:78–79; Williams to Winthrop, 14 August 1638, in Williams, *Correspondence*, 1:176; Jennings, *Invasion*, 258–59.

[8] "The Hartford Treaty with the Narragansett and the Fenwick Letters," *New England Historical and Genealogical Register* 46 (1892): 356; John W. Deforest, *History of the Indians of Connecticut from the Earliest Known Period to 1850* (Hartford, Conn., 1851), 160.

[9] Roger Williams to John Winthrop, 9 May 1639, in Williams, *Correspondence*, 1:196–97; see also 198, n 5.

for it he had the grudging respect of the New England magistracy. Many in New England remembered that large numbers of Narragansetts, on the other hand, had deserted just before the assault on the Pequot fort.[10]

The Narragansetts consequently felt themselves increasingly isolated in southern New England, aware both that the growing power of Uncas threatened their ambitions in the region and that the Bay Colony was an unreliable ally, more interested in securing title to the Pequot territory than in maintaining their friendship.[11] Miantonomo recognized the delicacy of his diplomatic position and attempted to preserve good relations with the Bay Colony, but events elsewhere in New England left him increasingly disenchanted. In September 1640 Bradford informed Winthrop that "the Narragansett sachem, Miantunnomoh, had sent a great present of wampum to the Mohawks, to aid him against the English." Officials in the Bay put little stock in these rumors, but they did summon Miantonomo to offer an explanation. The call to Boston undoubtedly intensified Miantonomo's hatred of Uncas, the apparent source of the rumor, and according to Winthrop the Narragansett sachem carried "home in his breast, as an injury, the strict terms he was put to both in this, and the satisfaction he was urged to."[12]

Rumors of Narragansett conspiracy continued to circulate. In the summer of 1642 an anonymous "relation" charged Miantonomo with attempting to confederate with Indian bands "upon the maine from the Dutch to the Bay and all Indian sachems from the Eastward." Lion Gardener confirmed these reports much later when he learned from the Montauk sachem Waiandance that Miantonomo planned to destroy the Indian bands friendly to the English and then, "with the Mowquakes and Mowhakes and the Indians beyond the Dutch, and all the Northern and Eastern Indians," fall upon the English and destroy them all, "man and mother's son."[13]

According to Gardener, Miantonomo was urging the Montauks on Long Island, former Pequot tributaries, to recognize the need for a united native response to English settlement. By 1642, he had come to accept the Pequots' earlier bleak assessment of the Indian future in New England. He invited the

[10] William Bradford, *Bradford's History of Plymouth Plantation*, ed. William T. Davis (New York, 1920), 338; Roger Williams to John Winthrop, 21 July 1640, in Williams, *Correspondence*, 1:203; Williams to Winthrop, c. late 1637, in Roger Williams, *Complete Writings*, 7 vols. (New York, 1963), 6:63–65.

[11] John A. Sainsbury, "Miantonomo's Death and New England Politics, 1630–1645," *Rhode Island History* 30 (1971): 117.

[12] John Winthrop, *Winthrop's Journal*, ed. James Kendall Hosmer, 2 vols. (New York, 1908), 7 September 1940, 2:6; 9 November 1640, 2:14–15.

[13] "Relation of the Plott," *MHS Coll*, 3d ser., 3 (1833): 161–64; *Winthrop Papers*, 1 September 1642, 2:74; Lion Gardener, "Lieft Lion Gardener His Relation of the Pequot Warres," *MHS Coll*, 3d ser., 3 (1833): 151–52; Marion Fisher Ales, "A History of the Indians on Montauk, Long Island," in *The History and Archaeology of the Montauk Indians*, ed. Gayenell Stone Levine (Lexington, Mass., 1979), 56; Sainsbury, "Miantonomo's Death," 117; Neal Salisbury, "Indians and Colonists in Southern New England after the Pequot War: An Uneasy Balance," in *The Pequots in Southern New England: The Fall and Rise of an American Indian Nation*, ed. Laurence Hauptman and James D. Wherry (Norman, Okla., 1990), 87.

Montauks to be "brethren and friends" with the Narragansetts, "for so are we all Indians as the English are, and say brother to one another." English settlement had devastated and divided native communities. Unless they came together, he warned, "we shall all be gone shortly, for you know our fathers had plenty of deer and skins, our plains were full of deer, as also our woods, and of turkies, and our coves of fish and fowl." The English, having taken their land, "with scythes cut down the grass and with axes fell the trees; their cows and horses eat the grass, and their hogs spoil our clam banks, and we shall all be starved." Miantonomo's appeal testified clearly to the pressure placed on Indian subsistence systems by expanding English settlement, a dangerous environmental and ecological assault on native ways of life. Waiandance, however, who only five years before had freed himself from Pequot overlordship, had little interest in replacing it with Narragansett dominance. Attempting to maintain his freedom of movement, he refused to join Miantonomo and then revealed "the Plott" to Gardener at Saybrook.[14]

Waiandance's report so terrified the colonists that Connecticut, Massachusetts, and Plymouth all placed themselves on a war footing. The Bay Colony ordered Miantonomo to Boston to face charges that he intended "to posesse himselfe of the Pecoits & theire country," that he had "drawn the Indians of Long Island, Block Island, & other pts thereabouts, being under the protection of the English, to pay him tribute," and that he harbored "divers Pecquits wch are runaway from us," or at least "countenance[d] & allow[ed] the Niantick sachem so to doe."[15]

Miantonomo blamed Uncas for the rumors and apparently convinced the Bay Colony magistrates of his innocence, for Winthrop wrote that "all this might come out of the enmity which had been between Miantunnomoh and Onkus, who continually sought to discredit each other with the English." Winthrop wrote to the more bellicose Connecticut council "to dissuade them from going forth" against the Narragansetts. "Upon receipt of this our answer," he noted, "they forbare to enter into war, but (it seemed) unwillingly, and as not well pleased with us."[16]

Though Miantonomo demonstrated for the English "good understanding in the principles of justice and equity, and ingenuity withal," it is likely that he had indeed engaged the neighboring Algonquian bands. His target, however, was not the English but the Mohegans. In the spring of 1643 Uncas accused Miantonomo of hiring a Pequot warrior to assassinate him. Before the Bay magistrates, Miantonomo and the accused Pequot vigorously denied Uncas's charges, asserting that Uncas had faked a wound in order to impli-

[14] Gardener, "His Relation," 154; John A. Strong, "The Imposition of Colonial Jurisdiction over the Montauk Indians on Long Island," *Ethnohistory* 41 (1994): 562.

[15] *MBR*, 6 and 8 September 1642, 2:23–28; *PCR*, 27 September 1642, 2:46; Winthrop, *Journal*, 1 September 1642, 2:74.

[16] Winthrop, *Journal*, 8 September 1642, 2:75–76, 79.

cate Miantonomo. The Bay Colony magistrates were not entirely convinced, but they did release Miantonomo and the Pequot.

By July the Narragansetts and Mohegans had gone to war. Sequassen, a River Indian allied with the Narragansetts and jealous of Mohegan over-lordship, attacked Uncas. The Mohegan sachem retaliated by killing seven or eight of Sequassen's men, wounding a dozen more, and destroying their houses. Miantonomo then inquired of Governor Winthrop at Boston whether they "would not be offended, if he made war upon Onkus," fulfill-ing, as he thought, his obligation to seek Puritan approval before attacking the Mohegans. Winthrop replied that "if Onkus had done him or his friends wrong and would not give satisfaction, we should leave him to take his own course."[17] Winthrop withdrew his qualified endorsement of Miantonomo's plan shortly thereafter, when word arrived that the Narragansett sachem, in June 1643, had murdered the Pequot suspected in the attempted assassina-tion of Uncas. "Fearing that his owne treachery would be discovered," Winthrop wrote, Miantonomo "stopped the Pequot's mouth by cutting of his head." With this act Miantonomo demonstrated his involvement in the plot to assassinate Uncas and forfeited whatever credibility he had retained among the Puritan leadership.[18]

The aggressiveness of the Mohegans and Narragansetts in pursuing their own objectives convinced metropolitan magistrates of the necessity for a union to oversee Indian and frontier affairs in New England more effi-ciently. The Confederation of New England, formed in 1643, defined itself as "a firme and perpetuall league of ffrendship and amytie for offence and defence, mutuall advice and succour upon all just occasions both for pre-serving & propagating the truth and liberties of the Gospell and for their own mutuall safety and wellfare." Eight Commissioners of the United Colonies, drawn equally from Plymouth, Connecticut, New Haven, and Massachusetts Bay, would determine "how all the Jurisdiccons may carry it towards the Indians, that they neither grow insolent nor be injured wthout due sattisfaccon, lest war break in upon the Confederates through such mis-carryages."[19]

The commissioners dealt immediately with the Narragansett-Mohegan war. Early in August 1643, Miantonomo, with one thousand warriors, "set upon Onkus before he could be provided for defence." Uncas emerged the victor, despite being outnumbered, and in the ensuing rout captured Miantonomo.[20] Uncas deposited his prisoner at Hartford, and waited "till

[17] Ibid., July 1643, 2:131–32; Vaughan, *New England Frontier*, 162–63.

[18] John Winthrop, *A Declaration of Former Passages and Proceedings betwixt the English and the Narrowgansetts with Their Confederation, wherein the Grounds and Justice of the En-suing Warre Are Opened and Cleared* (Boston, 1645), 2–3; William Hubbard, *A Narrative of the Troubles with the Indians in New England* (Boston, 1677), 6.

[19] Bradford, *History*, 382; *RUC*, 1:3–4, 6; see also *MBR*, 27 September 1642, 2:31.

[20] Winthrop, *Journal*, 6 August 1643, 2:134.

he might receive advice from the English how to proceed against him for sundry treacherous attempts against his life." Considering Miantonomo's

> ambitious designes to make himself universall Sagomore or Governor of all these parts of the Countrey, of his treacherous plotts by guifts to engage all the Indians at once to cutt of the whole body of the English in these parts wch were further confirmed by the Indians Generall preparacons, messages, & sundry insolencies and outrages by them committed against the English and such Indians as were subjects or friends to the English,

the commissioners concluded that "Uncas cannot be safe while Myantenemo lives."[21] Not only had Miantonomo, in the commissioners' eyes, violated the pact signed at Hartford in 1638, but he also stood accused of plotting against the English, of selling lands on the Shawomet neck to the heretical followers of Samuel Gorton, and killing the Pequot he had allegedly hired to assassinate Uncas.[22]

Consequently, the Commissioners ruled that Uncas might "justly put such a false & blood-thirsty enemie to death." They warned Uncas "that in the manner of his death all mercy and moderacon be shewed," and that the execution must take place in Uncas's "owne Jurisdiccon, not in the English plantacons." Miantonomo would be put to death by a Mohegan sachem, not an English court. English observers would accompany Uncas to witness the execution, and Hartford would supply the Mohegan sachem with protection "against any present fury or assault of the Nanohiggunsetts or any other" seeking to avenge Miantonomo's death.[23]

The commissioners' decision to permit Uncas to execute Miantonomo, however distasteful today, clearly accorded with the provisions of the Treaty of Hartford, negotiated five years before. Uncas, after capturing the Narragansett sachem, had turned him over to the English before taking any action, as required by the treaty. Miantonomo had aggressively pursued his own interests along the New England frontier but, unlike the more accommodating Uncas, had challenged the power of the united English in the region and disrupted the peaceful and orderly extension of English influence in southern New England. Miantonomo openly threatened English metropolitan control of the frontier, providing the commissioners with cause to "take part ... agaynst ye obstinate or refusing party."[24]

Uncas, who with an English escort led Miantonomo into the woods, ordered his brother to club the Narragansett sachem to death. A blow to the back of the head ended Miantonomo's life late in the summer of 1643.

---

[21] *RUC*, September 1643, 1:10–12; Bradford, *History*, 389.

[22] Winthrop, *Journal*, August 1643, 2:135; Sydney V. James, *Colonial Rhode Island: A History* (New York, 1975), 65; Sainsbury, "Miantonomo's Death," 118.

[23] *RUC*, September 1643; 1:11–12, 15; Winthrop, *Journal*, August 1643, 2:135.

[24] "Hartford Treaty," 355.

The execution of Miantonomo demonstrated the determination of the Commissioners of the United Colonies to secure English dominion along the frontier. At the same time, however, they still hoped to bring the reformed religion and English civility to New England natives. Late in July 1649 the Puritan-controlled Parliament in England passed an act "for the promoting and propagating of the Gospel of Jesus Christ in New England." The act created "The President and Society for the Propagation of the Gospel in New England."[25] The preamble to the society's charter recognized the early successes of individuals within the colonies in ministering to the Indians; many natives, through these efforts, had forsaken "their accustomed Charms and Sorceries, and other Satanical Delusions" to call "upon the Name of the Lord, and give great testimony of the power of God, drawing them from death and darkness, into the life and light of the glorious Gospel of Jesus Christ." New Englanders, however, had not undertaken this work on a large enough scale to effect the wholesale conversion of the New England Indians.[26]

The Society for the Propagation of the Gospel (SPG) therefore raised money in England and in the colonies to underwrite missionary activity in America. The Commissioners of the United Colonies would administer these funds, direct the activity, and report to the society on the progress of Indian education.[27]

In addition, the commissioners promoted projects on a smaller scale designed to "civilize" the New England Algonquians, such as Daniel Gookin's plan to allow "some encurragement towards the Imploying of the Indians att Naticke in spinning or other manufactory":

> Such Indians as shalbe willing to putt theire Children apprentices for convenient time proportionable to there age to any Godly English within the United Collonies with the consent of the Commissioners . . . shall receive yearly during theire Childrens apprenticeship one coate out of the Corporation stocke or from their masters besides meate, drinke and clothing convenient for theire Children whilest they continew with theire Masters.[28]

[25] C. H. Firth and R. S. Rait, eds., *Acts and Ordinances of the Interregnum, 1642–1660*, 3 vols. (Abingdon, England, 1982), 2:197–98. See also William Kellaway, *The New England Company, 1649–1776: Missionary Society to the American Indians* (New York, 1962), 83; Daniel Gookin, *Historical Collections of the Indians of New England*, rpt. (New York, 1972), 20.

[26] Firth and Rait, *Acts and Ordinances*, 197. For these early efforts, see "The Day Breaking, If Not the Sun-Rising of the Gospel with the Indians in New England (1647)"; Thomas Shepard, "The Clear Sun-Shine of the Gospel Breaking Forth upon the Indians in New England (1648)"; and Edward Winslow, "The Glorious Progresse of the Gospell amongst the Indians in New England (1649)," all in *MHS Coll*, 3d ser., 4 (1833).

[27] George Parker Winship, ed., *The New England Company of 1649 and John Eliot* (Boston, 1920), lxviii; Firth and Rait, *Acts and Ordinances*, 2:199; Commissioners of the United Colonies to the New England Company, September 1659, *RUC*, 2:217; Charles Chauncey to Robert Boyle, 2 October 1664, in *Some Correspondence between the Governors and Treasurers of the New England Company in London and the Commissioners of the United Colonies in America*, ed. John W. Ford (New York, 1970), 9; Kellaway, *New England Company*, 62, 75. In 1661, Parliament rechartered the Society for the Propagation of the Gospel as the New England Company. See Kellaway, *New England Company*, 41–45.

[28] *RUC*, September 1662, 2:280; September 1660, 2:251.

While engaging in projects designed to bring Christianity and civility to the Indians, the commissioners also needed to secure metropolitan dominion over the Anglo-American frontier by successfully managing relations between Indians and whites. To do so, they took care that no colonist sold arms or ammunition to the natives, or repaired weapons in the Indians' possession. They also hoped to reduce the likelihood of disputes between Indians and the frontier population by calling upon colonial governors to prevent "all Injuriouse carriages" toward the Indians and by forcing colonists to take responsibility for the ranging of their livestock and to fence both their own and the Indians' land.[29]

The commissioners could exert only limited control over Indian affairs, however. The New England Confederation initially promised to bring order to a chaotic situation where individual colonies aggressively pursued their interests at the expense of both their English neighbors and Native Americans. Yet the Confederation itself was weak: the commissioners met only once a year, in September, unless extraordinary occasions arose, and were largely powerless to deal with issues for which no consensus existed. Their responsibilities, then, were limited to dealing with crises originating in the individual colonies; they lacked power to dictate and enforce a uniform, metropolitan English policy toward the Indians that would prevent those crises from developing in the first place. This left unresolved critical problems that would eventually demand royal intervention.

The day-to-day administration of relations between Indians and whites remained with the individual colonies. Like the commissioners, colonial governments worked to limit contact between Indians and frontier whites. By attempting to regulate intercultural relations, they hoped to reduce the likelihood of an outbreak of violence that could jeopardize their security.[30]

The magistrates of the individual colonies limited access to the trade in wampum and furs by appointing "truck masters" and setting up licensing procedures. They also established trading houses to secure metropolitan oversight of frontier trade. They tried to curb the potentially deadly trade in arms and ammunition; during the 1640s all the colonies passed laws threatening severe punishment for those who supplied Indians with weapons. They prohibited Indians from handling English weapons within their settlements, and they outlawed the French and Dutch arms trade.[31]

In addition to English weaponry, metropolitan New Englanders saw alcohol as a serious threat to frontier security. The Indians, wrote one observer,

---

[29] *RUC*, September 1644, 1:21–23; July 1649, 1:143.

[30] *RICR*, 7 July 1640, 1:107–8; *PCR*, 11:183; *NHR*, 22 March 1654, 2:67. *CR*, 26 August 1642, 1:73; 3 June 1644, 1:106; 6 October 1652, 1:235.

[31] *CR*, 5 April 1638, 1:20; 11 June 1640, 1:52; 8 September 1642, 1:74; 14 October 1642, 1:79; 25 October 1644, 1:113–14; 18 September 1649, 1:197–98. *RICR*, 6 November 1638, 1:62–63; May 1647, 1:155, 2:29; 28 October 1652, 1:245–46. *MBR*, 2 June 1641, 1:322–23; 1 October 1645, 2:136–37; 9 April 1646, 1:138; 21 June 1650, 3:208–9; 6 May 1657, 3:424. *PCR*, 4 June 1639, 11:32; 7 December 1641, 1:152. *NHR*, 24 February 1645, 1:206.

"will part with all they have to their bare skins for [rum], being perpetually drunk with it, as long as it is to be had, it hath killed many of them." Thus instead of carrying "the knowledge of Christianitie," to the Indians, "we have taught them to commit the beastly and crying sins of our nation, for a little profit." The trade in rum, wrote another, was carried on by "ill-disposed people" who, "for filthy lucre's sake, do sell unto the Indians secretly." As a result, "that greate & crying sinn of Drunkenes reignes amongst them, to the greate dishonor of God & hazard of the lives and peace boath of the English & Indyans."[32]

When Indians obtained liquor, by English standards they drank to excess, producing displays that frightened English observers. Alcohol produced a potential for violent conflict along the frontier and created opportunities as well for the unscrupulous to defraud intoxicated Indians. All the New England colonies, consequently, passed acts severely punishing whites who provided Indians with alcohol. Drunken Indians were punished too, and magistrates permitted only licensed traders to sell alcohol.[33]

Colonial governments also tried to protect Indians from white land hunger by outlawing purchases of land directly from the New England bands. Requiring government permission, they hoped, would prevent aggressive frontiersmen from pressuring Indians into sales and eliminate the confusion produced when more than one group of Englishmen bought the same tract. The system worked well within the individual colonies, but broke down quickly when competing colonies authorized their inhabitants to purchase lands claimed by their English rivals.[34]

The laws passed by the New England magistrates were designed to consolidate metropolitan control on both sides of the frontier. Colonial governments punished Indians who violated English law but also penalized their own citizens for offenses committed upon Indians or their property. They worked to stabilize relations between the colonial population and their Indian tributaries by requiring these bands to "declare whoe is their Sachem or Chiefe," thus firmly establishing, for English purposes, the locus of responsibility within the tributary bands. In short, the New England colonies worked individually to extend their dominion over Indian bands within their territories and along the periphery of their settlements, hoping to centralize their control over the conduct of Indian-white relations.[35]

[32] John Josselyn, "An Account of Two Voyages to New England," *MHS Coll*, 3d ser., 3 (1833): 304; Gookin, *Historical Collections*, 11; CR, 3 October 1654, 1:263. The best statement on Indian drinking is Peter Mancall, *Deadly Medicine: Indians and Alcohol in Early America* (Ithaca, N.Y., 1995).

[33] PCR, 11:54, 184, 209, 235. MBR, 11 November 1654, 3:369; 6 May 1657, 3:425. CR, 4 October 1660, 1:354. RICR, 1:274, 279, 307–8, 413–14, 2:500.

[34] NHR, 4 January 1640, 1:27. PCR, 6 June 1643, 11:41. RICR, 4 November 1651, 1:236; 5 November 1658, 1: 403.

[35] CR, 5 April 1638, 1:19. For the operation of this process in one colony, see James P. Ronda, "Red and White at the Bench: Indians and the Law in Plymouth Colony, 1620–1691," *Essex Institute Historical Collections* 110 (1974): 200–215.

Provincial magistrates also passed laws and made provision for the acculturation and conversion of "those poore, lost, naked sonnes of Adam." The subjection of the Indians to English law and their conversion to English Christianity were tasks central to the metropolitan New World vision. The establishment of "Praying Towns" in the Massachusetts Bay Colony, beginning in 1651 with the founding of Natick under the supervision of John Eliot, combined both objectives in one program. Bay Colony magistrates expected the Algonquian bands to conform to Puritan proscriptions against blasphemy and idolatry, serious crimes whether committed by Indian or Englishman. Those practicing native religion within the colony or performing "outward worship of their false gods, or to ye devill," would be fined. These laws, "necessary & holesome" and intended "to reduce ym to civility of life," would be made known to the Indians through interpreters and ministers "chosen by ye elders of the churches every yeare, at ye Cort of Election."[36]

By the eve of the Algonquian rising in 1675, fourteen Praying Towns had been established in Massachusetts. At the same time, on Martha's Vineyard and the neighboring islands, the Thomas Mayhews, son and father, directed an even larger program of Indian conversion. With only a small English presence on the island, and largely insulated from the more disruptive elements of white society, the Indians on the Vineyard converted in large numbers after the 1650s.[37]

Puritan missionaries certainly saw little to admire in the social norms and cultural values of the neighboring Algonquian bands. Still, they believed that the Indians were reasoning and rational human beings who, upon recognizing their own cultural inferiority, would willingly embrace English standards of civility. Thomas Mayhew Jr., for example, celebrated "the notable reason, judgment, and capacitie that God hath given unto many of them; as also their zealous enquiring after true happinesse."[38]

Eliot proposed a thoroughgoing transformation of traditional native lifeways:

> The order of proceeding with them is first to gather them together from their scattered course of life, to cohabitation and civill order and Government, and

---

[36] CR, 14 September 1654, 1:265. MBR, 14 October 1651, 3:246; 4 November 1646, 2:177–78.

[37] Alden T. Vaughan and Daniel K. Richter, "Crossing the Cultural Divide: Indians and New Englanders, 1605–1763," *Proceedings of the American Antiquarian Society* 90 (1980): 32–33; James P. Ronda, "Generations of Faith: The Christian Indians of Martha's Vineyard," *WMQ*, 3d ser., 37 (1981): 370; William S. Simmons, "Conversion from Indian to Puritan," *New England Quarterly* 52 (1979): 218.

[38] Quoted in Winslow, "Glorious Progress," 77. See also John Eliot to Thomas Shepard, 24 September 1647, in Shepard, "Clear Sun-Shine," 59. For more critical discussions of Puritan missions, see Jennings, *Invasion*, 230; and Neal Salisbury, "Red Puritans: The Praying Towns of Massachusetts Bay and John Eliot," *WMQ*, 3d ser., 31 (1974): 29.

then to forme them (the Lord having fitted them) into visible Church-state, for the guidance whereof, I have instructed them, that they should look onely into the Scriptures, and out of the word of God fetch all their Wisedome, Lawes, and Government, and so shall they be the Lords' people, and the Lord above shall Reigne over them, and governe them in all things by the word of his mouth.

To effect this dramatic change, Eliot proscribed native customs and practices that he considered offensive, from premarital sex to killing "their lice be-tweene their teeth."[39]

Certainly many Algonquians found these strictures both needlessly op-pressive and absurd. As English pressure on native communities mounted to-ward the middle of the seventeenth century, however, a small but significant number of Indians found attractive the spiritual and material benefits accru-ing from a close association with English ministers. Eliot, for instance, pro-vided converts with English goods, which he hoped would effect change in native culture and aid in the "civilization" and "Christianization" of the In-dians. Native women who learned to spin would no longer serve as drudges, in Puritan eyes, to their lazy husbands. Native men who learned to farm and fence their fields took a huge step toward civility. English goods and tech-nologies provided Christian Indians with a means to adapt to a rapidly changing world in which an expanding white population altered the hunt-ing potential of the New England interior and occupied the choicest tracts of arable land, thus challenging traditional native ways of life.[40]

Many Indians converted for expedient purposes. Although non-Christian sachems often opposed the work of missionaries on the grounds that settle-ment in the Praying Towns effectively freed Indian converts from their trib-utary obligations, some converts saw in cooperation with English mission-aries a chance to expand their power in native communities. Waban, for instance, through these means rose from obscurity to become the principal native leader in Natick.[41]

In Waban's and other cases, however, conversion to Christianity seems to have been tied to native concepts of power, the efficacy of ritual, and the In-dians' perception of the relative strength of natives and Englishmen. Waban professed that he had "considered what the English do" only after a "great sikness" killed many Indians but left the English unscathed. Totherswamp, another convert, reported thinking in his heart "that if my friends should die, and I live, I then would pray to God." Soon after, he confessed, "God so wrought, that they did almost all die, few of them left; and then my heart feared, and I thought, that now I will pray unto God."[42] Similarly, the

---

[39] John Eliot, "Strength out of Weaknesse," *MHS Coll*, 3d ser., 4 (1833): 171; "Day Break-ing," 20.

[40] Harold Van Lonkhuyzen, "A Reappraisal of the Praying Indians: Acculturation, Conver-sion, and Identity at Natick, 1646–1730," *New England Quarterly* 63 (1990): 407–9.

[41] Ibid., 401–2.

[42] *MHS Coll*, 3d ser., 4 (1834): 231, 229.

younger Thomas Mayhew recalled the story of Ieogiscat, a sixty-year-old Indian on Martha's Vineyard,

> who was sick of a consuming disease, insomuch as the *Indian pawwawes* gave
> him over for a dead man: Upon which resolution of all the *Pawwawes* in the Is-
> land, the sick distressed Heathen upon a Lords day came unto mee . . . to desire
> me to pray unto God for him: And so when I had by reasoning with him con-
> vinced him of the weaknesse and wickednesse of the *Pawwaws* power; and that
> if health were to be found, it must be had from him that gave life, and breath,
> and all things; I commended this case unto the Lord, whereof he rejoyced, gave
> me thanks, and he speedily recovered unto his former strength.[43]

Such encounters planted in the minds of some Indians the seeds of doubt, a creeping suspicion that traditional religious practices no longer were adequate to secure the sacred power necessary to maintain native communities in an atmosphere of rapid and rending change. Indians in the vicinity of the Praying Towns debated vigorously the consequences of conversion to Christianity, some angrily and nativistically laying "the cause of all their wants, sicknesses, and death, upon their departing from their old heathenish ways," others seeing in Christianity a superior source of spiritual power. During the winter of 1649–50 Eliot reported, "It pleased God to worke wonderfully for the Indians, who call upon God in preserving them from the smal Pox, when their prophane Neighbours were cutt off by it."[44]

Yet even though some Indians found important sources of strength in Christianity, the number of converts remained relatively small. Eliot attributed the meager harvest to the necessity of putting first "flesh and sinewes unto these dry bones." The Spaniards, he wrote, had forced Indians to convert, and French Jesuits "would hire them to it by giving them coates and shirts." By following these tactics, he argued, "wee could have gathered many hundreds, yea thousands it may bee by this time, into the name of Churches; but wee have not learnt as yet that art of coyning Christians, or putting Christs name and image upon copper mettle."[45]

Despite the enthusiasm for their projects in Old England, and the support of the colonial governments, Eliot and other apostles to the Indians found that neighboring English settlements seldom shared their missionary zeal. "Our poor Indians," Eliot wrote in 1657, "are much molested in most places, in their proceedings in way of civility." Many settlers had little patience with

---

[43] Quoted in Winslow, "Glorious Progresse," 77.

[44] Mayhew quoted in Henry Whitfield, "The Light Appearing More and More towards the Perfect Day," *MHS Coll*, 3d ser., 4 (1834): 110; Eliot, "Strength out of Weaknesse," 165. The foregoing discussion draws much from Gregory Evans Dowd, *A Spirited Resistance: The North American Indian Struggle for Unity, 1745–1815* (Baltimore, Md., 1992), chap. 1.

[45] "Day Breaking," 14–15; John Eliot to Richard Baxter, 7 October 1657, in *Some Unpublished Correspondence of the Rev. Richard Baxter and the Rev. John Eliot, "The Apostle to the American Indians," 1656–1682*, ed. F. J. Powicke (Manchester, England, 1931), 22–23.

Indians, Christian or not, and in the decades after the Pequot War their land hunger overcame the original religious fervor of New England's founding generation. William Leverich, a minister at Sandwich in Plymouth, argued that the growing frontier population posed "a great stumbling Block" in his efforts to convert the Indians. "It is to be lamented," he wrote in 1651, "that . . . those looser sort of *English*" maintained little interest in their own religion, providing a poor example for the natives. These Englishmen, "rejecting of all Churches and Ordinances by a new cunning," Leverich believed, were "one of the last but most pernicious plot of the Devill to undermine all Religion, and introduce all Athiesme and profaneness."[46]

To civilize and Christianize the Indians, Puritan ministers needed government assistance, and magistrates responded when "unruly and disobedient persons" undermined metropolitan objectives along the frontier. But magistrates and ministers continually faced challenges from settlers unsympathetic to their policies and harshly intent upon extracting a livelihood from the thin New England soil.

The settlement and expansion of the town of Rehoboth, in Plymouth, illustrates these challenges. Relations between the Wampanoag bands originally inhabiting the region and the setters at Rehoboth were tense. Wampanoag villagers complained of beatings, theft, and abuse suffered at the hands of Rehoboth settlers, and the Plymouth magistrates intervened often to punish colonists for offenses committed upon the Indians. In the spring of 1655, for example, the Plymouth court punished John Woodcocke and Adonijah Morris for kidnapping and holding hostage a Wampanoag child "in lue of a debt . . . ought him" by the child's father. The court later convicted Peter Hunt, also of Rehoboth, of having "attempted the chastity of an Indian woman, by offering violence to her."[47]

The inability or unwillingness of the settlers to prevent their livestock from ranging in Indian fields proved the most serious and longstanding source of tension. The Wampanoags frequently complained to the provincial court "of great and unsufferable wronges don in theire corn by the horse and other cattle of the inhabitants of Rehoboth." The repeated orders by Plymouth magistrates for the Rehoboth settlers to maintain their fences, to erect pounds for holding stray animals, and to compensate Indians for their losses failed to reduce tensions, because cases of trespass were tried usually in town courts, where Indians had trouble collecting damages.[48]

---

[46] Eliot to Humphrey Atherton, 4 June 1657, *MHS Coll*, 1st ser., 2 (1793): 9; Leverich quoted in Henry Whitfield, comp., "Strength out of Weakness; Or, a Glorious Manifestation of the Further Progresse of the Gospel among the Indians of New England (1652)," *MHS Coll*, 3d ser., 4 (1834), 180–81.

[47] *PCR*, 6 March 1655, 3:174; 6 December 1659, 3:180.

[48] *PCR*, 3 July 1656, 3:106; 7 December 1652, 3:21; 3 June 1657, 3:119–20; 7 June 1659, 3:167; 13 June 1660, 3:192; 11:208–9, 227–28; See also Leonard Bliss, *The History of Rehoboth* (Boston, 1836), 44.

That the Wampanoags and Plymouth remained at peace was largely due to the longstanding bond of friendship between William Bradford and the sachem Massasoit, which dated back to 1621. By 1660, however, both men were dead, and a new and less tolerant generation occupied positions of leadership in both societies. Demographic growth and territorial expansion fostered an endemic instability along the frontier which metropolitan New Englanders could not control. The English colonies clashed as frequently with each other as they did with natives as they extended their territorial claims, producing tangled and contentious land disputes. As the orthodox Puritan colonies sought to carve up Rhode Island, moreover, even more complicated controversies developed.

The different strategies of land use employed by New England Algonquians and English settlers only exacerbated these tensions. Expansion brought the two populations into competition as they sought to control identical tracts of land but to exploit the resources there in different ways. The settlers used swamps and marshes for grazing cattle and allowed their hogs to root for food on coastal and estuarine mud flats. To natives, the wetlands were the source of raw material for native basketry, and the mud flats provided habitat for the shellfish that constituted an important element of their diet. As English settlers cleared the uplands, moreover, they eliminated shelter for wild animals and so altered the hunting potential of the region. And, as in Virginia, free-ranging English livestock frequently ravaged native cornfields, damaging a staple of the coastal Algonquian diet. When Indians killed English livestock found in their fields, and when English settlers retaliated, intercultural relations grew increasingly bitter. [49]

In short, native subsistence patterns and horticultural resources, dependent upon access to a limited supply of highly productive soil, were increasingly threatened at Rehoboth and elsewhere as Algonquian bands came into more and more frequent contact with an aggressive and expanding English frontier population.

II

The magistrates of the individual colonies and the Commissioners of the United Colonies failed to maintain order on the English side of the frontier and enjoyed no more success in controlling the Narragansetts and their al-

[49] Thomas, *Maelstrom*, 117–18, 120, 134, 197, 261; Peter A. Thomas, "Contrastive Subsistence Strategies and Land Use as Factors for Understanding Indian-White Relations in New England," *Ethnohistory* 23 (1976): 14; M. K. Bennett, "The Food Economy of the New England Indians, 1605–1675," *Journal of Political Economy* 63 (1955): 369–97; Virginia DeJohn Anderson, "King Philip's Herds: Indians, Colonists, and the Problem of Livestock in Early New England," *WMQ*, 3d ser., 51 (1994): 607–8. For supporting examples, see George Sheldon, *A History of Deerfield, Massachusetts*, 2 vols. (Deerfield, Mass., 1895), 1:75; J. H. Temple, *History of North Brookfield, Massachusetts* (North Brookfield, Mass., 1887), 70; "Records of the Particular Court of Connecticut, 1639–1663," *Collections of the Connecticut Historical Society* 23 (1928): 208; *Province and Court Records of Maine*, 6 vols. (Portland, Maine, 1928–75), 1:2.

lies, now implacably hostile to the Mohegans. Pessicus, "a young man of about 20," succeeded Miantonomo as Narragansett sachem. Neither he nor Canonicus had Miantonomo's leadership skills, and their weakness allowed Ninigret, the sachem of the allied Niantics, to assume a leading role in Narragansett affairs. Ninigret shared with Pessicus and Canonicus a desire to avenge Miantonomo's death.[50]

In October 1643 Pessicus sent wampum to Winthrop, desiring friendship "and withal that we would not aid Onkus against him, whom he intended to make war upon in revenge of his brother's death." Pessicus also accused Uncas of accepting a ransom for Miantonomo's life and demanded restitution. Winthrop accepted the gift but refused to allow the Narragansetts to attack the Mohegans. He then told the Narragansett sachem that even "if they sent us 1000 fathom of wampum and 1000 skins, yet we would not do that which we judged to be unjust, viz. to desert Onkus."[51]

Frustrated by the commissioners' steadfast determination to support Uncas, their "inhumane & cruell adversary," the Narragansetts acted to free themselves from the heavy-handed overlordship of the United Colonies. With the assistance of Samuel Gorton, who had his own reasons for undermining the hegemony of the United Colonies in New England, Pessicus and Canonicus in 1644 gave

> ourselves, peoples, lands, rights, inheritances, and possessions whatsoever, in ourselves and our heires successively for ever, unto the protection, care, and government of that worthy and royal Prince, Charles, King of Great Britaine."

They then wrote to the Massachusetts General Court as "subjects now . . . unto the same King and State yourselves are," declaring that in any "great matter" between them "neither yourselves nor we are to be judges; and both of us are to have recourse, and repair unto that honorable and just Government."[52]

The Narragansetts' direct submission to crown authority threatened the Puritan experiment and challenged the increasing autonomy of the United Colonies—especially Massachusetts Bay, which quickly sent messengers to the Narragansetts demanding an explanation. After Canonicus let the ambassadors stand in the rain for two hours, Pessicus determinedly announced his intention to wage war against the Mohegans. The Narragansetts would not allow Massachusetts or the United Colonies unchallenged dominion in southern New England.[53]

---

[50] Winthrop, *Journal*, 12 October 1643, 2:143; James, *Colonial Rhode Island*, 81–82; Timothy J. Sehr, "Ninigret's Tactics of Accommodation: Indian Diplomacy in New England, 1637–1675," *Rhode Island History* 36 (1977): 46.

[51] Winthrop, *Journal*, 12 October 1643, 2:143; February 1644, 2:157. For Pessicus's charges against Uncas, see *RUC*, 1:17, 2:415.

[52] *RUC*, 2:415; *RICR*, 1:134, 137. On the Gortonites, see James, *Colonial Rhode Island*, 28–32.

[53] Sehr, "Ninigret's Tactics," 46.

In June 1644 Narragansett warriors fell upon the Mohegans, killing "six of Onkus' men and five women." By the next spring, Roger Williams could report that "the Flames of Warr" were raging "next dore to us." The Narragansetts fought with a "Spirit of Desperacion . . . resolved to revenge the Death of their Prince and recover their ransome for his Life." In May 1645 an army of Narragansetts crossed into Mohegan territory. Both sides suffered heavy casualties, but the Narragansetts withdrew after a day-long battle. Again, the commissioners sent messengers to order Pessicus "to desist from warr upon Uncas."[54]

Pessicus received the messengers "with scorne and contempt" and announced that he would "have no peace without Uncas his head." If the English assisted Uncas, he "would procure the Mowakes against them," and together

> they would lay the English cattell on heapes as heigh as their houses, that no English man should stir out of his doore to pisse, but he should be killed.[55]

At an emergency meeting in July of 1645, the commissioners prepared for war against the Narragansetts. "The eyes of other Indians under the protection of Massachusetts and not at all engaged in this quarrell," the commissioners declared, "are . . . fastened upon the English with strict observacion, in what manner and measure they provide for Uncas his safety: If hee perish they will charge it upon them who might have preserved him, and no Indians will trust the English if they now broke engagements, either in the present or succeeding generations." Such a failure, continued William Bradford, would "expose the colonies to contempte and danger from the barbarians." Under so serious a threat to metropolitan dominion in New England, the commissioners believed they could not "but exercise force, when no other means will prevaile to reduce the Narigansets and their confederats to a more just and sober temper." Peace would be secured only when "some of ye chiefe Sachims deliver their Sonnes as Hostages or that some considerate part of the Countrey be yielded to the English for plantacons wherein there may be forts built by the English and mayntayned (at least in part) by a tribute from the Narrohiggansets."[56]

The Pequot War had taught the Narragansetts to respect English military strength. In August 1645 Pessicus and his cousin Mixanno arrived in Boston and signed a humiliating treaty of peace. The commissioners told the sachems that "the charge trouble & disturbance wch they had brought upon the Colonies by their unjust proceedings was great besides the damage Un-

---

[54] Winthrop, *Journal*, 23 June 1644, 2:172; Roger Williams to John Winthrop, 23 June 1645, in Williams, *Correspondence*, 1:225; *MBR*, 14 May 1645, 2:117; *NHR*, 20 June 1645, 1:167–68.

[55] Bradford, *History*, 391–92, 395–97; *RUC*, 1:54.

[56] *RUC*, 1:39, 55; Bradford, *History*, 397–98.

cas had sustayned." They required the Narragansetts to keep peace in the future with Uncas, to restore to the Mohegan sachem the captives they had taken, to pay a fine "of two thousand fathome of good white wampum," and to turn over hostages to the English as well. The treaty accomplished little, however, and it is clear that neither Ninigret nor Pessicus considered themselves subjects of the United Colonies. Their diplomacy was carried on with the continuing intent of avenging the death of Miantonomo and dislodging the Mohegans from the Pequot lands, in defiance of the directives of the United Colonies.[57]

The commissioners continued to fear the possibility of Narragansett alliance with neighboring Indians, particularly the Mohawks. Narragansett control of the coastal wampum supply, they believed, provided Ninigret and Pessicus with the means to secure Mohawk assistance—and the Narragansetts had, in fact, sent annual gifts of wampum to the Mohawks, probably to secure access to Dutch traders at Fort Orange.[58] Fear of Narragansett conspiracy intensified in 1646 when the commissioners uncovered a plot contrived by the River Indian sachem Sequassen to kill three Connecticut magistrates and pin the blame for the murders on Uncas.[59] Sequassen refused to respond to the commissioners' demand that he appear before them, so they sent Uncas to capture him for trial. Though the Connecticut magistrates acquitted Sequassen, he nonetheless planned to settle his score against Uncas. The involvement of the Narragansetts in this plot, the commissioners wrote in 1649, "was beyond all Rationall Deniall."[60]

The Narragansetts paid little attention to the coercive treaty of 1645. They neither turned over the hostages required of them nor paid the wampum demanded by the English. The Narragansetts insisted that their inability to pay the fine resulted from the defection of Caushawashott (Harmon Garrett), a wealthy half-Niantic, half-Pequot tributary, to the protection of Connecticut. The commissioners, however, believed that instead of paying their fines the Narragansetts had "by wampum hired the Mowhackes the Pocintuck Indians and others to cut of Unquas and his people, and in case the English defend him, then to fight with the English." The existence of the plot had been confirmed by both Williams and the Pocumtucks.[61]

Commissioners led by Humphrey Atherton traveled to the Narragansetts to demand payment of the fine and insist that Ninigret leave Uncas alone.

[57] *RUC*, 1:143, 45–46; Thomas, *Maelstrom*, 219. On the importance of English military might in Indian-White relations, see Patrick M. Malone, *The Skulking Way of War: Technology and Tactics among the New England Indians* (Baltimore, Md., 1991), 88–128.

[58] Roger Williams to John Winthrop Jr., 11 September and 10 October 1648, in Williams, *Correspondence*, 1:241–42, 251.

[59] Increase Mather, *A Relation of the Troubles Which Have Happened in New England* (Boston, 1677), 60–61.

[60] *RUC*, July 1649, 1:143–44; Deforest, *Indians*, 218–22.

[61] For the commissioners' complaints, see *RUC*, July 1647 and 12 September 1648, 1:85, 116; Roger Williams to John Winthrop Jr., 25 October 1649, in Williams, *Correspondence*, 1:299; Mather, *Relation*, 65–66.

Ninigret denied any involvement in the plot and demanded to be confronted by his accusers. He denied all charges, and the situation remained unresolved.[62] Indeed, over the course of the next few years the commissioners continued to send messengers to the Narragansetts, who continued to ignore the treaty of 1645. In 1649 Ninigret went so far as to plan for the marriage of his daughter to the brother of Sassacus, the former Pequot sachem, thus giving him a hereditary claim to the Pequot lands.[63]

By the 1650s even relatively minor bands on Long Island and in the Connecticut River valley were posing problems for the English. The lack of effective control in the region encouraged other groups to extend their influence into New England. The French made diplomatic inroads with the Eastern Abenakis of Maine and with various western Abenaki bands, specifically the Sokokis (Squakeags) in the upper Connecticut Valley. Only a lingering enmity between the French Algonquians of the St. Lawrence River valley and the Sokokis prevented the intrusion of French influence into the Connecticut River valley. At the same time the Dutch consolidated their grip on the lower Hudson Valley and may have considered sending support to Algonquian bands along Narragansett Bay. The Mohawks, apparently, had already established a sound relationship with the Narragansetts.[64]

Word of yet another Narragansett conspiracy in 1657 exacerbated fears of foreign involvement in New England. In April, Uncas informed Connecticut's governor, John Haynes, that Ninigret had spent the preceding winter with the Dutch on Manhattan. Since the English were then at war with the Dutch in Europe and on the high seas, Ninigret's visit raised the alarming prospect of combined Dutch-Narragansett activity against the English. The commissioners quickly called Ninigret and the sachems Pessicus and Mixanno before an emergency meeting of the United Colonies to answer "whether the Duch Govr hath engaged him and other Narragansetts Sachems and Indians to healp them fight against the English and how many." The sachems' emissary, Awashaw, pledged their loyalty to the English and denied the existence of any Dutch-Narragansett alliance.[65]

These pledges of loyalty failed to convince the commissioners. Throughout April and May they continued to receive reports of suspicious Dutch and Narragansett activity. Then in September word arrived that Narragansett warriors had attacked the Montauks on Long Island in retaliation for the earlier murder of several Niantics. Narragansett warriors killed two sachems and thirty others. The commissioners again sent a messenger to demand that Ninigret halt his attacks and return the thirty captives he had seized on Long Island.[66]

[62] *RUC*, September 1648, 1:118.
[63] John Endicott to John Winthrop Jr., 15 August 1651, *MHS Coll*, 4th ser., 6 (1863): 153–54.
[64] Thomas, *Maelstrom*, 237–38.
[65] *RUC*, April 1653, 2:4–12. Mixanno became a Narragansett sachem in 1647 after the death of Canonicus.
[66] *RUC*, April–May 1653, 2:12–13, 23–24, 53, 57; September 1653, 2: 88–90.

The order failed to impress Ninigret, who asked the messenger, Thomas Stanton, "what the English had to doe to desire or demaund his prsoners." Ninigret declared that "they should neither see them nor have them." While Stanton and Ninigret were exchanging words, "the Indians then surrounded them and sum of them charged theire guns with powder and bulletts and sum primed theire guns." This "tumultuous" and threatening behavior was for the commissioners sufficient evidence of Ninigret's guilt.[67]

Only the unwillingness of the Massachusetts commissioners to commit to an Indian war while England and the Netherlands were locked in combat averted hostilities in 1653. When the commissioners did decide on war in September 1654, after the Anglo-Dutch conflict had ended, some opposition to their decision still existed. Roger Williams recognized that any war against the Narragansetts would be fought in Rhode Island, which had the English settlements closest to the Narragansetts, and most exposed to Indian war parties. Moreover, if the United Colonies defeated the Narragansetts, they could claim—however tenuously—lands within Rhode Island by right of conquest and thus fulfill the longstanding desire of the orthodox puritan colonies to dismember their heretical brother. Williams thus viewed the impending war with Ninigret as a "fire wch now is kindling, the Fire of Gods Wrath and Jealousie wch if God graciously quench not, may burne to the Foundacions both of Indians and English togeather."[68]

Williams did not argue solely from self-interest; he believed that such a war threatened metropolitan interests in New England. The Narragansetts, he argued, had long been firm friends of the English, and "many hundreth English, have long experimented them to be inclined to peace and Love with the English Nation." Maintaining that friendship, he added, was strategically critical. The Narragansetts and Mohawks were "the 2 great Bodies of Indians in the Countrey; and they are Confederates and long have bene," so war with one would necessarily entail war with the other—too great a threat for New England to handle. Williams also suggested, quite sensibly, that it was difficult to convert Indians whom the commissioners were continually threatening to kill. He believed it "not only possible but very easie to live and die in peace with all the Natives of the Countrey."[69]

Williams stood alone by 1654. Frustrated by Ninigret's long chain of "hostile attempts and outrages," firmly convinced that the Narragansetts were no friends of the English, the commissioners sent 270 foot soldiers and 40 horses under Simon Willard to force the sachem to observe the treaty of 1645. Ninigret was to bear the cost of the expedition. He could comply with the commissioners' demands, Willard told him, or have "his head sett up upon an English pole." Confronting this rather unsavory choice, Ninigret

[67] *RUC*, September 1653, 2:94–95.
[68] Roger Williams to John Winthrop Jr., 9 October 1654, in Williams, *Correspondence*, 2:416.
[69] Roger Williams to the Massachusetts General Court, 5 October 1654, in ibid., 2:408–13.

signed a new treaty agreeing to turn over his Pequot tributaries within seven days. Like previous agreements, however, this one meant little. Ninigret did not turn over his Pequots, and Long Islanders continued to complain of Niantic-Narragansett raids.[70]

Throughout the remainder of the decade the Commissioners of the United Colonies failed to control the Algonquian bands of southern New England. Attacks by the Narragansetts upon the Montauks, by the Mohegans upon the Pocumtucks, and by the Pocumtucks and Narragansetts upon the Mohegans continued. The only success that could be legitimately credited to the commissioners was that native groups more frequently called upon the English to intervene in their own internal disputes. This was a mixed blessing at best, as competing Algonquian groups employed the threat of English military might against their aboriginal rivals. The commissioners could fine, they could threaten, and at times they could mediate and intervene, but they could not govern.[71]

In the spring of 1660 conflict erupted once again between the Narragansetts and the Mohegans. The Niantics renewed as well their attacks against the Long Island bands. The frustrated commissioners ordered Ninigret to pay an indemnity of 595 fathoms of wampum—500 for the recent raids and 95 for an earlier combined Pocumtuck-Narragansett assault on Uncas—and demanded his lands as security for the payment, due in four months. At this point, Humphrey Atherton, the leader of a group of land speculators which included Commissioner and Connecticut Governor John Winthrop Jr., lent the Narragansetts the wampum due in return for a mortgage payable in six months. When the two additional months did not make a difference, the Atherton Company foreclosed on the Narragansetts and Niantics, laying claim to all their lands, including a large chunk of territory within Rhode Island.[72]

III

The restoration of the Stuart monarchy in 1660, after nearly two decades of political and social turmoil in England, marked the renewal of the crown's attempt to curb the independence of the Puritan colonies and to obtain the metropolitan imperatives of dominion and civility. During the civil war and interregnum the New England colonies had established their virtual independence. Accustomed to governing themselves without royal interference, they posed a significant challenge to the imperial vision of Charles II.[73]

---

[70] *RUC*, September 1654, 2:114–15, 147–48; Vaughan, *New England Frontier*, 176.

[71] Thomas, *Maelstrom*; Deforest, *Indians*; Sehr, "Ninigret's Tactics," 51.

[72] Robert C. Black, *The Younger John Winthrop* (New York, 1966), 195; Richard S. Dunn, "John Winthrop, Jr., and the Narragansett Country," *WMQ*, 3d ser., 13 (1956): 72–73.

[73] J. M. Sosin, *English America and the Restoration Monarchy of Charles II* (Lincoln, Neb., 1980), 2, 74–76; Stephen Saunders Webb, *The Governors-General: The English Army and the Definition of Empire, 1550–1681* (Chapel Hill, N.C., 1979), 441.

Charles hoped to tighten his control over the empire and draw his "distant dominions and the severall interests and governments thereof into a nearer prospect and consultacon." The colonies, he wrote, "should be collected and brought under such an uniforme inspeccon and conduct that Wee may the better apply our royall councelles to theire future regulacon securities and improvement." Within weeks the newly-established Council for Foreign Plantations had before it numerous complaints against the United Colonies, as well as evidence calling their loyalty into question.[74]

The Puritans had traded with the Dutch and French in violation of the Navigation Acts, coined their own currency, and sheltered the regicides. They had also seized control from its proprietors of the province of Maine, a region "more important to the King, for trade, present and future, than all the rest of New England." The Puritan magistrates thus stood charged with tormenting the king's subjects, trading illegally with the king's enemies, sheltering the killers of the king's father, violating the king's laws, and usurping the rights of the king's favorites. For the purpose of correcting these abuses, conquering the Dutch colony of New Netherland, and allowing England to dominate the coast of North America, Charles appointed a royal commission in 1664.[75]

The royal commissioners—Samuel Maverick, Richard Nicolls, Sir Robert Carr, and George Cartwright—would enlist military support in New England for the conquest of New Netherland, hold hearings to resolve boundary disputes in New England, secure enforcement of the Navigation Acts, and investigate charges that the Puritan colonies had abridged the civil and religious liberties of the king's subjects. An additional set of secret instructions called upon the commissioners to persuade the Bay Colony magistrates to submit their charter for royal revision and review and to report on the state of relations between the colonists and the Indians.[76]

They found affairs in the colonies as bad as previous reports had led them to believe. Connecticut and Rhode Island, both reliant upon the crown's favor for resolution of their boundary disputes in the Narragansett country, cooperated with the commissioners, but Massachusetts defiantly refused each of their initiatives. Frustrated by the Bay Colony's decision to use "that authority wch [the king] hath given you to oppose that sovereignty which he

[74] Charles II's Patent Constituting a Council of Trade, 7 November 1660, *NYCD*, 3:30–31; Majesty's Commission for a Council of Foreign Plantations, 1 December 1660, *NYCD* 3:33; Sosin, *English America*, 93.

[75] Letter to Lord Chancellor Clarendon, after 19 December 1660, Captain Thomas Breedon to Council for Foreign Plantations, 11 March 1660/61, and Samuel Maverick to Clarendon, n.d., all in "The Clarendon Papers," *Collections of the New York Historical Society for the Year 1869* (New York, 1870), 24, 17–18, 33–34; [John Gifford?] to [Secretary Nicholas?], 1661, *CSP Col, 1661–68*, no.78; Stephen Saunders Webb, *1676: The End of American Independence* (New York, 1984), 226.

[76] Instructions to Commissioners, *NYCD*, 3:51–53; Robert C. Ritchie, *The Duke's Province: A Study of New York Politics and Society, 1664–1691* (Chapel Hill, N.C., 1977), 19.

hath over you," the commissioners decided that "wee shall not lose more of our labours upon you, but refer it to his majtys wisdom, who is of power enough to make himself to be obeyed in all his dominions."[77]

The commissioners found that provisions made for the "conversion of ye infidells" had been cynical and insincere. The colonists, wrote Carr, convert the Indians "by hiring them to come and heare Sermons. . . . The lives, Manners, & habits of those, whom they say are converted cannot be distinguished from those who are not."[78]

The commissioners also confirmed that in 1644 Pessicus and Canonicus had submitted "themselves, people, and country into his Royall Majesties protection." Ignoring this, the New Englanders had "disposed of a great part of [the Narragansetts'] country, pretending they had conquered it from the Pequod Indians."[79] In response to Puritan pretenses the royal commissioners formally received the Narragansetts as subjects of the crown, and did

> in his majestyes name, order, appoint, & command, that the said country from hence forward be called the King's Province, & that no person of what colony soever presume to exercise any jurisdiction within this the Kings Province, but such as receive authority from us or under our handes & seales, until his majesties pleasure be further knoune.

Further, because the "pretending" Atherton purchasers "knew that ye said country was submitted to his Majestie, as well by witnesses, as by ye said submission being eighteen years agoe Printed," the commissioners declared the Atherton claims null and void, and ordered the purchasers to "quit & goe of the said pretended purchased lands." Rhode Island would govern the King's Province until the crown's will was known.[80]

In sum, the royal commissioners concluded that the New England colonies had violated the fundamental tenets of metropolitan policy. Their aggressive and unwarranted land-grabbing had destabilized the frontier. Their commitment to the conversion of the natives seemed shallow and ineffectual. The United Colonies had demonstrated their inability to command the respect of neighboring Algonquian bands. They had, in other words, achieved neither dominion nor civility along the New England frontier.

What the commissioners and the crown would have preferred as an alternative to the policies pursued by the United Colonies is evident in New York, where Richard Nicolls became the Duke of York's first governor. With French and Iroquois communities to the north and a significant Dutch pop-

---

[77] Charles II to Governor and Council of Connecticut, 10 April 1666, CR, 2: 514; Charles II to Rhode Island, 10 April 1666, *RICR*, 2:149; *NYCD*, 23 April 1654, 3:51.

[78] Report of His Majesty's Commissioners concerning the Massachusetts, in *Documentary History of the State of Maine*, 24 vols., ed. William Willis et al., eds., (Portland, Maine, 1869–1916), 4: 294.

[79] *RICR*, December 1665, 2:128.

[80] *RICR*, 2:59–60, 128.

ulation remaining within the colony, Nicolls and his successor, Francis Lovelace, worked quickly to place English relations with the neighboring Algonquian, Munsee, and Iroquoian bands upon a firm and peaceful footing.

The Restoration governors of New York, in fact, constructed their policies with a close eye on what England's imperial rivals, the Netherlands and France, had accomplished in North America. The Dutch had been active in the Hudson and surrounding waters since at least 1609. Though some promoters of Dutch enterprise in the Americas, such as William Usselinx, dreamed of an empire that would devastate their Spanish enemies, plant prosperous colonies, and see to "the furtherance of the saving Gospel of our Lord Jesus Christ and the bringing of many thousands of men to the light of truth and to eternal salvation," most Dutch merchants interested in America hoped, rather less ambitiously, to profit from the fur trade.[81] The charter granted by the Dutch States-General to the West India Company in June 1621 thus bore little resemblance to Usselinx's grandiose designs.

Still, the desire to weaken the Spanish by preying upon their Atlantic trade and rolling back the advance of Catholicism remained, a product of the decades-long Dutch rebellion against the forces of Spanish imperialism. Chartered in 1621, the final year of a twelve-year truce between Spain and Holland, the West India Company provided Calvinists with a means to renew their battle against Spanish Catholicism.[82]

Dutch fleets did, in fact, maul Spanish shipping in the Caribbean. Meanwhile, the West India Company planted a series of tiny, peripheral outposts at Fort Orange (present-day Albany) in 1624 and at New Amsterdam (New York) in 1626. It viewed these small settlements as commercial operations where colonists, working for the company, would trade with the numerous Indian communities lining the Hudson River.[83] For this trade to succeed, the company need native cooperation. Therefore, it required that settlers and traders treat Indians fairly. The company's directors, in March 1624, ordered that the colonists "take especial care, whether in trading or in other matters, faithfully to fulfill their promises to the Indians . . . and not to give them any offense without cause as regards their persons, wives, or property, on pain of being rigorously punished therefor."[84]

---

[81] George L. Smith, *Religion and Trade in New Netherland: Dutch Origins and American Development* (Ithaca, N.Y., 1973), 5–6; Oliver A. Rink, *Holland on the Hudson: An Economic and Social History of Dutch New York* (Ithaca, N.Y., 1986), 52.

[82] Rink, *Holland*, 50–55; Paul Andrew Otto, "New Netherland Frontier: Europeans and Native Americans along the Lower Hudson River, 1524–1664" (Ph.D. diss., Indiana University, 1995), 126.

[83] Ian K. Steele, *Warpaths: Invasions of North America* (New York, 1994), 112; Allen W. Trelease, *Indian Affairs in Colonial New York: The Seventeenth Century* (Ithaca, N.Y., 1960), 35–40.

[84] Provisional Instructions for the Colonists, 18 March 1624, in *Documents Relating to New Netherland, 1624–1626, in the Henry E. Huntington Library*, ed. and trans. A. J. F. Van Laer, (San Marino, Calif., 1924), 17.

In two sets of "Further Instructions" issued to Director-General William Verhulst early in 1625, the company required that "in addition to good treatment" the Indians were to be "shown honesty, faithfulness, and sincerity in all contracts, dealings, and intercourse, without being deceived by shortage of measure, weight, or number, and that throughout friendly relations with them be maintained." Verhulst should "by small presents seek to draw the Indians to our service, in order to learn from them the secrets of that region and the condition of the interior." The directors hoped that well-treated natives would trade exclusively with the settlers at New Netherland, thus allowing the West India Company to monopolize the rich fur trade of the American interior.[85]

These economic, pragmatic, and expedient concerns always outweighed any interest in the souls of the natives. Dutch clergymen, when they did finally arrive in New Netherland in 1628, could hardly minister to a settler population that included a significant number of French-speaking Walloons, much less to the Indians. The Reverend Jonas Michaelius considered them not only "savage and wild, strangers to all decency, . . . uncivil and as stupid as garden poles" but "devilish men, who serve nobody but the Devil." In early New Netherland, commerce was king, and Indians were the source of future corporate assets.[86]

By the fall of 1626, at least one colonist could report optimistically "that our people are in good heart and live in peace there." Still, the Dutch settlements remained small, with most of the colonial population concentrated at the lower end of Manhattan Island. Company officials quickly became convinced that profits could accrue only through the establishment of permanent and growing settlements in the Hudson Valley. As a result, a new set of "Freedoms and Exemptions" issued by the company in 1629 named as "patroons" of New Netherland such individuals as Killian Van Rensselaer, willing to plant settlements of at least fifty persons over the age of fifteen. The company allowed generous provisions for the purchase and selection of lands for this purpose. The patroonship system, however, failed in its essential purpose: to increase the population of New Netherland. By the end of the 1630s only Rensselaerwyck, in the vicinity of Fort Orange, stood as testament to the West India Company's plan to develop bustling manorial estates along the river.[87]

Impatient with the lack of development in New Netherland, the States-General demanded that the West India Company find other ways to increase the population of its colony. In response, in the fall of 1638, the company abandoned the pretense of its monopoly over the fur trade—always unen-

[85] Ibid., 39, 55, 109–10; Otto, "New Netherland Frontier," 131–33.

[86] Jonas Michaelius, in *Narratives of New Netherland, 1609–1664*, ed. J. Franklin Jameson (New York, 1909), 126.

[87] Peter Schagen to States-General, 7 November 1626, *NYCD*, 1:37; Trelease, *Indian Affairs*, 36, 43; Smith, *Religion and Trade*, 12; Rink, *Holland*, 115.

forceable anyway—and opened the trade to all comers, granting land generously to those willing to remain in the colony as farmers. This change in policy did bring a sudden increase in population, but with this growth the West India Company lost what little control it had over Dutch-Indian relations. Settlers clashed frequently with natives in small conflicts over control of the land. As in the Chesapeake and New England, an absence of efficient metropolitan control over the frontier—here forfeited in the name of establishing a profitable colony—precipitated conflict between natives and newcomers as they sought to exploit identical frontier resources in ways that were seldom compatible.[88] Dutch cattle, one observer noted, "usually roamed through the woods without a herdsman, [and] they frequently came into the corn of the Indians which was unfenced on all sides, committing great damage there." This "led to frequent complaints on their part and finally to revenge on the cattle without sparing even the horses, which were valuable in this country."[89]

William Kieft, who became director-general in 1638, was temperamentally ill equipped to deal with the resulting tensions. A man as bloodthirsty and vindictive as he was weak and indecisive, Kieft surrendered control of the colony to the frontier thugs with whom he sympathized, provoking in the process a violent conflagration known as Kieft's War.[90]

The director-general clearly had little respect or affection for the small Munsee-speaking villages in the vicinity of Manhattan. These bands, in the decade and a half since Dutch settlement began, had become marginal to the fur trade—most of which now came through Fort Orange—and an obstacle to Dutch farmers on the lower Hudson. Seeking to make them useful to the colony, and in violation of West India Company policies, Kieft decided in September 1639 "to levy some contributions either in peltries, maize or wampum from the Indians residing hereabout" to defray the cost of building projects in New Amsterdam. No evidence exists to suggest how stringently Kieft enforced his tax policies, and very little building occurred, but Dutch-Indian relations in the lower Hudson Valley deteriorated rapidly thereafter.[91]

Kieft's exactions apparently were the final straw. Their lands pressed upon by a rapidly growing Dutch population, their fields trampled by Dutch livestock, the already hard-pressed Munsees took action. Indians attacked, and the Dutch retaliated, beginning a series of raids and counterraids that continued for several years. With the assistance of Mohawk warriors armed by

[88] NYCD, 1:110–14; Rink, *Holland*, 135–37; Otto, "New Netherland Frontier," 10–11; Trelease, *Indian Affairs*, 64.
[89] "Journal of New Netherland," in Jameson, *Narratives*, 273.
[90] NYCD, 1:104; Laurence M. Hauptman and Ronald G. Knapp, "Dutch-Aboriginal Interaction in New Netherland and Formosa: An Historical Geography of Empire," *Proceedings of the American Philosophical Society* 121 (1977): 172.
[91] "Resolution to Exact a Tribute . . .," 15 September 1639, NYCD, 12:6; Otto, "New Netherland Frontier," 177–78; Trelease, *Indian Affairs*, 65.

Kieft with muskets, the surviving Munsees—Wecquaesgeeks and Tappans mostly—were driven toward the Dutch settlements, establishing in February 1643 one camp near the fort at New Amsterdam and another across the Hudson at Pavonia. Kieft had little to fear from these shattered refugees. Nonetheless, at the behest of Indian-hating frontiersmen, he authorized attacks toward the end of that month. In a nighttime raid by Dutch forces at Pavonia, "young children, some of them snatched from their mothers, were cut in pieces before the eyes of their parents, and pieces were thrown into the fire or into the water; other babes were bound on planks and then cut through, stabbed and miserably massacred, so that it would break a heart of stone."[92]

If Kieft intended these attacks to "obtain any satisfaction for the bloodshed [so] that we may live here in peace," he badly miscalculated. At least eleven small Munsee bands began to prey upon isolated Dutch settlers, none of whom had been warned about the possible violent repercussions of Kieft's attacks. Native warriors "killed all the men on the farm lands whom they could surprise" and "burned all the houses, farms, barns, stacks of grain, and destroyed everything they could come at, so that they began an open and destructive war." Kieft was woefully unprepared to reap the whirlwind he had sown. By the autumn of 1643, with nearly 1,500 Munsee warriors storming the settlements under his charge, he could counter with only 60 soldiers, and 250 male settlers capable of bearing arms.[93]

The Indian attacks were effective. Farms along the lower reaches of the Hudson were destroyed, or abandoned as settlers fled to the relative safety of Fort Amsterdam. Not until the spring of 1644, when a combined force of Dutch soldiers and English mercenaries under the command of Pequot War veteran John Underhill killed nearly five hundred Indians in a bloody and fiery imitation of the Mystic fight, did the tide of the war finally turn against the Indians.[94]

The damage, however, had already been done. Perhaps a thousand Indians died in the fighting. Many settlers, with few prospects remaining in the war-ravaged outpost, returned to the Netherlands. The company concluded that Kieft's policies had left local Munsee bands "totally estranged from our people" and the colony lying "prostrate, the settlers hunted, their lands laid waste, the boweries and plantations, to the number of 50 or 60 burnt and laid in ashes, and what is worst of all, the Dutch name is through those cruel acts, despised to a most sovereign degree, by the Heathens of those parts." In the future, the Amsterdam directors advised, "the Colonists ought to settle nearer each other . . . with a view of being thus formed into villages and

[92] Quoted in Trelease, *Indian Affairs*, 72.

[93] Quoted material in Otto, "New Netherland Frontier," 186; Trelease, *Indian Affairs*, 73–76; and Steele, *Warpaths*, 116. See also "Resolution and Order to Attack the Indians," 25 February 1643, *NYCD*, 13:10.

[94] Otto, "New Netherland Frontier," 191.

towns, to be the better able to protect each other in time of need." They also ought to maintain a distance between themselves and the Indians, which "will prevent the cattle damaging the corn belonging to the Indians, which, added to excessive familiarity in associating with them, was the cause of many difficulties."[95]

The company next chose Peter Stuyvesant, a veteran of its outpost on Curaçao, to replace Kieft as director-general and bring order to Indian relations in New Netherland. The instructions issued to Stuyvesant reflect a clear desire to avoid violent conflict. "It is especially said of the native inhabitants of these territories," the Holland directors wrote, "that they must be governed with kindness and the former wars incline us to believe it." The colony needed Indians. Export duties on furs provided the company with much of its profit, and those furs could not be obtained with the colony at war. Furthermore, the company increasingly viewed peaceful relations with local natives as central to the protection of New Netherland from the rapidly growing English settlements to the east. Given the military weakness of the Dutch population, the company made sure Stuyvesant understood that he could not afford to alienate local Indians.[96]

Indeed, Stuyvesant worked to ensure stable Indian-white relations in New Netherland. He attempted to concentrate settlement to provide for the security of Dutch settlers while at the same time relieving pressure on Munsee lands in the Lower Hudson. Conflict over the land and its use, Stuyvesant recognized, lay at the heart of much of the colony's trouble with Indians.[97] He and his lieutenants punished settlers who provided Indians with alcohol because it was "a matter of dangerous consequence which may cause the ruin of the country." He authorized local sachems to seize "the brandy brought into their country for sale and those offering to sell it" and carry them to New Amsterdam for trial. He allowed the Mohawks, increasingly important in the fur trade, a supply of powder, shot, and weaponry to maintain their friendship. He limited the number of guns in the hands of colonists, both to ease the native fear of settlers that lingered from Kieft's administration and to reduce the ability of colonists to prey upon Indians.[98]

Despite these efforts, Stuyvesant confronted a series of challenges to effective West India Company control of the colony. At Fort Orange the director-general needed peaceful relations with the powerful Mohawks who dominated the regional trade in furs. Consequently, the oversight of Indian-white relations at the outpost became the most significant concern of the *commis* (later vice-director) and *commissarisses* Stuyvesant appointed.

[95] NYCD, 1:150–51, 251.
[96] Directors in Holland to Stuyvesant, 7 April 1648, NYCD, 13:27; NYCD, 14:186; Trelease, *Indian Affairs*, 85; Otto, "New Netherland Frontier," 210–11.
[97] NYCD, 13:64; Otto, "New Netherland Frontier," 211.
[98] NYCD, 13:218–19; A. J. F. Van Laer, ed., *Minutes of the Court of Fort Orange and Beverwyck*, 2 vols. (Albany, N.Y., 1923), 2:92.

The task was not easy. During the trading season, which lasted from May until October, large numbers of colonists swarmed into the fort seeking advantage in the fur trade. To obtain that advantage, some would ply Indians with alcohol.[99] Others sent brokers into the woods to intercept Indians before they could carry their furs to the market at Fort Orange. The native trappers, of course, wanted to shop for the best bargain, but according to Mohawk traders, these brokers violently prevented Indians from dealing with their rivals. Dutch brokers "when they are in the woods to fetch Indians beat them severely with fists and drive them out of the woods." The Mohawks asked "that no Dutchmen with horses or otherwise . . . be allowed to roam in the woods to fetch Indians with beavers, because they maltreat them greatly and presently ten or twelve of them surround an Indian and drag him along, saying 'Come with me, so and so has no goods,' thus interfering with one another, which they fear will end badly." The court at Fort Orange, seeing these attacks as "contrary to the welfare and the peace of this place," decided "to forbid all inhabitants of this place to go roaming the woods as brokers to attract Indians."[100]

Warfare did not break out in the vicinity of Fort Orange. Though Dutch traders continued to rough up Mohawks, and Indians killed roaming Dutch livestock and avenged insults suffered at the hands of traders, the limited pressure placed upon Mohawk subsistence patterns and the desire on the part of both Indians and colonists to trade preserved peace. They may not have liked each other, but that was beside the point. To obtain furs, the Dutch needed the Mohawks. To obtain furs from tribes farther west, the Mohawks needed Dutch weaponry. Out of mutual necessity Fort Orange became a pragmatic—however violent—meeting place, a middle ground where interdependence spawned by the fur trade forced Indians and settlers to tolerate each other.[101]

Elsewhere the story was much more violent. Late in the 1650s Dutch settlers began to occupy a fertile tract of land that they called Esopus, located roughly halfway between Fort Orange and New Amsterdam. They soon came into conflict with the Esopus natives, who complained of rough treatment suffered at the hands of an unruly Dutch population. In addition to beating and threatening Indians, the settlers apparently encroached upon native land, and again, their livestock damaged Indian cornfields. A small number of intoxicated warriors in May 1658 avenged these insults by murdering a colonist and burning two houses.[102]

The situation unfolding at Esopus alarmed Stuyvesant, who traveled to the settlement with several dozen men at the end of May. He encouraged the

---

[99] See, e.g., Van Laer, *Minutes of Fort Orange*, 2:32–33.

[100] Ibid., 2:32–33, 268–70.

[101] Hauptman and Knapp, "Dutch-Aboriginal Interactions," 170; Trelease, *Indian Affairs*, 115.

[102] Otto, "New Netherland Frontier," 224; NYCD 13:77–79, 102–3.

residents to move into a smaller number of better-defended sites "so that we may protect ourselves and our property by such means, to which the All-Good God may give his blessing against a sudden attack of the savages." They should not, however, attack the Indians before the fall. By then, the settlers would have had time to harvest their corn, and in the meantime, Stuyvesant thought, he could pursue peace through diplomacy. The director-general's visit, in fact, may well have cowed the Esopus Indians, or assured them of his peaceful intentions, for matters remained at least outwardly quiet along the Hudson for over a year.[103]

The Indians nevertheless continued to complain of ill treatment. Some said they had never been paid for land they earlier had ceded to the Dutch. As one Dutch observer noted, they claimed to have "patiently borne the blows, which each of us had often given them." Whereas at Fort Orange shared interests were powerful enough to maintain peace, at Esopus natives and newcomers competed for access to the land, and the result was conflict.

On September 21, 1659 frightened settlers attacked the Esopus Indians. Beginning the next evening native warriors retaliated. In October, Stuyvesant received word that "matters at the Esopus are in a bad condition; it is besieged by 500 to 600 savages, so that nobody can go in or near it." His correspondent, Andries Laurens, warned that "if Esopus receives no assistance, I am afraid, it will have no good end." Stuyvesant conceded that the Dutch should "make war on the Esopus Indians . . . and to carry it on against them as vigorously as possible," but he urged caution given the relatively small Dutch colonial population. In the spring of 1660 a number of attacks were launched against the Esopus Indians, and by July—with the assistance of Indians downriver who hoped to avoid being caught in the crossfire—the Dutch and Esopus Indians came to terms. Stuyvesant demanded that the Indians pay reparations, pledge not to kill roaming Dutch livestock, and give up a significant chunk of land.[104]

The 1660 treaty kept the peace for three years. In the meantime, the Dutch population increased and a new settlement, Nieuwdorp, was planted—against the wishes of the Indians. Pressed by the growing numbers of Dutch, Esopus natives attacked the colonists again in June 1663, reigniting the conflict. At the settlement of Wiltwyck, Stuyvesant learned, "an unexpected, sudden attack was made by them and pitiful, lamentable murders had been committed by them against us." The Indians, the report continued, "have burned 12 dwelling-houses in our village, murdered 18 persons, men, women, and children, and carried away as prisoners 10 persons more." Nieuwdorp was almost entirely destroyed, and some sixty-five persons were killed or captured.[105]

---

[103] *NYCD*, 13: 80–83.
[104] Ibid., 119, 136, 179–81; Otto, "New Netherland Frontier," 228.
[105] *NYCD*, 13:245; Otto, "New Netherland Frontier," 229.

Raiding continued throughout the summer. In September the Dutch successfully counterattacked, destroying an Esopus village and rescuing twenty-three captives. In May of the following year—shortly before the English conquest of New Netherland—Stuyvesant and the Esopus signed a treaty in which the defeated Indians ceded even more of their remaining land to the Dutch.[106]

Peter Stuyvesant was the most capable director-general the West India Company sent to America. Even he, however, spent much of his tenure resolving conflicts between Indians and whites. Though New Netherland's population was growing, and the colony was finally beginning to generate profits, relations along the Hudson were often tense.

From Governor Nicolls's perspective when the English took over, the Dutch had not secured effective control of the frontier, and he and Lovelace rejected the practice, continued under Stuyvesant, of allowing relative autonomy to fur traders, their often unsavory agents, and frontiersmen. They also recognized that to avoid problems like those that had unfolded at Esopus, the Restoration regime would have to alleviate the pressure placed upon Indian communities by growing Anglo-Dutch settlements. The English believed it imperative to place Anglo-Indian relations in the Hudson Valley upon a solid footing, for the presence of expanding French settlements on the St. Lawrence River might offer refuge to Indians disaffected with the English.

The French had planted their first permanent settlement in America in 1608 but did not achieve a degree of stability until the early 1630s at Quebec. They pursued policies directed to the same ends as those of the Spanish, the Dutch, and the English, seeking to extend their dominion overseas, establish a lucrative trading empire, and spread the Catholic religion. In 1603, for instance, Henry IV ordered his viceroy to New France "to lead the nations thereof to the profession of the Christian faith, to civilization of manners, an ordered life, practice and intercourse with the French for the gain of their commerce, and finally their recognition of and submission to the authority and domination of the Crown of France." These cardinal purposes of empire, in fact, were in New France closely intertwined. Trade was the earthly reward for bringing religion to the Indians, and neither commerce nor conversion could occur if Indians were treated poorly. The French considered the Indians reasoning and rational. Though they did not question the inferiority of native culture, they clearly believed that they could assimilate the Indians into a French colonial society in America.[107]

[106] Otto, "New Netherland Frontier," 232–33.

[107] Anthony Pagden, *Lords of All the World: Ideologies of Empire in Spain, Britain, and France, 1500–1800* (New Haven, Conn., 1995), 33–34; W. J. Eccles, *The Canadian Frontier, 1534–1760* (New York, 1969), 5; Henry IV quoted in Cornelius Jaenen, *Friend and Foe: Aspects of French-Amerindian Cultural Contact in the Sixteenth and Seventeenth Centuries* (New York, 1976), 153.

Armand Jean du Plessis, the Cardinal Richelieu, in 1627 developed an ambitious program of French colonial expansion designed to achieve these imperial objectives. Drawing support from government officeholders and a small number of merchants, noblemen, and clergy, Richelieu organized the Compagnie de Nouvelle-France, better known as the Company of One Hundred Associates, to gather the natural resources of Canada, plant thriving and stable agricultural settlements, and bring the Indians gently to an acceptance of Christianity and civility. In exchange for providing financial support to missionaries, defending French outposts from enemies both native and European, and shipping four thousand settlers to the colony within fifteen years, the Company of One Hundred Associates enjoyed a fifteen-year monopoly on all trade except fishing, the right to grant lands within the colony, and complete and perpetual control of the region's lucrative trade in furs.[108]

Like the Virginia Company, the One Hundred Associates was a private organization acting with crown support. Though profits clearly were important to the men who invested in the venture, it appears that they acted on a powerful religious commitment as well and that a desire to spread Catholicism overseas may in many cases have outweighed the desire for personal gain. Richelieu hoped "to introduce to the natives the knowledge of the true God, [and] to cause them to be civilized and instructed in the Catholic, apostolic, and Roman faith." This could be accomplished by missionaries and "French-born Catholics, who will by their example, lead these natives to the Christian religion and to civil life." The company's charter specified that any Indian who accepted Christianity and became a practicing Catholic would be viewed as a French subject with all the attendant rights and privileges, including a right to settle in France and to acquire and dispose of property like any other Frenchman. Few Indians, apparently, were interested in this offer, but it does reflect the powerful religious and assimilationist commitment upon which the Company of One Hundred Associates rested.[109]

French Jesuits thoroughly believed that the Algonquins and Montagnais they encountered along the St. Lawrence were "not so barbarous that they cannot be made children of God."[110] Jesuit fathers moved quickly into the interior, visiting the villages of Canadian natives. Some, however, questioned the efficacy of this approach. The Jesuit Superior Paul Le Jeune concluded in 1634, after spending the preceding winter with the seminomadic Montagnais, that the wholesale conversion and transformation of the Indians could

---

[108] Matthew Dennis, *Cultivating a Landscape of Peace: Iroquois-European Encounters in Seventeenth-Century America* (Ithaca, N.Y., 1993), 191; W. J. Eccles, *France in America* (New York, 1972), 27; Steele, *Warpaths*, 67–68.

[109] Richelieu quoted in James Axtell, *The Invasion Within: The Contest of Cultures in Colonial North America* (New York, 1985), 38.

[110] Quoted in ibid., 60.

most easily occur when natives settled in European-style agricultural communities.[111]

Late in the 1630s, for example, thirty-five to forty families of Christian Montagnais, along with a larger number of non-Christians, were living in the mission village at Sillery under the tutelage of Jesuit priests. Here, potential converts could be sheltered from the nasty habits of French Canadians while they made the transition from an Indian to a French way of life.[112]

Like those natives who converted to Christianity in New England, Indians who accepted the ministry of the Jesuit fathers did so for a variety of reasons. The devastation resulting from European colonization—disease and depopulation—affected Indians in New France as it did elsewhere, and many apparently tried to find explanations for their plight in a new religion. This may have been the case with the Mohawks who listened attentively to Jesuit missionaries in the wake of a 1666 French military expedition that left many Mohawk towns in ashes. Others followed kin into either Christian or traditionalist factions within native villages. Clearly the process of conversion produced divisions within indigenous communities, where kinship and affiliation influenced the decision as much as religion. For many Indians who encountered Jesuits, both in the St. Lawrence region and in Iroquoia, the shamanistic and magical powers displayed by the priests initially gained more converts than anything in their message. Jesuits, who often employed incense, bells, music, and display in their ritual, convinced many Indians reeling in a world of rapid change that their spiritual power was greater than that of the natives. Indians who found French Catholicism attractive, consequently, often accepted it on their own terms.[113]

French Jesuits nonetheless operated the most successful missions anywhere in North America. Their settlements, however, remained tenuous. Villagers at Sillery, for instance, frequently left to join war parties against the Mohawks, and at such times the rest abandoned the village to seek the greater safety of Quebec. During periods of warfare, common in the 1640s, Sillery took on the appearance of a ghost town.[114]

Warfare with Indians threatened all aspects of French colonial enterprise in America. It affected the flow of pelts into the settlements at Quebec, Montreal, and Trois Rivières. It diverted colonists from their agricultural pursuits, thus rendering it difficult for the Company of One Hundred Associates to establish self-sufficient American outposts. Warfare with Mohawk raiders in particular limited the effectiveness of French missions among the Hurons,

---

[111] James Ronda, "The Sillery Experiment: A Jesuit-Indian Village in New France," *American Indian Culture and Research Journal* 3 (1979): 2–3.

[112] Axtell, *Invasion*, 62; Jaenen, *Friend and Foe*, 178; Ronda, "Sillery Experiment," 7.

[113] Daniel K. Richter, *The Ordeal of the Longhouse: The Peoples of the Iroquois League in the Era of European Colonization* (Chapel Hill, N.C., 1992), 111–16; Ronda, "Sillery Experiment," 10–11.

[114] Ronda, "Sillery Experiment," 7–8.

the St. Lawrence communities, and the Iroquois. (The Mohawks were the easternmost of the Iroquois' Five Nations, with the Oneidas, Onondagas, Cayugas, and Senecas, respectively, to the west.) Because of the weakness of French settlements in relation to their more numerous neighbors, and because the success of New France hinged upon placid relations with the Indians, secular officials worked diligently to maintain peace between natives and newcomers. In the St. Lawrence the French placed few strains upon native subsistence, and this helped to relieve one important possible source of conflict. Others remained.

Unlike the New Englanders, for example, the French in Canada moved carefully in extending their laws over Indians. French law in theory held Indians to the same standards of responsibility as whites for their crimes. In practice, however, colonial authorities and Indian leaders constructed a judicial common ground where French legal procedure was twisted to accommodate the significant strength of neighboring Indians. New France simply could not afford to alienate Indians through the harsh imposition of foreign systems of crime and punishment.[115]

Despite these pragmatic policies, however, New France remained weak, fragile, and on the defensive. Iroquois warriors continually threatened the settlements. Mohawks, armed by the Dutch, wanted furs to trade at the market at Fort Orange and prisoners to replenish losses in population resulting from warfare and disease. To obtain them, they warred upon Huron, Montagnais, and Algonquin communities to their north, all allied with the French. Colonists frequently found themselves caught in the crossfire.[116]

By 1660 Mohawk raids had brought economic life in New France to a standstill. As farms located along the rivers were abandoned, food had to be imported to keep the colony alive. The Iroquois had defeated France's native allies; now they threatened to extinguish the colony itself.[117] These attacks peaked in 1661, when thirty-eight colonists were killed and another sixty-one captured. Jesuit missionaries pleaded for decisive assistance from France against the Iroquois on the grounds that "these barbarians must be exterminated, if possible, or all the Christians and Christianity itself will perish." The new king, Louis XIV, heard these calls. Firmly convinced that Canada if properly managed could enrich crown and colonist alike, he assigned Jean-Baptiste Colbert, his leading economic adviser, the task of developing a program for incorporating New France into an expansive and economically powerful French empire.[118]

---

[115] Jan Grabowski, "French Criminal Justice and Indians in Montreal, 1670–1760," *Ethnohistory* 43 (1996): 405–429.

[116] Richter, *Ordeal.*

[117] Marcel Trudel, *The Beginnings of New France, 1524–1663* (Toronto, 1973), 270–72; Robert A. Goldstein, *French-Iroquois Diplomatic and Military Relations, 1609–1701* (The Hague, 1969), 62.

[118] Steele, *Warpaths*, 72–73; Axtell, *Invasion*, 41, 48; Alisa V. Petrovich, "Perception and Reality: Colbert's Native American Policy," *Louisiana History* 39 (1998):73–83.

In 1663 Colbert revoked the charter of the Company of One Hundred Associates and transformed Canada into a royal colony. He brought to his task a broad metropolitan and imperial vision. He hoped, above all, to increase the economic strength of France, and for this purpose efficient colonial oversight was essential. Canada seemed especially valuable to Colbert as a source of the timber, pitch, and tar necessary to fit out an expanding French navy and merchant marine. His policies, similar to those pursued by the Restoration regime in the English colonies, would render France's overseas possessions subservient and useful to the empire.[119]

Colbert quickly set in motion administrative changes designed to give him effective control of affairs in the colony. He appointed a governor-general to oversee military and Indian affairs, and an intendant to administer justice, colonial finance, and civil government. These two officials would implement the policy changes he hoped to effect.[120]

Colbert expected colonists in New France to devote themselves to agriculture and the production of raw materials. The colony must become self-sufficient, and French-Canadians must cultivate the land. Colbert believed that the colony's traditional subsistence economy, with furs as its only export, could evolve rapidly into a diversified economy resting upon shipbuilding, mining, fishing, and agriculture. Considering an expanded colonial population a necessary precondition for these programs to succeed, he encouraged the emigration of soldiers and settlers from France, plus a significant number of young *filles du roi* to provide a more balanced sex ratio.[121]

More important, however, was weaning the colonists from their nearly single-minded devotion to the fur trade. "By means of this trade," Colbert wrote, "the *habitants* will remain idle a good part of the year, whereas if they were not allowed to engage in it, they would be obliged to apply themselves to cultivating their land."[122] It was an old story, and the French were no more successful in making it come true than the English. Jean Talon, Colbert's first intendant and the man charged with the delicate task of enforcing restrictions against *coureurs de bois*, illegal traders, wrote that

> one must not expect to make people here submissive and always respectful of the King's law and of those who represent his authority, since there has probably never been a country where so many people, even the foremost in every profession, have sought to deny it. [123]

---

[119] Eccles, *Canadian Frontier*, 60–62; Dennis, *Cultivating a Landscape*, 200–201; Steele, *Warpaths*, 75–76; Philippe Jacquin, "The Colonial Policy of the Sun King," in *The Sun King: Louis XIV and the New World*, ed. Steven G. Reinhardt (New Orleans, La., 1984), 76.
[120] Eccles, *Canadian Frontier*, 64, 67.
[121] Ibid., 69; Eccles, *France in America*, 75; Axtell, *Invasion*, 41.
[122] Quoted in Eccles, *Canadian Frontier*, 104.
[123] Quoted in Jacquin, "Colonial Policy," 80.

It was indeed an especially difficult task because harsh controls on *coureurs de bois* might cause them to defect to the English. Nonetheless, Colbert believed an overreliance on the fur trade dangerous, and he worked through his lieutenants to control it.

Like Richelieu, Colbert also called for the Christianization and "civilization" of the Indians. The presence of Christian Indians would testify to the ability of the French to spread the word of God and provide the colony with thousands of potential allies. Yet although Jesuits did persuade many Indians "to join civil society and abandon that manner of life which prevents them from becoming good Christians," Colbert still faced a formidable threat from the Iroquois. None of his plans for New France could succeed, he knew, in a colony constantly on the defensive.[124]

In 1665 he sent out the Carignan-Salières regiment, 1,100 men under veteran officers, to bring the Five Nations to heel. The ensuing campaigns by no means resulted in the conquest of the Iroquois, but they did result in the razing of the Mohawks' towns and the destruction of their food supplies. In June 1667 the Mohawks and the rest of the Five Nations, weakened already by disease and warfare with other Indians, negotiated a peace with the French at Quebec which would last for two decades. Colbert may have celebrated this success, but the elimination of the Mohawk threat did not enable him to achieve his metropolitan goals. Peace with the Five Nations opened the West to French traders, who poured into the Great Lakes region, or *pays d'en haut*, looking for furs. Colbert feared that so overextended a trading empire would be difficult and costly to defend. By 1681 he had conceded defeat. So many *coureurs de bois* were prowling about to the west that he could not punish, much less arrest or control, them all.[125]

Many of these traders, however, upon penetrating the *pays d'en haut*, succeeded in establishing what historian Richard White called a "Middle Ground," where Frenchmen and Indians engaged in a creative process of cultural compromise in which mutual self-interest drove them to accommodate one another.[126] The fact that these traders did not form agricultural settlements and generally did not disrupt Indian subsistence and land-use patterns gave the Middle Ground in the *pays d'en haut* a viability it did not have in the English colonies. Nicolls and Lovelace recognized that English agricultural settlements placed enormous pressure upon Indians, rendering any common ground extremely fragile. Only efficient imperial and metropolitan control could bring order to the Anglo-American frontier.

Nicolls quickly put into effect a body of laws for the governance of New York. A significant portion of this code, known as the "Duke's Laws" of

---

[124] Ibid., 78; Steele, *Warpaths*, 73.
[125] Richter, *Ordeal*, 102–4; Eccles, *Canadian Frontier*, 64; Steele, *Warpaths*, 76.
[126] Richard White, *The Middle Ground: Indians, Empires and Republics in the Great Lakes Region, 1650–1815* (Cambridge, England, 1991).

1664, dealt with the subject of Anglo-Indian relations. The Duke's Laws gave the governor the right to license the trade in furs, weapons, and alcohol. They prohibited the purchase of land from Indians without the permission of the governor and specified that "all Injuryes done to the Indians of what nature soever shall upon their Complaint and proofe thereof in any Court have speed redress gratis, against any Christian in as full and Ample manner . . . as if the Case had been betwixt Christian & Christian." Further, they required that "in all places within this Goverment the English and all others shall keep their Cattle from destroying the Indians Corne in any ground where they have right to plant," holding English *towns* responsible for the damage done by their wandering animals. The Duke's Laws, like the code developed two years before by Governor Sir William Berkeley for Virginia, reflected the powerful determination of the Restoration monarchy to secure control of its American frontiers, in New York, New England, and the Chesapeake, and to incorporate the people living there into the long-hoped-for Anglo-American, Christian New World empire.[127]

Nicolls and Lovelace set out to regulate relations between Indians and whites in the lower Hudson valley and at Albany, formerly Fort Orange. On Long Island, they appointed Commissioners for Indian Affairs to regulate land transfers between the Long Island sachems and the English settlers, and keep "ye Indyans in some Order & Decorum."[128] This was an attempt at sound and efficient administration, and the Long Island commissioners diligently executed their duties. Nicolls and Lovelace encouraged them as well to work with missionaries to advance "ye Gospell of Christ in the conversion of the Gentiles & bringing them to the knowledge of his Law."[129]

Although the two English governors enjoyed some success in stabilizing Indian affairs in New York, the crown's attempt to curtail the independence of the New England colonies was on the whole a failure. The royal commissioners had declared the Atherton Purchase null and void, but no one in New England listened. After the departure of the commissioners the New England colonies each continued to antagonize the Algonquian bands within its claimed boundaries, and did so increasingly without the oversight of the Commissioners of the United Colonies, who after 1664 met only once every three years. As the growing English population pressed upon the New England Indians, the governors of the Puritan colonies lost control of the frontier. Increasing friction there undermined English efforts to convert the Indians to Christianity. With the exception of the relatively small number of

---

[127] Charles Z. Lincoln, ed., *The Colonial Laws of New York from the Year 1664 to the Revolution*, 5 vols. (Albany, N.Y., 1894), 1:40–41.

[128] Lovelace to Commissioners of Indian Affairs at the Eastern End of Long Island, 8 February 1671, in *Minutes of the Executive Council of the Province of New York: Administration of Francis Lovelace, 1668–1673*, ed. Victor Hugo Paltsits (Albany, N.Y., 1910), 2:466–67; *NYCD*, 24 June 1672, 13:463; *NYCD*, 14 March 1667, 14:569–70, 595.

[129] Lovelace to Mr. James of Easthampton, 14 November 1668, *NYCD*, 14:610.

Indians settled in Eliot's Praying Towns, and those engaged by the Mayhews on Martha's Vineyard, most efforts yielded disappointing results. English settlers demonstrated increasing hostility toward all Indians during the 1660s and 1670s, as competition for control of frontier resources intensified.[130]

Indeed, the task of protecting the Indians from neighboring whites became steadily more difficult. Complaints from Indians of property damage and even personal violence suffered at the hands of an increasingly unruly white frontier population flooded colonial magistrates' offices.[131] The illegal sale of firearms to the Indians continued, as did the tide of alcohol flowing into Indian villages. Implicitly acknowledging their loss of control over English settlers, New England's leaders after 1670 tended to focus their enforcement efforts on the Native American recipients rather than the English suppliers of alcohol.[132]

The most severe challenge to New England metropolitans emerged in Plymouth, where the Wampanoags, under their new sachem Philip (Metacom), had grown increasingly unwilling to tolerate offenses committed by a frontier population pressing them from three sides. Because there had been "lately many rumers gon too and frow of danger of the rising of the Indians against the English, and some suspision of their plotting against us to cut us of," the Plymouth men called Philip before them in 1662, hoping to secure his loyalty.[133] Philip, stating that he earnestly desired "the continuance of that amitie and friendship that hath formerly bin between this government and his deceased father and brother," entered into an agreement in which he pledged his subjection to the English,

and particularly that hee will not att any time needlessly or unjustly provoake or raise warr with any other of the natives, nor att any time give, sell, or any way dispose of any lands . . . withouth our privity, consent, or appointment.[134]

Several months later Philip reviewed his understanding of the agreement in a letter to Plymouth's governor Thomas Prence. Philip stated that "this last sumer he maid that promis with you, that he would not sell no land in 7 yeares time, nor that he would have no English trouble him before that time."[135] Prence and Plymouth had intended this agreement as a device to

---

[130] Richard Baxter to John Eliot, 20 January 1656/57; Eliot to Baxter, 7 October 1657, in Powicke, *Unpublished Correspondence*, 21, 22–23; Eliot to Humphrey Atherton, 4 June 1657, *MHS Coll*., 1st ser., 2 (1793): 99; see also Vaughan and Richter, "Crossing the Cultural Divide," 45.

[131] *PCR*, 5:22, 31, 107, 213; 11:213. *CR*, 10 May 1666, 2:37; 21 May 1668, 2:88–89; 12 October 1671, 2:165.

[132] *PCR*, 4 July 1673, 11:234; *CR*, 25 May 1675, 2:257; *MBR*, 23 May 1666, 4 (pt. 2): 297; *MBR*, 15 October 1673, 4 (pt. 2): 564.

[133] *PCR*, 8 October 1662, 4:25.

[134] *PCR*, 6 August 1662, 4: 25–26.

[135] Philip to Governor Prence, [1662], *MHS Coll*, 1st ser., 2 (1793): 40. On the dating of this letter, see Jennings, *Invasion*, 290–91 n.

restrain Philip from selling land to "strangers," particularly settlers from Rhode Island or Massachusetts, both of which claimed Mount Hope, the neck of land on which Philip's village was located. From Philip's perspective, however, the agreement freed him from the hassle of any land sales to the English, ensuring the integrity of Wampanoag holdings for seven years.[136]

Despite the agreement, the Wampanoags continued to complain of damage done to their crops by ranging English livestock. In May 1667 reports arrived in Rhode Island that a frustrated Philip was plotting against the English. Within a month the Plymouth magistrates had called Philip before the General Court to answer charges that "hee was in complyance with the French against the English in New England." Philip denied the accusations, blaming them on his rival, Ninigret. The Plymouth magistrates could find no evidence to support their charges, but they did fine Philip £40 for their trouble.[137]

The Wampanoags were feeling in acute form what most Algonquian bands in southern New England had experienced since the middle of the seventeenth century. These village communities had played an integral role in the fur trade through the 1650s. As the supply of furs in New England dwindled, wampum assumed a critical role in keeping the trade alive longer than the indigenous beaver population alone could have done. Wampum, obtained from the coastal bands in exchange for English goods, was delivered to the Mohawks, who reciprocated with furs they pillaged during the Beaver Wars, fought to the north. But this exchange network, which, however tenuously, had tied the coastal Algonquians to the English and the Mohawk, had begun to unravel by the middle of the century.[138]

One cause lay in the commercial success of the colonies, which led to an influx of English currency and the retirement of wampum as legal tender. The resulting surplus of shell beads, which the English dumped in New Netherland (to the detriment of the Dutch), produced a devaluation of wampum, as well as a drop in demand for it among inland Indians. The coastal Algonquians thus found their role in the New England economy entering a state of decline. Increasingly isolated from the nascent Mohawk-English alliance, the coastal Algonquians drew closer to Algonquin-speaking bands in the interior—the Eastern and Western Abenakis—both allied with the French against the Mohawks.[139]

At the same time the English population expanded dramatically, contributing to the establishment in the 1660s and 1670s of a large number of

[136] PCR, 6 August 1662, 4:25–26; Jennings, *Invasion*, 291; Philip Ranlet, "Another Look at the Causes of King Philip's War," *New England Quarterly* 61 (1988): 82.

[137] RICR, May 1667, 2:193; PCR, 5 June 1667, 4:151; PCR, 2 July 1667, 4:164–66.

[138] Neal Salisbury, "Toward the Covenant Chain: Iroquois and Southern New England Algonquians, 1637–1684," in *Beyond the Covenant Chain: The Iroquois and Their Neighbors in Indian North America, 1600–1800*, ed. James H. Merrell and Daniel K. Richter (Syracuse, N.Y., 1987), 65.

[139] Neal Salisbury, "The Colonizing of Indian New England," *Massachusetts Review* 26 (1985): 456; Lynn Ceci, "The First Fiscal Crisis in New York," *Economic Development and Culture Change* 28 (1980): 839–47.

agricultural settlements in areas formerly left undeveloped. The English population of New England doubled in the quarter-century after 1650, and the metropolitan magistrates of the Puritan colonies did not couple this expansion with order. The New England Algonquians, then, becoming marginalized within New England, were encircled by expanding and aggressive English settlements.[140]

By 1671 the Wampanoags clearly had reached a crisis in their relations with the Plymouth colonists. Destruction of Indian fields by English livestock had become so great that the colony's General Court appointed men in each settlement "to view the damage done to the Indians by the Horses and Hoggs of the English."[141] In March of that year the court received reports that Philip and his men "were generally employed in making of bows and arrows and half pikes, and fixing up of guns," and that they had threatened some of the outlying settlements.[142]

The Plymouth magistrates immediately called upon Philip to meet them at Taunton. He came, and reportedly "did acknowledge that they had bine in a preparation for warr against us; and that not grounded upon any injury sustained from us, nor provocation given by us, but from theire owne naughty harts." The magistrates demanded that Philip turn over all his guns, "not being in a capasitie to be kept faitfull by any other bonds," and planned to force neighboring bands allied with him to submit to English overlordship.[143]

Philip ignored Plymouth's demands. He left behind the guns he had carried with him to Taunton, but the magistrates soon complained that "many guns are knowne still to be amongst the Indians that live by him." He paid little attention to Plymouth's repeated calls for him to come before the magistrates and was said to be exploiting divisions among the English by "indeavouring to render us odiouse to our naighbour collonie, by false reports, complaints, and suggestions." Thus by June Philip stood accused of violating the agreement he had reportedly entered into at Taunton.[144]

Because Massachusetts, however, in response to Philip's complaints, had decided to follow a moderate course, Plymouth was reluctant to proceed against Philip alone. The magistrates therefore invited the commissioners from Massachusetts and Connecticut, then in Boston, to come to Plymouth for "a faire and deliberate hearing of the controversy between our collonie and the said sachem, Phillip, he being personally present." The visiting commissioners, not surprisingly, found Plymouth's case persuasive and ordered Philip to submit himself to both crown and colony. At the end of September Philip acknowledged himself a subject of Plymouth, agreed to pay a fine of

[140] Salisbury, "Colonizing," 456; Evarts B. Greene, *American Population before the Federal Census of 1790* (Gloucester, Mass., 1966), 9.

[141] *PCR*, 5 June 1671, 5:62.

[142] Deposition of Hugh Cole at Plymouth Court, A.D. 1670, 8 March 1671, *MHS Coll*, 1st ser., 6 (1800): 211.

[143] *PCR*, 5 June 1671, 5:63–64.

[144] *PCR*, 5 June 1671, 5:63.

£100, and promised to sell no land without the consent of the Plymouth court. Plymouth had bullied him into a nominal subjection to English authority, but the colony had not established its dominion over the frontier. Philip, in fact, raised the funds necessary to pay the fines by selling land. With the money left over he bought guns.[145]

The treaty of 1671 did nothing to remedy the underlying sources of tension poisoning Indian-white relations in southern New England. Over the course of the next four years Plymouth continued to extend its jurisdiction over nearly every aspect of Native American life, at the same time failing to address effectively the conditions that threatened New England's tenuous peace. Algonquians, for their part, continued to bring complaints to the Plymouth court—in such volume that by 1673 the magistrates felt compelled to ban Indians from town when court was held. Indians were permitted only during the July and October sessions. The colony in effect created separate legal systems for Indians and for whites, the product of hardening provincial attitudes toward the natives.[146]

In January 1675 the events that led immediately to war occurred in Plymouth Plantation after the murdered body of John Sassamon, a Christian Indian, was found stuffed under the ice at Assowamsett Pond. Sassamon, literate in English and educated at Harvard, had earlier served as an interpreter and translator for Philip, despite his Christianity. He fell out with Philip when it was discovered that he had attempted to include in the sachem's will an enormous grant of land for himself.[147] He then joined the English at Nemsaket where he was on good terms with the colonists. In 1674, perhaps hoping to convert Philip, he returned briefly to the Wampanoags, where he saw enough to convince him that Philip had hatched a plan to attack the English. Sassamon provided this information to Plymouth's new governor, Edward Winslow, and he was killed a short time later. Three Wampanoag Indians were convicted of the murder and executed on June 8, 1675.[148]

The prosecution of Sassamon's alleged murderers brought Plymouth to the brink of war. During the trial, reports arrived daily that Philip planned to strike, and he gave "our people frequent alarums by drums and guns in the night." Philip was entirely disaffected with the English. In the middle of June he told Rhode Island's lieutenant governor, John Easton, that the English made the Wampanoags drunk "and then Cheted them in Bargens." If Indian sachems refused to sell land, he continued, the English frontiersmen would name a more compliant sachem "that would give or seall them there land." No matter how far the Indians removed from the settlers, "thay

[145] *PCR*, 23 August 1671, 5:77–79.

[146] Ronda, "Red and White," 210–211.

[147] "A Relacion of the Indyan Warre by Mr. Easton, of Roade ISLD," in *Narratives of the Indian Wars, 1675–1699*, ed. Charles H. Lincoln (New York, 1941), 7.

[148] *PCR*, 10:362; Jennings, *Invasion*, 294; Douglas Edward Leach, *Flintlock and Tomahawk: New England in King Philip's War*, (New York, 1958) 30.

Could not kepe ther Coren from being spoyled" by English livestock. Philip "thott when the English bott land of them thay wold have kept their Catell upone ther owne land." He complained that English alcohol had devastated his society. Philip and the Wampanoags felt besieged by an English population that had grown rapidly, spread across the countryside, and attempted to bring the Indians under colonial authority and acquire their land. Philip reminded Easton that when the Puritans first arrived in America fifty-five years before, his father, Massasoit, was "a great man and the English as a litell Child." At that time he had "constraened other Indians from ronging the English and gave them Coren and shewed them how to plant and was free to do them ani good and let them have a 100 times more land" than now Philip had for his own people.[149]

True to his Quaker leanings, Easton hoped the approaching conflict between the Wampanoags and Plymouth could be settled through arbitration. He expressed to Philip his desire that "the quarell might rightly be desided in the best way, and not as dogs desided ther quarells," through violence. Philip was suspicious. "All English agred against" his people, he told Easton, "and so by arbetration thay had much rong, mani miles of land so taken from them for English wold have English Arbetrators."[150]

At nearly the same time the Plymouth frontiersman Benjamin Church traveled to a dance held by Awashunks, the squaw-sachem of Sakonnet, demonstrating convincingly that at least some Indians were willing still to maintain friendship with the settlers. Awashunks informed Church that Philip had sent men "to draw her into a confederacy with him in a war against the English." Church assured her that the English intended peace and apparently convinced her that he spoke the truth. With the Wampanoag emissaries also at Sakonnet, armed and in war paint, Church was less diplomatic. He told Philip's men that "they were bloody wretches and thirsted after the blood of their English neighbors, who had never injured them." Church left the gathering convinced that Philip intended war. Colonists along the Plymouth frontier fled their homes in search of safer quarter.[151]

IV

Englishmen drew first blood late in June 1675, when two of them killed a Wampanoag Indian they caught rifling an abandoned house on the outskirts of Swansea. The next day, June 24, 1675, "the lad that shot the Indian and his father, and fief English more wear killed."[152]

---

[149] "Relacion of the Indyan Warre," 10–11.

[150] Ibid., 9.

[151] Benjamin Church, *Diary of King Philip's War, 1675–1676*, ed. Alan and Mary Simpson (Chester, Conn., 1973), 65, 69, 72; Nathaniel Saltonstall, "Present State of New England," in Lincoln, *Narratives*, 27–28; Leach, *Flintlock*, 34.

[152] "Relacion of the Indyan Warre," 12. Actually nine were killed at Swansea.

In the days after Philip's forces struck Swansea, the New England colonies prepared for war. Suspicious always of the Narragansetts, Massachusetts sent a delegation, escorted by Roger Williams, to secure their pledges of loyalty and a promise not to harbor Wampanoag refugees. The Narragansetts agreed to stay out of the war, but even Williams doubted their sincerity. He reported to John Winthrop Jr. that canoes had been regularly spotted passing between the Narragansetts and Wampanoags. Moreover, Williams did not believe that Philip would have attacked "had he not been assured to have bene seconded and assisted by the Monhiggins and Nahigonsicks."[153]

Fearing a widespread Indian uprising, the colonies worked to restrain their settlers from further alienating the neighboring Indians or providing them with the means to do damage to the English. The Connecticut Council ordered settlers at Northampton and Hadley to desist from bullying local Indians and told residents of Milford to ensure that "all fayre dealeings might be between them, and to advise them not to give them any just ground of provocations." The Bay Colony, similarly, ordered that "all trade with the Indians be prohibbited for the future" and quickly repealed an act that had allowed the treasurer to license colonists to sell weapons to the natives. In Plymouth the barter or sale of weapons became a capital crime.[154]

Within weeks New Englanders were convinced that all the Indians in the region had aligned against them. Certainly in the summer of 1675 this was not the case. As the New England colonies careened from disaster to disaster in the early months of the war, however, the desperate colonial governments managed to ensure the enmity of most of the New England Algonquian bands. Meanwhile, native groups watched and learned as their English neighbors demonstrated a unique vulnerability to ambush and surprise attack.

After Philip's forces razed Swansea, they fell upon the neighboring villages of Rehoboth and Taunton. On July 9 they attacked the small settlement at Middleborough. Most of the houses were burned. Shortly thereafter Philip's forces struck Dartmouth, in the southern part of Plymouth, where they burned thirty houses and killed "many People after a most Barbarous Manner; as skinning them all alive, some only their Heads, cutting off their Hands and Feet." The next week Nipmuck warriors destroyed Mendon, within thirty miles of Boston. The war was not going well, and the number of Algonquian groups taking part seemed to be growing.[155]

The colonists' own offensives against the Algonquians proved little more than ill-led and poorly executed exercises in futility that killed needlessly large numbers of Englishmen. An early attempt to trap Philip on the Mount

---

[153] Roger Williams to John Winthrop Jr., 25 and 27 June 1675, in Williams, *Correspondence*, 2:693–94, 698.

[154] CR, 25 August 1675, 2:353–54; 2 September 1675, 2:360. MBR, 9 July 1675, 5:44–45; 3 May 1676, 5:80. PCR, 1 June 1675, 5:173.

[155] Saltonstall, "Present State of New England," 30.

Hope peninsula failed to subdue the Wampanoag sachem but did result in the discovery of "some Heads, Scalps, and Hands cut off from the Bodys of some of the English, and stuck upon Poles near the Highway." An English attack on Philip early in August drove his forces into a swamp just west of the Pawtucket River, but the colonists failed to exploit their advantage, allowing Philip and his warriors to escape to the relative safety of Nipmuck country.[156]

With Philip still at large, Algonquian war parties devastated the New England frontier. Indians struck towns on the periphery of Plymouth and Massachusetts Bay, burning farms and forcing the abandonment of outlying areas there as well as in the Connecticut Valley. By far the worst English defeat came at Bloody Brook, five miles south of Deerfield. There eighty men, "the very flower of the County of Essex . . . were suddenly set upon, and almost all cut off."[157]

The provincial military system simply lacked the means to defend settlements scattered along nearly three hundred miles of frontier. The formal tactics of European warfare were better suited to the training ground than to the New England forest, and the rapid destruction of the Pequots in 1637 had given New Englanders little chance to adapt their tactics to American conditions. Thus handicapped in their efforts to fight the Indians on their own soil, English soldiers walked into a series of well-executed Algonquian ambushes. These attacks, wrote one Rhode Islander, "did ye English Great & sore damage, by reason of theyr unpreparednes at such unacspected times." In the fall of 1675 Governor William Leete of Connecticut complained that it was

> hardly feasable to extirpate [the Indians] in an ordinary way, they being so cunning in a sculking ambuscadoe maner, to make advantage of the woods, & so accurate markes men, aboue our men, to doe execution, whereby more of ours are like to fall, rather then of theirs, unlesse the Lord, by speciall providences, doe deliver them into our handes."[158]

The Lord, apparently, had little interest in doing so in the early months of the war. Even the famed Swamp Fight in December 1675, in which some six hundred Indians died (as many as half were women and children), was not an unqualified English military victory. In the middle of the Great Swamp near present-day West Kingston, Rhode Island, the Narragansetts had constructed

---

[156] Hubbard, *Narrative*, 19; Leach, *Flintlock*, 75–77.

[157] Hubbard, *Narrative*, 30.

[158] William Leete to John Winthrop Jr., 23 September 1675, *MHS Coll*, 4th ser., 7 (1865): 579; Douglas Edward Leach, ed., *A Rhode Islander Reports on King Philip's War: The Second William Harris Letter of August, 1676* (Providence, R.I., 1963), 34; Richard R. Johnson, "The Search for a Usable Indian: An Aspect of the Defense of Colonial New England," *JAH* 64 (1977): 639; Harold E. Selesky, *War and Society in Colonial Connecticut* (New Haven, Conn., 1990), 10.

an impressive fort, complete with breastworks and palisades, upon "a Piece of firm Land, about three or four Acres of Ground." Its defenders killed some two hundred Englishmen, including "six brave captains," before the attackers breached the palisade, drove off the warriors, and set the fortress ablaze. The poorly provisioned English troops, however, battered in the assault and weakened by the onset of winter, lacked the energy and determination to pursue.[159]

The Commissioners of the United Colonies had intended the campaign preceding the Great Swamp Fight to prevent an alliance between the Narragansetts and the Wampanoags. In October 1675 the commissioners obtained the signatures of seven minor Narragansett sachems on an agreement to turn over Wampanoag refugees under their protection. By November 2, however, the sachems still had not complied. The commissioners then raised a force of a thousand men, under the command of Governor Josiah Winslow of Plymouth, to force the Narragansetts to honor their agreement. Winslow never attempted to negotiate for the surrender of the Wampanoag refugees but set out to destroy the Narragansetts as quickly as possible. Whether or not the Narragansetts had previously intended to join Philip, the brutality of the battle ensured that the survivors of the Swamp Fight *would* ally with the Wampanoags.[160]

The New England metropolitans were not taking defeat well. Their inability to engage Philip's forces, and to prevent neighboring Algonquian communities from joining him, produced both fear and frustration in the provincial capitals. The success of the Algonquian rising demonstrated that provincial leaders had failed to govern the New England frontier effectively. When the Virginia Company showed a similar inability after 1622, the crown had taken over the colony. Massachusetts, the heart of Puritan New England, feared a similar fate.[161]

The Puritans' frustration with their inability to prosecute the war successfully manifested itself in a generalized viciousness characteristic of what was becoming, for New Englanders, a race war. Though colonial authorities attempted "to make a Distinction visible, betwixt our Friends *the Christian Indians*, and our enemie *the Heathens*," their policies generally transformed the former into the latter. As the war continued, Englishmen complained that "they cannot know a Heathen from a Christian by his Visage or Appareal."[162]

Colonial courts sold some captured Indians into slavery in the West Indies, "whereby damage from them may be prevented." Others they "condemned

---

[159] For accounts of the Great Swamp Fight, see Nathaniel Saltonstall, "A Continuation of the State of New England," in Lincoln, *Narratives*, 58–59; Hubbard, *Narrative*, 52–53; Leach, *Rhode Islander*, 36; George Madison Bodge, *Soldiers in King Philip's War* (Baltimore, Md., 1967), 185–98.

[160] *RUC*, 2 November 1675, 2:357; Leach, *Flintlock*, 126.

[161] Jennings, *Invasion*, 299.

[162] Saltonstall, "Continuation," 54, and "Present State of New England," 32.

unto perpetuall servitude . . . for and to the use of the collonie, as opportunity may present."[163] As colonial magistrates moved toward the frontier perspective that all Indians were potential enemies, Puritans gathered the Christian Indians who had settled in towns under provincial authority into concentration camps. In October 1675 the Massachusetts General Court ordered "that all the Naticke Indians be forthwith sent for, & disposed of to Deare Island, as the place appointed for their present aboade." Three weeks later the magistrates passed an additional act ordering "that none of the said Indians shall presume to goe off the said islands voluntarily, upon paine of death." The magistrates incarcerated the Praying Indians in response to the "desires of the Commonality," who thought them more likely "Preying Indians," who "have made Preys of much English blood."[164]

New Englanders also poured their wrath upon Englishmen accused of being friendly with natives. Arguing on behalf of the Christian Indians made Daniel Gookin "a Byword both among Men and Boys." Wrote Nathaniel Saltonstall, "the Commonalty were so enraged against Mr Elliot, and Captain Guggins especially, that Captain Guggins said on the Bench, that he was afraid to go along the Streets." The mob told the embattled captain that "you may thank yourself."[165] Lynch mobs roamed the streets of Boston in search of victims, ruthlessly putting to death suspect Indians and denouncing and threatening "Indian-lovers."[166]

As the war continued, New Englanders treated the Indians with increasing violence. Samuel Mosely, a Jamaican privateer who raised a company of "volunteers" from among "the most reckless and disreputable class in the colony," was one of the most notorious. Mosely cavalierly enslaved the Indians he captured or, on more than one occasion, gunned down his prisoners. Reporting to the Bay Colony's governor, John Leverett, on the interrogation of an Indian captured near Springfield, Mosely casually remarked that "this aforesaid Indian was ordered to be torn in peeces by Doggs and she was soe dealt with all."[167] In an act representative of the Puritan magistracy's frame of mind, the Plymouth court ordered that anyone who fired a gun in the colony for any reason "except att an Indian or a woolfe" would pay a fine of five shillings.[168]

---

[163] *MBR*, 21 February 1676, 5:72; *PCR*, 2 September 1675, 5:174. See also *PCR*, 4 August 1675, 5:173; and 22 July 1676, 5:207.

[164] *MBR*, 13 October 1675, 5:56–57 and 3 November 1675, 5:64; John Eliot to Robert Boyle, 17 December 1675, in Ford, *Correspondence*, 53–54; Saltonstall, "Present State of New England," 49; Daniel Gookin, *An Historical Account of the Doings and Sufferings of the Christian Indians in New England in the Years 1675, 1676, 1677* (New York, 1972), 485.

[165] Saltonstall, "Present State of New England," 40–41.

[166] Ibid., 41; Gookin, *Historical Account*, 482–516; Johnson, "Search," 626; Leach, *Flintlock*, 149, 151.

[167] Samuel Mosely to Governor Leverett, 16 October 1675, in Bodge, *Soldiers*, 69, 401; Saltonstall, "Present State of New England," 39–40.

[168] *PCR*, 4 October 1675, 5:177.

Ministers and magistrates attributed the colonies' failures in the war to the wrath of God. "I fear," wrote William Hubbard, that "God hath a controversie with New England, so now that the rod of affliction, hath not only budded and blossomed, but brought forth its fruit." All the colonial governments appointed days of fasting and humiliation and called for the moral regeneration of their people.[169] In Whitehall, however, "the chief if not only cause of the Indians making war upon the English" was thought to be "the tyrannical government of the Massachusetts." The king and his councilors believed that the petty New England governments had woefully mismanaged the frontier and needlessly provoked a war that killed the king's subjects and ruined the king's trade. The reported military prowess of the Puritans appeared illusory, as armed Algonquians set New England's frontier ablaze.[170]

The dawning of 1676 brought no change in New England's fortunes. In the first two months of the year Indians destroyed eight towns, ambushed English forces, and wiped out scattered garrisons. As Nathaniel Saltonstall wrote, "the Dispensation we lay under was Cloudy and Affrighting, Fresh Messengers (like Job's Servants) howrly arriving to bring Doleful Tidings of New Massacres, Slaughters and Devastations committed by the Brutish Heathens."[171]

The growing conflagration to the east alarmed the New York's new governor, Edmund Andros. He was "much troubled" in July 1675 by "the Christians misfortunes and hard disasters in those parts being so over powered by such heathen." As the Algonquian rising threatened to spread beyond New England into the Duke of York's domain, Andros took steps not only to secure New York's frontier but to extend dominion over all the subjects of the crown, both European and Native American.[172]

Andros was the consummate metropolitan. Promoted rapidly for his diligent service in the name of the king, he believed that order along the Anglo-American frontier, and thus the metropolitan imperatives of dominion and civility, could be obtained only through a dramatic reassertion of imperial power in the provinces. The crown, not narrow-minded provincials, must direct relations between Indians and the English. He saw scattered English settlements, each pursuing its own foreign policies, sometimes in unison with others but more often not, as inimical to the king's best interest.[173]

---

[169] William Hubbard, *The Happiness of a People in the Wisdome of their Rulers* . . . (Boston, 1676), 54; *MBR*, 3 November 1675, 5:59–63; *CR*, 26 August 1675, 2:355, and 22 November 1675, 2:383.
[170] Minutes of the Committee for Trade and Plantations Respecting the Case of Mason and Gorges, *CSP Coll*, 1675–1676, no. 721; Webb, *1676*, 206, 222, 227.
[171] Nathaniel Saltonstall, "A New and Further Narrative of the State of New England," in Lincoln, *Narratives*, 78; Webb, *1676*, 240.
[172] Edmund Andros to Go. Carteret, 4 July 1675, in *The Andros Papers: Files of the Provincial Secretary of New York during the Administration of Sir Edmund Andros, 1674–1680*, ed. Peter R. Christoph and Florence A. Christoph, 3 vols. (Syracuse, N.Y., 1989), 1:183.
[173] Webb, *1676*, 359; Richter, *Ordeal*, 135.

Andros recognized that closer ties with the Five Nations of the Iroquois could facilitate his imperial charge to contain the French on the northern side of Lake Ontario, secure the allegiance of New York's Dutch population, defend the duke's claims to the Delaware River drainage, and bring the detested Puritan colonies to heel. His predecessors, Nicolls and Lovelace, had laid the foundations for a solid Anglo-Iroquoian alliance. Upon this groundwork Andros hoped to complete the structure of crown rule in North America.[174]

Early in August 1675 Andros left the city of New York, stopping on August 5 at Esopus. There he confirmed an earlier peace with a local Mahican band before continuing on to Albany. Andros sent runners before him summoning the Iroquois, "the most warlike Indyans neare a hundred miles beyound Albany," to a meeting at the Mohawk castle at Tinontougen.[175] At that council the governor and the Iroquois ambassadors, led by Daniel Garacontié, discussed the resolution of warfare between the western Iroquois and the Susquehannocks, as well as with English colonists in the Chesapeake. Andros agreed also to settle a peace between the Mahicans and Mohawks, ending a decade of debilitating warfare. He pledged to protect the Mohawks from both the French and their enemies and to obtain the release of Mohawks held hostage by the Mahicans.[176]

By August 24 Andros had returned to Albany, which he placed upon a war footing lest it suffer the fate of so many Puritan towns. To secure friendly relations with Iroquoian groups coming there to trade, he authorized the town commissaries along with the commandant to sit as a Commission of Indian Affairs, thus continuing a technique of metropolitan oversight dating back to the administration of Richard Nicolls. Furthermore, he forbade "all barter or trade with the Indians outside the city of Albany," placing relations between Indians and colonists under the immediate oversight of his appointed agents. Convinced that in Albany "all things [were] settled, for the Magistracy, Militia and defence," Andros returned to New York at the end of the month.[177]

Andros called upon his lieutenants to follow closely the provisions of the agreements he had made not only with the New York Indians but with bands

---

[174] Treaty of George Cartwright with Mohawks and Senecas, 24 September 1664, *NYCD*, 3:67–68; Daniel K. Richter, "Ordeals of the Longhouse: The Five Nations in Early American History," in Richter and Merrell, *Beyond the Covenant Chain*, 24; Richter, *Ordeal*, 98–99; Salisbury, "Toward the Covenant Chain," 67.

[175] Edmund Andros, "A Short Account of the General Concerns of New Yorke," *NYCD*, 3:254.

[176] Francis Jennings, *The Ambiguous Iroquois Empire: The Covenant Chain Confederation of Indian Tribes with English Colonies from its Beginnings to the Lancaster Treaty of 1744* (New York, 1984), 141; Ted J. Brasser, "Mahican," in *Handbook of North American Indians*, vol. 15, *Northeast*, ed. William C. Sturtevant (Washington, D.C., 1978), 203–4.

[177] A. J. F. Van Laer, trans., *Minutes of the Court of Albany, Rensselaerwyck, and Schenectady, 1668–1685*, 3 vols. (Albany, N.Y., 1928), 2:17; *NYCD*, 3:254; Andros to Commissioners of the United Colonies, 16 September 1675, *RUC*, 2:453; Webb, 1676, 363.

farther south in the duke's domain along the Delaware. If treated well, he believed, the Iroquois and other native groups would provide valuable assistance to the pursuit of metropolitan goals. The governor's council accordingly resolved "that we ought not to breake wth our Indyans, upon Acct of
ye Warre betweene our Neighbours and their Indyans."[178]

Andros's informed diplomacy and broad metropolitan vision compared
favorably with the ineffectiveness of the Puritan regimes and spared the
duke's province the destruction meted out by Algonquian warriors in New
England. His careful awareness of the prerequisites for sound frontier defense and politic handling of his own relations with the New York and Long
Island bands, made "New York and its dependencies islands of interracial
symbiosis in a sea of red-white strife."[179]

Andros nonetheless prepared New York for the possibility that Algonquian
rage might spill across its borders. Philip and his allies had devastated the upper Connecticut Valley, and Andros believed that he planned to fall upon
Hartford by the middle of October. Fearing invasion, Andros sent Captain
Anthony Brockholes to Albany with instructions to persuade the Iroquois to
attack the Mahicans who had joined Philip, as well as other Hudson River
bands recruited to the Algonquian banner. Shortly after Brockholes departed,
word arrived of the devastating Algonquian assault on Springfield.[180] Andros
promptly modified his orders, calling upon Brockholes to persuade the Mohawks to attack not only the Hudson bands currently in rebellion but Philip's
forces as well. Brockholes must show no fear of the consequences of a
Wampanoag invasion but appeal instead to Mohawk interest. "The
Maques," Andros wrote, must "see tis ffriendship, not Apprehension or
Need of them, but for their Good," that they engage the Algonquians. He had
heard that they "and the Sinnekes are inclinable to a Warre wth the Indyans
to the East," and "if soe, though they have not yet attackt us, tis the Opinion
of my Councell, that twere well the said Maques were rather encouraged than
hindrd." Brockholes was to allow them "a ffree Markett for Powder, &c."[181]

Andros's Mohawk allies would bring to a close the Algonquian uprising
in southern New England. Early in January 1676, Andros received word that
Philip's forces had settled for the winter along the Hoosick River, fifty miles
from Albany. There, reports indicated, they had gained the support of the
Mahicans, several Hudson River Algonquian bands, and "5 or 600 French
Indyans with strawes in their noses"—probably Christian Mohawks who

[178] Council Minutes, 10 September 1675, in *A Narrative of the Causes Which Led to King
Philip's War of 1675 and 1676 with Other Documents*, ed. Franklin B. Hough (Albany, N.Y.,
1858), 71.
[179] Webb, *1676*, 353. See also proclamation by Andros, 16 September 1675, in Hough, *Narrative*, 75; Order to Disarm Long Island Indians, 24 January 1676, *NYCD* 14:712.
[180] For the best account of the damage, see John Pynchon to Governor Leverett and Assistants, 8 October 1675 in *Pynchon Papers*, ed. Carl Bridenbaugh, *Publications of the Colonial
Society of Massachusetts*, 61(1985), 1:157.
[181] Andros to Brockholes, 19 October 1675, in Hough, *Narrative*, 103.

had allied themselves with the French a decade before. The number of Indians encamped with Philip along the Hoosick may have approached three thousand.[182]

Andros commanded Brockholes to accept "old Maques Sachems, women & children into our townes" for protection and to supply the Mohawks "with [the] ammunicon, armes & all they wanted" to attack the Algonquians gathered at Hoosick. Plans for the assault progressed quickly. On February 4 Andros informed the Connecticut Council of his willingness to engage the Mohawks "in yor Indyan Warr upon Philip & North Indyans." First, however, he demanded to know "weather you would desire & admit our forces, Xtians or Indians, perticularly Maquase & Seneques, to pursue such ennemies, unto any part of yor Colony." Any aggression toward the Iroquois from Connecticut's bellicose frontier troops, Andros cautioned, would be ill advised, for the Mohawk force included "3000 or more good fighting men, and to farr to be easily forced."[183]

The New Englanders recognized the martial prowess of the Mohawks, and even Uncas had argued "that the said Mohucks were the only Persons likely to put an End to the War."[184] The New England colonies, however, and especially Connecticut, distrusted Andros. Before the war he had pressed the Duke of York's claim to all lands west of the Connecticut River, a tract that included all the colony's important towns. During the first month of the war, Connecticut had resisted Andros's attempt to land troops at Saybrook, ostensibly to assist in the river colony's war efforts. Now they saw lurking behind the New York governor's offers of military assistance the specter of Stuart absolutism.[185] Both Connecticut and Massachusetts Bay, moreover, suspected that the Albany arms trade was supplying not only Andros's Iroquoian allies but Philip's Algonquian confederates as well.[186]

Andros vigorously denied these charges. As he monitored the situation and learned from English scouts that Philip's gathered forces intended "first to destroy Connecticot this Spring, then Boston in the Harvest," he grew increasingly impatient with the Puritan governments. Word from Albany affirmed that a crisis was approaching. Andros ordered Brockholes to offer all possible encouragement to the Mohawks to fall on Philip's camp.[187]

---

[182] *CR*, 6 January 1676, 2:397; "A Short Account of the General Concerns of New York," *NYCD*, 3:255; "A Short Account of the Assistance Rendered by New-York to New England," *NYCD*, 3:265; *NYCD*, 14:715–16; Van Laer, *Minutes of Albany*, 2:48–49; Richter, "Ordeals," 24; Salisbury, "Toward the Covenant Chain," 70–71; Webb, *1676*, 367.

[183] *NYCD*, 3:265 and 13:509; Andros to Connecticut Council, 4 February 1676, *CR*, 2:406.

[184] Saltonstall, "New and Further," 88. See also Council of Connecticut to Andros, 13 January 1676, *CR*, 2:398–99.

[185] William Leete to Edmund Andros, 15 November 1677, *Andros Papers*, 2:160–61. James, duke of York, later asked Andros to postpone action on these claims; see Duke of York to Andros, 31 January 1676, *NYCD*, 3:235.

[186] Council of Connecticut to Andros, 31 January 1676, *CR*, 2:404–5.

[187] Andros to Council of Connecticut, 20 January 1676, *CR*, 2:404; Saltonstall, "New and Further," 88; Webb, *1676*, 368.

Then, late in February, aided by an early thaw of the Hudson, Andros "tooke ye first opportunity to goe up with an additional force and six sloops to Albany." Because Massachusetts Bay, Plymouth, and Connecticut had not "made us acquainted with their concerns and some of them slighted our friendly tenders, to continue our Endeavours as Christians and ye Kings subjects," he would act against Philip "without further application to the said Colonyes." Andros and his troops were not needed, however. Upon his arrival in Albany on March 4, the governor found "aboutt three hundred Maquaas Souldiers in towne, returned ye Evening afore from ye pursuite of Philip and a party of five hundred with him, whome they had beaten, having some prisoners & the crowns, or hayre and skinne of the head, of others they had killed."[188]

The Hoosick attack was the first of a number of blows that would signal the collapse of Philip's Algonquian uprising. Although it is possible to overstate the extent to which Andros "controlled" the Mohawks, there can be no questioning the success of his interracial diplomacy. Among the native forces gathered around Philip at Hoosick were "French Indyans" who had split from the Mohawks after 1665 and converted to Christianity; Mahicans, enemies of the Iroquois since at least the beginning of the seventeenth century; Algonquian bands from the upper Connecticut River valley with whom the Mohawks had fought incessantly since mid-century; and eastern and western Abenakis, allied with the French and hostile to the Iroquois. The Mohawks thus had cause for war with each of these, and their attack on Hoosick merely continued the bitter intertribal conflicts they had engaged in for the balance of a century. Recognizing and establishing an identity of interest between the king's subjects and the Mohawks, Andros took a sound first step toward establishing English dominion along the Anglo-American frontier.[189]

Philip still had considerable strength, and between March and June the Algonquian bands allied with him carried out fifteen assaults on surviving towns in the Connecticut Valley, hoping through these attacks to drive back English settlement in the region. These attacks failed, but the result was stalemate rather than setback; Algonquian groups had begun to plant corn in fields recently abandoned by settlers—a sign of growing confidence or, at least, an expectation that they could remain free from attack there long enough to harvest the corn in the fall. But Mohawk raiders shattered Philip's organization. The tide of the war had clearly turned, and the Mohawks were most responsible. Mohawk raids succeeded in cutting off the flow of weapons to Philip from Montreal, in demoralizing his forces, and driving the

---

[188] Andros, "Short Account," 3:255; Council Minute, 26 February 1676, *NYCD*, 13:493.
[189] Richard I. Melvoin, *New England Outpost: War and Society in Colonial Deerfield* (New York, 1989), 118–19, 119 n; Colin G. Calloway, *The Western Abenaki of Vermont, 1600–1800: War, Migration, and the Survival of an Indian People* (Norman, Okla., 1990): 78; Webb, *1676*, 355–404.

Algonquians from the relative safety of the Connecticut. Some of Philip's forces fled to Canada, others eastward. Many, like Philip himself, moved south toward revitalized colonial militias that had abandoned their scruples about fighting "Indian-style" and thus dramatically increased their effectiveness.[190]

King Philip's War ended where it began, on the Mount Hope peninsula. His people reeling from the slaughter that befell them at Turner's Falls in Connecticut and ravaged by disease and hunger, Philip was tracked down by a combined force of colonists and Christian Indians led by Plymouth's Benjamin Church. They killed Philip on August 12, 1676. Church ordered the sachem's body pulled from the mire where it had fallen, resolved "that forasmuch as he had caused many an Englishman's body to be unburied, and to rot above ground, that not one of his bones should be buried." Church hacked off the head, quartered the body, and hung Philip's dismembered corpse from four trees.[191]

Andros hoped to eliminate the conditions that he believed had contributed originally to the outbreak of war. Aware by the end of May that the Algonquians were effectively defeated, he announced that all "North Indyans" who settled in New York would "be protected, & a stop to be put to the Maques farther prosecuting sd. North Indyans."[192] In an attempt to subvert the Puritans' aggressive scramble for postwar spoils, Andros obtained the official grant of the King's Province for Rhode Island, itself a victim of Puritan bigotry and aggression. To prevent the Puritan colonies from making individual treaties with defeated Algonquian bands, the governor declared "that all Indyans, who will come in & submitt, shall be received to live under the protection of the Government" of the Duke of York.[193]

Pinched between Mohawk raiders and vengeful Puritans, large numbers of Connecticut Algonquians accepted Andros's offer and settled at the Mahican village of Schagticoke, near Philip's winter camp. There they escaped the wholesale enslavement, summary execution, and dispossession that characterized postwar Puritan "justice."[194]

The settled bands provided the duke's domain with a buffer against possible French invasion and tightened Albany's hold over the regional Indian trade. By settling the Algonquian refugees in the vicinity of Albany, moreover, Andros achieved oversight of the conduct of Indian diplomacy in southern New England. When the Connecticut Council requested permission "to

---

[190] Melvoin, *New England Outpost*, 112–21; Bodge, *Soldiers*, 242; Malone, *Skulking Way of War*, 119.

[191] Benjamin Church, *The History of the Great Indian War of 1675 and 1676, Commonly Called Philip's War*, rev. ed. (Hartford, Conn., 1851); Nathaniel Saltonstall, "The Warr in New England Visibly Ended," in Lincoln, *Narratives*, 105.

[192] Council Minutes, 29 May 1676, NYCD, 13:496.

[193] Council Minutes, 30 May 1676, NYCD, 13:496–97; Andros to Albany, 12 July 1677, *Andros Papers*, 2:72–73.

[194] Webb, *1676*, 357–58.

persue and to effect the utter extirpation of such as have imbrued their hands in the blood of many of his Majesties good subjects," and suggested that Andros "either grant us liberty to pass up your river . . . to persue and destroy those of the enemies that are in those parts; or doe something effectuall yourselfe, for the utter suppression of the enemie in those parts," he refused. When Massachusetts demanded that several hostile Indians now settled in New York be turned over, Andros coolly decided that "it is not proper."[195]

In protecting Algonquian refugees from the excesses of Puritan vengeance, Andros needed as well to protect them from the Mohawks, who pursued, with the governor's assistance, their own agenda. In the spring of 1677 Andros invited delegates from New England to meet with the Indians settled under his protection. The Mohawks agreed to halt their raids upon friendly Indians in New England, and to make peace with the Mahicans. They also agreed to commence hostilities against the Abenakis, (who were in conflict with settlers in northern New England).[196] The New Englanders, in turn, surrendered their right to treat with the New York tribes independently. Andros assured for himself oversight of New England Indian diplomacy when the Mohawks insisted that all future discussions between themselves and the Puritan colonies take place at Albany, in the presence of the governor.[197]

V

Philip's death brought to a close only the first chapter of the Algonquian rising that ravaged New England. Abenakis 250 miles to the north, along the densely forested coast of northern Massachusetts and the province of Maine, had struck out against the small pockets of English colonists there in September 1675, less than three months after Wampanoag warriors attacked Swansea. For the next two years Abenaki warriors—Sacos, Penobscots, Kennebecs, Pigwackets, and Androscoggins—would demonstrate to crown officials the vulnerability of the northern New England frontier.[198]

Massachusetts had usurped the right to govern the province of Maine, but by the 1670s it still had not established its authority there. This left the Maine frontier effectively free from any external English constraint. Alcohol

---

[195] Connecticut Council to Andros, 19 August 1676, *CR*, 2:470–71; Connecticut Council to Andros, 24 September 1677, in "The Wyllys Papers: Correspondence and Documents Chiefly of Descendants of Gov. George Wyllys of Connecticut, 1590–1796," *Collections of the Connecticut Historical Society* 21 (1924): 267–68; Council Minutes, 8 September 1676, *NYCD*, 13: 501.

[196] *CR*, 10 April 1677, 2:482; Order in Council, 28 March 1677, *NYCD*, 13:504; Webb, *1676*, 357–58.

[197] *NYCD*, 13:528–30. See also Lawrence H. Leder, ed., *The Livingston Indian Records, 1666–1723* (Gettysburg, Pa., 1956), 39–40.

[198] Hubbard, *Narrative*, 2:13; Dean R. Snow, "Eastern Abenaki," in Sturtevant, *Handbook*, 15:143; Gordon R. Day, "The Identity of the Sokokis," *Ethnohistory* 12 (1965): 237–49; Gordon R. Day, "Western Abenaki," in Sturtevant, *Handbook*, 15:148.

flowed freely into Indian settlements; European settlers, exchanging weapons with the Abenakis, often cheated native traders.[199] Thus a frontier population free from any governmental oversight poisoned the possibility of peaceful interethnic relations, and the Abenakis—though they benefited materially from their trade with the English and certainly desired its peaceful continuance—became increasingly impatient with their English guests.[200]

The outbreak of King Philip's War to the south exacerbated the tensions. The English frontier population, fearing that local bands might join with Algonquians of southern New England, demanded that the Abenakis surrender their guns and refused to sell them additional supplies of powder and shot. For the Abenakis, parting with their weapons meant the prospect of starvation during the long northern winter. Thomas Gardener, a colonial official at Sagadahoc, recognized the dangers inherent in so aggressive an ultimatum. "How," he asked, could the English "take Away their Armes whose livelyhood dependeth of it." Disarming the Abenakis would force them "to go to the french for Reliefe or fight Against us having nothing for their suport Almost in these parts but their guns."[201]

Shortly after the settlers demanded that the Abenakis surrender their weapons, a group of "rude and indiscreet" English sailors approached the wife and infant child of the Saco sagamore Squando and decided to test "whether the Children of the Indians as they had heard, could Swimme as naturally as any other Creatures." The child died soon after this sadistic episode, for which, Hubbard recorded, the Sacos alleged "some little colour or pretense of injury."[202] Elsewhere, English sailors captured otherwise peaceful Indians and sold them into slavery. Thereafter, wrote Gardener, the Indians fled "for fear from Any boats or English thay se & good Reason for thay well Know it may Cost them theyr Lives if the wild fisherman meet with them."[203]

Tension exploded into war in September 1675. Angered by the English murder of an Androscoggin spotted near some English houses, the Abenakis retaliated, falling upon settlements from Blackpoint south to Exeter, New Hampshire.[204] No clearer statement of their grounds for war appeared than in the letter from the Kennebec sachems to the Massachusetts General Court, attempting to explain to the magistrates "how we have been aroused." Their words echoed those of Philip.

[199] See *Documentary History of Maine*, 1 July 1677, 6:78–79.
[200] Kenneth M. Morrison, "The Bias of Colonial Law: English Paranoia and the Abenaki Arena of King Philip's War, 1675–1678," *New England Quarterly* 53 (1989): 369–71.
[201] Thomas Gardener to Governor Leverett, 22 September 1675, William Willis et al., ed., *Documentary History of Maine*, 24 vols. (Portland, Maine, 1869–1916), 6:91–92.
[202] Hubbard, *Narrative*, 2:29.
[203] Thomas Gardener to Governor Leverett, 22 September 1675, *Documentary History of Maine*, 6:92–93. Gardener's neighbors did not appreciate his criticism of their treatment of the Abenakis. They accused him of trading illegally with the Indians and shipped him to Boston, where later he managed to acquit himself of all charges.
[204] Morrison, "Bias," 373.

We love yo but when we are dronk you will take away our cot & throw us out of dore[.] If the wolf kill any of your catell you take away our guns for it & arrows[,] and if you see a engon dog you will shoot him[.] if we should do so to you cut down your houses kill your dogs take away your things we must pay a 100 skins[;] if we brek a tobarko pip they will prisson us becaus ther was war at naragans[.] you com here when we were quiet & took away our guns & mad prisners of our chief sagamore & that winter for want of our guns there was severall starved.

Angered by English duplicity and violence, even against Abenakis who had assisted the colonists, the sachems asked, "Is that your fashing to com & make pease & then kill us[?]" They feared that "you will do so agen."[205]

Soon the entire settlement was under attack. Richard Waldorne, a soldier, reported to the Massachusetts General Court that the Abenakis had fallen "upon Scarbrough & Sawco killing & burning." Abenaki attacks "filled all the Plantations about Pascataqua with fear and confusion . . . which caused most of them that lived scatteringly, at any distance from Neighbours, either to garrison their houses, or else to desert their own dwellings, and to repair to their next Neighbours that were better fortified then themselves."[206]

The dispersal of Philip's forces which began in the spring of 1676 added strength to the Abenaki onslaught, for some of the Algonquian refugees moved eastward.[207] In August a series of devastating raids forced the English to abandon all their settlements north of Casco Bay, leaving Blackpoint as the northernmost English garrison. As the Abenakis moved toward the isolated settlement, other alarming developments occurred. English colonists, hunkered down in their garrison, reported that the French were participating in and perhaps directing the Abenaki assault on northern New England. Blackpoint, unaided, could not hold out long. It fell during the summer of 1676.[208]

Like the northern settlers, Andros recognized how critical the situation in Maine had become. He was also aware that by intervening in the North he could place Indian relations there on a sound footing and at the same time remove the longstanding irritant posed by the Bay Colony's persistent interference in the region. Informed that "all said Easterne parts were wholly deserted by the Indyans, and then neglected by Boston, who had usurped it, butt now lost itt," and "dayley heareing of the number of captives, sloop and vesselles taken by the Indians," Andros had before him ample evidence of

[205] "Moxes and Indians W. H. & G, rec'd by Mrs. Hammond," 1 July 1677, *Documentary History of Maine*, 6:178–79.

[206] Hubbard, *Narrative*, 2:22.

[207] Petition from Thomas Gardener and others of Pemaquid, 21 August 1676, *Documentary History of Maine*, 6:118–19; Robert Earle Moody, "The Maine Frontier, 1607–1763" (Ph.D. diss., Yale University, 1933), 183.

[208] Andros, "Short Account," 3:255; *MBR*, 12 October 1676, 5:123; Emerson W. Baker, "New Evidence on French Involvement in King Philip's War," *Maine Historical Society Quarterly* 28 (1988): 8.

Puritan frontier mismanagement.[209] That was why, at the council held at Albany in April 1677, Andros secured Mohawk assistance against the Abenakis. He then informed the Bay Colony's governor, John Leverett, that the saints would not be allowed to treat the Mohawks as badly as they had treated other Native American groups. Leverett would, Andros wrote, "give sufficient Orders to any Out forces or places you have . . . being confident they will doe good service and not injure any Christian or Concerns."[210]

By June all of Maine's settlements "as farre as Piscattaway" had been destroyed by Abenaki raiders. Andros ordered Brockholes to sail "to the Duke's Territorys att Pemaquid and adjacent country" and there construct a prefabricated fort: "a wooden Redoutt with two gunns aloft, and an outworke with two Bastions in each of which two greatt guns, and one att the Gate."[211] Supplied with provisions for eight months, "sufficient ammunicion, stores of warre, and spare arms," Brockholes and the fifty men in his charge were to assist and provide intelligence for the Mohawks, while arranging peace with any neighboring Indians who returned all their English prisoners and captured ships. Such agreements were to all the "Neighbors of the Massachusetts and adjacent Colonyes if they accept itt."[212]

The Bay Colony magistrates tried to persuade Andros not to intervene in Maine, and one week later they landed a force at Blackpoint and attacked the Indians there. This botched attempt to secure a separate peace with the Abenaki bands cost the Bay Colony the lives of half the 120 men on the expedition. When the survivors approached the fort at Pemaquid, they were able to make "onely some questions and so returned" to Boston.[213]

A few days after the unsuccessful Bay Colony assault, Andros reported, "some Indyans came [to the fort] and, being informed who was there setled, offered submission, but not to Massachusetts." Andros refused to accept the Indians' terms; they must surrender to an English, not a provincial, authority. Within a month the Abenakis returned to Pemaquid, and "all submitted to include Boston and all Majesties subjects, & deliver to us all Christian captives and kettches taken which were in their possession."[214] Andros then sent the news of this agreement to Boston. The saints reluctantly accepted the treaty, Andros wrote, "which still continues & is all the peace (knowne) they have with Indyans."[215]

[209] "Account of Andros's Administration," *Andros Papers*, 2:468.

[210] Andros to Leverett, 4 April 1677, ibid., 2:35.

[211] "Account of Andros's Administration," ibid., 2:488; "Instructions for Anthony Brockles, Ensign Knapton, and Mr. M. Nicolls," 13 June 1677, *NYCD*, 3:248.

[212] "Instructions for Brockles," *NYCD*, 3:249; "Account of Andros's Administration," *Andros Papers*, 2:488; Webb, *1676*, 387.

[213] Edward Rawson to Andros, 22 June 1677, *Documentary History of Maine*, 4:376–77; Massachusetts Governor and Council, 10 July 1677, *Documentary History of Maine*, 6:186–87; "Account of Andros's Administration," *Andros Papers*, 2:488.

[214] "Account of Andros's Administration," *Andros Papers*, 2:488.

[215] "Short Account of the Assistance Rendered by New-York to New England," *NYCD*, 3:265; see also 254–57.

Andros hoped to extend his authority over the entire frontier population. It was lack of such oversight in the past, he believed, that had produced the war. By centralizing control over Indian-white relations in Anglo-America in his person, and by working with and through the Mohawks to establish the king's dominion over other Indians and frontier Englishmen, he forged the first links of what the Onondaga leader Daniel Garacontié would describe as the Covenant Chain. The Chain did not emerge completely formed in the summer of 1677—affairs to the south still awaited resolution—but Andros had taken the first steps toward the creation of a biracial diplomatic accord that helped pacify the Algonquians, stabilize relations between Native Americans and Englishmen, and remedy the problems produced by provincial frontier mismanagement.[216]

VI

The number of English casualties as a percentage of total population made the Algonquian rising of 1675 one of the bloodiest wars per capita in American history. But the costs of defeat were even more devastating for the New England Algonquians. Nathaniel Saltonstall estimated "that the Indians that were killed, taken, sent away, and now of late come in by Way of Submission, cannot in all, (Men, Women, and Children,) amount to fewer than Six Thousand." The longer-term dislocation caused by the war can only be guessed.[217]

Perhaps 2,500 English settlers died during the two years of raid and counterraid. Algonquian attacks retarded the advance of the frontier for twenty years, destroyed the material basis of New England's prosperity, and left a society mired in a state of intellectual, spiritual, economic, and physical crisis. With property carried off, farms burned, settlers killed, and livestock slaughtered, much of the New England interior remained a waste. Philip's forces destroyed sixteen towns in Massachusetts; four in Rhode Island— Warwick, Coventry, Westerly, and Charleston—were either abandoned or burned. The district of Maine could field one thousand soldiers before the uprising, men drawn from the thirteen towns and plantations scattered across the region; in 1680 only six of these settlements remained, the rest having been destroyed or abandoned. Fifty families had lived in the vicinity of the Kennebec River before the war; afterwards the region was a ruin, the entire population from Casco Bay eastward having fled.[218]

---

[216] Richter, *Ordeal*, 136; Webb, *1676*, 355–404.

[217] Leach, *Flintlock*, 243; Saltonstall, "New and Further," 97–98; Webb, *1676*, 243. On the costs of the war in general, see Michael J. Puglisi, *Puritans Besieged: The Legacies of King Philip's War in the Massachusetts Bay Colony* (Lanham, Md., 1991).

[218] Lois Kimball Matthews Rosenberry, *The Expansion of New England* (Boston, 1909), 57–58.

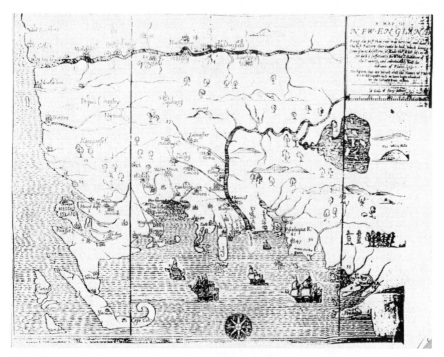

Map of New England in the Era of King Philip's War. The original caption read, "The figures that are joyned with the Names of Places are to distinguish such as have been assaulted by the Indians from others." From Hubbard, *Narrative.*

Aside from sheer physical damage, the Algonquian rising and its suppression had another cost: King Philip's War produced in New England an Indian-hating people, inclined to explicitly racist attitudes toward all Native Americans. At the most immediate level, the Puritan colonies sought to effect a near total separation from the Indians who had nearly destroyed them. Massachusetts placed its dependent Indians on reservations that closely circumscribed their freedom of movement. Though a small number of ministers continued to preach to Indians, missionary enterprise suffered. Only four Praying Towns remained inhabited after 1676, and the war brought both Indian convert and English minister into contempt with the white population.[219]

The frontier in particular increasingly manifested a virulent racism. In 1677, for example, a number of captured Saco warriors were brought into the outpost at Marblehead. The settlers there had suffered greatly during the war, losing both men and ships to Abenaki raiders. According to Robert

---

[219] *MBR,* 24 May 1677, 5:136; *PCR,* 1 November 1676, 5:215; Kellaway, *New England Company,* 117. For continuing Puritan efforts to minister to Indians, see Patrick Frazier, *The Mohicans of Stockbridge* (Lincoln, Neb., 1992).

Roule, who was attempting to escort the prisoners to Boston for trial, "the whole town flocked about them begining at first to insult them, and soon after, the women surrounded them, and drove us by force from them . . . and laid violent hands upon the captives." Then, Roule testified,

> with stones, billets of wood, and what else they might, they made an end of these Indians. We were kept at such distance that we could not see them till they were dead, and then we found them with their heads off and gone, and their flesh in a manner pulled from their bones. . . . they suffered neither constable nor mandrake, nor any other person to come near them, until they had finished their bloody purpose.[220]

Violence on the frontier affected attitudes toward Indians elsewhere. William Hubbard, the minister and historian, could not believe that the Algonquian rising emerged "from some Irregularities and miscarriages in our Transactions and Dealings with the Indians themselves." It was not the Commissioners of the United Colonies nor the Puritan magistrates who were the problem; rather, the war arose "only from such places & persons as border upon us round about, both Southward and Eastward, yet never were, nor would be, subject to the Laws of our Jurisdiction." In "many of these scattering Plantations," he said, "many were contented to live without, yea, desierious to shake off all yoke of Government, both Sacred and Civil, and so Transformed themselves as much as well they could into the manners of the Indians they lived amongst."[221]

There was some truth in what Hubbard said: New England metropolitans had failed to prevent their own citizens from engaging in the activities that ultimately provoked war with the Algonquians. New England's magistrates had failed to relieve the enormous pressure placed upon Indian subsistence systems by the English frontier population. Hubbard certainly was not alone in holding this opinion. Yet he could not explain the cause of the war solely in terms of the aggressiveness of the frontier population. Rather, he looked to the Indians and, in so doing, challenged the foundation of the metropolitan New World vision.

Hubbard remembered the story of George Thorpe, the ill-fated promoter of Henrico College, who had employed "the gentle means of Courtesy, Familiarity, and such like Civil Behavior" in his attempt to convert the natives. Hubbard, by 1677, could not accept such a program as a viable policy toward native peoples. Thorpe, he wrote, "was so full of Confidence and void of Suspition, that he would never believe any hurt of them, till he felt their cruell hands imbrued in his own blood."[222]

---

[220] James Axtell, "The Vengeful Women of Marblehead: Robert Roule's Deposition of 1677," *WMQ*, 3d ser., 31 (1974): 652.
[221] Hubbard, *Narrative*, 2:78, 77.
[222] Ibid., 86.

Hubbard himself shared "Master Stockam's opinion," thus demonstrating a great continuity in the metropolitan response to frontier crisis. The story of Thorpe, he believed, revealed "the naturall barbarousness and perfidiousness of [the Indians'] disposition," and Hubbard saw little reason to continue casting pearls before swine. The New England Algonquians, he said, were little different from those of Virginia. Though a remnant might be saved, he thought the vast majority "implacable and imbittered against us in their spirits, [and] may be for the sake of our Religion found hardened to their own Destruction." [223]

[223] Ibid., 87, 88.

5 *Elizabeth Bacon's Letter Home*

Elizabeth Bacon arrived in Virginia in the summer of 1674. The cost of her marriage to Nathaniel Bacon had been her ties to the comfortable world of the English gentry. Disinherited and disowned by a scornful father, living at what William Byrd called "the end of the world," she felt acutely the isolation and loneliness that characterized life on the Anglo-American frontier.

Nathaniel Bacon had purchased more than a thousand acres at "Curles," a stretch of land along the James River, twenty miles below the falls. Here Elizabeth Bacon resided while her husband planted his tobacco and profited from Indian trade. And here, as Virginia's hard-pressed frontier population dragged the colony into war with the Susquehannock and the Algonquian peoples of the fall line, she learned how violent and frightening frontier life could be.[1]

"I pray God," she wrote her sister in June 1676, to "keep the worst Enemy I have from ever being in such a sad Condition as I have been in." The "troublesome Indians," she reported, "have killed one of our overseers at an outward plantation which wee had, and wee have lost a great stock of Cattle, which wee had upon it, and a good crop that wee should have made there ... which is a very great losse to us."

Elizabeth Bacon's letter home expressed the fear, the anger, and the frustration that formed the litany of her husband's rebellious crusade against both the Virginia Indians and the administration of Governor Sir William Berkeley. "It would have grieved your heart, to hear the pitiful complaints of the people," she wrote, "the Indians killing the people daily and the Govern.: not taking any notice of it for to hinder them, but let them daily doe all

---

[1] Wilcomb Washburn, *The Governor and the Rebel: A History of Bacon's Rebellion* (Chapel Hill, N.C., 1957), 17–18; Marion Tinling, ed., *The Correspondence of the Three William Byrds of Westover, Virginia, 1684–1776* (Charlottesville, Va., 1977), 1:136.

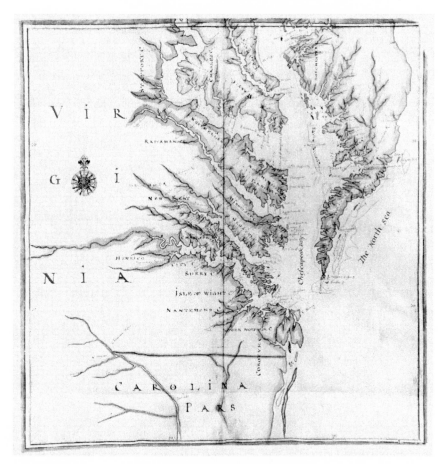

Map of Virginia, ca. 1677. Reprinted from Jeannette Dora Black, ed., *The Blathwayt Atlas* (1970). Courtesy John Carter Brown Library at Brown University.

the mischiefe they can." Were not the Indians such cowards, she believed, they would have destroyed English settlements the length of the frontier. As it was, with "the Governor so much their friend, that hee would not suffer any body to hurt any of the Indians," the damage they caused was grave enough.[2]

Elizabeth Bacon and the men who followed her husband faced too immediate a threat from the Virginia Indians, too great an obstacle to their economic aspirations, and too fierce a competitor for frontier resources to appreciate the metropolitan plan for securing an orderly frontier by maintaining peaceful relations with the natives. Her letter thus reflected the

[2] Egerton MSS 2395, fol. 550, British Library, London, *VCRP*.

attitudes of a population that felt itself the victim of both a deceitful and bloodthirsty enemy and an ineffective and inefficient provincial magistracy.

Where the Baconians saw a governor content to grow rich by coddling bloodstained savages, however, the metropolitans charged with governing the king's Old Dominion saw a bellicose frontier population intent upon extorting control of Indian land and producing endemic instability along the periphery of English settlement. The encroachment of white frontiersmen on native land, wrote Philip Ludwell, the colony's acting secretary of state, "fills us with complaints and will if not prevented keep our peace forever uncertaine."[3]

Governor Berkeley needed order along the frontier to secure a revenue for the crown and defend the colony from enemies both European and Indian. In this he succeeded reasonably well for much of the thirty-five years he spent in Virginia. When he finally lost control in 1676, it came as the result of a frontier rebellion precipitated by dramatic social and economic changes in Virginia and in the pressure applied by the "Seneca" upon the bordering Susquehannock and Doeg Indians. Bacon's Rebellion dramatically illustrated for the crown the decline in Berkeley's ability to govern the frontier. As in New England, the failure of metropolitans in the provinces to secure order for the crown produced a royalist and centralist response designed to increase direct imperial oversight in Indian affairs.

I

The series of raids undertaken in the years after 1622 by Sir Francis Wyatt battered Opechancanough's forces. Powhatan warriors engaged in so little offensive activity that the burgesses warned the colonists against becoming complacent. Many people, however, still clamored for war against the Powhatans. In 1629 the burgesses divided the colony into four military districts, launching raids from each district in November, March, and July "to doe all manner of spoile and offence to the Indians that may possibly bee effected."[4]

When Governor Sir John Harvey arrived in Virginia in the spring of 1630, he thus "found the colony engaged in a necessary war with the natives." Harvey prosecuted the war with vigor but also worked to secure order. His policies ran counter to the interests of powerful men in the colony such as William Claiborne and John Pott, frontier barons whose status within the colony depended upon their ability to exploit opportunities offered by the Anglo-American frontier.[5]

[3] Ludwell quoted in Washburn, *Governor*, 161.

[4] William Waller Hening, ed., *The Statutes at Large; Being a Collection of All the Laws from the First Session of the Legislature in the Year 1619* (Richmond, Va., 1809), 1:140–41.

[5] Harvey to the Privy Council, April 1630, *CSP Coll, 1574–1660*, 113, no. 85.

Harvey had traveled to Virginia in 1624 with a crown commission to investigate affairs under the Virginia Company. His report had lamented the weakness of the colony's fortifications, its scattered pattern of settlement, and its overreliance upon tobacco. It could succeed in the future, he wrote, only with "an established form of government settled amoungst them there, and another here in England; both managed by such men as maie bee subject & answerable in theire perticuler persons for all theire proceedinges to his Majestie and the Lords of his Majesties privy Counsell." [6] Upon taking office in 1630, Harvey set out to establish just such a government.

Harvey met opposition almost immediately. Nonetheless, acting on instructions from the Privy Council, he worked to curtail the colony's dependence upon tobacco and to diversify crop production. With help from the crown, he believed, Virginia could "bee made as Sicilye to Rome, the Granarie to his Majesties Empire, especiallie to all our Northerne Plantations." [7]

In order to effect this broad transformation of Virginia's economy, however, Harvey needed a peaceful and orderly frontier. To that end he improved the equipment and organization of the militia and tried to prevent contact between Indians and settlers. He built a palisade on the peninsula between the James and York Rivers. Indians were to be kept out, Englishmen—and their livestock—kept in. The palisaded peninsula would provide a secure base for Virginia's economic development. [8]

Harvey succeeded admirably. During the winter of 1631–32 local Indians began seeking opportunities to negotiate for peace. Harvey concluded a formal pact later in 1632 over the opposition of the more bellicose Council of Virginia members, and reported to the Privy Council in 1633 that "the country is on good termes with the Indians." [9]

Pott and Claiborne led the opposition to Harvey's policies. Pott had served as interim governor immediately prior to Harvey's arrival. Claiborne, a successful fur trader with Puritan ties and transatlantic connections, had established two thriving trading posts at Kent and Palmer's Islands in the northern Chesapeake region. Both men favored an aggressive policy against the Tidewater Algonquians; both hoped to open native land to English settlement and exploitation. Both, moreover, had made their reputations on the frontier as Indian fighters. Pott was known in Virginia Company circles as

[6] Governor Harvey's Report (1624), in "The Aspinwall Papers," *MHS Coll*, 4th ser., 9 (1871): 69–72.

[7] Harvey to Secretary Dorchester, 2 April 1631, *CSP Col*, 1574–1660, 129, no. 11; Privy Council to Harvey, January 1631, ibid., 125, no. 3; Harvey to Lords of the Council, 9 March 1632, in Robert C. Johnson, ed., "Virginia in 1632," *VMHB* 65 (1957): 459; Wilcomb E. Washburn, *Virginia under Charles I and Cromwell, 1625–1660* (Williamsburg, Va., 1957), 17.

[8] Harvey to Secretary Sir Francis Windebank, 14 July 1634, *VMHB* 8 (1900): 157; Hening, *Statutes*, 1:173–76, 198, 219; Washburn, *Virginia*, 5–6, 10; William L. Shea, *The Virginia Militia in the Seventeenth Century* (Baton Rouge, La., 1983), 53.

[9] Hening, *Statutes*, 167, 192–93; Captain Mathews to Sir John Wolstenholme, 25 May 1635, in *AM*, 3:35; Harvey to Privy Council, 20 February 1633, *CSP Col*, 1574–1660, 160, no. 73.

"the poisoner of the savages": he had killed 150 Indians by serving poisoned wine during a peace parley at Chiskiack in 1623. Claiborne, who had established a lucrative working relationship with the Susquehannocks, received a patent in 1626 for an "inventione" that he claimed offered "an assured way and means . . . to make [Indians] serviceable for many other services for ye good of the whole Colony." A few bugs remained in the device, however, so the war-weary council, of which Claiborne was a member, granted him an Indian prisoner to experiment upon. Both Pott and Claiborne opposed Harvey's effort to make peace with the neighboring Algonquian bands, to limit English territorial expansion, and to restrain "us from revenging ourselves."[10]

Relations between Harvey and his opponents reached a crisis in 1634 when the first Maryland settlers arrived. Lord Baltimore's proprietary grant had been carved from territory originally considered within the limits of Virginia. Even worse from the point of view of many Virginia settlers, Baltimore was a Catholic who envisioned his colony as a refuge for his co-religionists. His patent directly challenged Claiborne's interests in the northern Chesapeake. Claiborne's Kent Island post was within the chartered bounds of Maryland, and in Baltimore he saw a threat to his control of the Indian trade in the region. Claiborne encouraged the Susquehannocks, who themselves had much to lose should Maryland form a trading alliance with the nearby Piscataways or Patuxents, to stir up trouble within the colony. Harvey had little patience for Claiborne's renegade diplomacy. After the governor and commissioners of Maryland complained of the "evil practices of Captain William Clayborne with ye Indians to ye subversion of both colonies," Harvey removed him as secretary of state and ordered his arrest.[11]

By restraining Claiborne, Harvey was following his instructions to give Baltimore "friendly help and assistance in furtherance of his undertaking" and "to hold good correspondency with him and his planters and give them

---

[10] RVC, 2:478; Council Minutes, VMHB 26 (1918): 11; Captain Matthews to Sir John Wolstenholme, 25 May 1635, AM, 3:34; J. Mills Thornton III, "The Thrusting-Out of Governor Harvey: A Seventeenth Century Rebellion," VMHB 76 (1968): 19; J. Frederick Fausz, "Profits, Pelts, and Power: English Culture in the Early Chesapeake, 1620–1652," *Maryland Historian* 15 (1983): 19–20; Francis Jennings, *The Ambiguous Iroquois Empire: The Covenant Chain Confederation of Indian Tribes with English Colonies from Its Beginning to the Lancaster Treaty of 1744* (New York, 1984), 115.

[11] Petition of John Wolstenholme with Captain William Clayborne in Virginia to Privy Council, November 1633, CSP Col, 1574–1660, 172, no. 87; Thornton, "Thrusting-Out," 21; Washburn, *Virginia*, 22–23; H. R. McIlwaine, ed., *Minutes of the Council and General Court of Virginia, 1622–1632, 1670–1676* (Richmond, Va., 1924), 481; "Declaration of Sir John Harvey," VMHB 1 (1893): 429; J. Frederick Fausz, "Present at the Creation: The Chesapeake World That Greeted the Maryland Colonists," *Maryland Historical Magazine* 79 (1984): 7; Francis Jennings, "Pennsylvania Indians and the Iroquois," in Daniel K. Richter and James H. Merrell, eds., *Beyond the Covenant Chain: The Iroquois and Their Neighbors in Indian North America, 1600–1800,* (Syracuse, N.Y., 1987), 76–77. See also "Baltimore's Instructions," in *Narratives of Early Maryland, 1633–1684,* ed. Clayton Colman Hall (New York, 1925), 17–18.

such lawful assistance as may conduce to both their safeties and the advancement of the plantation of those countries." The king encouraged Harvey, late in the summer of 1634, to continue to protect Baltimore's "planters from the malice and injury of the Indians, or any other." The Virginia colonists, however—"soe averse" to the settlement of Maryland, observed Harvey, "that they crye and make it their familiar talke that they would rather knock their cattell on the heads then sell them to Maryland"—grew increasingly hostile toward a governor they saw as insensitive to the concerns of Virginia's frontier population.[12]

In April the governor's enemies began to plot his overthrow. Led by Pott, "the incendiary of these broils," they charged Harvey with ruling so arbitrarily "that noe Justice was done" in the colony. They also argued that by making peace with the Powhatans "the Governour would bring a second massacre among them." When Harvey accused his opponents of sedition, Pott ordered Harvey placed under arrest: "You must prepare yourself to goe for England . . . to answer the complainte that are against you."[13]

The "thrusting-out" of Governor Harvey in 1635 has been described as a response to his autocratic rule, his insensitivity to land rights obtained under the Virginia Company, and the assistance he offered Maryland's hated Catholics. All these factors were involved. A more important one, however, was that Harvey and his adversaries promoted distinctly different views of the Anglo-American frontier and its role within the empire. Harvey had tried to manage the colony's growth. He implemented the county court system and supported the construction of roads in an effort to improve administration at the local level.[14] At the same time, he tried to prevent the population from expanding onto Indian land. Through the four years of his governorship, for example, he issued only 98 patents for land; during the interim tenure of John West from 1635 to 1636, in contrast, 309 patents were issued. With the removal of John Harvey, frontier interests and frontier attitudes prevailed.[15]

The forces of frontier aggression that undermined Harvey would likewise challenge Sir William Berkeley, who arrived in the colony as governor in February 1642. Like Harvey, Berkeley supported the colony's developing local institutions. He reformed colonial defense and ensured that "all persons from the age of 16 to 60 be armed with guns, both offensive and defensive." Like Harvey, he also tried to prevent a scattered pattern of settlement and

---

[12] King to Governor and Council of Virginia, 12 July 1633, *AM*, 3:22–23; King to Governor and Council of Virginia, 29 September 1634, *AM*, 3:27; Harvey to Windebanke, 16 December 1634, *VMHB* 8 (1900): 161.

[13] Richard Kemp to Commissioners for Foreign Plantations, 17 May 1635, in "Aspinwall Papers," 145; Samuel Mathews to Sir John Wolstenholme, 25 May 1635, in "Aspinwall Papers," 131 n; *VMHB* 1 (1893): 425–30.

[14] Hening, *Statutes*, 1:224; Washburn, *Virginia*, 20; Thornton, "Thrusting-Out," 1–26.

[15] See Nell Marion Nugent, comp., *Cavaliers and Pioneers: Abstracts of Virginia Land Patents and Grants, 1623–1800* (Richmond, Va., 1934), 14–53.

the encroachment of settlers onto Indian lands. He promoted and organized frontier exploration, oversaw the Indian trade, and orchestrated the colony's defense against foes both European and Indian. His skills soon faced a formidable test.[16]

On April 18, 1644, Opechancanough led his second, and final, great rising against the English. As in 1622, he was reacting to the pressure placed upon his lands by the English frontier population. Nearly a century old, he was carried into battle on a litter. Even "in this low state," wrote Robert Beverley, Opechancanough and the Pamunkey, Weyanoke, Nansemond, and Chickahominy warriors he led killed four hundred colonists in a matter of hours and took many others prisoner.[17]

Berkeley quickly divided the colony into military precincts and ordered local militia leaders to prevent "the carelesse stragling of many people" that had exposed them to Indian attack. He had forts constructed at the falls of the James, on the Pamunkey River, and at the "Ridge of Chiquohhomine" north and west of Jamestown to serve as bases for raids into the Powhatan heartland. Though details of the ensuing campaigns are few, the English clearly directed their attacks against the Powhatan core chiefdoms: the Pamunkeys, Chickahominys, Nansemonds, Weyanokes, Powhatans, and Appomattocks.[18]

The English raids took their toll. By the spring of 1646 the governor and council recognized "the almost impossibility of a further revenge upon them." With the Indians "dispersed and driven from their townes and habitations, lurking up & downe the woods in small numbers," peace "would conduce to the better being and comoditie of the country."[19]

When Opechancanough showed no interest in an English peace, Berkeley personally led sixty horsemen out against the Pamunkey leader in the summer of 1646. They captured Opechancanough and carried him prisoner to Jamestown, where Berkeley ordered that he be "treated with all the Respect and Tenderness imaginable." An Indian-hating soldier, however, "resenting the Calamities the Colony had suffer'd by this Prince's Means," shot the *weroance* in his prison cell.[20]

The murder of "the great salvage kinge" led to the surrender of the Powhatan tribes to the English in October 1646. Opechancanough's succes-

---

[16] Edmund S. Morgan, *American Slavery, American Freedom: The Ordeal of Colonial Virginia* (New York, 1975), 146; Washburn, *Virginia*, 29–31; Instructions to Berkeley, *VMHB* 2 (1894): 281–82, 287; King's Commission to Sir William Berkeley, 9 August 1641, *CSP Col*, 1674–75, 84, no. 193; Hening, *Statutes*, 1:263, 255–56.

[17] Robert Beverley, *The History and Present State of Virginia*, ed. Louis B. Wright (Chapel Hill, N.C., 1947), 61–62; Helen C. Rountree, *Pocahontas's People: The Powhatan Indians of Virginia through Four Centuries* (Norman, Okla., 1990), 84.

[18] Hening, *Statutes*, 1:292–93, 300–301; Rountree, *Pocahontas's People*, 84–86; Shea, *Virginia Militia*, 64–65.

[19] Hening, *Statutes*, 1: 318.

[20] Beverley, *History*, 61–62.

sor, Necotowance, acknowledged English dominion over the Powhatan chiefdoms by agreeing "to hold his kingdome from the King's Ma'tie of England, and that his successors be appointed or confirmed by the King's Governours from time to time." In return, the English agreed to defend the weakened Algonquian bands "against any rebells or other enemies whatsoever." Necotowance ceded to the English all lands between the York and James Rivers, from the falls eastward to the bay, and accepted the English demand that "it shall be lawfull for any person to kill any such Indian" who entered the region. To protect the Indians from further frontier aggression, Berkeley reserved to Necotowance the right "to inhabit and hunt on the north-side of Yorke River, without any interruption from the English."[21]

The treaty of 1646 laid the foundation for English metropolitan Indian policy for the next three decades. Berkeley recognized that English territorial aggression had provoked the 1644 massacre and that no order could exist along the frontier unless Indians were guaranteed possession of land free from English interference. The success of Berkeley's program, as implemented in the treaty, would depend in the future upon the governor's ability to control the English frontier population. That this population grew rapidly after 1640 rendered his task extremely difficult.[22]

II

With Opechancanough's death, the chiefdom forged by Powhatan collapsed as a functioning political entity. Necotowance was the last Pamunkey to rule over the Algonquian peoples of coastal Virginia. By 1648 he had disappeared from the historical record, either deposed or deceased. Totopotomoy, another Pamunkey, replaced him but represented only his own tribe in dealings with the English.[23] The Powhatans had steadily lost territory in the James and York River drainages since the 1630s. By the middle of the century the tribes of the Powhatan core area had been isolated in small pockets of land, surrounded by English settlers who now far outnumbered the native inhabitants of the region.[24]

Berkeley recognized that as the English population grew, land hunger and soil exhaustion could still threaten frontier order. In 1647 he ordered settlers in the Northern Neck and "other remote and straying plantations on the

---

[21] Ibid., 63; Grand Assembly of Virginia to Commons, 17 March 1646, in *Proceedings and Debates of the British Parliaments Respecting North America*, ed. Leo Francis Stock, 2 vols. (Washington D.C., 1924), 1:182; Hening, *Statutes*, 1:323–24.

[22] Wesley Frank Craven, *The Southern Colonies in the Seventeenth Century, 1607–1689* (Baton Rouge, La., 1949), 363; Warren M. Billings, " 'Virginia's Deploured Condition,' 1660–1676: The Coming of Bacon's Rebellion" (Ph.D. diss., Northern Illinois University, 1968), 191–92. On this population growth, see Morgan, *American Slavery*, 180–84.

[23] Rountree, *Pocahontas's People*, 86–89.

[24] Ibid., 82–29, 105–27.

south side of Patomeck River, Wicokomoko, Rappahannock, and Fleets Bay" to leave Indian lands because such settlement jeopardized the peace of the colony. [25] Scattered settlements violated the treaty and could not be defended. Berkeley feared that they would provoke an Indian attack, involving the colony in a long and expensive war.

The settlers who had moved into the region wanted fresh land where they could plant tobacco and range livestock. A year after Berkeley ordered the Northern Neck settlers removed, several burgesses petitioned the governor for permission to settle north of the Rappahannock. They cited "the great and clamorous necessities of divers of the inhabitants occasioned and brought upon them through the mean produce of their labours upon barren and over-wrought grounds and the apparent decay of their cattle and hoggs for want of sufficient range." Berkeley acknowledged "the substance of their desires but for reasons of state . . . importing the safety of the people in their planting, did think fitt to restraine them to a further limitation of time." The governor ordered that no one settle in the region until September 1649, apparently to allow the governor and his council time to obtain title to the lands in question. [26]

Despite Berkeley's efforts, conflict and competition between Indians and Englishmen for access to and control of land was nearly inevitable. English planters generally chose sites for tobacco plantations with three considerations in mind. They needed navigable water to transport the crop to market, freshwater springs for drinking water, and high-quality silty and sandy loam soils suitable for hoe cultivation. Similar considerations pertained to the Algonquians' selection of sites for settlements. As in New England, then, settlers and Indians grappled for control of identical tracts of land which they employed in different and incompatible ways. [27]

Berkeley tried to ease tensions wherever possible. Despite a shortage of labor in seventeenth-century Virginia, he outlawed Indian slavery and called upon the assembly to prohibit the theft of Indian children. He required that those apprenticed voluntarily to the English not be sold, or treated, like slaves. To smooth the process of intercultural trade in the cash-starved Virginia economy, the assembly under Berkeley set prices for Indian roanoke and peak, shell beads that some colonists circulated as money. Berkeley also called for the repeal of that provision in the treaty of 1646 which allowed English settlers to kill Indians who entered the English reserve between the James and York Rivers, pointing out that the colony had been

---

[25] Quoted in Washburn, *Virginia*, 40.

[26] Hening, *Statutes*, 1:353.

[27] Stephen R. Potter, *Commoners, Tribute, and Chiefs: The Development of Algonquian Culture in the Potomac Valley* (Charlottesville, Va., 1993), 220–21. See also Lewis R. Binford, *Cultural Diversity among Aboriginal Cultures of Coastal Virginia and North Carolina* (New York, 1991); and Timothy Silver, *A New Face on the Countryside: Indians, Colonists, and Slaves in the South Atlantic Forests, 1500–1800* (Cambridge, England, 1990).

subject to manye prejudices by Reason of the Latitude, and Generallitye of such allowance, and that the breach of the peace may probablye be the Consequence thereof through the Rashness, and un-advicedness of Divers persons whoe by such Act Rather vindicate some private mallice, then provide for theire owne, or the Publick Indempnitye.[28]

Berkeley directed his Indian policy, as embodied in the peace treaty of 1646 and subsequent enactments, toward relieving the nearly constant tension and violence that had characterized the Virginia frontier for a quarter-century. Even though he was forced to surrender the government in the spring of 1652, following Roundhead victories in the English civil war, the Commonwealth regime that replaced him continued his policies in confronting challenges that had originated during Berkeley's first administration. During the Commonwealth period the Virginia Assembly passed laws prohibiting acts of vigilante justice against Indians. It declared in 1656 that "no Indians that are in our protection be killed, not committing what would be a felony in an Englishman, And that two oathes at least must be evidence of the said felony." Indians could be prosecuted for trespass, but the punishment could not extend "to death or maimeing."[29]

In March 1656 the Commonwealth government undertook a program to "civilize" the Indians. Recognizing that the "invasions of our neighbouring and bordering Indians . . . humanely have bin only caused by our extreame pressures on them and theire wanting of something to hazard & loose besides their lives," the assembly provided that for every eight wolves' heads brought in by the Indians, their headman would receive a cow; this would be "a step to civilizing them and to making them Christians" by instilling in them a sense of private property and moving them toward the settled form of agriculture and herding which English metropolitans considered "civilized." The assembly declared further that

> If the Indians shall bring in any children as gages of their good and quiet intentions to us and amity with us, then the parents of such children shall choose the persons to whom the care of such children shall be intrusted and the country by us their representatives do engage that wee will not use them as slaves, but do their best to bring them up in Christianity, civility and knowledge of necessary trades."[30]

Like Thorpe and Wyatt, the Commonwealth regime would endeavor to assimilate the Powhatans into an Anglo-American colonial society.

---

[28] Warren M. Billings, ed., "Some Acts Not in Hening's *Statutes*: The Acts of Assembly, April 1652, November 1652, and July 1653," *VMHB* 83 (1975): 63–65; Rountree, *Pocahontas's People*, 92.

[29] Hening, *Statutes*, 1:415.

[30] Ibid., 1:393–96. For related enactments, see 64–65, 410, 546.

The Commonwealth governors recognized, however, that the fundamental source of conflict between Algonquians and English settlers in Virginia, and the principal barrier to attaining metropolitan objectives in North America, was competition between Indians and Englishmen for control of the land. The governors received "many Complaints . . . touchinge wrong done to the Indians in takeinge away theire lands, or fforceinge them into such narrow Streights, and places That they Canott Subsist, either by plantinge, or huntinge." They feared that the Indians might be "Justlye Driven to dispaire" by English aggression and "attempt some Desperate Course for themselves." Earlier enactments had tried to remedy this situation, "yet never the lesse many English doe Still Intrench upon the Said Indian lands." Consequently, the assembly, in the hope that "the Indians might by all faire, and Just usage be reduced to Civilitye and the true Worshipp of God . . . ordained and En-acted that all the Indians of this Collonye Shall, and may hold and keepe those seates of Land that they now have, And that noe person, or persons whatsoever, be suffered to Intrench or plant uppon Such places as the Indians Claime, or desire" without permission from the governor, council, or com-missioners. And to relieve frontier pressure, the Assembly decided that no grants of land would be made "untill the Indians be first served with the pro-portion of fiftye Acres of land for each Bowman."[31]

Through these means the Commonwealth governors hoped to secure peace-ful relations with the Indians, an orderly frontier, and, as well, the Christian-ization and "civilization" of the Indians. Still, problems developed, especially on the Eastern Shore and in the new counties north of the York River.

English settlement on the Eastern Shore began slowly. In 1624 only 76 Eng-lishmen resided on the peninsula, while the Indian population totaled some 2,000, grouped loosely into two tribal headings—the Accomacks and Occo-hannocks—united under the leadership of the "Laughing King of Acco-mack." Within a decade the English population climbed to nearly 400 and had reached 1,000 by 1649, exacerbating tensions between frontier planters and neighboring Indians.[32] By the end of the 1640s these tensions had esca-lated into open conflict, as frontier barons like Edmund Scarburgh and Philip Taylor pursued their own Indian policy, based on a desire to monopolize the limited Eastern Shore fur trade and engross as much land as possible.[33]

[31] Billings, "Some Acts," 68, 72.

[32] J. Douglas Deal, *Race and Class in Colonial Virginia: Indians, Englishmen, and Africans on the Eastern Shore during the Seventeenth Century* (New York, 1993), 11–16; Jennings Crop-per Wise, *Ye Kingdome of Accawmacke; or, The Eastern Shore of Virginia in the Seventeenth Century* (Richmond, Va., 1911), 40–41, 57; Susie M. Ames, *Studies on the Virginia Eastern Shore in the Seventeenth Century* (Richmond, Va., 1940), 6; Christian F. Feest, "Nanticoke and Neighboring Tribes," in *Handbook of North American Indians*, vol. 15., *Northeast*, ed. William C. Sturtevant (Washington, D.C., 1978), 240.

[33] Deal, *Race and Class*, 19, 26–27. On Scarburgh's land acquisitions, see Nugent, *Cavaliers*, 119, 121, 139, 183, 225, 305, 418, 419, 425, 452, 453, 536. On Taylor, see Susie M. Ames, ed., *County Court Records of Accomack-Northampton, Virginia, 1640–1645* (Charlottesville, Va., 1973), 56, 235, 265.

In the spring of 1650 Governor Berkeley lectured the Eastern Shore commissioners on the importance of maintaining peace with "the Langhinge Kinges Indyans," who had "beene ever most faithfull to the English And pticulerly that neither they nor their kinge in the last bloody massacre could bee induced to engage wth our Enemyes agt us." The Laughing King had "kept the remote Indyans at least Newtrall in a tyme when a genrall combination agt us had beene if not ruinous att least of unsupportable prejudice to us in that Connection." Such steadfast friendship would not continue "unlesse wee correspond wth them in Acts of Charitye & Amytie Especially unlesse wee abstain from Acts of Rapine & violence which they say we begine to doe by taking away their land from them by prtence of ye sale of a pte." In the "Name of the Peace & Safety of the Country," the governor ordered the commissioners to "suffer noe Land to bee taken from them But what shall be allowed both in Justice and Convenience by the fall Court."[34]

Berkeley's eloquent appeal had little effect, and by late summer of 1650 rumors of Indian conspiracy began to circulate among frightened settlers on the Eastern Shore. The Nanticokes, who lived on the northern part of the peninsula in Maryland, had reportedly recruited a number of smaller Algonquian groups to join them in a plot to poison English wells and then to launch an assault upon the survivors.[35] In April 1651 Edmund Scarburgh "did in a hostile manner contrary to the known laws of Virginia . . . raise a body of men, and march among the Indians to take or kill the king of Pocomoke." Scarburgh and his band "shot at the Indians, slashed them, cut their bows, took Indian prisoners, [and] bound one of them with a chain."[36]

Scarburgh's attack "caused the Indians to gather themselves together in great multitudes to invade the country to the great danger of the peoples' Lives and estates." His fellow planters, who apparently did not share his enthusiasm for tormenting Indians and feared the consequences of his vigilantism, sent him and his supporters to Jamestown for trial.[37] Scarburgh maintained considerable influence at Jamestown, however, and he managed to convince Berkeley and the council that the threat of Indian conspiracy on the Eastern Shore was real, and the council dropped all charges against him, finding that he and the others "did as honest & carefull men ought to have done."[38]

Interracial tensions continued to mount on the Eastern Shore after the acquittal of Scarburgh. Early in 1652 native villagers at Oanancocke complained to the Northampton County Court that so many Englishmen had

[34] Berkeley to the Commissioners of Northampton County, April 1650, WMQ, 5 (1896–97): 82–83.

[35] Deal, *Race and Class*, 25–26.

[36] Northampton County Records, 10 May 1651, VMHB 5 (1897–98): 33–34.

[37] Ibid., 34.

[38] Northampton County Records, Deeds and Wills, 1651–54, quoted in Deal, *Race and Class*, 28.

settled upon their lands "that the Indians are now straightened from their hunting, (a great part of their relief consisting thereupon) and also they have declared that lately divers of our people have been in their woods and laid out land even unto the very town of Oanancocke, which if they should part with they should wholly destroy the inheritance of themselves & their posterity." The county court's demand that no one settle on Indian land without compensating the Indians' "Great Men" went unheeded, and an uneasy wariness characterized relations on the peninsula for the rest of the decade.[39]

North of the York River, pressure from the frontier population produced a pattern of Indian relations similar to that on the Eastern Shore. English settlers pouring onto lands on both sides of the Rappahannock River dispossessed the natives and allowed their livestock to run roughshod in Indian fields. Late in the fall of 1654 the Rappahannocks retaliated, offering "divers injuries and insolencys" to the inhabitants of Lancaster, Northumberland, and Westmoreland Counties. The assembly instructed a combined militia force drawn from these counties to march to the Rappahannock town "and demand and receive such satisfaction as [they] shall thinke fitt for the severall injuries done unto the said inhabitants, not using any act of hostility but defensive in case of assault." The assembly's attempt to procure redress for the counties while avoiding bloodshed failed when the meeting turned into a brawl in which the Rappahannock *weroance* was killed.[40]

Two years later the court of Rappahannock County (lately separated from Lancaster) signed peace treaties with the Rappahannocks and Mattaponis, pledging to treat the Indians as Englishmen. Neither treaty, however, reversed the tide of white expansion. In 1660 the Mattaponis complained of pressure from frontiersmen to abandon their village near the headwaters of Piscataway Creek. Two years later Englishmen burned the *weroance*'s house. Governor Berkeley, recently returned to power, ordered the militia commander to make reparations, but the Mattaponis did not collect until 1667. By that time most of the tribe had moved back to their old home near the head of the Mattaponi River. The Rappahannocks fared little better. They suffered continual pressure from aggressive English frontiersmen, who coerced sizable chunks of land from them.[41]

Farther north, along the Potomac, frontier barons such as Giles Brent, Gerard Fowke, George Mason, and John Lord tried to oust the Potomack Indians from Westmoreland County. The four men were members of the county commission charged with the management of local Indian affairs. When several English settlers were murdered in 1660, the commissioners devised a plan to extort a cession of land from the Potomacks. Their *weroance*,

[39] Northampton County Records, July 1652, *VMHB* 5 (1898): 36–37.
[40] Hening, *Statutes*, 1:389; Rountree, *Pocahontas's People*, 118.
[41] Old Rappahannock County Records, *WMQ*, 2d ser., 18 (1938): 298, and 16 (1936): 592. See also Rountree, *Pocahontas's People*, 93, 113–14; Lancaster County Records, *WMQ* 4 (1895–96): 178–79.

Wahanganoche, was required by treaty to turn over Indians suspected of murdering Englishmen and did so in this case. But Fowke allowed the suspects to "escape" and then claimed that Wahanganoche had never delivered them. The commissioners charged the *weroance* with high treason and imprisoned him.[42]

Changes in the colony's political and social structure rendered the governor's control over events such as these increasingly ineffective. The English population of Virginia increased eightfold in the decades after 1634, so that by the 1660s the homes of 40,000 Englishmen were scattered below the falls of the major rivers. The county court system, implemented by Governor Harvey in 1634 to cope with the administrative and political difficulties caused by rapid population growth and territorial expansion, originally conceived of the counties as agencies of local government with narrowly circumscribed powers. By 1660, however, the county court had become the branch of colonial government with the most immediate impact upon the life of the local planter. As the number of Englishmen in Virginia increased, so too did the number of deeds, wills, indentures, lawsuits, and disputes that required governmental attention. Delegating responsibility for such activity to the counties lightened the burden carried by the provincial government but decreased metropolitan control in the localities.[43]

The reliance on county courts consequently produced a decentralized political system in Virginia. The county court constituted an intervening authority between governor and colonist, and men of local wealth and power exploited the opportunities it offered to carve out sizable political domains for themselves. To manage the Anglo-American frontier effectively, the governors of Virginia required the assistance of county officials. When men such as Scarburgh, Brent, Mason, and Fowke rose to positions of local prominence, however—men whose attitudes toward Indians had been shaped along the frontier—the governor could restrain them only with great difficulty.[44]

III

This, then, was the administrative system Sir William Berkeley inherited when the assembly recalled him in 1660, just a few months before Charles II returned to the throne of England. Once again Berkeley worked to obtain English dominion along the frontier.

[42] Gregory Waselkov, "Relations between Settlers and Indians," in *Westmoreland County, Virginia*, ed. Walter Biscoe Norris (Montross, Va., 1983), 21.

[43] On English population, see the 1634 census in *VMHB* 8 (1900): 32; Morgan, *American Slavery*, app.; Warren M. Billings, "The Causes of Bacon's Rebellion: Some Suggestions," *VMHB* 78 (1970): 411; Billings, "The Growth of Political Institutions in Virginia, 1634–1676," *WMQ*, 3d ser., 31 (1974): 228.

[44] Billings, "Causes," 411; Billings, "Growth," 228–32; Washburn, *Virginia*, 48–49; Washburn, *Governor*, 20.

Early in 1662 the Virginia Assembly undertook a codification of the colony's laws. Berkeley had sailed for England in April of 1661 to obtain royal support for his scheme to develop Virginia's economy. He left his lieutenant, Francis Moryson, in charge of guiding the legislation through the House of Burgesses. There can be no question that the body of laws reflected the views of both men. Under their codification, wrote Robert Beverley, "the Church of England was confirm'd the established Religion, the Charge of Government sustain'd, Trade and Manufacture were encouraged, a Town projected, and all the Indian Affairs settled."[45]

Moryson and Berkeley understood that "the mutuall discontents, complaints, jealousies, and ffeares of English and Indians proceed chiefly from the violent intrusions of diverse English made into their lands." As a result, both sides sustained injuries, and a cycle of "reports and rumours . . . of the hostile intentions of each to the other" tended "infinitely to the disturbance of the peace of his majestys country." The 1662 enactment reveals the metropolitan sense of the scale of frontier abuse.[46]

Moryson recognized the need to restrict the right of Englishmen to buy Indian land. "Laws prohibiting the purchase of any Indians lands," the codification read, had been "fruitles and ineffectuall" in the past because it was as "easy to affright [the Indians] to a publique as well as a private acknowledgement" of the sale. "Corrupt interpreters" added "to this mischiefe by rendering [Indians] willing to surrender when indeed they intended to have received a confirmation of their owne rights, and redresse of their wrong." Allowing these abuses to continue "must needs have involved the country into an inevitable and destructive warre." The governor, council and assembly therefore declared

> that for the future noe Indian king or other upon any pretence alien and sell, nor noe English for any cause or consideration whatsoever purchase or buy any tract or parcell of land now justly claymed or actually possest by any Indian or Indians whatsoever; all such bargaines and sales hereafter made or pretended to be made being hereby declared invalid, voyd and null, any acknowledgement, surrender, law or custome formerly used to the contrary notwithstanding; and further that the Indians properties of their goods bee hereby assured and confirmed to them, and their persons soe secured that whoever shall defraud or take from them their goods and doe hurt and injury to their persons shall make such satisfaction and suffer such punishment as the laws of England or this country doe inflict, if the same had bine done to an Englishman.[47]

---

[45] Moryson dedicated the published version of the body of laws to Berkeley, "who of the most and best of them, was the only Author." See [Francis Moryson], *The Lawes of Virginia Now in Force* (London, 1662), dedicatory epistle; Beverley, *History*, 66; Stephen Saunders Webb, *The Governors-General: The English Army and the Definition of Empire, 1569–1681*, (Chapel Hill, N.C., 1979), 334–36.

[46] Hening, *Statutes*, 2:138.

[47] Ibid., 138–39.

The laws required that Englishmen settled on Indian land without proof of title vacate their claims and empowered the governor to appoint "such uninterested persons as he shall think fitt, to enquire into and examine the severall claimes made to any part of our neighbouring Indians land." Englishmen settled within three miles of any Indians were "to helpe the Indians to ffence in a corne ffield proportionable to the number of persons the said Indian towne doth consist off," though the Indians were responsible for maintaining the fences in a good state of repair. County courts were to allow unarmed Indians to fish and gather shellfish and wild fruits "for the better reliefe of the poor Indians whome the seating of the English hath forced from their wonted conveniences," a reflection of the critical environmental strain placed upon Native American communities by expanding English settlements. Finally, the body of laws outlawed acts of vigilante justice committed upon Indians.[48]

In subsequent years Berkeley continued to call for legislation designed to prevent disorder along the frontier. The assembly's requirement that tributary Indians, those who had surrendered after the final Anglo-Powhatan war in 1646, assist in the apprehension of Indians who had murdered Englishmen, was an attempt on the governor's part to secure justice quickly and to eliminate the incentive for vengeful frontiersmen to carry out bloody acts of vigilantism. The sale of arms to Indians was punished by a fine of 10,000 pounds of tobacco or two years' imprisonment. The assembly also attempted to prevent a scattered and vulnerable pattern of settlement by stipulating that no "frontier plantations" be seated unless the party included "fowre able hands well armed."[49]

The legislation did not, however, put an end to violence on the frontier. In the fall of 1661 planters in Rappahannock County found, at the farm of Richard White,

> the body of Jo[?]uelly Massacred in the house of the aforesaid White his skull Splett on the forehead down to the [?] his Skull beaten in the side [?] of his head over His Eye moreover neere the doer of the said house we found the body of Thomas White sonn of the aforesaid Richard stripped naked with his skull beaten in over the Eye also we found the skull of Daniel Pignell servant to the said Richard White beaten in the side of the head with an ax as we conceive by the bigness of the hole in the Skull.[50]

Northern Neck natives resisted English encroachment upon their lands, and acts like the attack on White's farm occurred more often as the decade progressed. By 1663 the council felt it necessary to call upon "the kings of

[48] Ibid., 139–41, 155–56.
[49] Ibid., 209, 215, 218–19, 237.
[50] Rappahannock County Records, Deeds, Book 2, 9 September 1661, 201–2, WMQ, 2d ser., 18 (1938), 297–98.

Potomack and all the rest of the northerne Indians Weroances" to "deliver such hostages of their children or others as shalbe required" to ensure their good behavior. If they did not, they would "be declared as an enemy and proceeded against accordingly."[51]

Whether or not the Indian leaders complied with this demand, relations between Indians and Englishmen in the Northern Neck deteriorated. Settlers continued to occupy Indian lands regardless of Berkeley's orders, and Indians continued to retaliate. By the summer of 1666 Rappahannock County officials apparently had convinced Berkeley of the seriousness of the situation. The "Northern Indians" (Nansemonds, Rappahannocks, Portobaccos, and Patomacks), he believed, had combined with "foreign Indians" to threaten the frontier. Berkeley consequently authorized the Rappahannock County militia to launch a campaign "to Destroy all these Northern Indians" and sell the captive women and children into slavery to defray the cost of the expedition. The members of the county court shared Berkeley's opinion "that the Late Execrable Murders are & have bin Committed by a Combination of our Northern Indians prticularly by the Doagges conjunct wth our Neighbour Indians above." In July Berkeley and the council declared war against the Doegs and the Northern Neck nations. The Patomacks disappeared entirely from the historical record shortly thereafter. The English attacks significantly weakened the Northern Neck natives and succeeded in driving the Doegs, at least temporarily, back into Maryland.[52]

Edmund Scarburgh continued to wage his private war against local natives on the Eastern Shore, enlarging his considerable domain at their expense. By 1664 he had patented more than 20,000 acres and by the end of the decade he had acquired 10,000 more, making him by far the peninsula's largest landowner.[53]

With the exception of Scarburgh, most Eastern Shore planters lived in relative peace with the Accomacks (now called Gingaskins) and Occohannocks. Disease and, later, alcohol took an enormous toll among Indians on the peninsula, and their capacity to resist English expansion deteriorated rapidly after midcentury. Scarburgh, however, loved bullying the weak, and he certainly hated Indians. By 1670 rumors of an Indian conspiracy directed

[51] Hening, *Statutes*, 2:193–94.

[52] William Berkeley to Major General Smythe, 22 June 1666, and Rappahannock County Court to Berkeley, n.d., Rappahannock County Deeds, bk. 3, 57–58, in *Extracts of Records, 1664 May 27–1692 July 14, Concerning Relations with the Indians* (Virginia Historical Society, Richmond) 591. The Doegs had been active along the periphery of English settlement in Maryland as well. The Maryland Council made peace with the Doeg and other Potomac Valley Indians on 20 April 1666, but isolated Doeg attacks apparently continued. See Peace Treaty, 20 April 1666, and "Petition of Thomas Allcock," April–May 1666, in *AM*, 2:25–28, 71. The increasing frequency with which the phrases "foreign" and "Northern" Indians were used by Virginians testifies to the growing numbers of Susquehannocks and Doegs active in the Northern Neck. See also Rountree, *Pocahontas's People*, 95, 122.

[53] Nugent, *Cavaliers*, 119, 121, 139, 183, 225, 305, 418, 419, 425, 452, 453, 536, 554, 555; Ames, *Studies*, 25.

at him once again began to circulate. Berkeley, recognizing that the source of Indian discontent lay in Scarburgh's continued acts of aggression against the natives, ordered him arrested and drew up an impressive indictment. Scarburgh had "contrary to my order and the peace long since established between us & the Indians unjustly & most tyranously oppressed them by murthering, whipping, & burning them, by taking their children by force from who are their parents & many other waies to the apparent hazzard of the said Peace established as aforesaid." It was less the prosecution of Scarburgh, however, than his death in 1671 that returned the Eastern Shore to its relative tranquility.[54]

Sir William Berkeley consistently tried to establish peaceful relations with Virginia's Indians. He recognized, correctly, that the metropolitan objectives of dominion and civility could not be attained without order, and that endemic frontier disorder resulted primarily from English pressure on Indian land. Frontier aggression could disrupt both economic activity in the colony and the crown's customs revenue. Warfare with the Indians, moreover, would absorb the limited resources Berkeley had at his disposal to defend the colony from the periodic threat of Dutch invasion. As he explained to the king in 1667, the Virginians were "a people press'd at our backes with Indians, in our Bowills with our Servants . . . and invaded from without by the Dutch."[55]

Berkeley recognized as well that a disorderly frontier reduced the likelihood that any Indians would convert to Christianity. "The Heathen," wrote a Berkeley supporter in England in 1662, "enter frequently into some of the remote dispers'd habitations of the Christians," and "premises considered, what can they see which should make them in love with their Religion?" According to this author, "They see their families disordered, their Children untaught, the publick Worship and Service of the Great God they own, neglected." Little chance existed "that any rationall Heathen should be perswaded to commit their Children to the teaching and education of such Christians, whom they shall perceive to want Schooles of Learning (the means of both) for their own."[56]

But Berkeley, a firm believer in the colony's potential, thought that he could govern Virginia's frontier, remedy its problems, and attain for the crown the metropolitan imperatives of dominion and civility. During his trip to England in 1661 the governor admitted

[54] Accomack County, Deeds and Wills, 1664–1671, p. 166, quoted in Deal, *Race and Class*, 39; Rountree, *Pocahontas's People*, 124–25.

[55] Berkeley to King, 1667, Colonial Office: Colonial Papers 1, General Series, 1574–1757, Public Record Office (hereafter C.O. 1), C.O. 1/21, 111, VCRP. See also Berkeley to King and Privy Council, C.O. 1/30, 114–15, VCRP; Washburn, *Governor*, 160–62.

[56] "Virginia's Cure," in *Tracts and Other Papers Relating Principally to the Origin, Settlement, and Progress of the Colonies in North America*, ed. Peter Force, 4 vols. (Washington, D.C., 1836), 3, no. 15: 7.

that *Barbadoes* sends a better commodity into England, then Virginia yet does, but withall it must be acknowledged, that one Ship from Virginia brings more money to the Crown, than five Ships of the same burthen do from the Barbadoes.

"But," he added, "had we ability or skill to set forward those staple commodities I mentioned, of Silk, Flax, Hemp, Pitch, Pot-Ashes, and Iron, a few yeares would make us able to send more Ships laden with these, then now the Barbadoes do with Sugar." Virginia, in Berkeley's view, was central to the prosperity of the Restoration Empire.[57]

The governor's plans resemble the earlier efforts of the Virginia Company to diversify economic activity in the Old Dominion. Settlers would gather in towns, where artisans could establish their crafts and find a market for their wares. A population settled in towns would require food; consequently, planters would at last have an economic incentive to raise corn and other grain for sale to townsfolk. Berkeley wanted to encourage also those willing to try their hands at ironworking, glassmaking, spinning and weaving, silk-worm growing, and ship-building. He hoped to insulate settlers from the vagaries of an unpredictable market, while increasing the profitability of the tobacco produced by reducing the supply.[58]

Berkeley failed, however, to reduce the colonists' commitment to tobacco. Between 1637 and 1640 an average of 1,395,063 pounds of tobacco had been exported annually; in 1669 the export figure exceeded 9 million pounds. Ever since the 1630s frontier barons had turned their attention away from the control of local corn and fur supplies and toward the accumulation of large tracts of land for speculation and tobacco culture. Berkeley had proposed in 1663 that taxes be levied on land rather than polls, in an attempt to discourage the engrossment of large tracts as well as to relieve pressure on Indian lands, but even in this he failed to overcome the opposition of frontier planters.[59]

Overproduction of tobacco ensured that the price offered for the crop in English ports would remain low. At the same time restrictions on colonial trade, as manifested in the Navigation Acts passed under both the Commonwealth and the restored monarchy, eliminated legal opportunities for English planters to circumvent low English prices and high customs duties by selling directly to the Dutch.[60]

[57] William Berkeley, *A Discourse and View of Virginia* (London, 1663), 5.

[58] Morgan, *American Slavery*, 187–88; John C. Rainbolt, *From Prescription to Persuasion: Manipulation of the Eighteenth-Century Virginia Economy* (Port Washington, N.Y., 1971), 6.

[59] Lewis Cecil Gray, *History of Agriculture in the Southern United States to 1860*, 2 vols. (Washington, D.C., 1933), 1:213. Between 1665 and 1688, the average tobacco export reached nearly 14.5 million pounds per year, and 35 million by 1700. See Jon Kukla, "Order and Chaos in Early America: Political and Social Stability in Pre-Restoration Virginia," *AHR* 90 (1985): 285; Morgan, *American Slavery*, 193.

[60] Warren M. Billings, John E. Selby, and Thad W. Tate, *Colonial Virginia: A History* (White Plains, N.Y., 1986), 78–79.

War with the Dutch from 1664 to 1667 and again from 1672 to 1674 further damaged the tobacco trade, as ships were either captured on the high seas, converted to military use in England, or burned at anchor by Dutch raiders. The reduction in the size of the fleet drove up shipping costs, while the produce of most planters rotted at dockside for want of transport. Crown policies during the war did not help the situation. Charles II and his councilors ordered Berkeley to build an expensive fort at the mouth of the James River. The governor argued that the fort was useless because "the Entrance into the Province is so large that any enemys ship may ride out of all possible danger to the greatest cannon in the world." Berkeley's prediction proved correct when, in July 1673, a small Dutch fleet destroyed the tobacco ships lying at anchor in the James River.[61]

The king's grant of the Northern Neck to a number of investors in 1663 and his proprietary grant of all the colony's public lands to Lords Culpeper and Arlington in 1674 added to Virginia's considerable fiscal woes by throwing land titles throughout the colony into confusion. Berkeley was forced to send "agents to address the King to vacate those Grants" and faced the humiliation of having to levy taxes to buy back from court favorites the land he governed in the king's name.[62]

Against this backdrop of economic crisis Virginia acquired a new social structure. Throughout the seventeenth century the number of English indentured servants surviving their terms of servitude increased. Once free, they looked for land of their own. But finding it more and more difficult to obtain land suitable for tobacco culture that had not already been claimed, the growing ranks of freedmen moved to the frontiers, where they too competed with Indians for control of the land.[63]

Life there was difficult, and the chances for economic advance poor. Some small farmers, through luck and determination, did join the ranks of wealthy planters, but for the vast majority profits were meager, and whatever economic independence they achieved was often tenuous at best. In Gloucester County in the second half of the seventeenth century, for example, less than 20 percent of those individuals whose initial land patents were for less than 200 acres managed to obtain additional land in the county. Of those who patented between 200 and 399 acres, only about one-quarter obtained additional holdings. The increase in taxation to pay for useless forts and castles, the king's capricious generosity, and the collapse in tobacco prices caught small planters on the frontier in a mounting cycle of debt that forced

---

[61] Berkeley and Council in Virginia to Secretary Lord Arlington, 13 July 1666, *CSP Col, 1661–68*, 396, no. 1241; extract of letter to Mr. Hammond, 3 September 1673, *NYCD*, 3:205–6.

[62] Beverley, *History*, 75; Morgan, *American Slavery*, 245; Sister Jean de Lourdes Leonard, "Operation Checkmate: The Birth and Death of a Virginia Blueprint for Progress," *WMQ*, 3d ser., 24 (1967): 69–71.

[63] Morgan, *American Slavery*, esp. 218.

many of them back into the tenantry or servitude they had hoped to escape. The tax burden alone amounted to a figure between a quarter and a half of the average planter's income, making living even at a subsistence level difficult. With more stringent trade regulations, falling tobacco prices, and the elimination of the Dutch market as an alternative to crushing English customs duties, the future for Virginia's tobacco planters looked bleak indeed.[64]

Governor Berkeley, as the king's representative in the colony, bore the brunt of the growing popular discontent. Henry Norwood, a loyal supporter of the crown and the colony's treasurer, as early as 1667 could lament the "extream and grievous taxes" the colonists "ly under Continually and yet the tobbaccoes that are Raised not Expended to the desired end." Few of Virginia's former servants, it appears, respected the governor. The political system seemed unresponsive to the needs of ordinary settlers. Since 1661, no election had been held for seats in the House of Burgesses. The governor maintained the same group in power, periodically proroguing the assembly when it suited his needs. This assembly worked with the governor to exclude the heavily-taxed former servants from power. In 1670, for instance, the burgesses voted to disfranchise those "who having little interest in the country, doe oftner make tumults at a election to the disturbance of his majesties peace, then by their discretions in their votes provide for the conservation thereof, by making choice of persons fitly qualifyed for the discharge of soe greate a trust." Thereafter, only property holders could vote.[65] Forts that bought no security—a closed provincial elite that seemed to be headed by a corrupt and avaricious governor intent upon engrossing the wealth of men of more moderate and limited means, a political system unresponsive to local needs, and a general constriction in opportunity—all served to weaken Berkeley's position in the colony at a time when he badly needed the support of the people.[66]

In this environment the English failed entirely to notice changes occurring in Native American communities which rendered conditions along the frontier extremely volatile. Ever since the final defeat of Opechancanough in 1646, the Algonquian groups scattered along the peripheries of English settlement—members of the component bands that had constituted Powhatan's chiefdom—had become marginalized, as English settlement advanced up the rivers. By 1660 at least, despite metropolitan efforts, some were serving as slaves for life.[67] Even though growing numbers of natives were slowly be-

---

[64] Stephen Saunders Webb, *1676: The End of American Independence* (New York, 1984), 19; Billings, "Virginia's Deploured Condition," 167; Rainbolt, *Prescription*, 18; Morgan, *American Slavery*, 227; James Horn, *Adapting to a New World: English Society in the Seventeenth-Century Chesapeake*, (Chapel Hill, N.C., 1994), 292.

[65] Hening, *Statutes*, 2:280.

[66] Richard L. Morton, *Colonial Virginia*, (Chapel Hill, NC 1960), 219–20; Horn, *Adapting to a New World*, 373–74.

[67] In March 1662 a Powhatan Indian "was sold for life time to one Elizabeth Short by a king of the Wainoke Indians." The Weyanoke *weroance*, the Assembly declared, "had no power to sell [the Powhatan] being of another nation." The Assembly, with the imperatives of dominion and civility clearly in mind, ordered the Powhatan freed, "he speaking perfectly the English tongue and desiring Baptism." See Hening, *Statutes*, 2:155.

coming anglicized as English settlements surrounded their own, intensifying competition for control of land continued to produce racist views of the Indians. In other words, those Indians who had been overrun by English expansion, rendered tributary, and now found themselves living *among* the English, benefited little by Anglicizing, because the resistance of Indians on the frontier intensified racial animosities within the colony.[68]

At the same time, tribes stronger than the Powhatan remnants, refugees fleeing Iroquois aggression, moved into the region. The strongest of these, the Doegs of Maryland and the Susquehannocks, by the mid-1670s had nowhere else to go. They were caught in a vise between the Maryland English, the Virginia frontier, and the Iroquois.[69]

The Susquehannocks, after February 1675, occupied a fortified site along the banks of the Potomac River, opposite present-day Mount Vernon. They had settled there at the invitation of Governor Charles Calvert, soon the third Lord Baltimore, who recognized that western Iroquois assaults upon the Susquehannocks jeopardized his interests in Maryland. An understanding of the events that led to Calvert's offer and the Susquehannocks' acceptance is necessary to an understanding of the origins of Bacon's Rebellion.[70]

When the Marylanders decided to drive William Claiborne from his Kent Island post, the proprietary government gained not only his enmity but that of the Susquehannocks as well. After attacking Maryland's fur-trading allies, the Piscataways, at two villages along the Potomac and sacking Jesuit storehouses along the Patuxent in the summer of 1642, the Susquehannocks killed a number of settlers near St. Mary's City. That September, Maryland declared war against "the Sesquihanowes, Wicomeses, and Nantacoque Indians," all considered "enemies of this Province" and therefore to be "proceeded against by all persons."[71] In the summer of 1643 Maryland launched two attacks. The first of these ended inconclusively, as the Susquehannocks avoided English firepower, and in the second the Susquehannocks routed the Marylanders, capturing fifteen prisoners whom they promptly tortured to death.[72]

The Mohawks and western Iroquois complicated the tense relationship between Maryland and her Indian neighbors when they turned south in 1651 to challenge Susquehannock dominance in the northern Chesapeake. Though the arrival in 1652 of their old friend William Claiborne—at the head of a parliamentary commission intent upon "reducing" Maryland—smoothed the passage toward a peace agreement between the Susquehannocks and the

---

[68] Rountree, *Pocahontas's People*, 89. The tributary Indians in 1670 numbered probably between 2,500 and 3,000. A census in 1670 listed the number of bowmen at 725, and the accepted multiplier of four Indians per hunter gives a total of 2,900. See *VMHB* 14 (1907): 289; and W. Stitt Robinson Jr., "Tributary Indians in Colonial Virginia," *VMHB* 67 (1959): 49–64.

[69] Webb, *1676*, 4; Hening, *Statutes*, 2:153.

[70] *AM*, 19 February 1675, 2:428–29.

[71] Hall, *Narratives*, 136, 138; Proclamation of Lieutenant Governor Leonard Calvert, 13 September 1642, *AM*, 3:116–17.

[72] Jennings, *Ambiguous Iroquois Empire*, 120.

Marylanders, the source of the ensuing treaty itself must be seen as a product of the Susquehannock desire to avoid fighting a war on two fronts. Thereafter, in return for the cession to Maryland of large tracts of land on both shores of Chesapeake Bay, the Susquehannocks were able to devote their attention to the Iroquois.[73]

Mohawk involvement in the war would not last long. After the Dutch captured New Sweden on the Delaware River in 1655, the Mohawks dropped out of the fighting. The Susquehannocks and Mohawks no longer had to compete for access to Dutch trade, since each group now had its own vested interest in a Dutch trading center, the Mohawks at Fort Orange and the Susquehannocks at New Amstel. Each attempted to control the access of foreign tribes to its Dutch post, but neither had an interest any longer in intruding upon the claims of the other.[74]

The same circumstances did not apply for the western Iroquois. Warfare between the Susquehannocks and the Five Nations disrupted the fur trade in the Maryland-Delaware region. To increase their profits, the Dutch at New Amstel hoped to persuade the western Iroquois to carry their furs to Dutch posts on the Delaware. Because the Mohawks jealously guarded what they saw as their primary right to trade at Fort Orange, the Dutch offer no doubt was attractive to western Iroquois traders who sought European goods. To carry their furs to the Dutch, however, the western nations first had to pass through Susquehannock territory—and pay for the privilege.[75]

The increase in Dutch activity on the Delaware concerned Lord Baltimore, who saw in Dutch efforts to trade with the western Iroquois an attempt to weaken the English in Maryland. Good relations with the Susquehannocks thus became a means for Baltimore to secure his frontiers. On May 15, 1661, Maryland and the Susquehannocks agreed to a new peace treaty in which the two sides pledged to "assist one the other against the Ennemies of either nacon." The English agreed also to send fifty men to the Susquehannocks "to cause some Spurrs or flankers to be layd out for the Defence of the Indian Forte" and to "assist against the Assaults of their Ennemies."[76]

The Susquehannocks held their own quite well, largely owing to the formidable arsenal they had accumulated through their ties to both the Delaware Dutch and the Maryland English. In 1663 the Senecas, accompanied by Onondagas and Cayugas, gathered eight hundred warriors for an assault upon the Susquehannock fort. The Iroquois warriors were "surprised"

---

[73] The peace treaty is printed in *AM*, 5 July 1652, 3:275–78. See also Jennings, *Ambiguous Iroquois Empire*, 121.

[74] Francis Jennings, "Glory, Death, and Transfiguration: The Susquehannock Indians in the Seventeenth Century," *Proceedings of the American Philosophical Society* 112 (1968): 25–26.

[75] Barry C. Kent, *Susquehanna's Indians* (Harrisburg, Pa., 1984), 38; Jennings, "Glory."

[76] Articles of Peace, 15 May 1661, *AM*, 3:420–21; instructions to Captain John Odber, 21 May 1661, *AM*, 3:417. See also Jennings, *Ambiguous Iroquois Empire*, 127–28; Kent, *Susquehanna's Indians*, 39.

to find the "defenses so well-planned," with the fort secured "on one side by the stream, on whose banks it was situated, and on the opposite by a double curtain of large trees, flanked by two bastions erected in the European manner, and even supplied with some pieces of Artillery." Unable to take the stronghold through a direct assault, the Iroquois "resorted to their customary subtlety, in order to gain by trickery what they could not accomplish by force." They offered to send in twenty-five envoys to treat for peace and buy provisions for the trip home. Before they could surprise their hosts, however, they were seized, placed on scaffolds, and burned alive in front of their kinsmen.[77]

The Susquehannocks later carried the war into the heart of Iroquoia, destroying Onondaga defenders in 1666 at the same time that French forces were razing the Mohawk towns. Both sides suffered severely from war and disease, however, and despite their military victory, the Susquehannocks returned home seriously weakened.[78] By the 1670s the western Iroquois had regrouped and renewed their offensive. Sometime during the summer of 1673, reports arrived in French Canada that Iroquois war parties had "utterly defeated the Andastogues [Susquehannocks], their ancient and most redoubtable foes." Although the extent of the Susquehannock defeat is debatable, the western Iroquois did convince the Maryland English that they now were the dominant aboriginal power in the region.[79]

The renewal of the western Iroquois offensive coincided with the short-lived Dutch reconquest of New Netherland in 1673. Calvert feared that the Dutch would incite the Iroquois against the Maryland English. Placing the good of the colony ahead of that of its Indian allies, and convinced that the Susquehannocks could no longer provide a viable counterforce to Iroquois aggression, the Maryland Assembly voted for "a Peace to be made wth the Cynicoes Indians," even though such a peace must "bring a Warre wth the Susquehannoughs."[80]

Calvert recognized that "should the Susquehannah Indians be permitted to live among the Respective friend Indian nations," the results could "be of Dangerous Consequence to the Province in General." He feared that Englishmen might be caught in the crossfire as western Iroquois raiders fell upon the Susquehannocks. Consequently, when "some of the Great Men of the Susquehannahs . . . Desired to know what part of the Province Should be

---

[77] Daniel K. Richter, *The Ordeal of the Longhouse: The Peoples of the Iroquois League in the Era of European Colonization* (Chapel Hill, N.C., 1992), 98; *JR*, 48:77, 79; *AM*, 1:471–72.

[78] Webb, *1676*, 290. They also renewed their peace with Maryland. See *AM*, 29 June 1666, 3:549–50; *JR*, 49:147–49.

[79] *JR*, 49:251. See also "Mathew's Narrative," in *Narratives of the Insurrections, 1675–1690*, ed. Charles M. Andrews (New York, 1915), 18. For assessments of the Susquehannock defeat, cf. Elizabeth Tooker, "The Demise of the Susquehannocks: A Seventeenth Century Mystery," *Pennsylvania Archaeologist* 54 (1984): 1–10; and Jennings, *Ambiguous Iroquois Empire*, 140.

[80] *AM*, 1 June 1674, 2:377–78.

Allotted for them to live upon," the governor suggested to them "a Place above the falls of Potomack."[81]

For the Susquehannocks, the Maryland proposal provided the opportunity for a strategic withdrawal. A sojourn on the Potomac would allow this intensely trade-oriented people, driven from the Delaware fur trade, to redirect their activities toward the Potomac Valley. Relocation also offered a respite from Iroquois aggression. For the Marylanders, the relocation of the Susquehannocks gave the proprietary government, at long last, a chance to establish order along its borders. Sending the Susquehannocks to the Potomac frontier, however, where they settled in an abandoned fort well below the falls, placed the retreating Indians in close quarters with frontiersmen from western Maryland and Virginia. These settlers would pressure the Susquehannocks as they had the coastal Algonquians before them. The results would devastate both Indian and English societies in the Chesapeake.

IV

In July 1675 "certeine Doegs & Susquehanok Indians on the Maryland side" of the Potomac "stole" some hogs from Thomas Mathew, a Northern Neck planter who had "abused and cheated them, in not paying for such Indian trucke as he had formerly bought of them." Mathew was not the sort to take an Indian insult sitting down. He gathered together his neighbors, pursued the responsible Indians across the river, and proceeded to beat some and kill others in order to reclaim his livestock. To the Doegs and Susquehannocks this was merely one more example of how Mathew treated Indians. In retaliation a Doeg "Warr Capt. with some Indians came over to Potomake and kill'd two of Mathews his servants, and came also a second time and kill'd his sonne."[82]

Upon learning of the Doeg attack Giles Brent and George Mason gathered the militia and set off at daybreak in pursuit of the killers. At a fork in the trail they split their forces. Within a mile Brent stumbled across a Doeg village and called the Indians to parley. The Doeg leader "came Trembling forth and would have fled" had not Brent grasped his scalplock. When the *weroance*, denying any knowledge of the attack on Mathew's farm, slipped free, Brent shot and killed him. The brief but bloody firefight that ensued left another ten Indians dead. Meanwhile, the noise of the gunfire "awakened the Indians in the Cabin which Coll: Mason had Encompassed." When they rushed out, the frontiersmen opened fire, killing fourteen Susquehannocks before Mason realized he had the wrong Indians.[83]

[81] *AM*, 19 February 1675, 2:428.
[82] Colonial Office: America and West Indies 5, Original Correspondence, 1606–1807, Public Record Office (hereafter C.O. 5) C.O. 5/1371, 188, *VCRP*.
[83] Ibid.; "Mathew's Narrative," 17.

With confusing reports flowing in from the north, Berkeley ordered John Washington and Isaac Allerton to undertake "a full & thorough inquisition . . . of ye True Causes of ye severall Murthers & Spoyles & by wt Nation or Nations donne." After completing their investigation, they were to "demand satisfaction and take such further course in this Exegency as shall be thought requisite and necessary."[84]

Instead of investigating, Washington and Allerton rendezvoused late in September with a Maryland force under the command of Thomas Truman. The Doegs by this time had dispersed into the backcountry, but the Susquehannocks had gathered in their Potomac fortress, a formidable defensive position which the English lacked the manpower to storm or the artillery to knock down. Instead, they resolved to lay siege to the stronghold. When five headmen came out to parley, the English "caused the [Indian] Commissioners braines to be knock'd out," an action "being Diametricall to the Law of Arms."[85]

After killing the Susquehannock emissaries, the Virginia and Maryland militia conducted such "a negligent siege" that the entire native garrison escaped in mid-October. They "resolved to imploy there liberty in avenging there Commissioneres blood, which they speedily effected in the death of sixty inosscent soules." Then, "Forsaking Maryland" the Susquehannocks crossed the Potomac

> and thence over the heads of Rappahannock and York Rivers, killing whom they found on the upmost Plantations untill they came to the Head of James River, where . . . they Slew Mr. Bacon's Overseer whom He much Loved, and one of his Servants, whose Blood Hee Vowed to Revenge if possible.

Having avenged their losses, the Susquehannocks sent messengers to Governor Berkeley with an offer to conclude a peace, but Berkeley refused to treat with them. The Susquehannocks thereafter gradually withdrew in small numbers into the backcountry.[86]

Though the number initially killed by the Indians was relatively small, frightened reports from the frontier naturally magnified the scale of Indian violence, creating a unified call for swift and violent retribution.[87] Facing these demands, Berkeley commissioned his lieutenant-governor, Sir Henry Chicheley, to raise troops against "the Murderers." Before the troops

---

[84] Westmoreland County Records, Deeds and Wills, fol. 232, *WMQ* 4 (1895–96): 86.

[85] "The History of Bacon's and Ingram's Rebellion," in Andrews, *Narratives*, 47–48. See also "Mathew's Narrative," 18–19; Westmoreland County Deeds and Wills, 1665–77, fol. 288, *WMQ*, 1st. ser., 2 (1893–94): 39–40; AM, 2:481–88, 500–501; C.O. 5/1371, 188, VCRP.

[86] "Cotton's Narrative," in Force, *Tracts*, 1, no. 9: 3; "Bacon's and Ingram's Rebellion," 48–49; "Mathew's Narrative," 19–20.

[87] Rountree (*Pocahontas's People*, 97) and Washburn (*Governor*, 33) emphasize the small number of casualties, without considering how frontier fears would magnify the scale of violence. Webb, (1676, 4), suggests a much higher number of casualties.

marched, however, Berkeley countermanded his order and disbanded the force. He then instructed frontier planters to draw together, ten men in a house, as a means of defending themselves from Indian attack. The recall of Chicheley stunned the colony, angered a frontier population who had heard that help was on the way, and destroyed the governor's credibility. Berkeley appeared, at best, indecisive and, at worst, cowardly.[88]

The Indian warfare on Virginia's frontier held for Berkeley a frightening prospect. The governor believed that as a result of King Philip's War to the north "the New England men will not recover their wealth and Townes they have lost this twenty coming yeres." One hundred miles of territory had been devastated for want of secure defenses, and New Englanders had added to their problems by marching out recklessly in search of Indians, falling victim in due course to well-planned native ambushes. Berkeley thought it possible that "the beginning of the New England troubles were the cause of ours," and that he too faced a massive Indian uprising aimed at eliminating the English presence in North America.[89]

Berkeley's own experience in Indian warfare, along with the example of New England, thus militated against an offensive strategy. His recommendations to the March assembly were intended to remove control of the war from the hands of such frontier thugs as Brent, Mason and Washington and to secure the allegiance of the tributary Indians. He proposed to construct a series of forts at the heads of the major rivers. Five hundred men, a quarter of those mounted, would man the forts, with troops constantly ranging between them in search of natives. In order to prevent another disaster like Mason and Brent's attack, however, the assembly ordered that no "ffort, habitation or number of the enemy settled or fortifyed" be attacked without permission from the governor.[90]

The frontier population found little to its liking in the governor's plan. The scattered forts, Berkeley's opponents argued, would not halt Indian incursions, and the enemy, after learning "where these Mouse-traps were sett," would bypass them "without any detriment to theire designes." For those already burdened with high taxes, moreover, the levies required to construct the forts seemed like a useless waste of money or, worse, "a Designe of the Grandees to engrosse all their Tobacco into their owne hands." Thus, at a time when Berkeley most needed the support of the frontier population, "the sense of this oppression and the dread of a common approaching calamity made the giddy-headed multitude madd, and precipitated them upon that rash overture of Running out upon the Indians themselves."[91]

[88] C.O. 5/1371, 189, VCRP; Washburn, *Governor*, 25–26.
[89] Berkeley to Williamson, 1 April 1676, VMHB 20 (1912): 245–46; Berkeley to Mr. Ludwell, 1 April 1676, C.O. 1/36, 67–68, VCRP; Jennings, *Ambiguous Iroquois Empire*, 147; Washburn, *Governor*, 25–26.
[90] Hening, *Statutes*, 2:327, 330–32; Egerton MSS 2395, fol. 539, VCRP.
[91] "Bacon's and Ingram's Rebellion," 50; C.O. 5/1371, 189, VCRP; Berkeley and Council to Charles II, 25 January 1676, C.O. 1/37, 33, VCRP. For defenses of Berkeley's policy, see

Berkeley received petitions from the frontier counties in the spring of 1676, requesting commissions to attack the Indians. "The poore distressed subjects in the upper parts of the James River" asked the governor to allow them to appoint officers and "to take armes in defence of our lives and estates which without speedy prevention lie liable to the Injury of such insulting enimmies." Everywhere, royal commissioners would later report,

> the common cry and vogue of the Vulgar was, away with these Forts . . . wee will have warr with all Indians which come not in with their armes, and give Hostages for their Fidelity and to ayd against all others; wee will spare none, and [if] wee must be hang'd for Rebells for killing those that will destroy us, let them have us, wee will venture that rather than lye at the mercy of a Barbarous Enemy, and be murdered as we are etc.[92]

Nathaniel Bacon shared these concerns. In his mid-twenties when he came to Virginia, Bacon was described as "indifferent tall but slender, blackhair'd and of an ominous, pensive, melancholly Aspect, of a pestilent and prevalent logical discourse tending to athiesme in most companyes." He was "not given to much talke, or to make suddain replyes, of a most imperious and dangerous hidden Pride of heart, despising the wisest of his neighbours for their Ignorance, and very ambitious and arrogant."[93] Bacon had received ample assistance in establishing himself in Virginia. A cousin both to Governor Berkeley and Nathaniel Bacon Sr., one of the king's councilors in Virginia, the younger Bacon was honored with appointment to the governor's council and granted a license to engage in trade with neighboring Indians. With these connections he quickly became one of the most prominent planters on the upper portion of the James River.[94] In April he had gathered with his friends in Henrico County to drink and make "the Sadnesse of the times their discourse." These men persuaded Bacon to cross the James into Charles City County, "to goe over and see" the volunteers then gathering for a march against the Susquehannocks. The fearful backcountry settlers implored Bacon to "becom there Guardian Angle, to protect them from the cruilties of the Indians."[95]

His supporters tried to obtain a commission for him, but the governor refused. Bacon, the governor's supporters argued, simply did not see the wisdom of Berkeley's policy. The governor advised Bacon against becoming a mutineer and, when Bacon refused to abandon his preparations for a

---

"Answer of Alexander Culpeper to the Objections against Sir William Berkeley," 4 December 1677, C.O. 5/1355, 230–39, VCRP; William Sherwood to Joseph Williamson, 1 June 1676, *VMHB* 1 (1893): 168–69; and esp. Washburn, *Governor*, 31–32.

[92] C.O. 1/36, 139, VCRP; "Commissioners' Narrative," in Andrews, *Narratives*, 11. See also C.O. 1/37, 29, VCRP; C.O. 5/1371, 127, VCRP.

[93] Washburn, *Governor and the Rebel*, 18.

[94] Ibid., 17–18.

[95] "Commissioners' Narrative," 110–11; "Bacon's and Ingram's Rebellion," 52.

campaign against the Indians, proclaimed him a rebel on May 10 and removed him from his seat on the council. The next day Berkeley dissolved the assembly, which had sat for fourteen years, and called for new elections. The new burgesses, he said, would deal with the Indian problem and air any grievances against his administration. He promised that if his policies were the principal source of discontent in the colony, he would petition the king to recall him from service in Virginia.[96]

By the time Berkeley proclaimed him a rebel, Bacon had already commenced his march against the Indians by chasing the Pamunkeys into the Dragon Swamp. The Pamunkey were no threat to the English, but Bacon's forces, "coveting the good land" the Pamunkey occupied, attacked them anyway. He had little success, however, in finding the Susquehannocks. With his provisions nearly exhausted, Bacon and his men came to the village of the Occaneechees, "a nation," according to Berkeley, "who were ever friends to the English and seated in an Island very well-fortified by nature."[97]

It is likely that the Occaneechees, intensely involved in intercultural exchange, expected to trade with the rebels. Their *weroance*, Posseclay, fed Bacon's men and then offered to attack a group of Susquehannocks camped twenty miles from the village. They returned from the attack victorious and "brought in Divers prisoners most of which the Indians Knockt in the head in the sight and instance of the Inglish." The Occaneechees also brought "in a considerable quantity of beavor and a considerable quantity of Beads the only Indian Coyne."[98]

Bacon promptly claimed the treasure. "The Indians modestly replied that . . . they had got it with the hazard of their lives and that they knew not how any one besides themselves could pretend any title to it." Bacon so pretended by opening fire. "About 50 Indians were blown up in their Cabins, [and] some killed in the fort" into which the Occaneechees retired. The Indians, now aware of Bacon's poor manners, fought back fiercely. With "Night approaching," the English withdrew, "leaving a drum and some men behinde and soe Mr Bacon and those of his men which were left, retired in a disorderly manner, Eleven of his Company being killed, and severall mortally wounded."[99]

Bacon's rebellious attack upon the friendly Occaneechees and Pamunkeys, the governor's supporters believed, destroyed metropolitan Indian policy in

---

[96] William Sherwood to Joseph Williamson, 1 June 1676, C.O. 1/37, 1, *VCRP*; Egerton MSS 2395, fol. 546, *VCRP*; Billings, "Virginia's Deploured Condition," 22.

[97] William Berkeley to Sir Henry Coventry, 2 February 1677, in Wilcomb E. Washburn, ed., "Sir William Berkeley's 'A History of Our Miseries,'" *WMQ*, 3d. ser., 14 (1957): 407.

[98] Ibid. See also "Virginia's Deploured Condition," in "Aspinwall Papers," 406. For Occaneechee trade activities, see H. Trawick Ward and R. P. Stephen Davis Jr., "The Archaeology of the Historic Occaneechi Indians," *Southern Indian Studies* 36–37 (1988): 1–128.

[99] "Virginia's Deploured Condition," in "Aspinwall Papers," 167.

Virginia. Because of Bacon, Philip Ludwell wrote, "we have not now, that we know of, hardly 100 ffriend Indians on all or Borders Round, & at least 1500 enemies more than wee needed to have had." Bacon's activity exhausted Berkeley, throwing the aged governor into such fits of despondency and frustration that he could write, in mid-May, "to spare none that has the name of an Indian for they are now all our enemies." Two days before the assembly was scheduled to convene in June, Berkeley informed Secretary of State Henry Coventry that "I am not able to support my selfe at this Age six months longer and therefore on my Knees I beg his sacred majesty would send a more Vigorous Governor."[100]

The Virginia Assembly that gathered in Jamestown on June 5, 1676, was packed with Bacon's sympathizers, and the rebel himself had been elected burgess from Henrico County. Though he did not dare challenge openly the governor's proclamation from the month before, he did sneak into town the night of June 6 to confer with supporters but was captured the next morning. On bended knee he admitted his errors and begged Berkeley for a pardon. Aware that as many as two thousand Indian-hating, heavily taxed Bacon adherents had entered town, "armed and resolved to rescue him out of our hands," the governor prudently pardoned the rebel and on June 10 restored him to his seat on the council. Four days later Bacon left town, ostensibly to visit his sick wife.[101]

During Bacon's absence, Berkeley lectured the burgesses on the foolishness of warring indiscriminately against all Indians. The assembly conceded that a distinction might exist between Indian enemies and Indian friends but allowed the governor little else. "Forasmuch as wee are not altogether satisfied that all Indians are combined against us, and are our enemies," and that "wee are taught as well by the rules of our sacred religion, as those of humanitie, that we ought not to involve the innocent with the guiltie," the assembly, defining guilt broadly, enacted "that all such Indians shall be accounted and prosecuted as enemies that either already have, or hereafter shall forsake theire usuall and accustomed dwelling townes without licence obtained first from the honourable governor ... as alsoe such Indians as shall refuse upon demand to deliver up into the hands of the English all such armes and ammunition of what kind or nature soever." In short, Indians who fled from armed Englishmen, along with Indians who resisted their English assailants, were accounted enemies by the June assembly.[102]

---

[100] Ludwell to Joseph Williamson, 28 June 1676, *VMHB* 1 (1893): 180; Berkeley to Henry Coventry, 3 June 1676, quoted in *The Old Dominion in the Seventeenth Century: A Documentary History of Virginia, 1606–1689*, ed. Warren M. Billings (Chapel Hill, N.C., 1975), 272; Morgan, *American Slavery*, 260.

[101] William Sherwood to [?], 28 June 1676, C.O. 1/37, 40, VCRP; Washburn, *Governor*, 51–52; Webb, *1676*, 32.

[102] Hening, *Statutes*, 2:341–42. See also H. R. McIlwaine, ed., *Journals of the House of Burgesses of Virginia*, 13 vols. (Richmond, Va., 1905–15), 2:65.

Except for an act by the burgesses petitioning the crown to continue Berkeley in office, June was a disastrous month for the governor's Indian policy. The Baconian assembly ordered that several of the forts established by the act of the March assembly be abandoned and their garrisons redistributed, and that a force of a thousand men, "whereof the one eighth part to be horsemen and dragoones bee forthwith raised in order to the prosecuting this Indian warr." Furthermore, all trade with Indians was prohibited; Indians captured in war were to be made slaves; land abandoned by Indians would be sold to defray the costs of the war; and even friendly Indians were to be disarmed and permitted to hunt only with bows and arrows. And finally, after storming the capital with "att least 400 foote ye Scum of the Country, & 120 horse," Bacon extracted from Berkeley at gunpoint a commission to raise volunteers and march against the Indians.[103]

By the end of June, then, frontier interests had triumphed in Jamestown, and Bacon had governmental sanction for his crusade to exterminate Indians. The metropolitan Sir William Berkeley, who recognized "that I could doe the King little service by dying for him," had been powerless to resist. Finally exhausted and defeated by the frontier interests he had sought to contain for thirty-four years, he retired to his plantation at Green Spring.[104]

The governor could not remain inactive for long, however. Late in July he received a petition from residents in Gloucester County, complaining of Bacon's appropriation of horses and weapons "to the great disturbance of the peace of this county." Berkeley, energized by what he saw as a hint of support, granted the county the right to resist Bacon and denied that Bacon's commission had any validity.[105] The governor's attempt to raise forces in the county failed, however, when the recruits realized they were to march against Bacon instead of Indians. The troops thought the notion of attacking Bacon repellent, for he had engaged "the comon enimy, who had in a most barberous manner murthered som hundreds of our deare Brethren and Country Men." Finding no one to support him, and aware that rebel forces were on the way, Berkeley once again defiantly proclaimed Bacon a rebel and then fled across the Bay to the Eastern Shore.[106]

With Berkeley gone, Bacon consolidated his control over the colony. On July 30 he issued his "Declaration in the Name of the People" from Middle Plantation, condemning the governor for "greate unjust taxes" that bought no security, for monopolizing the Indian trade through his licensing prac-

---

[103] McIlwaine, *Journals*, 2:66; Hening, *Statutes*, 2:341–48, 350–51, 351–52; William Sherwood to Joseph Williamson, 28 June 1676, *VMHB* 1 (1893): 171.

[104] Berkeley to Sir Henry Coventry, 2 February 1677, in Washburn, "Berkeley's 'A History,'" 409.

[105] "Humble Petition of the County of Gloster," and "The Governor's Answere to yt Peticon," in "Aspinwall Papers," 181–83.

[106] "Bacon's and Ingram's Rebellion," 56; Isle of Wight County Grievances, C.O. 1/39, 223–24, *VCRP*.

tices, and for having "protected, favoured, & Imboldened the Indians agt his Maties loyall subjects, never contriveing, requireing, or appointeing any due or propr meanes of satisfaccon for their many Invasions, Robbories, & murthers comitted upon us." Bacon denounced as well the recall of Chicheley's force from its Indian targets, "when we might with ease have distroyed ym." For these crimes, Bacon condemned Berkeley and his supporters "as Traytors to ye King & Country."[107]

In a "Manifesto" issued shortly thereafter, Bacon made clear the racist, Indian-hating basis of his campaign against the governor. A "main article of our Giult," Bacon declared, "is our open & manifest Aversion of all, not onely the Foreign but the protected & Darling Indians, this wee are informed is Rebellion of a deep dye." He asserted that all Indians were

> wholly unqualifyed for the benefitt and Protection of the Law, For that the law does reciprocally protect and punish, and that all people offending must either in person or Estate make equivalent satisfaction or Restitution according to the manner and merit of ye Offences, Debts or Trespasses; Now since the Indians cannot according to the tenure and forme of any law to us known be prosecuted, Seised, or Complained against, Their Persons being difficulty distinguished or known, Their many nations languages, and their subterfuges such as makes them incapable to make us Restitution or satisfaction would it not be very giulty to say They have bin unjustly defended and protected these many years.[108]

After rallying the countryside against Berkeley and securing oaths of allegiance to support him against both the governor and the crown, Bacon sent his "navy," commanded by Giles Bland, to Accomack to apprehend the governor, while he marched off in search of Indians.

Bacon led his forces again toward the falls of the James in search of the Susquehannocks. Not finding his prey, he turned next toward "the Freshes of Yorke" to fall once more upon the Pamunkeys. Even though "it was well knowne to the whole country that the Queen of Pamunkey and her people had nere at any time betray'd or injury'd the English," to Bacon and his followers "it matter[ed] not whether they bee Friends or Foes Soe they be Indians." Bacon tracked the Pamunkeys to their refuge in the Dragon Swamp and fell upon them, killing several and taking forty-five prisoner, as well as plundering the village of the "Indian matts, Basketts, matchcotes, parcells of Wampampeag and Roanoke ... in Baggs, skins, Furrs, Pieces of Lynnen, Broad cloth, and divers sorts of English goods (wch the Queene had much value for)." The queen of Pamunkey, Cockacoeske, fled to the woods, where she struggled to survive.[109]

[107] C.O. 1/37, 128, VCRP.
[108] C.O. 1/37, 179, VCRP.
[109] "Commissioners' Narrative," 123, 127.

While Bacon was busy scattering the Pamunkeys, his naval forces had been captured on the Eastern Shore, enabling Berkeley to return to Jamestown early in September with troops recruited in Accomack County. Bacon regrouped his followers and, with their loot and Indian prisoners, marched "with a marvellous cellerity" on the capital, arriving on the evening of September 13. The governor's forces outnumbered those of Bacon by at least two to one. Nonetheless, the rebels dug trenches and settled into a siege of Jamestown. Berkeley's ships' cannon failed to dislodge them from their positions, and the rebels easily turned back a sortie by Berkeley's soldiers.[110]

Bacon and his followers subsequently began a concentrated assault upon Berkeleyan morale. First, he took "the wives and female Relations of such Gentlemen as were in the Governor's Service against him" and placed them "in the Face of his Enemy, as Bulwarkes for their Battery." Then he put the captured Pamunkeys up on the entrenchments, reminding everyone in Jamestown that they were risking their lives for an Indian lover. Combined with the effect of Baconian artillery fire, these ploys caused morale in the town to reach a critical ebb. Berkeley's forces drifted away until "only some 20 gentlemen" could be found willing to stand by him. Once again Bacon forced the governor to abandon the provincial capital in favor of refuge on the Eastern Shore. Bacon entered Jamestown unopposed on September 19. That night he set the town on fire.[111]

V

Bacon's Rebellion began in the spring of 1676, the result of a dispute between metropolitans and frontiersmen over the conduct of Indian policy. Before it reached its conclusion, it had evolved into a movement directed against the authority of the king's governor in Virginia. The supporters of William Berkeley could not appreciate the fears and pressures that drove frontiersmen to take up arms and could conclude only that the rebellion had "not proceeded from any real fault in ye Governmt but rather from the lewd dispositions of some persons, of desperate fortunes, lately sprung up amongst us."[112]

To observers in England, affairs in Virginia took on a much different hue. Reports of Indian warfare, "extreme and grievous taxes," and planters unable to grow their tobacco flooded the offices of the king's secretaries of state and other powerful men close to the crown. These officials in London found it difficult to escape the conclusion that royal authority in Virginia faced a serious challenge from both Indian warfare and internal rebellion.[113]

[110] Ibid., 132–34; "Bacon's and Ingram's Rebellion," 70.

[111] "Commissioners' Narrative," 132–35; Webb, *1676*, 63.

[112] Philip Ludwell to Mr. Secretary Coventry, 14 April 1677, C.O. 5/1355, 152–55, VCRP.

[113] Thomas Holden to James Hickes, 11 November 1676, *CSP Col, 1661–68*, 424, no. 1310 (misdated 1666); Henry Norwood to Joseph Williamson, 17 July 1676, ibid., 484, no. 1532

The crown needed an orderly Virginia. To fulfill their absolutist aspirations and rule without Parliament, the Stuart sovereigns needed the £100,000 in customs revenue collected on Virginia tobacco. By causing "the neglect of one year's planting there," Bacon's Rebellion struck at the heart of the Stuart imperial design.[114]

In September 1676 the king directed Secretary of State Sir Henry Coventry to allow "Sir William Barkley's petition to give him leave to retire for his ease and recovery of his strength," royal recognition that the governor's "age and infirmities" rendered him "totally unsuitable to the execution of so weighty a charge as the management of the King's affairs." He then appointed Herbert Jeffreys, Sir John Berry, and Francis Moryson to a royal commission to investigate the causes of the rebellion. They were accompanied by 1,100 English troops, sent to secure order in Virginia.[115]

Berry and Moryson, arriving late in January 1677, discovered that Bacon had died the preceding October, that the rebels were defeated, and that the governor had since occupied himself in the plunder of his enemies' estates. The royal commissioners requested Berkeley's assistance in provisioning the English force and emphasized as well the need to reestablish peace with the neighboring Indians. They then issued a declaration to his "Majesty's loving subjects of Virginia" inviting colonists to voice their grievances.[116]

The order Berkeley had established after Bacon's death was clearly tenuous. Having not settled a peace with the tributary Indians, he had left the frontier subject to native incursions. His pursuit of vengeance against the Baconians, furthermore, promised continued instability. On February 27 Berry and Moryson, joined now by Jeffreys and most of the royal troops, called upon the Virginia General Assembly, gathered at Green Spring, to make peace with the Indians. "The Breach and Violation" of Berkeley's peace with the neighboring Indians, they argued, had been "accompanyed with soe ill consequences, as well to yourselves in Generall by interrupting the Freedome & debarring you the Benefit of your owne Trade and Labours, As also the Greate Detrement and losse which thereby redounds to his Majestie in his Royall Revenues and Customes in England."[117]

(misdated 1667); Holden to Williamson, 3 January 1676, State Papers Office 29, Domestic, Charles II, 1660–85, Public Record Office (hereafter S.P. 29), S.P. 29/378, 19, VCRP; Holden to Williamson, 28 August 1676, S.P. 29/385, 15, VCRP; Holden to Williamson, 25 September 1676, S.P. 29/385, 164, VCRP; Morgan Lodge to Williamson, 23 June 1676, S.P. 29/382, 122, VCRP; See esp. Baconian Giles Brent to the King, 28 April 1676, C.O. 1/36, 54, and to Thomas Povey, 8 July 1676, C.O. 1/37, 84, VCRP.
   [114] Commons Debate, 12 March 1677, in Stock, *Proceedings and Debates*, 412; Webb, *Governors-General*, 342; Webb, *1676*, 189; Washburn, *Governor*, 93.
   [115] Secretary Sir Henry Coventry to the Attorney General, 16 September 1676, *CSP Col, 1674–75*, 449, no. 1032; Commission of Charles II to Herbert Jeffreys and Others, 3 October 1676, C.O. 5/1355, 83–85, VCRP; Washburn, *Governor*, 95.
   [116] C.O. 5/1371, 25ro–27ro, VCRP.
   [117] C.O. 5/1371, 78–80, VCRP; Thomas Notley to [?], 22 January 1677, C.O. 1/39, 20–23, VCRP; Commissioners to the Assembly, Governor and Council of Virginia, 27 February 1677,

The commissioners appealed then to the Indian-hating elements in the assembly, that "inconsiderate sort of men, who so rashly and causelessly Cry up a Warr with, and seeme to wish and ayme at an utter Extirpation of the Indians," asking that they

> lay their handes on their hearts, and seriously consider with themselves, Whither it be not a base Ingratitude, a namelesse Prodigie of Infatuation and mere madnesse in such men as would make a Breach with or strive to destroy and Extirpate those Amicable Indians (who are soe far from hurting them or us), That wee must justly confesse they are our best guards to secure us on the Frontiers from the Incursions and suddaine assaults on those other more Barbarous Indians on the Continent, who never can be brought to keep a peace with us, But will still continue our most Implacable & Mortall Enemies; And the more their daylie Murders and Depredations are upon us, the more earnestly it inforces this Argument for a Peace with the Frontier Indians.[118]

The Green Spring assembly spent most of its time punishing rebels and did little to bring order to the colony's relations with its Indian neighbors.[119] For the king's commissioners, who wished to return Indian affairs to their Berkeleyan *status quo ante bellum*, the assembly's activity provided additional evidence that the colonial leadership had lost sight of metropolitan concerns.

The commissioners spent much of February and March collecting grievances from the counties. The complaints they received demonstrate that the origins of the rebellion lay in an opposition to heavy taxes and a frontier rejection of metropolitan Indian policy; their responses reveal their determination to have peace and order along the Virginia frontier.

Most of the counties argued that Berkeley had responded too slowly to the Indian threat. Representatives from Charles City County complained, for example, that the governor "slighted and rejected the grate and lamentable cries of bloud, rapine, devastation, and distraction that came to his ears, from most of his Maties distressed country, and tooke noe suffitient course to prevent or revenge the same." Others ridiculed the fort plan; to petitioners from Isle of Wight County it was one more example of cowardly behavior by a government that "more and more oppress[es] with great taxes." Furthermore, the governor's ban on attacking Indians without his permission was a "lenity," wrote the men from Gloucester County, that "gave the Indians incouragement to persist, in their bloody Practice; and was Occa-

---

Bibliotheca Pepsyiana 2582, Magdalene College, Cambridge University (hereafter Pepys 2582), VCRP.

[118] Commissioners to the Assembly, Governor, and Council of Virginia, 27 February 1677, Pepys 2582, VCRP; Ibid. See also Francis Moryson to Sir William Jones, October 1676, Pepys 2582.

[119] The assembly's enactments are in Hening, *Statutes*, 2:397–406.

sion, in part of the Peoples arming themselves without command from their Superiors in a Rebellious mannir."[120]

The commissioners replied that "these Complainants never consider that the breach of the Peace, and occasion of Bloodshed has still been on the side of the English." In response to the economically troubled settlers' call for a war against all Indians, the commissioners noted the irony of this

> wild Request to have a war with all the indians of a Continent, and this by Voluntary Contributions proposed to bee carryed on; when if these Requesters were to be try'd upon any just occasion they should be the first that would cry out of the charge, and be unwilling to pay 6 pence towards it.[121]

The request of petitioners from a number of counties that "the Indians taken in the late warr be made slaves" found support in the enactments of the Green Spring assembly.[122] Most of the enslaved Indians, however, belonged to the Pamunkeys or other tributary nations. The commissioners consequently thought this proposal "inconsistent with his Maties Royal Goodnesse and honor." In response to the complaint that Berkeley and his favorites had monopolized the Indian trade, the commissioners conceded that "wee conceave this a reall greevance and a great occation of the warr wth the Indians." They did not, however, abandon the concept of a tight regulation of intercultural exchange; they proposed that the trade be open to all "at two, or more prefixt tymes in the yeare at appointed Marts, and Clerks appointed to take and give just accounts of what Stores of Powder, shot, & Armes are disposed of from tyme to tyme."[123]

The commissioners received no assistance from the aged governor, who viewed them as meddlesome intruders with no real understanding of the complexities of managing a frontier colony three thousand miles from Whitehall. Fiercely proud of his nearly four decades of service to the crown, Berkeley reacted with violent indignation to the suggestion that the Baconian rising resulted in any way from a defect in his leadership. He refused to comply with the request that he account for all confiscations and seizures of rebel property, that he immediately settle a peace with the Indians, and that he cooperate with the crown's efforts to restore metropolitan rule in Virginia. Jeffreys, Berry, and Moryson certainly understood that the Indian war resulted from frontier pressures on Indian land, but they recognized as well that the governor's credibility in the colony had been seriously damaged, that his continued prosecution of Bacon's followers did nothing to endear him to

---

[120] Gloucester County Grievances, C.O. 1/39, 243, *VCRP*; Charles City County Grievances, Pepys 2582, *VCRP*; Isle of Wight County Grievances, C.O. 1/39, 223, *VCRP*.

[121] Nancymond First Grievances, C.O. 1/39, 247, *VCRP*; Henrico County Grievances, C.O. 5/1371, 163, *VCRP*.

[122] Surrey County Grievances, C.O. 5/1371, 156, *VCRP*; Hening, *Statutes*, 2:404.

[123] Surrey County Grievances, C.O. 5/1371, 156, *VCRP*; James City County Grievances, C.O. 5/1371, 149, *VCRP*; Henrico County Grievances, C.O. 1/39, 238–39, *VCRP*.

the populace, and that the spirit of disaffection remained strong. Consequently, they believed that metropolitan order could not be restored while Berkeley held the reins of government.[124]

On April 27, 1677, Jeffreys proclaimed himself "Governor and Captain Generall of Virginia" in "all matters, causes, and things as well Civill, as Military." He pledged to remove all corrupt and incapable officials, to encourage the propagation of the gospel in Virginia, to examine the qualifications of the clergy, and to report his findings to the Bishop of London, in whose diocese Virginia lay. Jeffreys also announced that he would "with all convenient Expedition most sharply and vigorously prosecute a just warre with, and extirpation of, such of our Indian Enemies as shall not adhere to, accept, and maintaine a good Peace and League with us." For those "other amicable Indian Neighbours as shall seeke or receive His Majesties Royal Overtures of Peace and amity, I shall most readily imbrace, and earnestly endeavour to conclude and preserve such a peace with them, as may not only be a firme and lasting one, but such as shall be most agreeable to his Majties Honor and Interest."[125]

Berkeley questioned Jeffrey's right to proclaim himself governor and argued that nothing in the commissioners' instructions warranted such an action. He signed his objection "William Berkeley Governor of Virginia till his most sacred Majesty shall please to determine otherwise of me." The king, however, had already decided the governor's fate. Secretary Coventry informed the petulant Berkeley in mid-May that his decision not to return to England angered the monarch, who had "very little hopes that the people of Virginia shall be brought to a right sense of their duty to obey their Governors when the Governors themselves will not obey the King." Jeffreys was ordered to put Berkeley on the next ship home "should he still be reluctant to obey his orders to that effect." Berkeley returned to England in May 1677, a failure in the eyes of the king and died from "grief of mind" shortly after landing.[126]

Jeffreys and subsequent governors would continue to struggle with the members of Berkeley's "Green Spring faction" for control of the colony. In the critical area of Indian policy, however, Jeffreys succeeded, where Berkeley had failed, in restoring metropolitan control. At the end of May 1677 he negotiated a treaty with the Nottoways, Weyanokes, Nansemonds, and Pamunkeys "for the firm Grounding and sure Establishment of a good and just Peace with the said Indians . . . (Founded upon the strong Pillars of Recip-

[124] See Nicholas Spencer to Lord Baltimore, 24 May 1677, C.O. 1/40, 188, *VCRP*; Morton, *Colonial Virginia*, 1:280.
[125] Declaration of the Governor and Captain Generall of Virginia, 27 April 1677, C.O. 1/40, 67, *VCRP*.
[126] Berkeley to Jeffreys, 28 April 1677, C.O. 1/40, 68–69, *VCRP*; Colonial Office: Board of Trade 389, Entry Books, 1660–1803, Public Record Office (hereafter C.O. 389), C.O. 389/6, 194–98, 201, *VCRP*; Webb, *Governors-General*, 363–64.

rocal Justice) by Confirming to them their Just Rights." The Indians agreed to pay tribute to the English. In return they would "hold their Lands and have the same Confirmed to them and their Posterity, by Patent under the Seal of his Majesties Colony ... in as free and firm manner as others His Majesties Subjects." They were guaranteed possession of this land so long as they maintained "their due Obedience and Subjection to His Majesty, His Governour and Government, and Amity and Friendship towards the English."[127]

Jeffreys acknowledged in the treaty that "the mutual Discontents, Complaints, Jealousies and Fears of English and Indians" had been

> occasioned by the Violent Intrusions of divers English into their Lands, forcing the Indians by way of Revenge, to kill the Cattel and Hogs of the English, whereby Offence and Injuries being given and done on both sides, the Peace of his Majesties Colony hath been much disturbed, and the late unhappy Rebellion by this means (in a great measure) begun and fomented, which hath Involved this Countrey into so much Ruine and Misery.[128]

To prevent these "evil consequences" the parties agreed that no English would settle within three miles of any Indian town. Those encroaching would be removed by the governor. Furthermore, crimes committed against Indians by Englishmen would be treated "as if such hurt or injury had been done to any Englishmen; which is but just and reasonable, they owning themselves to be under the Allegiance of His most Sacred Majesty."[129]

The treaty secured the Indians as military allies for the Virginia English. As in earlier accords, they promised to report "any March of strange Indians near the English Quarters or Plantations" and join with English militia forces for campaigns against hostile natives. Furthermore, the parties agreed "that no Indian (of those in Amity with us) shall serve for any longer time then English of like Ages should serve by Act of Assembly, and shall not be sold as Slaves."[130]

Jeffreys, with the obvious assistance of Moryson, thus reestablished the peaceful and mutually beneficial protective relationship that Berkeley had established after the defeat of the Powhatan chiefdom in 1646. The new treaty reaffirmed the metropolitan principle that the interests of the crown would be best served when Indians were treated well, secured in the possession of their lands, and protected from an aggressively expanding English frontier population. Bacon's Rebellion had been predicated upon the frontiersmen's hatred of Indians, which was rooted in competition for control of the land. With the "Treaty of Middle Plantation," Bacon's poorly executed

---

[127] *Articles of Peace*, (London, 1677), 4–6.
[128] Ibid., 6–7.
[129] Ibid., 8.
[130] Ibid., 10, 11, 13.

program of extermination was supplanted by an attempt to reestablish metropolitan dominion.[131]

VI

While Herbert Jeffreys and the royal commissioners worked to restore order within Virginia, Edmund Andros considered the safety of his own colony. Like Berkeley, he feared a continentwide Indian uprising directed against all English settlement in America. With colonies on both sides of New York immersed in Indian war, the situation looked dangerous indeed. Andros maintained a supremely strategic vision of England's relations with the American Indian nations, however, and saw in the damage done by frontiersmen in Maryland and Virginia an opportunity to secure English metropolitan objectives along the entire Anglo-American frontier.

As early as February of 1676 Andros had tried to contact the beleaguered Susquehannocks. When a meeting with two sachems finally took place in June, he made them an offer they could hardly refuse. Expressing his sympathy for the "troubles" that had befallen the Susquehannocks, he told the sachems "that if they are afraid and not well where they are," they could resettle under the Mohawks in New York, and "bee wellcome and protected from their Ennemys." Andros assured them that at his approaching conference with the Five Nations he would "take care the Maques and Sinneke [would] bee at peace with them" and that he would also "make peace for them with Virginia and Maryland."[132]

The two sachems, having no authority to conclude a peace with the English, told Andros that they must return to consult with their people. The governor assured them that his offer was good and that upon their return "they should say whether they will come into the Government or no."[133]

The Susquehannocks, under Andros's plan, would strengthen the Mohawks, allowing them to compensate for the population losses caused by disease, warfare, and defection to French Jesuits along the St. Lawrence River. The infusion of Susquehannock manpower, moreover, would significantly strengthen Andros's primary weapon against the French and bring him the allegiance of one of the most aggressive and successful trading people in early America.[134]

Neither the western Iroquois (collectively referred to as "Seneca" by the English) nor the Marylanders, however, relished the notion of a Mohawk

[131] See the Minutes of the Board of Trade, 18 October 1677, C.O. 391/2, 132, VCRP.
[132] Minutes of a Meeting with the Susquehanna Sachems, 2 June 1676, in *The Andros Papers: Files of the Provincial Secretary of New York during the Administration of Sir Edmund Andros, 1674–1680*, 3 vols., ed. Peter R. Christoph and Florence R. Christoph (Syracuse, N.Y., 1989), 1:377–78; Webb, *1676*, 373–75; Jennings, *Invasion*, 149–51.
[133] *Andros Papers*, 1:378–79.
[134] Webb, *1676*, 374–76.

guardianship over the Susquehannocks. The western Iroquois had engaged in war with the Susquehannocks for a generation, and nothing less than the complete absorption of their enemies, they told Andros, could be accepted. For the Marylanders, who had never relinquished their claims to Delaware Bay, a Susquehannock force acting on Andros's orders would put a stop to their ambitions in the area, as well as deprive them of Susquehannock trade.[135]

The range of obstacles that Maryland and the western Iroquois could toss in front of Andros increased during the summer of 1676 when Susquehannock refugees, fleeing frontier violence and Iroquois aggression, settled along Delaware Bay and requested from Maryland "a peace and trade as formerly with the English." Maryland's lieutenant governor, Thomas Notley, viewed this "Overture of Peace" as "a blessing from God unhoped for" and quickly took steps to secure a treaty with the Susquehannocks. Notley believed that Andros had negotiated a peace earlier that summer between the Susquehannocks and the "Cinigos." "This notwithstanding," he wrote Berkeley, the Susquehannocks had approached the English in the bay, indicating that the tribe was unwilling to play the pawn in Anglo-Iroquois power politics. If Notley could negotiate a separate peace with the Susquehannocks, effectively detaching them from Andros, the Chesapeake colonies would gain a buffer nation to protect their northern and western frontiers, as well as a valuable trading partner. Notley's Piscataway and Mattawoman allies, however, wanted war with the Susquehannocks. They agreed to "march with the English to the new ffort they have built, or otherwise to pursue the Susquehanoughs, and be obedient to the English Commanders with whom they shall be Ordered to march."[136]

Andros obviously caught wind of events in Maryland but was uncertain whether Notley would attempt to make peace with the Susquehannocks or attack them and, under the pretence of "pursuing" them into Delaware, lay claim to the Duke of York's territory there by right of conquest. Aware that the Calverts had long aspired to the control of Delaware Bay and might exploit the opportunity offered by a weakened Susquehannock population, Andros sent instructions to his lieutenant there, John Collier, that "the Militia in the severall places bee well armed, duly exercised, and kept in good order and Dissipline." Collier was then to deliver two ultimatums, one to Notley and one to the Susquehannocks.[137]

First, Andros demanded to know Maryland's "Resolves about the Suscohannes" and informed Notley that unless Maryland showed cause to the contrary, he would "admitt them within this Government, rather then hazard

---

[135] Jennings, *Ambiguous Iroquois Empire*, 150; Jennings, "Glory," 37; Webb, *1676*, 375.
[136] Lt. Governor Thomas Notley to William Berkeley, 6 August 1676, AM, 15:122–23; Council Minute, 17 August 1676, AM, 15:126.
[137] Commission to John Collier, 23 September 1676, NYCD, 12:556. For Maryland's plans, see Helmer Wiltbank to Governor Andros, 26 February 1677, NYCD, 12:571.

their being obliged to refuge wth a grudge and rancour in their hearts, further off, if not wholly out of our reach." He would not allow Maryland to disrupt his diplomatic strategy. Second, recognizing fully the explosiveness of a Susquehannock presence on the Delaware, even within the duke's domain, he instructed Collier to invite the Susquehannocks to New York proper, and "to lett them know, that though they shall receive no harme from the Governmt, I will not now undertake to Secure them from others where they are; And therefore such as shall not come in, will do well to bee vigilant on their guard till they can bee well assured."[138]

Andros received unexpected help from the western Iroquois in December when they attacked an encampment of Susquehannock refugees at the head of the Chesapeake. With the Mohawks and Lenapes already joined under Andros, Notley recognized that "Sennico" control of the Susquehannocks would be fatal for Maryland, leaving its frontiers unprotected and its opportunities for trade and expansion to the west and north severely curtailed. Seeing the opportunity for another end-around, Notley informed Baltimore that he would "take all imaginable care to be at peace both with the Sennico and Susquehannoch, especially the Sennico if to be obtained, they being the greatest and most considerable Nation."[139]

Given Maryland's ambiguous policy and the western Iroquois' desire to be lords over the Susquehannocks, Andros continued his efforts to obtain the removal of the latter to New York. On March 12, 1677, the governor's council ordered that all "strange Indyans" coming to New York "may live & be incorporated under" the Indian nations, Iroquoian and Algonquian, living in the duke's domain.[140] Less than a month later, on the eve of his departure for Albany to meet with the Mohawks and delegates from Connecticut and Massachusetts, Andros reiterated his offer to the Susquehannocks. If they would resolve "to leave off ye Warre, they shall have a convenient place assigned them to their content, or may goe and live with ye Maques, or any other our Indyans, [and] if they doe not like it, then they have liberty to go back where they will." They should not, however, stay in the Delaware region, "it being not safe for them."[141]

By the end of April, Notley in Maryland recognized that the western Iroquois raids had accomplished their design and that the Susquehannocks had "Submitted themselves to and putt themselves under the protection of the Cinnigo's or some other nation of Indians resideing to the northward of this Province, & within or neer unto the Territoryes of his Royall Highnesse the Duke of Yorke." An alliance of the Susquehannocks and western Iroquois laid Maryland's frontiers open to ruin. It was necessary to settle a peace quickly, and since the "said Indians doe now reside for the most part within

---

[138] Commission to John Collier, 23 September 1676, NYCD, 12:557.
[139] Notley to Baltimore, 22 January 1677, AM, 5:153; Webb, *1676*, 377.
[140] Council Minute, 12 March 1677, NYCD, 13:503; Webb, *1676*, 377.
[141] See the Order in Council, 6 April 1677, NYCD, 12:572.

the Territory of his said Royall Highnesse, or at least cannot be treated with but by a journey to be had through his said Highnesses Territory," Notley had no choice but to ask Andros to mediate a peace. The "Preservation of His Majesties Subjects in these parts from plunder and destruction by the Northern Indians," he wrote Jeffreys later, "obliged me to send an agent to New Yorke by the means of Col. Andros to come to a treaty with the Heads of all the severall nations who were in a possibility of annoying of us."[142]

The Maryland Council selected Henry Coursey to treat with Andros on behalf of Maryland, Maryland's Indian allies, and Virginia. The council instructed Coursey to stop first at New Castle in order to inform himself "of the true State of the Susquehannoughs."[143] Coursey found that nearly all had followed, or been taken, to New York by the western Iroquois, nor were there any "Cinnigoes" in the area with whom he could treat independent of Andros.

Coursey arrived in New York on June 6, 1677, and experienced a fate similar to that of the New England delegates two months before. Andros, who controlled access to the Iroquois, revised the draft treaty proposals from Maryland, forcing Coursey to recognize that the Iroquois could be dealt with only on his terms and establishing his preeminence in the Anglo-Iroquoian alliance. Specifically, objecting to the demand that the western Iroquois deliver to the Marylanders any Susquehannocks suspected of criminal activity, Andros removed all references to the Susquehannocks from Coursey's proposals. The parties to the treaty would be the Iroquois and their dependents on one side and the southern colonies on the other, with Andros playing a critical role as mediator.[144]

At the end of July, finally satisfied with Coursey's proposals as revised, the New York governor permitted the Maryland envoy to meet with delegates from the Five Nations. Exhausted by a generation of warfare but pleased to replenish their ranks with refugees from New England, Maryland, and Virginia, each of the Five Nations accepted the proposals. In words that would give a name—the "Covenant Chain"—to the diplomatic and metropolitan product of the gathering at Fort James, the instrument that reestablished dominion along a redefined frontier in the wake of the wars of 1675 and 1676, the great Onondaga leader Daniel Garacontié accepted Coursey's peace offering and said that "wee desyre now yt all wch is past may be burried in oblivion and doe make now ane absolut Covenant of peace wch wee shall bind wth a chayn."[145]

---

[142] Council Minute, 30 April 1677, *AM*, 15:150; Notley to the Governor of Virginia, 22 June 1677, C.O. 1/40, 247, *VCRP*.

[143] Notley's Instructions to Coursey, 30 April 1677, *AM*, 15:150–53.

[144] Council Minute, 12 March 1677, *NYCD*, 13:503; Jennings, *Ambiguous Iroquois Empire*, 158–59; Webb, *1676*, 384–85.

[145] Onondaga Answer to Coursey, 21 July 1677, in *The Livingston Indian Records, 1666–1723*, ed. Lawrence H. Leder (Gettysburg, Pa., 1956), 43.

The Covenant Chain succeeded admirably. For the Iroquois it brought peace at long last to the Five Nations, replenished population lost to disease and warfare, and left them the dominant power—with English assistance—in the vast areas beyond English settlement. For Andros and the English it secured their frontiers from invaders both European and Indian and granted New York a position of unquestioned preeminence in intercultural exchange throughout English America. By drawing the winners and losers of the intercultural warfare of 1675 and 1676 into one powerful and expansive organization, Andros and his Iroquois allies resolved at once the Indian conflicts that had destabilized the first Anglo-American frontiers, from the Penobscot to the Roanoke, and built a foundation for future efforts to attain the metropolitan imperatives of dominion and civility.[146]

[146] Webb, *1676*, 359; Jennings, "Glory," 43–44.

Conclusion

Edmund Andros asserted English dominion in North America. In so doing, he redefined the ideal envisioned and expressed a century before by Thomas Hariot and Richard Hakluyt and adapted it to the new realities of the Anglo-American frontier.

The metropolitan vision of the *ideal* Indian put forward by the Elizabethan promoters of English expansion held little attraction for the *actual* Indian. Native Americans could have followed the path of civility the metropolitan English had charted for them, but doing so would have meant nothing less than the forfeiture of their culture and religion. Hariot and Hakluyt never appreciated this. They viewed Indians within the framework of an emerging metropolitan paradigm, one that comprehended trade relations with the natives in terms of securing the economic, social, and political health of the realm; conversion of the natives in terms of both religious conflict between Catholic and Protestant powers and an understanding of England's history; and alliance with the natives in terms of imperial competition for control of North America.

In this context, Hariot and Hakluyt celebrated the Indian's potential but not Indians themselves. For them, Indians were constantly in a state of becoming. They believed that Indians would readily abandon their cultural and religious practices and beliefs when offered the English example. Brazenly Anglo-centric, Hariot and Hakluyt nonetheless thought of Indians as prospective and vital members of an English society abroad. They emphasized always the responsibility of the English, through education and catechesis, to bring the natives slowly and gently to an embrace of the reformed religion and English standards of civility.

Success, for them, depended upon the ability of English metropolitans to control the frontier and its inhabitants, European and Native American.

The Anglo-American Empire, ca. 1677. Reprinted from Jeannette Dora Black, ed., *The Blathwayt Atlas* (1970). Courtesy John Carter Brown Library at Brown University.

Metropolitans hoped to obtain an orderly frontier by regulating and controlling the occasions when Indians and Europeans came into contact. They hoped to restrain the frontier population from encroaching upon Indian lands, from provoking a frontier crisis that could threaten the security of their colonies and the king's dominions. Hariot, Hakluyt, and Sir Walter Ralegh at Roanoke; Sir Francis Wyatt and George Thorpe at Jamestown; the metropolitan promoters of settlement in New England—all recognized that they could not obtain their objectives without an orderly frontier.

English metropolitans failed in this, the challenge of the first Anglo-American frontiers. They failed both because of native resistance and because the attitudes of most colonists toward the Indians had been forged along what Winthrop Jordan has called "the bloody cutting edge of the English thrust into the Indians' lands."[1] Indians pursued their own interests independent of the English, and when they cooperated they did so as much as possible upon

---

[1] Winthrop D. Jordan, *White over Black: American Attitudes toward the Negro, 1550–1812*, (Chapel Hill, N.C., 1968), 89.

their own terms. Meanwhile, metropolitans found their policies challenged by a frontier population that competed regularly with Indians for control of frontier resources.

These colonists had little patience for the metropolitan program that combined frontier administration with missionary zeal. Whereas the metropolitans advocated secure and regular patterns of settlement, control, and peaceful relations with the Indians, the resistance of a frontier population that extracted its livelihood from frontier soil produced an endemic instability. That this dynamic undermined metropolitan policies in the New World is clear in Morgan Godwyn's lament to Governor Berkeley that the conversion of the Indians in Virginia was "lookt upon, by our new race of Christians, as so idle and Ridiculous, so utterly needless and unnecessary, that no man can forfeit his Judgement more, than by any proposal looking or tending that way."[2] The more philanthropic elements in the metropolitan world view thus were subordinated as governors and imperial officials struggled to maintain order along the frontier.

In this respect, the English experience in America bore much resemblance to that of their imperial rivals. The Spanish, the Dutch, and the French all initially viewed peaceful Indian relations as central to the success of their colonies. For a time, and in places, Europeans shared a middle ground with the natives among whom they had settled. Dutch traders in the vicinity of Fort Orange and French traders in the Great Lakes Region are by no means the only examples of relatively peaceful European-Indian interaction. Still, this middle ground, wherever it developed and especially in the English colonies, always remained tenuous. It would not endure the harsh environmental and cultural conflict that occurred when settlers began to compete with native communities for control of the land and its resources.

By the closing decades of the seventeenth century, frontier interests and attitudes toward Indians had prevailed in English America, and the coastal Algonquians retreated. The native population on Martha's Vineyard and Nantucket, which numbered near three thousand on each island at midcentury, had been reduced by disease to one-third its original strength. In 1674 Daniel Gookin reported that of the Massachusetts Indians "there are not of this people left at this day above three hundred men, besides women and children." The "Pawtuckett" were "almost totally destroyed . . . so that at this day they are not above two hundred and fifty men." During King Philip's War, which soon followed—a war that originated in frontier pressure on native land—provincial forces slaughtered large numbers of Indians, sold others into West Indian slavery, and left many with no choice but to resettle in New York, further reducing New England's Algonquian population.[3]

---

[2] Morgan Godwyn, *The Negro's and Indian's Advocate* (London, 1680), 172.
[3] Sherburne F. Cook, "The Significance of Disease in the Extinction of the New England Indians," *Human Biology* 45 (1973): 492–93; Daniel Gookin, *Historical Collections of the Indians of New England* (1674), rpt. (New York, 1972), 89.

Farther south, Robert Beverley recorded an equally devastating decline in the native population of the Tsenacommacah. In 1705 Beverley wrote that "the Indians of Virginia are almost wasted." Together "they can't raise five hundred fighting men. They live poorly, and much in fear of the Neighbouring Indians." On the Eastern Shore the Occahannocks, Beverley reported, had only "a small number yet living," and there remained at the village of Oanancocke "but four or five families." On the mainland the Weyanokes were "almost wasted, and now gone to live among other Indians." The Appomattocks had not "above seven Families," while the Rappahannocks were "reduc'd to a few Families, and live scatter'd upon the English seats." Surviving Algonquians, in Virginia as in New England, lost their political autonomy, faced intensified threats to their cultural integrity, and suffered disruptions in their traditional subsistence routine as English settlers pushed into the interior.[4]

In one sense, Edmund Andros succeeded in resolving the conflict between metropolitans and frontiersmen by eliminating the source of contention between them. The Algonquian losers of King Philip's War—those not enslaved or dispossessed or forgotten and marginalized on tiny reserves in New England—settled in New York under the protection of the Duke of York and his Mohawk allies. The Susquehannocks, with the urging of Andros and the Senecas, accepted the guardianship of the western Iroquois nations. By placing Indians out of the reach of aggressive and land-hungry English settlers, Andros secured dominion along the frontier. But by implicitly accepting the premise that Englishmen and Indians could not live in peace together, he also effectively abandoned for a time the ideal that had formed so fundamental a part of the English New World vision.

In another sense, however, Andros redefined the Anglo-American frontier and, through cooperation with an Indian power, provided a foundation for the renewal of metropolitan efforts in North America. Andros recognized that the crown's interests in the colonies—religious, economic, and imperial—depended upon peaceful relations with the Indians but that these could never be attained "so long as each petty colony hath or assumes absolute power of Peace and Warr, which cannot be managed by such popular Gov-

---

[4] Robert Beverley, *The History and Present State of Virginia*, ed. Louis B. Wright (Chapel Hill, N.C., 1947), 232–33; James H. Merrell, " 'The Customes of Our Countrey': Indians and Colonists in Early America," in *Strangers within the Realm: The Cultural Margins of the First British Empire*, ed. Bernard Bailyn and Philip D. Morgan (Chapel Hill, N.C., 1991), 120. Much recent research has explored the strategies Indians used to preserve a degree of cultural autonomy once white settlements surrounded their communities. See Daniel Mandell, " 'To Live More like My Christian English Neighbors': Natick Indians in the Eighteenth Century," *WMQ*, 3d ser., 48 (1991): 552–79; Paul R. Robinson and Glenn W. La Fantasie, "Scattered to the Winds of Heaven: Narragansett Indians, 1676–1880," *Rhode Island History* 37 (1978): 66–83; Frank W. Porter III, "Behind the Frontier: Indian Survivals in Maryland," *Maryland Historical Magazine* 75 (1980): 42–54; Patrick Frazier, *The Mohicans of Stockbridge* (Lincoln, Neb., 1992); James H. Merrell, *The Indians' New World: Catawbas and Their Neighbors from European Contact through the Era of Removal* (Chapel Hill, N.C., 1989), 167–284.

ernments as was evident by the late Indian wars in New England."[5] Warfare in the Chesapeake and New England had destroyed the coastal Algonquians as an effective barrier to English settlement. Colonists in New England, in Virginia, and at points between no longer confronted the scattered pattern of Algonquian village communities, already reduced by disease, that had punctuated the haphazard line of English settlements in America. They faced now a new frontier defined and occupied by the Iroquois, a people with a more pronounced militant tradition than the coastal Algonquians, more cultural coherence, and a long history of confederation and cooperation, who could pose a formidable obstacle to frontier expansion.[6]

Andros and the Iroquois formalized this frontier with the Covenant Chain, a series of treaties based upon the melding of Iroquoian condolence council forms with the aims of English diplomacy. The resulting agreements benefited both the Iroquois and New York, and Andros could not have attained his goals without Indian assistance. The Covenant Chain secured the eastern and southern borders of Iroquoia and gave the Five Nations access to thousands of potential allies settled under their protection in the duke's domain, as well as support from the English. Iroquois warriors and hunters now could look westward for fresh sources of fur and were guaranteed safe access to the Albany market, where furs fetched a higher price than in New France. Andros and his lieutenants regulated this market tightly, and the abuses suffered by Indians in previous decades declined dramatically in number.[7]

With Iroquois assistance, Andros demarcated a frontier line between the English and Indians in North America. He established the duke's province of New York as the locus of metropolitan control over Indian affairs, and the Iroquois, in turn, recognized Albany as the only legitimate site for councils with signatories of the Covenant Chain. English influence among the Five Nations increased at the expense of the French. Under the aegis of the Society for the Propagation of the Gospel in Foreign Parts, a renewal of missionary activity, centered at Fort Hunter, occurred during the tenure of Andros's successors. The Anglo-Iroquoian alliance proved an enduring one, and the "Faithful Mohawk," whose allegiance was considered "absolutely necessary for the security of the Province of New York and the rest of your Majesty's Dominions in that part of America," in many ways remained more loyal to the interests of the crown than did the English colonists. The Covenant Chain secured nearly a century of peace for New York and the older areas of settlement and laid the basis for renewed efforts to attain the metropolitan imperatives of dominion and civility.[8]

[5] Edmund Andros to William Blathwayt, 16 September 1678, *NYCD*, 3:271.
[6] Stephen Saunders Webb, *1676: The End of American Independence* (New York, 1984), 410–12.
[7] Daniel K. Richter, *The Ordeal of the Longhouse: The Peoples of the Iroquois League in the Era of European Colonization* (Chapel Hill, N.C., 1992), 136–37; Webb, *1676*, 359.
[8] John Wolfe Lydekker, *The Faithful Mohawks* (Port Washington, N.Y., 1968), 4; Council of Trade and Plantations to the Queen, 2 June 1709, *CSP Col, 1708–9*, 328, no. 524.

Indeed, the aspirations of Thomas Hariot and Richard Hakluyt would remain a central part of metropolitan discourse through the removal period in
the nineteenth century. The desire to incorporate Indians into an Anglo-
American, Christian, New World empire would endure, as is evident in the
course Anglo-Indian relations took in the Restoration proprietary colonies
of Carolina and Pennsylvania. The proprietors of Carolina, like promoters
of settlement elsewhere, hoped to derive a profit from their colony, plant a
defensible settlement that would secure the southern frontier of English
America and Christianize and civilize the Indians. Under the Fundamental
Constitutions, drafted by Anthony Ashley Cooper and John Locke and ap-
proved in 1670, the proprietors required that their colonists treat Indians
justly.[9]

Few settlers in Carolina took the directives seriously, however. Owing to
the proprietors' lack of initiative, and their own considerable opportunism,
the "Goose Creek Men"—Barbadian immigrants who had settled along the
so-named tributary of the Cooper River—seized control of affairs in the
colony, ignored the proprietary monopoly on Indian trade, and began enslaving area natives. In response, the proprietors in 1680 appointed a commissioner "to take care that no Indians that are friendly and that live within
200 miles of the territory be made slaves or sent out of the country without
special orders." The commissioners' purpose was "to redress injuries done
to the Indians, not to involve the Proprietors in war."[10]

The proprietors prohibited any person from settling on land "within two
miles, on the same side of a river, of an Indian settlement." Furthermore,
they required that settlers who took up "lands near the Indian settlements
must help them to fence their corn that no damage be done by the hogs and
cattle of the English." Regarding the enslavement of Indians, they declared
simply that "we cannot answer it to God, the King, our inhabitants, nor our
own consciences, that such things should continue."[11]

Yet the proprietors never succeeded in curtailing the activities of frontier
settlers which jeopardized the colony's peace. In 1707 they intensified their
efforts to achieve a meaningful control, and the provincial legislature appointed a commission to oversee Anglo-Indian relations. The nine commissioners granted the licenses now necessary to participate in Indian trade;
they also designated an agent who would reside for most of the year among
the Indians, resolve disputes between Indians and traders, and establish a
sound foundation for peaceful intercultural exchange.[12]

[9] J. Leitch Wright, *The Only Land They Knew: The Tragic Story of the American Indians of the Old South* (New York, 1981), 116.

[10] *CSP Col, 1677–80*, 526, no. 1357.

[11] Proprietors of Carolina to Governor, 5 June 1682, *CSP Col, 1681–85*, 242, no. 540; Proprietors of Carolina to Governor, 30 September 1685, *CSP Col, 1681–85*, 510, no. 1284.

[12] Converse D. Clowse, *Economic Beginnings in Colonial South Carolina, 1670–1730* (Co-
lumbia, S.C., 1971), 142–43; Merrell, *Indians' New World*, 66.

Some of these agents, such as Thomas Nairne, energetically pursued their assignment, recognizing that peace with Indians was essential so that "the English American Empire may not be unreasonably crampt up." Disaffected Indians, Nairne feared, could easily enter the orbit of the Spanish at St. Augustine or the French at Mobile, thus threatening the security of Carolina. Nairne was no Indian lover. Though he steadfastly believed that the SPG should devote its energies to sending missionaries among Carolina Indians, he also believed that those uninterested in listening to God's word could be enslaved. This, he felt, would be better than allowing them to learn Christianity from Spanish or French Catholics. Still, Nairne was firmly convinced that the nature of Anglo-Indian relations in the Carolina interior should be regulated tightly in the name of securing both dominion and civility.[13]

Few agents were as conscientious as Nairne, however, and in the second decade of the eighteenth century effective metropolitan regulation of the Carolina frontier collapsed. The resulting conflicts, the Tuscarora War beginning in 1711 and the Yamasee War in 1715, threatened the very existence of the colony as angry Indians avenged insults—including the confiscation of land and the enslavement of native women and children—suffered at the hands of unscrupulous backcountry traders. Warriors killed nearly four hundred colonists during the Yamasee War. With reports arriving in London of settlers "reduced to such a dismall extremity that nothing but yr. Majesties royall and most gracious protection (under God) can preserve us from ruin," the Council of Trade and Plantations anxiously desired "to know what there Lordships have done or intend to do towards the security of that Province."[14]

The Yamasee War discredited the proprietors in the eyes of the colonists and, worse, the crown. The commission granted in 1720 to South Carolina's first royal governor, Sir Francis Nicholson, demonstrates that the Council of Trade and Plantations recognized fully the importance of the colony. Because of the war, Nicholson's commission read, the Carolinas had

fall'n into such disorder and confusion, yt the publick peace and administration of justice . . . is broken and violated, and the said province become wholly void of defence against any foreign enemy, or even against the incursions of the barbarous Indians, whereby the Southern frontier to our Plantations on the Continent of America, and one of the most fruitfull of all our Colonies, is in great danger of being depopulated, and the trade and advantages thereof forever lost from the Crown of Great Britain. [15]

[13] Thomas Nairne to [Earl of Sunderland?], 10 July 1610, *CSP Col, 1710–11*, 241, no. 632.
[14] Address of Representatives and Inhabitants of South Carolina to King, 13 May 1718, *CSP Col, 1717–18*, 252–53, no. 536; *CSP Col, 1717–18*, 3 April 1718, 230, no. 486.
[15] Council of Trade and Plantation to the Lords Justices, 16 August 1720, *CSP Col, 1719–20*, 100–101, no. 192.

As elsewhere, the failure to secure metropolitan objectives invited royal intervention in American affairs.

While the proprietors of Carolina were struggling to hang on to their colonial outpost, William Penn had commenced his "Holy Experiment" along the banks of the Delaware and Schuylkill Rivers. When Charles II gave Penn control over a considerable tract of land, both the crown and the proprietor intended the colony to serve metropolitan ends. Charles granted the charter "out of a commendable desire to enlarge our English Empire, and promote such usefull commodities as may bee of benefit to us and our Dominions, as alsoe to reduce the Savage Natives by gentle and just manners to the love of civill Societie and Christian Religion."[16]

As for Penn, though he more clearly articulated a desire to secure justice and respectful treatment for Indians than any other metropolitan promoter of settlement in seventeenth-century America, the policies he pursued certainly were not without precedent. In the "Conditions or Concessions" granted to the first group of settlers in July 1681, Penn ordered "that noe man shall by any wayes or meanes in word or deed, affront or wrong any Indian, but he shall Incurr the Same Pennalty of the law as if he had Committed it against his Fellow Planter."[17] He worked to monitor the fur trade so "that the Natives may not be abused nor provoked," and he won the trust of neighboring Indians. "I would have you well to observe," he wrote to native leaders in October of 1681,

> that I am very sensible of the unkindness and Injustice that hath been too much exersised towards you by the People of thes parts off the world, who have sought themselves, and to make great Advantages by you, rather then be examples of Justice and Goodness unto you, which I hear, hath been a matter of trouble to you, and caused Great Grudgeings and Animosities, sometimes to the shedding of blood, which hath made the great God angry. But I am not such a man.[18]

Peaceful relations with neighboring Indians, Penn knew, were essential for his colony's success and consistent with his Quaker beliefs. He believed that Indians and whites could live together in peace. But although Penn's diplomacy provided a solid foundation for his colony, he soon lost control of affairs in Pennsylvania to settlers who simply did not share his concerns. James Logan, the proprietor's secretary and himself a man committed to aggressively exploiting the Anglo-American frontier, wrote that neighboring

---

[16] Pennsylvania Charter, in *Minutes of the Provincial Council of Pennsylvania* (Philadelphia, 1852), 1:17; Stephen Saunders Webb, "The Peaceable Kingdom: Quaker Pennsylvania in the Stuart Empire," in *The World of William Penn*, ed. Richard S. Dunn and Mary Maples Dunn (Philadelphia, 1986), 173–94.

[17] "Conditions or Concessions to First Planters," in *The Papers of William Penn*, ed. Richard S. Dunn and Mary Maples Dunn (Philadelphia, 1982), 2:100.

[18] Penn to the Kings of the Indians, 18 October 1681, in Dunn and Dunn, *Papers of William Penn*, 2:128.

Delawares were "much abused by having their corn (which they never use to fence) destroy'd by the Cattle of these new-comers whom they know not."[19] A familiar refrain, this, as Englishmen and Indians competed for control of frontier resources they employed in different and incompatible ways.

Settlers on the Pennsylvania frontier demonstrated as great a hunger for land as colonists elsewhere, and by the end of the seventeenth century the Lenapes of Pennsylvania found themselves pressed by the Iroquois to the north, Conoys and Susquehannocks to the west, and very rapidly growing English settlements. As early as the 1720s, Indian and European interests began to clash sharply. The result, in Pennsylvania as elsewhere, was conflict, violence, and increasingly harsh attitudes toward natives. The Lenapes were driven westward. Indians in the colony learned quickly to distinguish between William Penn himself and the men and women who settled along the frontiers of his colony, a distinction that explains at least in part the periodic fury unleashed by natives upon the Pennsylvania frontier.[20]

The nature of Anglo-Indian relations in Carolina and Pennsylvania was in many ways consistent with the pattern established in New England and the Chesapeake. Promoters of settlement in English America continued to pursue peaceful relations with the Indians among whom they settled. They continued to believe that peace would enable colonies to prosper and to remain secure from both European and Native American enemies, thus providing a base for the expansion of Christianity and civility.

This ideal, indeed, informed the thought of Cadwallader Colden, who argued in his 1727 history of the Iroquois that "if care were taken to plant in them and cultivate that general Benevolence to Mankind, which is the true Principle of Vertue, it would effectually eradicate those horrid Vices occasioned by their Unbound Revenge." Then, Colden continued, "the Five Nations would no longer deserve the Name of Barbarians, but would become a people whose Friendship might add Honour to the British Nation, tho' they be now too generally despised." To those who thought of the Iroquois as hopelessly primitive, Colden responded that "the present state of the Indian Nations exactly shows the most Ancient and Original Condition of almost every Nation; so I believe, here we may with more certainty see the Original Form of all Government, than in the most curious Speculations of the Learned." Like all the world's societies, Colden implied, the Iroquois would progress.[21]

---

[19] Logan quoted in Francis Jennings, "Brother Miquon: Good Lord!" in Dunn and Dunn, *World of William Penn*, 208–9. See also Thomas J. Sugrue, "The Peopling and Depeopling of Early Pennsylvania: Indians and Colonists, 1680–1720," *Pennsylvania Magazine of History and Biography* 116 (1992): 3–31.

[20] See Eric Hinderaker, *Elusive Empires: Constructing Colonialism in the Ohio Valley, 1673–1800* (Cambridge, England, 1997), 126–28, 157–61; Jane T. Merritt, "Kinship, Community, and Practicing Culture: Indians and the Colonial Encounter in Pennsylvania, 1700–1763" (Ph.D. diss., University of Washington, 1995), 161, 178.

[21] Cadwallader Colden, *The History of the Five Indian Nations Depending on the Province of New York* (New York, 1727), v, xvii.

The metropolitan vision was apparent in 1753 as well when the New England minister Samuel Hopkins called upon his audience to treat the Indians "who live among us, and upon our borders, in a just, kind and charitable Manner" in order "to attach them to us, and the British Interest." At the same time Hopkins emphasized the importance of sending missionaries whose efforts might, "by the Blessing of God, serve to remove their Barbarity, correct their Manners, reform their Lives, promote in them virtuous Sentiments, and by Degrees form them to true Religion."[22] The vision was also apparent in Parliament's 1763 plan to demarcate a line separating Indians and whites so that natives "should not be molested or disturbed in the possession of . . . their hunting grounds," and again in William Johnson's ultimately unsuccessful effort to protect Indian lands in the Treaty of Fort Stanwix in 1768.[23] It continued to be apparent in Thomas Jefferson's earnest desire to transform the Indian into something very much approaching the American yeoman ideal, and in the arguments of many who opposed Andrew Jackson's policy of Indian removal early in the 1830s.[24]

The ongoing presence of metropolitan programs for incorporating the Indians into a Christian and Anglo-American empire, however, was matched by the persistence of harsh frontier assessments of native culture. Indians and whites may have been able to get along at times and in places, but English settlers who moved into a region invariably employed the land in ways that bred conflict with natives. Clearing the land, for instance, altered the hunting potential of a given area. Roaming English livestock foraged in unfenced Indian cornfields. As Indians and English settlers thus sought to use identical environmental resources in ways that were seldom compatible, the result was conflict. In Virginia and in New England, frontier attitudes—"Master Stockam's opinion"—prevailed.

As the dynamic of frontier and metropolitan conflict played itself out on subsequent American frontiers, metropolitan planners came to regard the removal of the Indians out of the path of white settlement as the only hope for obtaining dominion and civility. The Covenant Chain served reasonably well as George Washington's "Chinese Wall," but only for a time; so too the frontier line proclaimed by Parliament in 1763. In the face of mounting Indian resistance and increasing frontier pressure on Indian lands, metropolitans reluctantly recognized that no order could exist along the frontier while Indians and Anglo-American settlers remained in close contact.[25]

---

[22] Samuel Hopkins, *An Address to the People of New England Representing the Very Great Importance of Attaching the Indians to Their Interest* (Philadelphia, 1757), 3, 18–19.

[23] Peter C. Mancall, *Valley of Opportunity: Economic Culture along the Upper Susquehanna, 1700–1800*, (Ithaca, N.Y., 1991), 91.

[24] On Indian removal, see Jeremiah Evarts, ed., *Speeches on the Passage of the Bill for the Removal of the Indians Delivered in the Congress of the United States* (Boston, 1830); and Francis Paul Prucha, ed., *Cherokee Removal: The William Penn Essays and Other Writings by Jeremiah Evarts* (Knoxville, Tenn., 1981).

[25] See Francis Paul Prucha, *American Indian Policy in the Formative Years: The Indian Trade and Intercourse Acts, 1780–1834* (Cambridge, Mass., 1962).

Indian removal in this sense was the logical, if tragic, outcome of the process of Indian-white relations as they developed in North America. Frontier settlers wanted the land and needed to eliminate the Indian presence if they were to obtain it. Metropolitans, on the other hand, wanted peaceful relations with the Indians which would allow them to frame strategic alliances, to profit by establishing elaborate trade networks and avoiding the expense of costly wars, and to bring Christianity and civility to the Indians. To many in the 1830s the Cherokees and the rest of the so-called "Five Civilized Tribes" represented the fulfillment of the metropolitan plan, native peoples who had adopted the mores and values and material culture of Anglo-American society. In this view the Cherokees were white in every sense of the word save for the color of their skin: they farmed, many spoke English, they celebrated American political culture, and they practiced Christianity. Americans holding this opinion vehemently opposed Jackson's, and the frontiersmen's, policy of coerced removal in 1830. Most, however, accepted removal as the only alternative to continued disorder along the frontier, as well as a means to buy the Indians time and protect them until benevolent metropolitan plans could come to fruition.

Index

Abenakis: alcohol and, 166–167; alliance with New England Algonquians, 112; attacked by Mohawks, 169–170; and English settlements, 167–168; and French, 132; and fur trade, 90, 98; and King Philip's War, 166–170; lynching of, 171–172; and Maine settlers, 167

Accomack Indians, 184, 190

Agriculture (European): contrastive subsistence strategies, 4–5; effect on Indian subsistence, 4

Agriculture (Native American): Carolina Algonquians and, 33; in New England, 95; pressures on, at Roanoke, 36, 39; threatened by tobacco culture, 67. *See also* Indians: subsistence systems

Albany (NY), Andros at, 161. *See also* Fort Orange

Alcohol: and Abenakis, 166–167; toll on Eastern Shore Indians, 190; trade in, limited, 122–123

Alexander, William, 84

Algonquins (Canada), 145, 147

Allerton, Isaac, treachery of, 199

Amadas, Philip, voyages to Roanoke, 26–27

Ancient Britons, Indians compared to, 12, 53–54

Andros, Sir Edmund: arms Mohawks, 163; and Anglo-American frontier, 217, 220–221; and Covenant Chain, 215–216; distrusts Maryland, 213–214; enlists Mohawks, against Abenakis, 169; and Iroquois, 161–162, 164–166; offers refuge to New England Algonquians, 165; and Province of Maine, 168–170; pursues orderly frontier, 160–166, 168–170, 215–216; and Rhode Island, 165; and Susquehannocks, 212–216

Androscoggin Indians, 166

Anglo-Dutch Warfare: and New England Indians, 132–133; and tobacco trade, 193

Appomattock Indians, 55, 220

Aquascogoc, 31, 35

Argall, Samuel: captures Pocahontas, 64; governs Virginia, 67–68

Arms and Ammunition: Andros supplies Mohawks with, 163; illegal trade in, with Indians, 151; Ma-Re Mount settlers and, 93–94; Powhatans acquire, 59, 68; settlers required to stockpile, in early New England, 90; trade in, regulated, 90–91, 122, 150, 156, 189

Arrohatocs, 55

Atherton, Humphrey: invalid title of, 136; and Narragansett lands, 131, 134; purchase of, ruled null and void, 150

Awashunks, 155

Bacon, Elizabeth, and frontier life, 174–176

Bacon, Nathaniel: attacks friendly Indians, 203, 205; background, 201; burns Jamestown, 206; death of, 207; mentioned, 174; obtains commission, 204; proclaimed rebel, 202; supporters of, control Assembly, 203–204

Collier, John, 213–214
Colonies, importance of, to crown, 2
Commissioners, Royal, of 1664: conquer New Netherland, 135; investigate New England colonies, 135–137
Commissioners, Royal, in Virginia: collect county grievances, 208–209; pursue orderly frontier, 207–212
Company of One Hundred Associates, 145–148
Connecticut (Colony): calls for vengeance, refused, 165–166; claims to land in, 102; controls on frontier settlers, 156; cooperation with Royal Commissioners, 135; distrust of Andros, 163; Dutch claims to, 98–99; fear of Narragansett conspiracy, 118; Fort Saybrook established, 102–103; and Pequot War, 109–116; settlement of, 100–103, 107; settlers threaten Pequots, 101–103; support for Uncas, 116–117; treaty of 1638, 116
Conoy Indians, 225
Conquistadors, 14–15
Cooper, Anthony Ashley, 222
Council for Foreign Plantations, 135
Council of Trade and Plantations, 223–224
Coursey, Henry, 215
Covenant Chain, 170, 215–216, 221
Coventry, Sir Henry, 207
Cradock, Matthew, 90
Crashaw, William, 52
Curio-collecting, 20
Curles, Bacon's plantation at, 174
Cushman, Robert, 83, 88, 92

Dale, Sir Thomas, 60; campaign against Powhatans, 63–65; departs Jamestown, 67
Dartmouth, 156
Dasemunkepeuc, 31, 44
Davies, Sir John, 30–31
de Bry, Theodor, 9–10
Dennis, Matthew, 3
De Rasieres, Isaac, 98
Discourse on Western Planting, 27
Disease: among Carolina Algonquians, 42; attachment to traditional religions weakened by, 9; hepatitus epidemic, in New England, 84–85, 94; Indian beliefs about, 9–10; and Indian conversion, 125–126; Indians killed by, at Roanoke, 9; smallpox in New England, 85, 99–100; in Spanish colonies, 15

Doeg Indians: attack on Mathew's farm, 198; driven into Potomac Valley, 195; war declared upon, 190
Dowd, Gregory Evans, 33
Downing, Emmanuel, 88
Drake, Sir Francis, 16
Dudley, Thomas, 103
Dutch, colonies in America, 5; compared to English, 219; and Connecticut River Valley, 98–99; English conquest of, 135–136; fur trade in, 138–139; goals of, 137; in Hudson Valley, 132; Indian friendship pursued, 138, 141; patroonship system, 138; and wampum, 96

Eastern Shore (Virginia): frontier population of, 185–186; settlement of, 184
Easton, John, 154–155
Edward VI, 13
Eliot, John: and frontier population, 126; "Praying Towns" and, 124–127; threatened by mob, 159
Elizabeth I, 12, 27
Encomenderos, 14–16
Endicott, John: attacks Block Island and Pequot Harbor, 105–106; and Christianity, 84; Gardener and, 106; and Ma-Re Mount, 94; and martial discipline, 90
English colonization, origins, 12–14
Ensenore, 38, 43–44
Esopus, Dutch and Indian conflict at, 142–144
Ethnocentrism, 33
Exeter (New Hampshire), attacked by Abenakis, 167

Felipe II (Spain), 16, 48
Ferrar, John, and Henrico College, 69
Ferrar, Nicholas, and Henrico College, 69–70
Fishing, 12
Five Nations. *See* Iroquois
Fort Hunter, 221
Fort Orange: Dutch settlement at, 131; founded, 137; Stuyvesant's plans for, 141–142
Fowke, Gerard, 186–187
France, Colonies in America: compared to English, 5, 219; diplomacy with Abenakis, 132; early efforts, 144; fur trade in, 144–150, 221; middle ground in, 149; warfare with Indians, 146–150

191–192; Indian population decline in, 220; laws of, codified, 188–189; population growth in, 187; socio-economic crisis in, 192–194

Virginia Company of London: connections to Ralegh's circle, 50; dissolved, 50; Henrico College and, 70; martial law imposed by, 60; objectives, 50–54; pursues orderly frontier, 61; racism and, 79; response to massacre, 76–77; Sandys' reforms, 68–80; settlement planted at Jamestown, 54–55

Waban, 125
Wahanganoche, 187
Wahginnacut, 97
Waiandance, 117–118
Waldorne, Richard, 168
Wampanoag Indians: ally with Narragansetts, 158; disease and, 84; pledge loyalty to English, 151; Rehoboth settlers and, 127–128. *See also* King Philip's War; Philip
Wampum: manufacture of, 96; metropolitan concern, 103; Narragansetts and, 96; and native culture change, 95; New England fur trade and, 98; retired as legal tender, 152; value of, 98
Wanchese: abandons English, 38–39; travels to England, 26–27
Washington, George, 1, 226
Washington, John, treachery of, 199, 200
Waterhouse, Edward, 79
Weapemeocs, 32, 40
Werowocomoco, 57–58
Wessagusset, 91–92
West, John, 179
West India Company (Dutch): founded, 137; need for increased population in colonies, 138; treatment of Indians, 140–141. *See also* Dutch, colonies in America
West, Thomas (Lord De La Warr), 60; imposes martial law, 61; leaves Virginia, 63
Western Niantic Indians, and Saybrook, 107
Westmoreland County (Virginia), 186
Weston, Thomas, 91–92
Wethersfield, 107
Weyanoke Indians, 180, 220
Whitaker, Alexander, 66–67
White, Bruce, 37
White, John: at Durham House, 20; and Indian potential, 12; interest in Indians, 8;

paintings of, 23; at Pomeiooc and Secotan, 35
White, John (of Dorchester), 83–84, 86, 88–89
White, Richard, 3–4, 149
White, Richard (of Virginia), farm attacked, 189
Wienshauks, Pequot settlement at, 110
Williams, Roger: and Connecticut, 115; conversion of the Indians and, 86–87; fears war with Narragansetts, 133–134; and King Philip's War, 156; and Narragansett-Mohegan warfare, 130; and Peach murder, 81–82; and Pequot War, 111
Wiltwyck, 143
Windsor, (Connecticut), 107
Wingina: abandons Roanoke, 43–44; changes name, 39; conspiracy of, alleged, 39–46; death of, 45; disillusionment with English, 38–39; joins English in prayer, 38; mentioned, 26, 35; rallies support among Roanokes, 43; Ralph Lane and, 42; territory of, 31; war with neighbors, 32
Winslow, Edward: Christianity and, 83; colonists, 88; fur trade and, 98; Wessagusset and, 92
Winslow, Josiah, 158
Winthrop, John: aboriginal title to land, 85–86; Brewster message and, 103; Christianity and, 84; Connecticut settlers and, 100–101; defends Uncas, 129; disease among Indians, 85; Endicott mission and, 105; Miantonimo and, 119; motives for migration, 83; murder of John Stone and, 99–100; Pequots and, 104; river Indians and, 97
Winthrop, John Jr.: mentioned, 134; King Philip's war and, 156; Pequots and, 103–104; Saybrook and, 102–103
Wituwamut, killed, 92
Wood, William, 96
Woodcocke, John, 127
Wyatt, Sir Francis: attacks on Powhatans, 77–78, 176; governs Virginia, 73; mentioned, 50; metropolitan policies of, 74, 218; on cause of massacre, 76

Yamasee War, 223
Yeardly, George, governs Virginia, 70–72
Youghtanund Indians, 55